D0174851

Also by David Hajdu

Lush Life: A Biography of Billy Strayhorn

Positively 4th Street: The Lives and Times of Joan Baez, Bob Dylan,
Mimi Baez Fariña and Richard Fariña

THE TEN-CENT PLAGUE

 # TEN-CENT PLAGUE

The Great Comic-Book
Scare *and* How It
Changed America

DAVID HAJDU

Farrar, Straus and Giroux

New York

Farrar, Straus and Giroux
18 West 18th Street, New York 10011

Distributed in Canada by Douglas & McIntyre Ltd.
Printed in the United States of America
First edition, 2008

Owing to limitations of space,
illustration credits appear on page 435.

Library of Congress Cataloging-in-Publication Data
Hajdu, David.
    The ten-cent plague : the great comic-book scare and how it changed
America / David Hajdu. — 1st ed.
        p.   cm.
    Includes bibliographical references.
    ISBN-13: 978-0-374-18767-5 (hardcover : alk. paper)
    ISBN-10: 0-374-18767-3 (hardcover : alk. paper)
    1. Comic books, strips, etc.—United States—History—20th century.
2. Comic books, strips, etc.—Social aspects—United States.   I. Title.

PN6725.H33 2008
302.23'2—dc22

                                        2007025024

Designed by Abby Kagan

www.fsgbooks.com

1 3 5 7 9 10 8 6 4 2

For Jake, Torie, and Nate

Contents

THE TEN-CENT PLAGUE

Prologue

Sawgrass Village, a tidy development about twenty-five miles east of Jacksonville, Florida, is named for the wild marsh greenery that its turf lawns displaced. It has 1,327 houses, each of them pale gray on the outside. On the inside, the one at 133 Lake Julia Drive is a dream shrine—a temple not to the past, like many other homes of retirees, but to a life imagined and denied. All the walls in its eight rooms, as well as the halls, are covered with framed paintings by Janice Valleau Winkleman, who moved there from Pittsburgh with her husband, Ed, in 1982, when he ended his four-decade career in sales (first, chemicals, then steel products). She had been painting almost every day for nearly thirty years. Having shown artistic talent at an early age, she had taken some formal training in fine art and illustration, and, at age nineteen, she began working professionally, drawing for Quality Comics in Manhattan. Then, one evening eleven years later, she came home from work and never went back.

For more than fifty years after that, Winkleman made no mention of the fact that she had had artwork prominently published as Janice Valleau. Her daughter Ellen grew up reading comic books without knowing that her mother had once helped create them.

In 2004, the Winklemans' living room held seventy-four paintings—vigorous watercolor seascapes with violent waves, rendered in heavy blues and blacks; an acrylic of two seagulls suspended in flight, positioned upright in a golden-brown sky and surrounded by other gulls darting about them in every direction; watercolor after watercolor of old sailing ships, moldering in dry dock; a few abstracts of angular shapes and patterns done in pastel; portraits of exotic, alluring young women, one of them topless, with her face either unfinished or painted over. The images—at once lovely and tortured, all skillfully done but madly varied—could occupy a graduate art student or a psychoanalyst for some time.

At age eighty-one, Winkleman was a fragile woman, weakened by age and illness, though she still painted when she felt up to it, usually one or two days each week. "I like art—it's important to me," she said in a small but firm voice. Her eyes were bright behind grand, squarish glasses that covered most of her face. She sat straight-backed in a thin-cushioned metal chair that went with the desk in a half-room that also had her easel and taboret, a few boxes of art supplies, and a tea set. Her hands formed a teepee on her lap. She wore a pressed linen house dress and well-used tennis shoes, and she kept her legs crossed tightly with her calves angled back under the chair, as if to hide the shoes. Hanging in a frame on the wall to her right was the original pen-and-ink art to the first page of a *Blackhawk* comic-book story drawn by one of her old studio mates, Reed Crandall. In the days when they were working together, Winkleman had sneaked the page home in her portfolio, because she admired Crandall's dynamic compositions and sure line.

"I wanted to be a magazine illustrator, but I loved comics, too," she said, pointing her teepee toward the *Blackhawk* page. "I would have been happy being in any kind of art at all."

Why, then, had she stopped working professionally half a century earlier? The paintings all over her house show that Winkleman had the skill and the versatility to have done commercial illustration. She had the experience in comics and the affection for the medium to have continued in that field. With the imagination she applied to some of her canvases, she might even have pursued fine art professionally. Why not?

"My God," she said. She separated her hands and slapped them on her lap, then slowly brought them back together. "I couldn't go back out there—I was scared to death. Don't you know what they did to us?"

In the mid-1940s, when Janice Valleau was thriving as an artist for Quality Comics, the comic book was the most popular form of entertainment in America. Comics were selling between eighty million and a hundred million copies every week, with a typical issue passed along or traded to six to ten readers, thereby reaching more people than movies, television, radio, or magazines for adults. By 1952, more than twenty publishers were producing nearly 650 comics titles per month, employing well over a thousand artists, writers, editors, letterers, and others—among them women such as Valleau, as well as untold members of racial, ethnic, and social minorities who turned to comics because they thought of themselves or their ideas as unwelcome in more reputable spheres of publishing and entertainment.

Created by outsiders of various sorts, comics gave voice to their makers' fantasies and discontent in the brash vernacular of cartoon drawings and word balloons, and they spoke with special cogency to young people who felt like outsiders in a world geared for and run by adults. In the forties, after all, the idea of youth culture as it would later be known—as a vast socioeconomic system comprising modes of behavior and styles of dress, music, and literature intended primarily to express independence from the status quo—had not yet formed; childhood and young adulthood were generally considered states of subadulthood, phases of training to enter the orthodoxy. Comic books were radical among the books of their day for being written, drawn, priced, and marketed primarily for and directly to kids, as well as for asserting a sensibility anathema to grown-ups.

Most adults never paid much mind until the comics—and the kids reading them—began to change.

During the early postwar years, comic books shifted in tone and content. Fed by the same streams as pulp fiction and film noir, many of the titles most prominent in the late forties and early fifties told lurid stories of crime, vice, lust, and horror, rather than noble tales of costumed heroes and heroines such as Superman, Captain Marvel, and Wonder Woman, whose exploits had initially established the comics genre in the late thirties and early forties. These unprecedented dark comics sprouted from cracks in the back corners of the cultural terrain and grew wild. Unlike the movies and the broadcast media, comic books had no effective monitoring or regulatory mechanism—no powerful self-censoring body like the film industry's Hays Office, no government authority like the FCC imposing content standards. Uninhibited, shameless, frequently garish and crude, often shocking, and sometimes excessive, these crime, horror, and romance comics provided young people of the early postwar years with a means of defying and escaping the mainstream culture of the time, while providing the guardians of that culture an enormous, taunting, close-range target. The world of comics became a battleground in a war between two generations, delineating two eras in American pop-culture history.

"Comic books are definitely harmful to impressionable people, and most young people are impressionable," said the psychiatrist Fredric Wertham, author of an incendiary tract, *Seduction of the Innocent*, which indicted comics as a leading cause of juvenile delinquency. "I think Hitler was a beginner compared to the comic-book industry.

"The time has come to legislate these books off the newsstands and out of the candy stores."

Churches and community groups raged and organized campaigns against comic books. Young people acted out mock trials of comics characters. Schools held public burnings of comics, and students threw thousands of the books into the bonfires; at more than one conflagration, children marched around the flames reciting incantations denouncing comics. Headlines in newspapers and magazines around the country warned readers: "Depravity for Children—Ten Cents a Copy!" "Horror in the Nursery," "The Curse of the Comic Books." The offices of one of the most adventurous and scandalous publishers, EC Comics, were raided by the New York City police. More than a hundred acts of legislation were introduced on the state and municipal levels to ban or limit the sale of comics: Scores of titles were outlawed in New York, Connecticut, Maryland, and other states, and ordinances to regulate comics were passed in dozens of cities. Soon, Congress took action with a set of sensational, televised hearings that nearly destroyed the comic-book business. Like Janice Valleau, the majority of working comics artists, writers, and editors—more than eight hundred people—lost their jobs. A great many of them would never be published again.

Through the near death of comic books and the end of many of their makers' creative lives, postwar popular culture was born.

Page-one news as it occurred, the story of the comics controversy is a largely forgotten chapter in the history of the culture wars and one that defies now-common notions about the evolution of twentieth-century popular culture, including the conception of the postwar sensibility—a raucous and cynical one, inured to violence and absorbed with sex, skeptical of authority, and frozen in young adulthood—as something spawned by rock and roll. The truth is more complex. Elvis Presley and Chuck Berry added the soundtrack to a scene created in comic books.

It is clear now that the hysteria over comic books was always about many things other than cartoons: about class and money and taste; about traditions and religions and biases rooted in time and place; about presidential politics; about the influence of a new medium called television; and about how art forms, as well as people, grow up. The comic-book war was one of the first and hardest-fought conflicts between young people and their parents in America, and it seems clear, too, now, that it was worth the fight.

1. Society Iss Nix

The first mission of the funny pages was to convoke the lower classes. Near the end of the nineteenth century, decades before the rise of comic books, more than thirty daily newspapers were competing for the allegiance of New York's reading public, and publisher Joseph Pulitzer decided to experiment with his populist *New York World* to increase its appeal to the public that did not read, at least not English. He purchased one of the few printing presses capable of mass-producing full-color pictures on newsprint and introduced the Sunday color supplement: a four-page, seventeen-by-twenty-three-inch carnival of illustrated stories on ostensibly exotic and titillating subjects (Paris! Ballerinas!), political cartoons, and what quickly became America's first comics sensation and licensing bonanza, a cartoon series published as *Hogan's Alley* but popularly known by the nickname of its leading character, a bald little boy in a yellow nightshirt. Written and drawn by Richard Felton Outcault, a former technical illustrator, "The Yellow Kid" was set in the gutters of Manhattan's Lower East Side and depicted the rowdy antics of a gang of young scruffs. The Kid himself, whom Outcault and no one else called Mickey Dugan, was a crude but strangely endearing caricature of the immigrant poor—barefoot, ugly, inarticulate, concerned only with base pleasures, and disposed to violence. He rarely spoke, and then did so in a marginally intelligible pidgin jumble of ethnic clichés: "De phonograph is a great invention—nit! I don't think—wait till I git dat foolish bird hom. I wont do a ting te him well say!" His pals, much the same, were all vulgar stereotypes: oil-smeared Italians throwing tomatoes; Negroes with gum-bubble lips, snoozing or cowering in fear; scowling Middle Easterners in fezzes, waving scimitars—comrades in egalitarian minstrelsy. Some scenes included a goat who fit companionably with the kids. Apart from occasional adult trespassers such as cops or dogcatchers, tokens of civil order who would be duly subjected to horrific abuse, the residents of *Hogan's Alley* were juveniles delinquent in many ways.

Within a decade, the popularity of the Yellow Kid led to the creation of dozens of newspaper cartoons and strips, including a duplicate Kid in the *New York Journal* when William Randolph Hearst bought the paper, a color press of his own, and most of Pulitzer's staff, including Outcault and his feature. (The *World* continued to publish *Hogan's Alley* with the Yellow Kid and his crew drawn by another artist, to the confusion of both papers' readers and the enrichment of their attorneys.) The best of the strips lingered around the Lower East Side: *Happy Hooligan*, which followed a gleeful lout in his travails with the law, and the *Katzenjammer Kids*, in which a pair of immigrant German twins, Hans and Fritz, incited havoc in all quarters of society. As one of their favorite victims, "der Inspector," noted: "Society iss nix" in the Katzenjammers' hands. (This time, Hearst commissioned an artist on his staff, Rudolph Dirks, to create a strip on the model of *Max und Moritz*, a series of illustrated stories published in Germany, and the artist came up with the Katzenjammers, Hans and Fritz; in time, Dirks jumped over to Pulitzer with the Kids, and Hearst hired a mimic to continue the strip anyway, resulting again in look-alike comics with the same characters, done by different artists for two papers.) Happy Hooligan was essentially the Yellow Kid with clothes on, a few years older and more delinquent; Hans and Fritz were the Kid doubled and made more juvenile.

In their earthiness, their skepticism toward authority, and the delight they took in freedom, early newspaper comics spoke to and of the swelling immigrant populations in New York and other cities where comics spread, primarily through syndication (although locally made cartoons appeared in papers everywhere). The funnies were *theirs*, made for them and about them. Unlike movements in the fine arts that crossed class lines to evoke the lives of working people, newspaper comics were proletarian in a contained, inclusive way. They did not draw upon alleys like Hogan's as a resource for refined expression, as Toulouse-Lautrec had employed the Moulin Rouge, nor did they use Hooligan's clashes with the law for pedagogy, to expose the powerful to the plight of the underclass, as John Steinbeck would utilize Cannery Row. The comics offered their audience a parodic look at itself, rendered in the vernacular of caricature and nonsense language. The mockery in comics was familial—intimate, knowing, affectionate, and merciless.

Comic strips were just beginning to sprout when some protective citizens noticed this unclassified species from Lower Manhattan and set out to uproot it. Articles censuring the various hooligans in the Sunday supplements began appearing in national magazines—that is, in a stratum of publishing then commonly regarded as more literate and more responsible than the mass-circulation newspapers; after all, unbridled sensationalism made Hearst and, to a lesser degree, Pulitzer, as notorious as the Yellow Kid for whom their brand of journalism was named. In a snorting critique published in the August 1906 issue of *The Atlantic Monthly*, Ralph Bergengren called the supplements "humor prepared and printed for the extremely dull" and "a thing of national shame and degradation." Chastising cartoons such as the *Katzenjammer Kids* for their vulgarity and crude draftsmanship, Bergengren ranted, "Respect for property, respect for parents, for law, for decency, for truth, for beauty, for kindliness, for dignity, or for honor, are killed, without mercy . . . Lunacy could go no farther than this pandemonium of undisguised coarseness and brutality . . ."

The criticism echoed already familiar charges against the dime novels of the late nineteenth century, which had delivered short, readable doses of blood and thunder to a working-class readership, thereby imperiling Victorian propriety. Comic strips essentially supplanted the dime novels and, in their accessibility to nonreaders in the immigrant population, surpassed the books in popularity. To watchdogs of American esteem in the early post-Victorian years, the earthy and raucous pages of the Sunday funnies threatened to devalue the United States' emerging status as a civilized world power. Magazine articles derided comic strips as infantile, brutal, unsophisticated, and subliterate; and the funnies were all that, though by design—a possibility lost to critics applying the standards of other forms of art and literature created for one class to a new form invented for another class. Indeed, much of the early criticism of newspaper comics condemned them as lower-class, as if that status alone were cause for condemnation. Even the charge of juvenilia was entwined with class bias in a day when people of low social rank, like those of color, were often conflated with children.

Ladies' Home Journal, in an article titled "A Crime Against American Children," published in January 1909, tore the Sunday supplements apart for undermining literacy and glorifying lawlessness and savagery:

Are we parents criminally negligent of our children, or is it that we have not put our minds on the subject of continuing to allow them to be injured by the inane and vulgar "comic" supplement of the Sunday newspaper? One thing is certain: we are permitting to go on under our very noses and in our own homes an extraordinary stupidity, and an influence for repulsive and often depraving vulgarity so colossal that it is rapidly taking on the dimensions of nothing short of a national crime against our children.

Other magazines, including *The Nation* and *Good Housekeeping*, found the Sunday supplements most offensive because they were published on Sunday, the Christian Sabbath. When Hearst introduced the color section of the *Journal*, he promoted it as "eight pages of polychromatic effulgence that makes the rainbow look like a lead pipe!" How could Sunday school compete with the thing that topped the rainbow? The supplements transformed Sunday in millions of American homes, Christian and otherwise, and not only for children. At a time when the newspapers were not only the primary form of mass communication but the only form (notwithstanding the mail) in many households, the leaping distance from gray sheets of type, dotted with tiny line drawings, to pages filled with bold colors was a vast one greatened by the sordid, anarchic content of those pages. If Pulitzer and Hearst could not steal the day from the God of Christ, they certainly made it hard for His people to keep holy.

A few newspapers around the country responded to this criticism with gestures such as shifting the arrangement of their comics features so one more temperate—say, Carl Schultze's *Foxy Grandpa*, an anomaly among early strips, in which a family elder regularly outwitted the prankster tots—would appear before the woolly stuff. But papers running strips ignored the dissent from another sphere. By 1914, the events of the Great War came to dominate the news in magazines and newspapers across the world. This was not the time for a war over comics.

Over the first two decades of the twentieth century, the funnies deepened through experimentation. They grew wilder, freer, and more varied in subject matter and style, infusing the huge pages onto which they were printed, as well as the kitchens in which they were read, with the spirit of adventure. Working in a young field with few traditions or conventions and little supervision other than that of editors satisfied with good newsstand sales, talented artist-writers pushed comics forward by pulling them in every direction. Winsor McCay, a grade-school dropout with staggering capacities of inventiveness and prolificity, concocted a string of fanciful strips for *The New York Herald*, culminating with *Little Nemo in Slumberland*, a majestically crafted amalgam of art nouveau design and surrealistic story content first published in 1904, the year Salvador Dalí was born. George Herriman, a "colored Creole" from New Orleans who allowed others to mistake him for Greek, took comics further into the realm of dreamscape with his poetic valentines to sadomasochism between the species, *Krazy Kat*, created for the Hearst syndicate in 1911. E. C. Segar, a modestly talented draftsman from rural Illinois who had a knack for storytelling, explored the narrative potential of comics, entwining humor, suspense, and adventure in *Thimble Theater*, which began in 1919 for Hearst and took on a second life ten years later, when Segar brought an odd new character into his troupe of comedic grotesques, a fist-happy hooligan named Popeye. These artists' work, along with that of other important comics innovators such as C. W. Kahles (*Hairbreadth Harry*), James Swinnerton (*Little Jimmy*), Harry Hershfield (*Desperate Desmond*), and Percy Crosby (*Skippy*), brought newspaper strips into creative maturity by tapping their childlike determination to play where they weren't supposed to go.

Like jazz and film, popular arts that also took form around the turn of the century, newspaper strips were not well received in the cultural establishment until the years after the First World War, when a new perception of the United States as having some parity with Europe helped spark a surge of interest in American culture. At the same time, serious critics were thinking about modernism, and some began to veer into disreputable neighborhoods of the arts with eyes (and ears) open to native modes of expression concerned more with novelty than with tradition. Gilbert Seldes discovered *Krazy Kat*. A high-spirited intellectual, Seldes was the editor of the venturesome literary journal *The Dial*, for which he published "The Waste Land" and hired Eliot, Mann, and Gorky as foreign correspondents. In 1924, while vacationing in Paris, he completed his book *The Seven Lively Arts*, a manifesto of critical democratization that challenged (as it defined) aesthetic elitism, arguing the intrinsic merits of popular entertainment such as the movies, ragtime, vaudeville, popular song, and the comics. As Seldes wrote,

> With those who hold that a comic strip cannot be a work of art I shall not traffic. The qualities of "Krazy Kat" are irony and fantasy— exactly the same, it would appear, as distinguish *The Revolt of the Angels*; it is wholly beside the point to indicate a preference for the work of Anatole France, which is in the great line, in the major arts. It happens that in America irony and fantasy are practiced in the major arts by only one or two men, producing high-class trash; and Mr. Herriman, working in a despised medium, without an atom of pretentiousness, is day after day producing something essentially fine. It is the result of a naive sensibility rather like that of the *douanier* Rousseau . . . In the second order of the world's art it is superbly first rate.

An explorer, rather than a liberator, Seldes had no intent to take comics off the streets of their provenance, the aesthetic turf of *Hogan's Alley*, but to show that low places are not always as bad as they look from the outside.

■　■　■

After nightfall on Saturdays, when their Sabbath had passed, the Eisner family often spent the last hours of the day together at the dining table of their four-room railroad flat in the Pelham Bay shtetl of the Bronx. Shmuel Eisner—Sam, since he had arrived in New York from Vienna in the first months of the Great War—would bring in the bulldog edition of the *New York Journal*, and he would read the stories about love nests and robberies to his wife, Fannie, who had grown up poor on the

Lower East Side and had never learned to read. William—Willie (later Bill, and finally Will)—the older of their two sons, would lay out the funnies, unfold a sheet of brown wrapping paper saved from the groceries, and try to replicate the drawings in pencil. By the age of eight, in 1925, he could make the simple, big-foot characters in E. C. Segar's *Thimble Theater* well enough to upset both parents. His father, a failed landscape painter who ended up working as a furniture "grainer," simulating wood-grain patterns on white-metal beds, disapproved of his son's indifference to realism, and his mother feared that drawing cartoons would keep the boy from learning practical skills.

Will Eisner, recalling those evenings many years later, said, "The comic strips in the newspapers of the time were everything to me, as they were for every other kid I knew then. They made me want to be an artist, and that was a cause of great concern to my parents, because my father was an elitist in his heart, and my mother was a peasant and a very practical woman. I turned out a little like each of them, so I would always have that internal struggle. My dream from the time I was quite young was maybe someday to be a newspaper cartoonist." He was a "cocky and frustrated" boy, by his own account, a kid whose skill at a form of entertainment for children made him impatient for adulthood. "The comics were something I felt was within my grasp, something I knew that was a part of my world, but something also that could maybe take me out of that world and take me out of the ghetto."

The Sunday papers were art class for innumerable children of the Depression years, and some skill at drawing cartoon characters imparted social status in every schoolyard. (Ronald Reagan, another child of the twenties, also could emulate Segar, as he demonstrated in the doodles he made at meetings during his presidency.) For poor kids with strong artistic inclinations, moreover, the funnies often represented the near whole of their exposure to art. "They were full of vivid drawings, the Sunday supplements, and they were all the art I saw when I was young," said Creig Flessel, an artist born in 1912 and raised on a five-acre farm in central Long Island. His father, a black-smith, catered to the horse and buggy trade. "They also had great sto-ries about the French underground and murderers and rape and arson and everything. They provided quite an education. I wasn't a good stu-dent at school, but I could draw. What I learned about art when I was a kid, I learned from those wonderful and free color drawings on Sun-days. I saved them and stared at them all week."

Between 1929 and 1934, as Will Eisner and tens of millions of chil-dren of early-century immigrants were coming of age, newspaper comics shifted in tone and style. They drew more explicitly from the pulp magazines of the time, such as *Amazing Stories* and *Dime Detective Magazine*, whose formula of sensational adventure stories, dynami-cally told, had proven appealing to the adolescent boys and working-class men who were also core readers of the comics pages. Chester Gould's *Dick Tracy* appeared as a daily strip in 1929, followed that year by Harold Foster's *Tarzan* and soon after by Alex Raymond's *Flash Gordon* (a superior response to *Buck Rogers* of 1929) and Milton Can-iff's *Terry and the Pirates*. Their tales of extravagant heroism, physical prowess, and wile gave opulent expression to the fantasies of male adolescence, and the bold but essentially realistic (or literal) artwork of Foster, Raymond, and Caniff conferred upon the comic strips a new kind of legitimacy. If the adventure strips were lacking the cryp-tic visual poetry of *Little Nemo* or *Krazy Kat*, they represented some-thing with more currency to many comics readers: a working-class ideal of skilled craftsmanship in the service of manhood.

A generation of young artists took Harold Foster, Alex Raymond, and Milton Caniff as idols. "I started out copying the big three, the three giants, when I was only seven or eight," said Everett Raymond Kinstler, a hungry, ambitious kid from Upper Broadway who quit school at sixteen to do comics. "I admired them, because they could draw well—Milton Caniff, especially. He worked in a medium of imagination, but he made it realistic—he made it real, through great draftsmanship."

Will Eisner, likewise, regarded Caniff as an elevating figure. "He had drama and adventure, and his storytelling was so lucid and clear—it had heft, it had cohesion," Eisner said. "His characters were real people to me, and that made him an artist to me."

Eisner attended DeWitt Clinton High, an all-boys school in the Bronx, where he demonstrated a deft touch with the various visual media young art aspirants try, as well as with cartoons; and, at fifteen, he had his first publication, in the school paper: a cluttered but vigorous pen-and-ink sketch of a tenement block whose fortunes were beginning to turn. (It ran over the headline "Bronx's 'Forgotten' Ghetto Revealed; 'Is School for Crime,' Doctor Says.") He applied to Syracuse University and was accepted with a scholarship to study fine art, but he left high school near the end of his fourth year, in the spring of 1935, without graduating. "My father had finally given up trying to work in any area of art, even wood graining, which was close to the bottom rung, and went into business—the fur business," because of some family connections there, Eisner recalled. "He was a terrible businessman. We were wiped out, and my mother took me aside, and she said to me, quietly, 'Look, your father can't make a living. You're the head of the family now.'" As he considered what kind of job to look for, Eisner thought of the Saturday evenings he had spent with his parents. His father, perennially hoping to find better work, would end the night's reading with selections from the help-wanted ads, and his voice would drop whenever he hit a word that appeared in descriptions of some of the best jobs: "restricted."

Shopping on avenues where he expected no obstacles, Will Eisner applied for a position as the art director of a new magazine called *Eve*, sponsored by Tetley Tea and "Dedicated to the Modern American Jewess." He was hired, at eighteen, on the merits of his portfolio of felicitous illustrations in a variety of modes, and let go, two months later, because the editor considered the drawings of vamps and prizefighters that Eisner contributed (under his own name and pseudonyms) lowbrow. "They wanted classy, WASPy *Vanity Fair* kind of things, to make the readers feel like they were assimilating," Eisner said. He turned to the printing trade, a field in which Jews had progressed rapidly in the early twentieth century, and took an apprenticeship at a small outfit, Bronfman Press on Varick Street in Lower Manhattan, to bring in money while he worked on ideas for original newspaper comics. By year's end, Eisner had created and shopped samples of two strips: *Harry Carey*, a lighthearted detective series rendered in the Segar vein, and *The Flame*, a stylish adventure feature about a suave crime-solving mystery man much like Leslie Charteris's pulp hero, The Saint. Neither sold.

These were the glory days of unsold comic strips, however—an auspicious time to be rejected by the newspaper syndicates. A great many creatively inclined people under the comics' thrall, including kids younger than Will Eisner, were inventing characters, writing, and drawing sample stories in rows of comics panels, and mailing them to the syndicates listed in *Writer's Markets and Methods*. The process, like that of making cold submissions in every arm of publishing, kindled young hopes and incinerated them efficiently, until 1935.

In February of that year, Malcolm Wheeler-Nicholson, a professional eccentric and small-time entrepreneur, opened a secondary market for unsuccessful comics ideas in the form of a magazine called *New Fun*, a thirty-six-page, black-and-white, tabloid-size (ten-by-fifteen-inch) collection of previously unpublished comics created with newspaper syndication in mind; it was a hodge-podge of kiddie stuff such as *Oswald the Rabbit* and adventure stories about cowboys and swordsmen geared for children. Some of the material was old goods, dating from the twenties; some of it new; some, fun. Although *New Fun* had a ten-cent cover price and was sold on newsstands through the distributors of *McCall's*, Wheeler-Nicholson created it not to attract ordinary readers but to impress newspaper comics syndicators, in hopes that they would buy the rights to the characters from him. *New Fun*, then, was a comic book made as a sales kit for a brokerage operation. As Wheeler-Nicholson wrote to Jerry Siegel, a teenager in Cleveland who had been working with a high-school friend to develop ideas for the syndicates, "I see these magazines more or less as brochures to interest the newspaper syndicates in an idea. It's much easier to sell a comic strip if you can show it in already published form."

Wheeler-Nicholson had made specialties of guile and stealth in packaging a far more unlikely product: himself. A writer for pulp magazines such as *Thrilling Adventures* and *Argosy* in the twenties and early thirties, he had earned his living by spinning tales of his own extraordinary, otherwise undocumented adventures as a military hero and lothario. A few highlights: As a major in the U.S. cavalry during the First World War, he had commanded secret missions beyond the Western Front; he had been shot in the head and survived; he had been a leader in the United States' undisclosed alliance with the Russians to repel the Bolsheviks; having uncovered a Prussian conspiracy in the ranks of his superiors, he had alerted the president, only to find himself court-martialed on a false charge; while in Russia, he had been seduced by a lady-in-waiting to the king—or was it a duke?—who arranged their passage to America, where they were married.

Wheeler-Nicholson ran the *New Fun* operation out of three airless rooms in the rear of a building full of garment dealers on Fourth Avenue and Twenty-eighth Street, and he marched about it with an air of grand burlesque. He invariably wore a long gray double-breasted cloak, yellowing spats, and a tattered, black wide-brimmed beaver hat. He carried a walking stick and used a cigarette holder. His face was round and pale, his nose broad and red, and his teeth green. When he met a new artist or writer or, for that matter, a new messenger boy, he removed his hat and bowed.

"The major was very quiet and polite—he had almost a European, English manner, and he couldn't be trusted to tell you the time," recalled Creig Flessel, who worked under Wheeler-Nicholson. "He had this wonderful idea to take comic strips that kids were sending in to the newspapers and publish them, to give them exposure, so he never had to pay for anything. That was good, because he didn't have any money. But he ran out of samples [of newspaper strips] and started asking the kids to do new comics just for him." Jerry Siegel and his partner, Joe Shuster, submitted *Henri Duval of France, Famed Soldier of Fortune* and *Dr. Occult, the Ghost Detective*, the first rendered on brown paper, the second on the back of wallpaper.

New Fun had some antecedents. Popular newspaper comics had been reprinted in various kinds of books and magazines from time to time since the Yellow Kid, and samples of unsold newspaper strips had found their way onto news racks as early as 1929 (in a tabloid put together by George Delacorte, the founder of Dell publishing). Most of those reprints had been produced as giveaways: *Buy so many boxes of such-and-such cereal, and receive a free funny book*, the precise contents of the latter left as vague as those of the cereal. Comic strips, having been created for an intrinsically disposable medium, were thought of as worthless after they were printed; they derived their value from their freshness, like produce and journalism (and, to a degree, works of modernism). Accordingly, a reprint collection that would come to be regarded as the first comic book, *Funnies on Parade*, from 1933, was never intended for sale but was used as a free premium for Procter & Gamble. Someone working at Eastern Color, the printing company that handled the presswork for most of the Sunday supplements in the Northeast—perhaps Maxwell Charles Gaines, a commission salesman, perhaps Harry Wildenberg, his sales manager—figured out how to produce a small, cheap promotional item by (a) printing eight pages on each sheet of standard newsprint and (b) doing so on the shop's third shift, during the press downtime. Its success as a sales gimmick led later that year to a second book of newspaper reprints, *Famous Funnies*, which Gaines marketed as a radio-show promotion for Wheatena, Canada Dry soft drinks, Phillips' Dental Magnesia, and other products. The next February, Gaines put a ten-cent price sticker on an edition of *Famous Funnies*; he arranged for national sales through a major distributor, American News Company, and started producing issues monthly. Comic books were on the newsstands, though they still contained old material until *New Fun*.

Such was the making of a tenuous new form of American popular art: a vehicle for giving away used goods of diminished value became a forum for selling discarded goods and new goods by people who could not compete with the makers of the used goods when they were new. "It was wide open—nobody knew what they were doing," said Joe Kubert, a Polish-born son of a butcher, who was ten years old in 1936 when he took the subway to Manhattan from Brooklyn, walked into the offices of an early comic-book studio, and was given work as an artist. "If you wanted to do comics and you had a little bit of talent—hell, even if you didn't have any talent—there was work for you. Maybe you had a lot of talent but you had a different kind of style, something unique and different, that the art directors in the slick magazines didn't like. You could be a genius, you could be a nobody, a little kid from Brooklyn like me, or some kind of nut. The doors were open to any and all."

In the spring of 1936, Will Eisner was picking up minor commercial-art jobs around Pelham Bay—a poster for the tailor shop, an ad for the dry cleaner—when he bumped into a friend from DeWitt Clinton High, Bob Kahn. The two had palled around as teenagers under an unspoken pact of mutual exploitation. Kahn, who loved cartooning and dancing, had shown talent at the latter, and Eisner had been shy with girls; Kahn had set Eisner up on double dates, and Eisner had involved Kahn in school art projects, often helping him with the drawing. Affable, energetic, and unimpeded by awareness of his limitations, Kahn was quick to pursue the new comic-book field and sold a few gag cartoons about a hillbilly character, Hiram Hick, to a monthly hybrid called *Wow What a Magazine*, under the name Bob Kane. "Bob was a very vapid kind of guy, and his talent was quite limited," Eisner said. "The big thing he was working on at that time was a thing called *Peter Pupp*, which was an imitation of Disney. That was the limit of his capacity. But he was very aggressive, and he had an immensely leathery skin, so that no matter how much humiliation he suffered, it didn't even register with him." Eisner, who had a folder of unsold ideas for newspaper strips, asked his old friend if he thought *Wow* might be interested in his work.

"Of course," said Kahn/Kane, as Eisner recalled. "They buy from everybody."

Eisner brought a portfolio of his comics samples to the magazine's offices, which were a pair of rooms on one floor of a garment-center factory that made men's shirts, in addition to *Wow*, rendering literal the scrappy young comic-book business's reputation as a rag trade. Eisner had trouble getting the attention of the editor, Samuel Iger, who called himself Jerry. Iger, rushing out of the building to tend to an emergency at the magazine's printers, several blocks south on Fourth Avenue, told Eisner to tag along and show him his artwork as they walked. At the printing plant, Eisner drew upon his apprenticeship at Bronfman Press and solved the emergency by cleaning some burrs off the engraving plates with a burnishing tool. Back at the shirt factory, Iger agreed to buy a four-page story about a rugged adventurer Eisner had created, "Scott Dalton." Or so went the story of Eisner's entry into comics as he liked to tell it—as an Aesopian fable of casual heroism, hidden virtue, and vindication through the lessons of hard experience.

Wow published *Scott Dalton*, followed by revised versions of Eisner's *Harry Carey* (now *Harry Karry*) and *The Flame* before going under with its fourth issue. New comic books were popping up so quickly, however, that Eisner saw an opportunity to satisfy both the artist and the breadwinner within him. "Most comic books were publishing compilations of daily strips, rejects, or new material so poor I wouldn't put it in my trash can," Eisner said. "I thought, well, pretty soon they're going to run out of old material, and they're going to need good new stuff. So I called Jerry Iger." Over lunch at a doughnut shop near the *Daily News* building on Forty-second Street, which Eisner thought of as the epitome of big-time publishing, Eisner proposed starting a manufacturing partnership: a studio to produce ready-to-print comic-book stories for publishers looking to try the comics business without worrying about the craft, an idea derived from the model of sweatshop subcontractors common in the piece-goods trades. Similar comics studios were opening around the same time, including one run by Harry Chesler, a former advertising man out of Chicago who was supplying pages to Comics Magazine Company, an outfit begun in 1935 by two former employees of Major Wheeler-Nicholson. Eisner said he could bankroll the company, although he had only fifteen dollars to his name—the payment for an advertisement he had done for a grease solvent—and he said he was twenty-five, although he was nineteen. Iger was thirty-two, but broke from a divorce in progress, his second one, and he was hungry.

The Eisner and Iger Studio opened in the first weeks of 1937 in a ten-by-ten-foot, fifteen-dollar-a-month room in a brown, formerly red, brick office building on Forty-first Street and Lexington Avenue, a block south of Grand Central Terminal. It was occupied mainly by bookmakers, numbers operators, and miscellaneous transients. Iger handled the sales and the lettering of the dialogue in the word balloons, while Eisner did the writing and artwork—at first single-handedly (except for a few contributions from Iger, who could do simple children's cartoons); in time, with a staff of artists and writers under him. As with many good partnerships, the principals appeared to be ill suited. Eisner was bigger than he seemed, thick all around and slumped from too many hours at the drawing table. His face was long and sober, though he could laugh heartily, if not easily, at himself. He wore gray Scotch-tweed suits and smoked a pipe, and he never brought up his unfinished education or his age. Some artists who worked under him at Eisner and Iger, such as Chuck Mazoujian and Bob Fujitani, found him aloof. None described him as less than brilliant at what he was doing—or just learning to do at the same time he was trying to teach it to his staff.

"Will Eisner treated what he did very seriously, like a serious art form, from the very beginning," remembered Bill Bossert, an artist who worked at Eisner and Iger and later became an art instructor and watercolorist. "He never looked down on comics. Of course, most people did, and I did, too. It seemed a little weird to me that he wanted us to put so much effort into comic books. I'd say he was compensating for his age, but we were all kids."

Jerry Iger was a feisty, small-framed man with a pencil mustache and well-tonicked black hair. He had an underbite that thickened his speech when he was upset, which was often. Iger was comfortable with women and men of every station, a trait that Eisner envied. "He was something of a blowhard—very, very aggressive," Eisner said. "Jerry thought of himself as a ladies' man. He was always in nightclubs every weekend. Monday morning, there was always some babe that would show up in net stockings, and she'd say, 'I met your partner. He gave me a job.' He was that kind of guy—he would walk up and see anybody. I was in awe of the fact that he would go up and see Randolph Hearst, if necessary." In emulation of Hearst, he started going by the name S. M. Iger.

"The camaraderie in that studio was really lovely," said Lee Ames, an artist at Eisner and Iger. "We were all bound by the fact that we denigrated Jerry. He was a swarthy little asshole of a guy who had no interest in anything but the bottom line. I could never understand how he and Will could have been together for any reason. The contrast between them was wonderful."

Like every port in the uncharted comic-book business, the Eisner and Iger Studio harbored a flotilla of artists and writers of many flags; they drifted in and found the place welcoming. Comic books, even more so than newspaper strips before them, attracted a high quotient of creative people who thought of more established modes of publishing as foreclosed to them: immigrants and children of immigrants, women, Jews, Italians, Negroes, Latinos, Asians, and myriad social outcasts, as well as some like Eisner who, in their growing regard for comic books as a form, became members of a new minority. "I wanted to be a fine artist," said Nick Cardy (Nicholas Viscardi), a scrappy Italian-American from the Lower East Side whose first artwork was miniature sculpture, crafted with the small blade of a broken pen knife from discarded broom handles and other pieces of wooden trash. When Cardy was fourteen, in 1934, a mural of athletes he had painted for his school, Forsyth Junior High, was reproduced in the *New York Herald Tribune*. "I found, first of all, that I couldn't afford the oil paints. To buy oil paints, they were very expensive, and I couldn't afford the canvas. Then I thought I could go into illustration. There was some beautiful illustration, excellent work being done in illustration in the 1930s—Harold von Schmidt, Dean Cornwell, Howard Pyle. Good artists—not Degas, but good. That was a step down from fine art, but that would be all right, but I realized that I couldn't do that, either. I didn't know what to do or where to go. I didn't have a suit to wear to see anybody, and I think those shops were pretty closed. I didn't think I had a chance at breaking in, and I needed to make a living. I needed money—right away, to live. So I went into comic books, and I liked it there."

The Eisner and Iger Studio, the Chesler shop, and others to follow applied the industrial method to the creative process, producing comic-book pages by assembly line. Eisner (or, sometimes, Iger or someone else in the studio) would hatch an idea for a character—say, Sheena the Jungle Queen, whom both Eisner and Iger would lay claim to creating. Eisner would usually design the character, then pass on the development of that character and the crafting of a story to his chief writer, Audrey "Toni" Blum, a would-be short-story writer who came to the studio soon after her father, Alex Blum, a portrait artist from Philadelphia who had found his clientele diminished after the Depression. Then an artist—often Eisner or Bob Powell (Stanley Pulowski), a brusque, combative Polish-American with a keen design sense—would take the typed story and "break it down" into comics panels roughed out in simple sketches. Another artist—perhaps Alex

Blum or Chuck Mazoujian, a high-spirited young Armenian artist with a delicate illustrative style—would take the "breakdown" and make tight pencil drawings of the main characters. Another—Andre LeBlanc, a quiet, gravely serious artist with a lyrical approach, born in Brazil (where he later returned to become a much honored illustrator)—would pencil the secondary characters. The next—Bob Fujitani, a Japanese-American teenager just starting out, or Jack Kirby (Jack Kurtzberg), a cocksure New York kid who had attended Pratt Institute in Brooklyn at the age of fourteen and loved comics—would pencil in the backgrounds. Finally, an inker—Powell, back for double duty, or Lou Fine, a meticulous draftsman (whose legs were crippled from polio) so versatile and deft that he could work in pen or brush without pencil sketches—would render all the pages of the story in ink, bringing to them some unity and a patina of personal style. When he handled the penciling, Fine used a mechanical pencil with no eraser. Someone outside the studio, often a technician at an engraving plant, would add the colors, usually but not always using color guides provided by Eisner. He liked to describe his operation as "an Egyptian galley going down the Nile," a charming image, its slavish implications notwithstanding.

The work produced at Eisner and Iger was, at its best, violently stylish. In features such as *Muss 'Em Up*, a noirish, black-and-white one-shot about a trench-coated vigilante, and *Hawks of the Seas*, a swashbuckler series set in the seventeenth century or thereabouts (and produced in black and white for sale to publishers overseas who thought they were buying reprint rights to a successful American newspaper strip), Eisner betrayed his debts not only to the much imitated adventure strips of Raymond, Foster, and Caniff, but also to film, especially the Warner Bros. gangster pictures and Errol Flynn adventures of the period. Muss 'Em Up Donovan, the titular hero, administers justice with the cavalier brutality of James Cagney or George Raft. ("Send an ambulance for Mike and his pal," Donovan says in one frame. "They were resisting an officer—so I sort of MUSSED 'EM UP!!") The drawings were composed like camera shots, with sharp, expressionistic angles and deep shadow effects that mirror the way the lens, not the eye, registers depth of field and light. Jules Feiffer, the cartoonist and playwright, was struck deeply by *Muss 'Em Up* as a boy. "*Muss 'Em Up* was full of dark shadows, creepy angle shots, graphic close-ups of violence and terror," Feiffer wrote as an adult. "Eisner's world seemed more real than the world of other comic book men because it looked that much more like a movie . . . When one Eisner character slugs another, a real fist hits real flesh. Violence was no externalized plot exercise; it was the gut of his style."

■ ■ ■

At some point in 1937, Creig Flessel could not recall exactly when, Major Malcolm Wheeler-Nicholson began keeping unlit butts in his cigarette holder. As the end of the year approached, there would sometimes be nothing in it, until the major found an ashtray with a salvageable piece of a cigarette. Wheeler-Nicholson was broke; despite having kept expenses down by buying cheap and paying his artists and writers late, if at all, he could not keep up with his printing bills and begged the printer, Harry Donenfeld of Donny Press, for a break. Donenfeld, a brash publisher of girlie magazines such as *Juicy Tales* and *Hot Tales* as well as a printer, was a crafty deal-maker. He had floated Wheeler-Nicholson in the past in exchange for pieces of his business. He understood the major's predicament, having played a key role in creating it, and responded by buying him out. Donenfeld and a partner, Paul Sampliner, took over the publication of Wheeler-Nicholson's comics, including the major's new title, *Detective Comics*. "I believe they call that 'the old squeeze,'" said Flessel. "I never saw the major again."

Among Wheeler-Nicholson's items of unfinished business was a new book, *Action Comics*. The major had prepared only a dummy issue for the purpose of registering the title for copyright, and both of its stories were lifts from the first issue of *Detective Comics*: "The Murders of Cap'n Scum," written and drawn by Flessel, which was featured on the mock-up cover—a close-up image of a ghoulish, hooded killer holding up a long knife dripping with blood; and "The Streets of Chinatown," an adventure about Slam Bradley, a two-fisted detective conspicuously similar to Roy Crane's "Captain Easy" of the newspaper comics. Bradley was another contribution by the Cleveland partners Jerry Siegel and Joe Shuster, whom Wheeler-Nicholson had been using regularly. The major may or may not have been planning to run Siegel and Shuster's unusual new character, "Superman," in *Action Comics*; independently, however, Sheldon Mayer, a clever young artist-writer working for the publishing jobber M. C. Gaines in newspaper syndication, noticed samples of Superman on Gaines's reject pile and passed them on to *Action*'s new editor, Vincent Sullivan, who had been a writer on Major Wheeler-Nicholson's staff. "I thought it was good," Sullivan said.

Superman, the man of steel in the guise of the mild-mannered reporter Clark Kent, was not a wholly original creation sprung from the depths of adolescent dreams; he merely seemed their fulfillment. Developed primarily by Siegel, who read science fiction and pulp magazines as well as comic strips, Superman was a mix of ideas swirling around the soup of junk culture in the 1930s: the super-strong protector of lesser creatures (Burroughs's Tarzan, publishers Street and Smith's Doc Savage—the "Man of Bronze" with the first name Clark); the hero with the secret identity (Zorro in the movies, the Shadow and the Green Hornet on the radio, the Spider in the pulps); and the costumed crime fighter (all of the heroes with secret identities, including the Phantom, Lee Falk's newspaper-strip character, who wore a purple leotard). He had dozens of distant ancestors in classical mythology, of course, as well as a prominent one among the religions to follow. There was obvious precedent for the basic story of Superman, in which a wise and mighty father in the heavens sends his only son to Earth, where he performs miraculous feats for the benefit of mankind.

Siegel and Shuster, both of whom were Jews, were tapping multiple traditions and theologies. According to Bob Oksner, a contemporary of theirs who fell into comics after getting a master's degree in education at Columbia, "There's no question in my mind that Jerry saw Superman as a kind of projection of his own self-image or his own fantasies about himself. Jerry was Jewish, like I am—like a lot of people in comics in those days—and the rest were Italian. Superman was the story of an unfairly denigrated person who knows that he had the ability to prevail in the end, whoever that person may be." A viable metaphor for Jesus, Superman was also Jewish.

Portrayed in Siegel's early stories as the "Champion of the Oppressed," avenging battered wives and vindicating the unduly punished, Superman spoke directly to survivors of the Depression; he was an immigrant (from another planet) himself, and he embodied the Roosevelt-era ideal of power employed for the public good. Children found special satisfaction in Superman, a fantasy adult wholly unlike other adults, perfect in his childlike purity, who wields amazing powers to undo the wrongness in the grown-up world and who treats the doing like play. With his debut on the cover of the premiere issue of *Action Comics*, published in June 1938, Superman distinguished comic books not only from newspaper funnies but from all the major forms of entertainment then popular—magazines, radio, and the movies.

We find Superman on that first cover, unidentified, hurling an automobile onto a boulder while several men run in fright; it is not clear until the inside pages if the fellow in the colored tights is a hero or a villain. Pulp stories in magazines and on the radio had told of fantastical doings in words and sounds, but did not show them unraveling in pictures; and movies had brought larger-than-life heroes such as Tarzan and Zorro to audiences in black and white, although the technology of the day made superhuman heroics prohibitively difficult and expensive to depict. Whatever Jerry Siegel could imagine and Joe Shuster could draw or suggest with a few brushstrokes—a man leaping over skyscrapers, outracing a locomotive, towing an airplane on his back, snuffing a time bomb in his hands—kids could now see, and in full color. The special effects in *Action Comics* No. 1 cost Joe Shuster about a dollar and a half, the going price of a kit of cartooning supplies.

Superman caught on fast. After a few months, a survey by National Periodicals (later known as DC, as in *Detective Comics*) found children asking news sellers for its Superman character by name, and the editors started promoting him on every issue of *Action*; by its nineteenth issue, *Action* was selling some 500,000 copies per month, more than four times as much as any other comic. In 1939, National started publishing a comic book named *Superman*, and the company spun off a syndicated Superman strip. By 1940, *Superman* comics were selling 1,250,000 copies per month, and the daily strip was appearing in three hundred cities. Newspapers were following the comic books' lead.

Imitations and variants flourished in superabundance: Amazing Man, Wonder Man, Sandman, Doll Man, the Flash, Master Man, Hawkman, the Whip, Hourman, Roy the Superboy (no relation), Captain America, Captain Marvel, Bulletman, Johnny Quick, Aquaman, and Wonder Woman, all published by the end of 1941. Bob Kane created a flying hero he called Bird-Man, whom he refined into Batman with considerable aid from an uncredited collaborator, Bill Finger. Imbued with gallantry, righteousness, physical strength, and patriotism, the bright, kinetic fabulism of superhero stories took the comics far from the tawdry chaos of the early funny pages. *Action* and its ilk were not so much outlets for the errant impulses of their artists, writers, and readers, or vehicles for them to challenge social convention or authority, as blunt credenda of virtue and testaments to the goodness of America. With Superman, the comics assimilated. As much as the Yellow Kid reveled in the immigrant experience, the red-and-blue man gloried in the American way.

 **It Was Work**

Harry "A" Chesler, Jr., the comic-book packager, applied the "Jr." to his name or dispensed with it as he saw fit, and put quotation marks around the initial because he thought they were stylistically correct, and he had a point. When he was asked what the "A" stood for, he said, "Anything"; indiscrimination was his middle name. Stubby and gray-skinned, he dressed in striped shirts and a suit vest that often but not always matched the pants; he kept a derby laid flat atop his head, all day, indoors; and he was usually smoking a cigar, proportionately stubby and also gray, with the label intact—a fancy label that could impress anyone who did not know much about cigars. Chesler, a stickler for efficiency, minimized the creative effort required of his artists to render him in caricature. He set up his studio in a long, open workspace, last used by a wholesaler of buttons and zippers for the garment trade, on the fourth floor of 276 Fifth Avenue, a ten-story, half-block-long building north of Twenty-ninth Street. Chesler filled the room with rows of used desks, which were cheaper than drawing tables, and he lorded over the shop as if it were a gangland fiefdom: Anyone arriving at work five minutes late would be docked an hour's wages; and on payday, he would sit behind the desk in his office, summon the artists, one by one, and ask each of them, "How much do you need this week to get by?"

Late in 1939, Irwin Hasen joined Chesler's staff. Hasen was just beginning to work professionally in art and, at twenty-one, was still living with his parents, who had had a furniture business go bankrupt and were rock-skipping from apartment to apartment in Manhattan to avoid going under. Hasen was an all-around artsy fellow who could have passed for Mickey Rooney's more effervescent, smaller brother. He had taken some drawing classes at the National Academy of Design and the Art Students League, but abandoned his first aspiration, fine art, as impractical. He had a good compositional sense and applied himself to his assignments for Chesler, among the first of which was a detective story about a counterfeiting ring, published by Timely. Not long after Hasen stacked the pages and submitted them to his boss, Chesler walked over to his drawing table and told him, "Good work, kid! That's a hell of a job you did! I'm going to play that up big!" At the end of the day, as Hasen cleared up his materials, he realized that he had inadvertently given Chesler only the top page of the story he had done. All the sheets of drawing board underneath it were blank.

"That's when I learned something about the comic-book business at that point in time," Hasen said. "It was going gangbusters, no matter what you did, and nobody was really paying any attention. Nobody cared what the heck was actually on the pages. It's true—they could be blank, and nobody would notice. I wouldn't be surprised if Chesler sent those pages to the printer."

The ghetto of comics was becoming a boomtown. By 1940, the population of Americans eighteen and under had been growing steadily for years and was now at a record high of more than forty-five million. Superman and his costumed progeny bounded into the world at a good time, or the time fostered their propagation. Young people were buying more and more comics every month—and not only the ones about superheroes, but books with adventures of every sort, as long as they were depicted in panels and word balloons: stories of cops and robbers, cowboys, spies, knights, flying aces, jungle men and, in a mark of the medium's benevolence toward adolescent males, jungle women. The number of comic books published ballooned from about 150 in 1937 to nearly 700 in 1940, expanding in course the numbers of writers, artists, letterers, and others necessary to make the pages. Comics were in their gold-rush period, a frenzied era of speculation, experimentation, easy rewards, and a kind of aesthetic lawlessness, through the lack of clear, established standards and the limited accountability within the trade. The people creating and publishing comic books were competing by improvising, trying practically anything, rejecting almost nothing, in a freewheeling spirit of innovation entwined with opportunism born, for many, of desperation.

"It was a medium coming up, it was new, and I was new, and it would accept people like me, because it didn't know where the hell it was going, and I didn't know what the hell I could do, either, and that made it easy and exciting," said Tom Gill, a resourceful Canadian-born artist, raised mainly in Flatbush, Brooklyn. Gill had started drawing spot illustrations for the New York *Daily News* in 1931 and gravitated to comic books in the late 1930s. (He would go on to teach cartooning at the School of Visual Arts for decades.) "I couldn't go be an illustrator and stuff like that—that was so set, and everything was established. But here, it was a free atmosphere. There was room for you to grow and experiment."

Some young comics artists, such as Jerry Robinson, an undergraduate at Columbia who did some ghosting for Bob Kane on *Batman* after class hours, exulted in the new medium's freedom. "Basically we were kids ourselves, so we were writing what excited us, which our audience then related to," said Robinson. "We were inventing the language as we went along, and some of us had an awareness of that. Every time we did something that we didn't think had been done before, it was exciting—maybe something like the whole first page as a splash page to introduce the story or breaking out of the panel format. Really, what we were trying to figure out how to do was give a perception of time, cross-cutting, and setting the scene, and establishing character, and we had to break away from the conventions of newspaper comics to do that."

Freshman artists and writers who found themselves working together in comics learned their craft over each other's shoulders, and their primary gratification apart from the pay of $15 to $25 per page was self-satisfaction or the approval of their peers. "Oh, it was like a college class for me," said Bob Lubbers, a comic-loving Long Island native who started drawing for the Centaur company in 1940, at age eighteen. "All I'd do is walk around and see what the other guys were doing. We all did that. We would catch some trick—somebody was using a Japanese brush or applying some different kind of light to light the scene, or different angles. Everybody had his strengths, and we rooted each other on and stole everything we could from each other. I thought Nick Cardy had the prettiest girls, Artie Saap was the best draftsman. I think Johnny Celardo had great compositions and did great animals, and then there was Joe Doolin, who was a cover man, and he was as tight as you could possibly be, but the covers looked posed—they sort of lacked a continuum of action in that he was so tight. We all took mental notes and robbed each other blind."

Low expectations granted comics creators vast license. Sold next to the candy on newsstands and drugstore racks, comic books were generally thought of as another nutrient-free but essentially harmless confection for kids. They were not just infantile, but something less worthy of adult consideration: junk. "A lot of guys looked their noses down on comics—they thought it was kid stuff," said Mickey Spillane, the pulp writer, who did more than a dozen manic cops-and-robbers stories for comic books, beginning in 1940. "So it was kid stuff? It was work. You can call it kid stuff, comic books, garbage, you name it—labels like that, guys put on things so they don't have to think about them. That's just the way I like it. Leave me alone—I'll go about my business and do what I want. If it's any good, somebody will pay for it, and a kid's dime buys the same cup of coffee."

A forum for artists and writers who were outsiders of all sorts, comic books spoke cogently to young people as they struggled to come to terms with adult society. "I decided when I was quite young that there was a certain element of nonsense going on in the grown-up world—a lot of people who were supposed to be older and wiser but were really in a world of their own, and I developed an inability to accept nonsense from people just because they're older and supposedly wiser," recalled Al Jaffee, the cartoonist and writer, who, at age nineteen in 1940, started working for Quality Comics. Raised in Lithuania, Savannah, and the Bronx, Jaffee had first learned to use cartoons to satirize authority and conformity while a student at the High School of Music and Art in Manhattan. "When I went into comics, the business was full of misfits like me. If you were inclined to point out the silliness of the world, as I was, nobody in the business was going to stop you." One of Jaffee's first creations was a big-foot hero, a caricature of comic-book heroes, called Inferior Man. Published in *Military Comics* by Quality, Inferior Man pointed to the comics' ability to defy the norms, including the just-forming conventions of the comics medium.

Erratic, inelegant, often clumsy, but boundlessly energetic and wide-eyed, early comic books appealed to youngsters as a kindred species. Kids recognized in comics something resolutely, gloriously unadult. The books were "less grown-up" than "everything, including the Sunday funnies," recalled Jules Feiffer, who, at eleven years old in 1940, was an avid comic-book fan and already writing and drawing stories of his own, for pleasure, though the work (pieces of which he would keep for the rest of his life) was as good as some published in comics at the time. "The rowdiness, the crude drawing, the cheap printing, the fact that they were looked down upon—these are the things that made them attractive," said Feiffer. "There was practically nothing else that we thought of as ours in those days."

At ten cents a copy, comics, like sodas and candy bars, were among the few things children of the post-Depression years could afford to buy by saving the pennies they could pick up on the sidewalk or earn by running errands, and they instilled a pride of ownership rooted not in adult conceptions of value, but in their absence. Parents considered comics worthless; therein lay their worth to kids. "I really loved comics . . . [and] I'd have to say that I probably loved comics so much, like I did, because my parents didn't give a damn about them," said Martin Thall, a New York City kid, ten years old in 1940, who, like Feiffer, was inspired by comics to become a cartoonist himself. "I went to the newsstand every day looking for new ones, and if they weren't there, I would stare at the old ones again, every day, like I would find something new [in them]. My buddies and me talked about them all day. If you didn't know about comics, you were a nobody." Comics were capital in the social economy of childhood, void among adults.

Nearly all young people—boys and girls, loners, athletes, scholars, and debutantes—read comic books, and most of their parents did not. To read comics was to belong to a vast yet exclusive club, one whose membership was restricted primarily by age. "Everything else was 'Ladies and gentlemen,' and comic books were, 'Hey, boys and girls!'" remembered Ted White, who, as a boy in Falls Church, Virginia, began looking at comics before he could read. (White would grow up to be a major comic-book collector.) There were two stores in downtown Falls Church that sold comics: Ware's Pharmacy, at the main crossroads, and, a quarter-block from there, Murphy's Five and Dime. After school, White and a few of his friends would walk together, first to Ware's, where they would stand around the magazine racks, pretending to browse, rushing through as many of the latest comics as they could before they were shooed away for loitering; then they would head to Murphy's and pick up what they hadn't finished reading. By the time he was eight, White had read hundreds of comics, although he owned only about a dozen, all tattered and smudged, many with covers long molted and lost. "We all passed them around, like sacred objects, until they fell apart," White said. They kept their favorites—*All-Star Comics* were White's—in shoe boxes hidden in the backs of their closets and under their beds, hoards of illicit treasure.

Will Eisner so prospered in the factory production of this treasure that he moved with his parents into a sumptuous nine-room apartment on Riverside Drive on Manhattan's Upper West Side, a colony of Jewish affluence; still, a curiosity about the comic-book medium's creative capacity—combined with illimitable confidence about his own ability to exploit it—led him to cash in his share of the partnership with Iger, so he could experiment more freely. By 1940, Eisner had accepted an offer from a venturesome publishing gadfly, Everett "Busy" Arnold, to produce a different sort of comic, a hybrid of newspaper strips and comic books that would be distributed as a supplement to Sunday papers served by the Des Moines Register and Tribune Syndicate, and he was promised creative independence. Since the newspapers had a readership of adults as well as children, Eisner reasoned, the venture offered him a vehicle to transcend the juvenilia of the superhero craze.

"I made my bones, as my Italian friends put it, but I wanted to go on, and along came the opportunity to produce for another market, the newspaper market—adults," Eisner said. "I saw no future for me in the comic-book market, because I thought, well, I'd be doing the same thing again and again and again. Most comic books were very insipid, and that's all the publishers expected from us. Even the highly successful *Superman* and *Batman* had inane stories. Comic books then were regarded as a very cheap, low art form, and I was not proud of being part of it. I was always embarrassed to explain where I was working and what I was doing. To say you were a comic-book artist in those days was like saying, 'I sweep floors,' 'I'm a super.'

"At the same time, I felt comic books were underrated—I felt they had untapped potential, at that time. I thought that most of the guys in comics underestimated their readers. I think they wrote down. Remember, I was younger than everybody else in my studio, so I was living with this idea that, 'Hey, don't underestimate me because of my age.' As a matter of fact, I got into a confrontation with the guys at Eisner and Iger over this. I said in an interview that, when I made the decision to do the Spirit, I thought that comic books could be an art form, a literary art form, and the guys in the shop said that I was being uppity." Paraphrasing Eisner, *The Philadelphia Record* reported:

> The comic strip, he explains, is no longer a comic strip but, in reality, an illustrated novel. It is new and raw in form just now, but material for limitless intelligent development. And eventually and inevitably it will be a legitimate medium for the best of writers and artists. It is already the embryo—Eisner apologizes a little for the trite phrase— of a new art form.

■ ■ ■

Sterling North, a grandson of Midwestern homesteaders, grew up during the first decades of the twentieth century in Edgerton, Wisconsin, a farm town that he evoked as a hammock daydream of heartland wonderment in a series of books for young readers. He attended the University of Chicago and worked for many years as a reporter and columnist for *The Chicago Daily News*, a literate independent paper, for which he wrote frequently on his main subjects of interest, childhood and literature. In the May 8, 1940, edition of the *News*, there was an article by North in the left column of the "Books and Authors" page; it combined a review of the spring season's offerings for children with a narrative of the delight in literature that he and his wife shared with their young son and daughter. North began the piece by introducing the family members and announcing that one of his own juvenile books had sold 30,000 copies and that the most recent, *Greased Lightning*, had been selected for the Junior Literary Guild. He then provided a rapturously sensual account of how his family experienced newly published books:

The packing from around the new books is hastily thrown into the fireplace. We spread out all over the floor of the living room and the sunlight comes in through the many-paned windows. Then the fun begins—because new books are fun. Even the way they smell is delightful; the texture of paper and binding is exciting.

In the text to follow, North found much to praise in many of the season's titles, such as *That Mario*, "the adventures of a lazy little boy of the Philippines," *Quest of the Cavaliers*, about De Soto and the Spanish explorers, and *Bill and the Bird Bander*, "a book about bird banding, bird migration and the curious habits of birds which should make more than one young reader wish to become a professional ornithologist."

To the right of this article, boxed and centered on the page, was a companion piece by North. It was headlined "A National Disgrace (And a Challenge to American Parents)," and this is what it said:

Virtually every child in America is reading color "comic" magazines— a poisonous mushroom growth of the last two years.

Ten million copies of these sex-horror serials are sold every month. One million dollars are taken from the pockets of America's children in exchange for graphic insanity . . .

The bulk of these lurid publications depend for their appeal upon mayhem, murder, torture and abduction—often with a child as the victim. Superman heroics, voluptuous females in scanty attire, blazing machine guns, hooded "justice" and cheap political propaganda were to be found on almost every page.

The old dime novels in which an occasional redskin bit the dust were classic literature compared to the sadistic drivel pouring from the presses today.

Badly drawn, badly written and badly printed—a strain on young eyes and young nervous systems—the effect of these pulp-paper nightmares is that of a violent stimulant. Their crude blacks and reds spoil the child's natural sense of color; their hypodermic injection of sex and murder makes the child impatient with better, though quieter, stories. Unless we want a coming generation even more ferocious than the present one, parents and teachers throughout America must band together to break the "comic" magazines.

But, of course, the children must be furnished a good substitute . . . And never before in the history of book publishing have there been so many fine new books for children . . .

The shame lies largely with the parents who don't know and don't care what children are reading. It lies with unimaginative teachers who force stupid, dull twaddle down eager young throats, and, of course, it lies with the completely immoral publishers of the "comics"—guilty of cultural slaughter of the innocents.

But the antidote to the "comic" magazine poison can be found in any library or good bookstore. The parent who does not acquire that antidote for his child is guilty of criminal negligence.

In large part, Sterling North's critique of comic books was little more than a double echo of earlier indictments of the Sunday newspaper supplements and their predecessors, the dime novels that North mentioned. (The "national shame" of *The Atlantic Monthly* in 1906 became North's "national disgrace.") The charges of vulgarity, prurience, and an absorption with violence returned, and North's supporting description of comic-book pages as filled with portrayals of superhuman derring-do, titillating women, gunfire, and vigilantism was not inaccurate, broadly speaking. The reference to "cheap political propaganda" is less well founded; early comic books were mostly apolitical, although, in their penchant for bestowing great powers upon the weak, they could have struck a conservative such as North as suspiciously left-leaning. North inflated the prevalence of and oversimplified the function of "mayhem, murder, torture and abduction" in the comics; heroes such as Superman and Captain Marvel, the role models of their stories, were superhumanly virtuous and supremely devoted to prevailing over wrongdoing of every sort. Kids were scarcely enticed to glory in the limited and functional mayhem that transpired in most comic books of 1940. Yet North was telling in his claim that violence was part of comics' appeal to young readers. This was his only acknowledgment of the fact that comic books had any appeal whatsoever to children, a tacit recognition of the fascination with both good and evil that has always been a part of how young people come to terms with the adult world. Otherwise, North's piece served as a denial of the possibility that comic-book readers were reading comic books by choice: The dimes of children were "taken" by the tens of millions "in exchange for . . . insanity," like Faustian lures; comic books were "sold," but not purchased. North appeared discontented with the prospect that young people might prefer a kind of book wholly unlike the ones he was writing.

Comic books, in their boisterous crudity, were antithetical to the genteel asceticism that Sterling North grew up with and carried over to his work; Northeastern, urban, and vaguely ethnic, if not overtly Jewish, comics came from and conjured a place far from Edgerton, Wisconsin. (The sweatshops of Fourth Avenue had little access to sunlight and no fireplaces.) North's comments about comic books' substandard writing and draftsmanship were not only sweeping and simply wrong in the case of some of the art, they suggested a contempt for vernacular expression, a parochial reverence for technique, and an obedience to tradition and orthodoxy at the expense of individual expression—attitudes that modernist critics such as Gilbert Seldes had been challenging for years. Likewise, North's scorn for the comics' cheap printing seemed to betray a bias against modes of expression produced economically enough for the lower classes—or children—to afford. To North, comics pages had no more value than the packing materials he and his family burned in their hearth.

North infused his vilification of comic books with a fury rare in his journalism and virtually absent in his gentle, elegiac fiction. It was as much a work of activism as one of criticism, as North signaled with the second part of his title, "And a Challenge to American Parents."

Arguing that children need a "good substitute" for comics (such as, presumably, the books North wrote or wrote about), he clearly saw comics and traditional books as mutually exclusive; he thought young bodies could not digest both literary junk food and nourishment.

After North's piece appeared, young comics lovers such as Sam Kweskin, a Chicago native, found parents more interested suddenly in what kids were reading in their bedrooms. Kweskin, like Will Eisner, had taught himself to draw by copying the Sunday funnies on sheets of grocery paper. "My mother would make three trips to the butcher for three soup bones, so she could bring me back more wrapping paper," said Kweskin, who, in adulthood, worked for a few years as an artist for Timely. His youthful ability was such that he was admitted, on scholarship, to a program for young people at the Art Institute of Chicago during the summer before his senior year of high school. (Bill Mauldin, who later became a Pulitzer Prize–winning political cartoonist, was a classmate.) When "A National Disgrace" was published in the *News*, Kweskin was just about to graduate and start his first job, as a night-shift copy boy at the *Chicago Tribune*. "I remember that someone, another woman in the apartment building where we lived, gave my mother a copy of that [article] to read, because we didn't get the *Daily News*," Kweskin said. "My father died when I was eleven, and my mother treated me like the man of the house, but I remember that she came over to me, and she said she wanted to take a look at the drawings I had been making. I was a Hal Foster nut—I even made a pilgrimage to see him in his studio [in Evanston, Illinois] when I was sixteen. So I was just copying Foster. She took a good look, and she smiled, and that night, when she was cleaning up the scraps from dinner, she took that page from the *News*, and she dumped the scraps onto it. She didn't say anything, she just kept right on cleaning. Oh, how I loved her for that.

"When I started working at the *Trib*, I heard talk about what a reactionary that fellow North was. But, there, you have to consider the source—I don't know if anybody at the *Trib* ever read a word of the

News, and that was the whole problem with this whole thing, if you ask me. A lot of people said things about comics, and I don't know if they ever read them."

Within a year of its initial publication, some forty newspapers had reprinted "A National Disgrace" in full or in part, according to a follow-up article by North ("The Antidote to Comics") published in the March 1941 issue of the National Parent-Teacher Association's magazine. "The 'comics' magazines, in our opinion, are furnishing a pre-Fascist pattern for the youth of America through emulation," North wrote, updating his argument for the day. "The chances of Fascism controlling the planet diminish in direct proportion to the number of good books the coming generation reads and enjoys."

The charge closest to North's heart, that comic books endangered the readership of traditional children's books, resonated well with other potential victims of such a threat. Librarians were early to respond in outrage over the "Comics Menace," in the phrase of the title of an article in the June 1941 edition of *Wilson Library Bulletin* that criticized "the highly colored enemy," comic books, mainly for not being printed in black and white, and for being written in "objectionable" vernacular language.

In the psychiatric and psychological communities, where menaces, real or imagined, are real either way but call for explication rather than campaign warfare, one of the first prominent statements on the comic-book question was temperate and sympathetic. Dr. Lauretta Bender, a child psychiatrist associated with New York's Bellevue Hospital, presented a paper on comics at the annual meeting of the American Orthopsychiatric Association, held in New York in February 1941. Working in collaboration with a colleague in her practice, Dr. Reginald S. Lourie, Bender drew upon the history of newspaper strips, the scant literature on comic books (including North's article), and both psychiatrists' clinical experience with patients who read comics. They found a great deal of benefit in comic books and virtually no harm. "The comic . . . is the folklore of the times, spontaneously given to and received by children, serving at the same time as a means of helping them solve the individual and sociological problems appropriate to their own lives," Bender said in her presentation. "Comic books may be said to offer the same type of mental catharsis to [their] readers that Aristotle claimed was an attribute of the drama . . . Well balanced children are not upset by even the more horrible scenes in the comics, as long as the reason for the threat of torture is clear and the issues are well stated."

While verifiable data on comic-book sales were impossible to come by, seven million to ten million comics were estimated to have sold each month, for annual gross revenues of $8 million to $12 million, in 1941. The same year, traditional children's books grossed about $2 million. Comic-book publishers—prospering entrepreneurs who, a few years earlier, had been printers, pornographers, and jobbers on the fringes of legitimacy—were little concerned with Sterling North and a few thousand do-gooders with mimeographed handouts. Still, Harry Donenfeld of National Periodicals (DC), whose history as the publisher of girlie pulps would bear little scrutiny in schools and churches, devised a way to shield his companies from charges of insalubrity: Beginning in the summer of 1941, each comic published by National and its allied company, All-American Comics, included a full-page house ad promoting a new Editorial Advisory Board. Its shifting roster of part-time members comprised "professional men and women who have made a life work of child psychology, education, and welfare," including Pearl S. Buck, Nobel laureate; Josette Frank, staff advisor of the Children's Book Committee of the Child Study Association; William Moulton Marston, psychologist, sexual theorist, scholar of the principles behind the polygraph machine, and contributor to *Family Circle*; Colonel C. Bowie Millican, chief reviewer of publications for the U.S. Army; Dr. Robert Thorndyke, a professor in the Department of Educational Psychology at Columbia; and Gene Tunney, former heavyweight champion and Shakespeare buff, who once lectured on the bard at Yale. It was a board befitting the comic books: accessible, attention-grabbing, a bit strange, and not quite middlebrow, but, rather, a collision of lowbrow and high.

Organized by M. C. Gaines, who had been a schoolteacher (and perhaps a principal) several jobs before he got to All-American Comics, the Editorial Advisory Board was intended to mollify parents and preempt critics through the fact of its existence, rather than the effects of its actions, which were few. The members of the board were paid honoraria and sent occasional memos outlining a few sample storylines. It was a phantom board; yet, as a spectral presence at National and All-American, it had a bit of influence on the work produced at both companies. "I reported to Shelly Mayer, the editor there, who was a guy I knew from when we were both apprentices for the same cartoonist, and we never showed anything to any board for anybody's approval," said Harry Lampert, who had joined All-American comics late in 1938. He grew up in a Jewish pocket of Harlem and learned to draw from books his mother purchased through an art correspondence school; unable to afford the whole course, she convinced the school to let her buy the texts alone. Lampert served an apprenticeship to a gag cartoonist for the *Daily Mirror*, Ving Fuller, brother of Sam Fuller (then a crime reporter, later a filmmaker with a newspaperman's eye), and he considered them both influences on his spare, punchy drawing style. "We didn't have to get anything approved, because Shelly knew what we were supposed to do—we all knew. They had a policy there where we were supposed to walk the straight and narrow. We knew we had to keep the action a little tamed down, and so we did."

Martin Nodell, a veteran of the Chicago Academy of Art and the Art Institute of Chicago, moved to New York seeking work in theater art that never came, and he started doing comics for small companies in 1938. Two years later, he joined Lampert at All-American. "I worked at a couple of other places [Ace and Fox Comics], and they were the anything-goes kind of operation," said Nodell. "The first thing I did for Sheldon Mayer was the Green Lantern, which I created [with writer Bill Finger, in 1940]. He ran a clean shop. Of course, the war came after that, and things were fine and dandy as long as the bad guys were Nazis and Japs."

By the end of 1941, American families were absorbed with dangers clearer and more present than comic books. Much as the First World War had snuffed early criticism of newspaper strips, the Second damped the debate over comic books before it caught fire. In fact, the idea of superheroes began to seem acutely patriotic—a simple, democratic, home-grown symbol of American might and surety of purpose.

Less than four weeks after *The Chicago Daily News* published Sterling North's diatribe, one of its rivals, the *Chicago Sun*, introduced Will Eisner's new project, a sixteen-page supplement to the Sunday edition at first called the *Weekly Comic Book* and soon renamed for its lead feature, *The Spirit*. The series started out tentatively but developed in the course of its first year to vindicate Eisner's faith in the ability of the comic book to hold an audience of all ages. The characters were human, even the Spirit (despite his name)—a detective without portfolio who had no superpowers and wore no costume (aside from a token mask that Eisner treated as a blue skin graft around the eyes); the stories were fairly sophisticated—intimate fables of human folly, developed from gestural crime situations; the pacing was languid; and the drawing, cartoonish yet realistic—comics with dimension and weight. (The *Weekly Comic Book* also included two lesser series by other artists and writers working under Eisner: *Lady Luck,* about a gorgeous socialite, Brenda Banks, who fought crime in a kelly-green ensemble accented with a veil and a broad-brimmed hat; and *Mr. Mystic*, a rewrite of *Yarko the Great*, an old idea of Eisner's lifted from Lee Falk's newspaper strip, *Mandrake the Magician.*)

There was not much to the Spirit as a character: Private detective Denny Colt was taken for dead, although he was really alive, and he encountered (as often by happenstance as by intent) various troublemakers (typically, exotics such as spies and smugglers, many of them

47

vamps smitten with the Spirit). That was it—no parents from outer space, no wizards or genies, no incantations, no kit of gadgets and weapons. He never behaved spookily, and no one in the stories seemed to think he was supernatural; he got punched and kissed, and he bruised and kissed back. The idea of the Spirit was a positioning statement of objection to comic-book ideas, brazenly cursory, a mark of contempt for the gimmickry passing for characterization in many of the comics of its time.

There was not much crime in the Spirit stories, either—at least not after the early episodes. Much as Orson Welles and Alfred Hitchcock used trash sources as excuses to explore emotional terrain, Eisner tended to focus on psychological themes such as loneliness, betrayal, and despair against a translucent scrim of cops-and-robbers doings. In "Two Lives," for instance, Eisner interwove the stories of unrelated captives, an incarcerated hood and a milquetoast fellow trapped in a bad marriage; they both escaped, were mistaken for one another, and were returned to the wrong prison. Before long, Eisner was dispensing with the pretense of crime situations—and with the Spirit himself. In some of the series' best stories, the Spirit barely appeared in his own comic book. Instead, Eisner presented a goofy nobody named Gerhard Shnobble on the day he discovers he has the power to fly, or Adolf Hitler on a secret reconnaissance mission, roaming the subways and hobo jungles of New York in a twist on *Death Takes a Holiday*. Both Shnobble and Hitler found enlightenment in Eisner's hands but suffered for it by the last panel. Shnobble, reveling in his uniqueness among men, was accidentally hit by a gunshot meant for the Spirit and fell to his death before anyone saw what he could do. Hitler, converted to goodness by his exposure to America, decided to give a speech reversing all his policies but was assassinated by a warmongering lieutenant. The Spirit's world often seemed a bleak, even godless one, not so much part of an irrational or existential universe, but one worse, rigged in the Devil's favor.

Like Welles and Hitchcock, again, Eisner was interested in form, and he began experimenting with the architecture of his medium in the same period as *Citizen Kane*, *The Magnificent Ambersons*, and *Lifeboat*. One Spirit story was told from the point of view of a murderer, all the images rendered in the ovals of the killer's eyes. Another one took place in the "real time" of the ten minutes Eisner calculated the reader would spend reading it. The text for another was all rhyming verse. Another had no dialogue and unfolded in pantomime. One meta-episode included scenes of Eisner as both author of the tale at hand and a key part of it. Imaginative and ambitious, yet still "a comic-book man," Eisner seemed to be trying to push out the boundaries of the comics form from within, as if he were one of his own characters, another misunderstood victim of an unfair system, struggling to escape.

The setting was Eisner's native New York, at first cited as Manhattan, then left unnamed (under pressure from a syndicator fearful of alienating readers elsewhere, according to Eisner), and later called the generic Central City. There was no centrality in the mise-en-scène, however; in its architecture, weather, population, and culture, the home of the Spirit was strictly Old World Northeastern urban—more specifically, lower-middle-class ethnic. Like Eisner in his youth, the people he drew lived in tenements near elevated tracks, gathered on their stoops, and rode the subway to work. They had strong features and wore heavy clothes that could use a pressing. Jules Feiffer, who was one of Eisner's assistants early in his career, later wrote that, despite the former Denny Colt's Irish-sounding first name, Feiffer grew up presuming the Spirit was Jewish, like Eisner and him. The character is exceptional and held in suspicion by those outside his circle of compatriots. "I suppose he was Jewish, insofar as the fact that he was the product of my experience, and I put a little of myself in him," Eisner said. "I never felt like I really fit in anywhere. I certainly didn't feel like I belonged in the superhero field, where everyone was basically trying to do the same thing. I believed in doing my work my way, because it was my work. I thought, well, okay, I'll just ignore everybody else and proceed in the manner I want, because, candidly, I believed I would prevail." In essence, the Spirit was the fantasy image of every outsider, a force of superior cool strolling through a landscape of woeful normalcy.

To small-town kids such as the young John Updike, the Spirit provided a map to a darkly compelling place. "After the relatively innocent good-against-evil adventures of Superman, Batman, and Plastic Man, Will Eisner's Spirit made an alarming and indelible impression," recalled Updike, who grew up in Shillington, Pennsylvania, near Reading. "The vertiginous perspectives, the long shadows, the vivid pools of blood, the artist's blithe violation of the tidy limits of the panels, and curious moral neutrality of the noir hero—all this formed, for me, an unsettling transition into what I now realize was the adult world."

Eisner's deal with Busy Arnold called for him to oversee the production of two standard-format comics magazines, *Hit Comics* and *Police Comics*, for his partner's company, Quality Comics, in addition to generating the Spirit newspaper insert. (Once he felt confident that his two audiences were sufficiently distinct, Eisner started using the same Spirit stories in both *Police Comics* and the weekly supplement.) The content of Quality's line, especially the artwork, justified the company name and demonstrated that not all comics artists were caught in a cycle of imitation during the superhero boom. Arnold, a former salesman for the Great Buffalo Press who had helped two of Major Wheeler-Nicholson's ex-employees launch the short-lived company Centaur Comics, fancied himself a classy guy with refined tastes and a keen eye for talent. Soft in the middle and small featured, he was boyish at the age of thirty-nine in 1941. Arnold wore custom-made double-breasted suits, and he parted his hair high on his head, like Rudy Vallee, whom he resembled. He lived with his wife in Greenwich, Connecticut, and with his girlfriends at 10 Park Avenue in Manhattan.

An amateur photographer, Arnold had a portfolio of eight-by-tens of a pair of well-acquainted women frolicking nude in the sand in Palm Beach, which he used as a social lubricant in meetings with male colleagues. Arnold laughed often and paid well. "You could buy a lot of macaroni working for Busy," said Tony DiPreta, an artist from Stamford who was employed for a time doing color work in Arnold's production facility in Greenwich. "You couldn't help but like the guy, if you were an artist, and he gave you all the leeway in the world. The only thing he wouldn't tolerate is messy borders on the page. The borders had to be absolutely perfect, like his hair."

There is a photo of Busy Arnold taken at the Stork Club. In the center we see his companion for the evening, a staff artist who was a good inker and was also a ravishing young woman. She is wearing a ribbon-striped taffeta gown and long black gloves on arms folded across her chest. Her hair is pulled back, aging her a bit beyond her twenty years, and she is giggling. To the right, we see one of Busy Arnold's hands, a part of his arm, and a bit of his side as he leans out of camera view. "Oh, Busy was all right," recalled the woman in the picture, Janice Valleau Winkleman. "He just liked to go out, and he took the guys in the studio out sometimes, too. But his wife didn't like me very much. I don't think she liked Busy very much."

The daughter of a Paine Webber executive, Janice Valleau had contracted polio as a girl and used leg braces on and off until young adulthood, when her body strengthened enough for her to walk on her own. She learned to draw by copying magazine illustrations with art supplies her older brother bought for her. After high school, she enrolled in the Phoenix Art Institute, a small school on the floor above a stationery store on Madison Avenue and Forty-fourth Street; oriented to practical training in marketable art skills such as commercial illustration and design, it sought to attract women entering the wartime workplace by promising "Art Training that gets you somewhere" in ads alongside those for the School of Famous Graduates Fashion Academy, the Washington School for Secretaries, and the New York

School of Applied Design for Women. Valleau wanted to do lush, painted illustrations like the ones she tried to make at home.

"The school was really not much, and, I don't know why, but that was the place my parents sent me," she said. "My brother went to Lehigh University, and the Phoenix Art Institute is where I went. When I graduated, they sent me down to MLJ [later better known as Archie Comics]. Bob Montana [Archie's creator] went to the Phoenix Art Institute, and he hired me. That was okay. Then I went to Quality to work for Busy, and he was great—he really was.

"Busy wanted to have the best people around him. We were his little stars. We could be as creative as we wanted to be, and he loved it. I made the characters look however I wanted, and I designed their clothes, I decorated their houses. I gave them their personalities. That was exciting, and I really liked it. I never thought of doing comics, and when I did [them], I realized, this is great—I couldn't do anything like this anywhere [else]."

In a rare capitulation to a comic-book artist, Arnold had granted Will Eisner, the savvy businessman, rights to the Spirit character. Arnold then assigned another of his artists, Jack Cole, to create an exact duplicate of the Spirit, called Midnight—same plain blue suit and blue fedora, same gratuitous blue mask, same movie-idol features, same mysterious identity, same urban setting. Arnold introduced the feature in the January 1941 issue of *Smash Comics* as insurance against the Spirit: If Eisner was drafted and killed in the war or otherwise unable to deliver his product, Arnold had a replacement up and running. He made only one change, presumably minor to Arnold's thinking: He replaced the Spirit's comic-relief sidekick, Ebony, a Negro boy, with a talking monkey in a child's cap.

3. Crime Pays

Let us consider the contours of American popular culture in the days between the rise of Superman and the escalation of American involvement in World War II, by way of the films of James Cagney.

In 1938, the year of *Action Comics* issue No. 1, Cagney appeared in *Angels with Dirty Faces*, a Warner Bros. melodrama, directed by Michael Curtiz, about a pair of young scamps from the New York slums who are lured by fate to opposite extremes: One of them, Rocky Sullivan, grows up to be a notorious but endearingly roguish gangster (Cagney); the other, Jerry Connolly, becomes an altruistic but disarmingly earthy priest (Pat O'Brien), who serves in the old friends' boyhood neighborhood. The two reunite in competition for the souls of a new brood of delinquents, portrayed by the Dead End Kids. (The small troupe of young actors had come to Hollywood from Broadway in 1936 as accessories to the screen rights to Sidney Kingley's Broadway hit, *Dead End*, a social-realist drama about immigrants in Upper Manhattan.) *Angels with Dirty Faces* gives us two Rockys. A juvenile actor, Frankie Burke, plays Sullivan as a boy, one very much like the real Cagney in his youth: wily, combative, a street fighter scrapping his way out of the tenements. Cagney, as the adult Sullivan, presents a variation on the cinematic archetype he introduced in *The Public Enemy* of 1931 and refined in a stream of gangster movies that established the genre: a tinderbox of malevolent glee, robbing, killing, and smashing grapefruits into girlfriends' faces for the thrill of breaking rules. The first Rocky, like the Dead End Kids in this film, reinforced the prevailing view of children as rudderless vessels that could go wrong or right, depending solely upon how adults steer them. The second, an update of the outlaw antihero long common to folk tales of many kinds, was a durable artifact of the Depression—a projection of the widespread sense of economic inequity and disillusionment with authority during Prohibition. James Cagney, like his frequent costars Humphrey Bogart, Edward G. Robinson, and George Raft, helped implant a romantic conception of gangsters in the American consciousness, where it would stay for the rest of the century and into the twenty-first.

In 1942, the year America threw its full weight into the war, Cagney starred in *Yankee Doodle Dandy*, a musical biography, also directed by Curtiz for Warners, about George M. Cohan. Cagney's brother Bill, a film producer, had told Jack Warner, the head of the studio, "We should make a movie with Jimmy playing the damnedest patriotic man in the country," and they decided on Cohan. A specialist in ecstatic sing-along jingoism such as "It's a Grand Old Flag," the First World War rallying call "Over There," and "Yankee Doodle Boy," Cohan was a one-man morale campaign, and Cagney portrayed him like a human fireworks display. The image of Cagney, the insolent tough guy in all those crime dramas, now ebullient—grinning, singing, and dancing before rows of flag-waving chorines—seemed to embody America's potential to keep faith and tap hidden resources for Uncle Sam. At the film's premiere in Los Angeles, no tickets were sold; you bought a war bond to get in. Warner Bros. announced that the proceeds would help fund the construction of three Liberty cargo ships, with the names of each contributor engraved in the captains' tables.

Crime Pays

All the entertainment arts—the movies, radio, the comics, even pulp magazines—did service as instruments of wartime booster-ism. Comic books, an outlet for many young Jews, were particularly zealous in their creative assault on Fascism. A few comics characters joined the war effort before the United States did: Timely's Sub-Mariner was battling Nazi submarines as early as February 1940, and the same company's flag-adorned hero, Captain America, was punching out Hitler himself on the cover of his first issue in March 1941. After Pearl Harbor, almost every superhero stopped fighting traditional crime, abandoning murderers, kidnappers, and bank robbers to focus on saboteurs, spies, scientists working for the Axis, and other domestic threats. Judiciously, comics editors tended to grant most superhumanly endowed characters wavers from trench-combat duty, avoiding the issue of why they failed to use their powers to end the war in a few panels. In addition, Superman, Batman, Daredevil, the Sub-Mariner, and others not only contributed to the war effort in the narrative domain, but often broke out of their stories with exhortations to their real-world readers to pitch in by taking their wagons around their neighborhoods and collecting scrap metal and glass. All the titles of National and All-American Comics now included a letter from Secretary of the Treasury Henry Morgenthau, Jr., imploring readers to buy a ten-cent War Savings Stamp every week "to pay for part of a gun, plane or ship which your fathers, brothers or uncles are using for the defense of our country." Hitler appeared on the covers of no fewer than fifty comics, including one issue of *Thrilling Comics* that showed the führer in bed, tucked under a red quilt decorated with little swastikas, as a group of boy heroes, the Commando Cubs, raided his house.

Charles Biro heard the comic books singing "Yankee Doodle Boy" and saw opportunity in the absence of dirty faces.

The youngest of several sons of Hungarian immigrants, Biro grew up on East Eighty-second Street in Yorkville, two blocks from the apartment Cagney had moved into at age two. The neighborhood was poor and tough, and it was apportioned ethnically, building by building: The first four or five tenement houses on the north side of Eighty-second Street heading west were Hungarian; the next few were German; toward the end of the block, a small building was Polish. One of Biro's childhood friends, Rudy Palais, lived with his five brothers and sisters in a sizable German-Austrian building on Eighty-first. Most of the families in the area were Catholic, and the children who did not attend parochial school went to P.S. 157, where Biro and Palais (following Cagney by a few years) met.

"It was a rough-and-tumble kind of place," recalled Rudy Palais. "It wasn't like you see in the movies, really—it was rougher. You had to know how to fight. The thing for me was art, and that didn't go down too well, unless you were quite good at it, and then it earned you a degree of respect. You didn't have to fight as much. That's what brought Charlie and I together. He wanted to be an artist—as a matter of fact, he told everybody what a great artist he was, but he couldn't draw a thing.

"I was rather skilled, because my dad taught me, and we used to draw together," said Palais, whose father was a draftsman for a Brooklyn manufacturer of components for diving apparatus used at the nearby Naval Yard. "Charlie was always inviting me over to his house. He'd say, 'Oh, Rudy—come on over, we can draw together, okay?' And I'd say, 'All right'—I liked to draw, he liked to draw. And every time I came over to his place, he would make an excuse to go off into another room to do his artwork, and then he would come back in and show me what he did, and it was surprising, because it seemed to me that it was beyond his years."

When the boys were in the sixth grade, Biro was boasting about his talent to their teacher, a Miss Smith, and she asked him to come up to the blackboard and draw something for the class. As he headed forward, she asked Palais to join him. Biro made a tic-tac-toe board, and Palais made a lion crouching in attack, which he had mastered the night before. "I found out eventually that one of Biro's older brothers had a pantograph [a mechanical device for replicating images]," said

Palais. "I found out a long time later, after we started working together, that he used it his whole life, even when he was a big success in comics. He never learned to draw. I never saw anything worse than his stuff, really. But he was a talker, and that gave him an edge, I believe."

After graduating from Stuyvesant High School, Biro took some courses at the Grand Central School of Art, which advertised below the Phoenix Art Institute in the classified sections for professional schools. In 1936, at age twenty-five (several years older than most others in comics), he landed at the Harry "A" Chesler shop, where he contributed light filler cartoons such as *Goobyland* and *Topsy Turvy* until he was appointed shop steward. "He was a very strong sort of guy, but he couldn't really contribute very much, in terms of the art," recalled Irwin Hasen, who joined the studio during Biro's last days with Chesler. "He was a lot more interested in the stories than he was in the art." A few inches taller than six feet, Biro had an athletic build and a squat face with ruddy cheeks and eyes that arched upward at the temples; he appeared to be scowling, even when he smiled. He dressed conventionally—white shirt, dark suit, conservative tie—and looked uncomfortable; he darted, rather than walked, and when he was standing alone, he sometimes shadow-boxed. He spoke, with a trace of a Hungarian accent, in elliptical sentences peppered with carefully articulated multisyllabic words, often used correctly, according to Hasen and others in comics who found him imposing. Biro had a pet monkey who often sat on his master's shoulder while Biro drew. After three years with Chesler, Biro moved (laterally or, arguably, down a step) to MLJ Publishing, where he helped create standard-issue characters such as the costumed Steel Sterling and the Army hero Sergeant Boyle for *Blue Ribbon*, *Zip*, and *Pep* comics. He left MLJ during the summer of 1941, in order to help yet another enterprising veteran of the printing business, Leverett Gleason, start yet another comics company. A few months later, *Pep* introduced a new comics character—a teenager adapted from the Andy Hardy movies by Phoenix Art Institute alumnus Bob Montana, called Archie—inaugurating a transformation of the modest, derivative MLJ into a lucrative and influential comic-book publisher.

Gleason, the former advertising manager for Eastern Color (the printer that had published *Famous Funnies* in 1933), hustled like a proud capitalist and talked like a frustrated socialist. He set up a small company in partnership with a failing publisher, Arthur Bernhard, who brought with him one title, *Silver Streak*; a strong original character from that comic, Daredevil (and his stronger nemesis, the Claw); and a healthy supply of paper despite the restrictions of wartime rationing. (Gleason finagled a way around the limited paper allocations permitted to new publishers by using Bernhard's old firm as a front.) To produce the pages, Gleason hired Charles Biro, and Biro brought on an artist-writer with whom he had worked at both the Chesler studio and MLJ, Bob Wood. "Lev Gleason was a very clever businessman and a social idealist," recalled Jerry Robinson, who was friends with both Biro and Wood and who collaborated with them and a few others on the first comic titled for the Daredevil character, produced in a rented room over three days and nights in order to meet the deadline for a paper allotment. "He went to Charlie, whom he knew and respected for his ability to organize. And then, [Biro] could also write—and damn well. I think Gleason had the idea to do something with social relevance, and he tried to set up the business almost like a kind of cooperative. He said to Charlie, 'Listen, there's money to be made in this business, and if we work together, I'll make sure you get your share of it. I'll split the pie.' Charlie tried to bring me in with the same kind of talk, and I think Charlie did very well there eventually. Gleason told him, 'Come up with something that everybody else isn't doing,' and he wouldn't mind if it happened to be topical."

Biro had a tabloid sense of topicality, framed by his youth on the streets of Yorkville and an urban bachelorhood spent working with fringe operators for subsistence wages and drinking away those wages after hours. As he liked to tell the story of his great inspiration for a new comic book, describing the events a decade after the fact: He was in a midtown bar one night when a strange man approached him and offered him the opportunity for a discreet encounter with a female acquaintance in a nearby hotel. The man showed Biro a photograph of the woman, an attractive brunette, and Biro demurred, unopposed to the offer on principle but attuned to something fishy. The next day, Biro picked up the morning paper and, according to one of the versions he would tell, found a picture of the man from the night before under the headline "Police Nab Oleomargarine Heir in Kidnapping." In another version, the paper ran the photo that he had been shown of the woman, under a similar headline. In a third, he read that the stranger had not only kidnapped the young lady, but killed her. (Minot "Mickey" Jelke III, inheritor to the Good Luck margarine company, was once arrested on charges of running a high-society prostitution ring; the *New York Times* headline "Oleo Heir Is Seized in Vice Raids Here" appeared on August 16, 1952, ten years after Biro placed the event in his talk.)

"Bob Wood loved to hear Charlie tell that—it made him laugh," recalled Pete Morisi, an artist and writer who worked for Gleason's company under Biro and Wood. "Wood was a strange guy. I stayed away from him." Understood to have grown up in blue-collar South Boston, Wood rarely discussed his background or his life outside of comics. Six years younger than Biro, pale, slovenly, and inarticulate, he appeared to have little in common with his chief advocate other than a compatibly primitive drawing style and a feeling for the violence in the comics Biro wrote.

Biro's idea, to devote a comic book to tales of felonious vice, was a cartoon update of the true-crime pulp magazines that had flourished since the twenties, a stew of titles made with a few cheap ingredients (*True Crime, True Detective, True Detective Mysteries, Front Page Detective, Crime Detective, Spicy Detective, True Gang Life*, and the all-embracing *True*). In some of the stories he had done for Gleason's *Daredevil Comics* ("The Killer Who Hated Death," "Death Is the Referee"), Biro had shown a facility with gruesome content, and, in recounting his experience with the kidnapper, Biro proved to have a disencumbered conception of the truth, appropriate to the true-crime genre. He took as the name for his new comic a phrase in popular currency, the title of a series of documentary-style short subjects from MGM that dramatized how real-life law enforcement officers had solved criminal cases: *Crime Does Not Pay*. The first issue was published in June 1942, as No. 22 of a magazine identified in small type as "formerly *Silver Streak* comics" (thereby saving Gleason the $100 fee for registering a new publication with the post office). Under the title, a tagline announced it as "The First Magazine of Its Kind!"

Crime Does Not Pay was unique, though not because it portrayed foul play in drawings and word balloons. As readers of the Sunday funnies had known for nearly fifty years, all sorts of wrongdoing—truancy, petty thievery, defacing property, bloodless variations on assault—had always been mainstays of the comics pages. Of course, most of that cartoon impropriety was conducted by children, albeit upon adults. By the 1940s, the juvenile pranksterism of old-style newspaper strips had become so ingrained in the popular consciousness that it no longer seemed improper. Indeed, the once-scandalous comic-strip pages won acknowledgment as a necessary literary evil by the childrearing expert Josette Frank. As she wrote in her popular handbook for parents, *What Books for Children?* (first published in 1937 and updated in 1942, after she joined National and All-American Comics' Editorial Advisory Board):

> However unacceptable they may be to adults, the comic strips continue to appeal to children; and for valid reasons. For here is action, swift, sudden, effective and usually unexpected . . . Furthermore, in the comics somebody usually does something which the young reader is himself forbidden to do—and swift retribution follows. It may be that the child reader here experiences vicariously both the pleasure of transgressing and the expiation of his guilty feelings

via the pictured culprit who is punished . . . We might not like to believe that nice little boys and girls think it funny for children to wring chickens' necks, but apparently they do. They think it funny, but also they know it to be wicked . . . How far such stories meet a deep psychic need of childhood we can only surmise. That they *do* fill such a need seems evident.

The token retribution paid to the mischief-makers in traditional funnies was certainly swift—a threatening shake of a rolling pin or kick on the behind in the last panel. Most of the space in the strips and all of the fun was in the doing of the misdeeds, the source of their potency as outlets of fantasy for the very young (or otherwise underempowered). By contrast, the newspaper adventure strips and adventure-hero comic books, intended for slightly older audiences, were, for the most part, more vigorously and conventionally moralistic; they inverted the funnies' dramatic proportions, turning the troublemakers into secondary characters and making their punishers the protagonists. Right prevailed over wrong in action and character—not only in the good guys' inevitable victory over the bad, but in the heroes' characterization. A villain such as Batman's chief nemesis, the Joker, may have been compelling in his weirdness and menace, but he had such narrow dimensions (he resembled a circus clown and robbed banks) that he earned no empathy. Only a small handful of fairly complex heroes, such as Batman, the Spirit, and his copy Midnight, played on the line between the law and criminality, being heroes whose loyalties were suspect to others in their stories; and virtually every comic-book hero tended to use illegal or socially unacceptable methods—destruction of property, unprovoked assault, taking suspects without charges, and sometimes letting them slip out of the sky to their deaths. A few heroes worked outside the law; nearly all, above it; but none worked against it.

Comic books had carried accounts of realistic crimes, solved by people not wearing tights, years before Charles Biro went to work for

Lev Gleason. One of the first, a feature based on FBI case histories, had been J. Edgar Hoover's idea. Hoover, who used the press to build a personal myth that he made the foundation of his empire within the federal government, subscribed to all five Washington newspapers, mainly for the comic strips, Hoover told writer Jack Alexander of *The New Yorker*. His favorite characters were Dick Tracy and Secret Agent X-9, because, as Alexander wrote, Hoover "consider[ed] them highly important influences in creating a public distaste for crime and de-rive[d] a keen inward satisfaction from seeing their flinty-jawed heroes prevail over evil."

In May 1936, at Hoover's initiative, the *Philadelphia Ledger* Syndi-cate introduced the newspaper strip *War on Crime*, subtitled *True sto-ries of G-men activities from the files of the Federal Bureau of Investigation*. A few months later, *Famous Funnies* reprinted *War on Crime* in comic-book form. The cover showed a group of cartoon men, boys, and a dog, all dancing and cheering at the sight of a billboard, upon which had been plastered a close-up, black-and-white photograph of a grim fellow in a suit; he is pointing a tommy gun straight at the reader of the cover, his eyes squinting behind the sights. The story inside follows a trio of hoods trying to keep a kidnapped state police officer hidden in their car as they cross the bridge between Phillipsburg, New Jersey, and Easton, Pennsylvania—a ramshackle byway photographed exten-sively by Walker Evans in harrowing WPA photographs nothing like the sunny, generic imagery of the *War on Crime* drawings. Hoover had stipulated that he and his associate Clyde Tolson approve every word and drawing, ensuring that the series had all the fire and grit of a folder of press releases.

Crime also permeated the tales of heroism in nearly all comic books, since it was the thing crime fighters fought. Jerry Siegel and Joe Shuster had created a pair of features about law enforcement officers: The jurisdiction of one, *Calling All Cars* (later retitled *Radio Squad*), was local; the other, *Federal Men*, national; both were published two years before Siegel and Shuster went interstellar with Superman. In

December 1936, Centaur packaged one of the first comic books devoted to a single theme, *Detective Picture Stories*, which was ripe with pulpy, noirish features such as Will Eisner's *Muss 'Em Up* and homicide procedurals such as "The Murder of Miser Flint," written and drawn by Joseph E. Buresch. "Whatever you wanted to do, you could go ahead with it—you could get away with murder, and I thought, Well, that gives me an idea," recalled Buresch, who was nineteen when he started contributing to *Detective Picture Stories* and already had two years' experience doing newspaper strips in his native Pennsylvania. "I went ahead and did what I wanted, and I put a little murder in there, and I had fun. I didn't give any kind of consideration to the person reading the thing, because I didn't think anybody was going to read it, and if they did, I sure as heck didn't know who they were."

Crime Does Not Pay was the first comic magazine of its kind not in the fact that it portrayed criminality but in the weight and the shape of that portrayal. The logo represented the product well: The opening word, CRIME, appeared in heavy, three-dimensional block letters two and a half inches tall, occupying nearly a third of the cover, and the other three words ran at a height of five-sixteenths of an inch, set inside a black banner that tricked the eye into reducing them further. The rest of the cover was a tempest of excess. For the first issue, a column running down the cover's left side showed a stack of heads cut out from black-and-white photographs, all of notorious killers and gangsters—Louis "Lepke" Buchalter (shown behind cartoon prison bars); "Hollywood's Panther Man" (his eyes pointing toward a drawing of a hangman's noose); and "Mad Dogs" Anthony and William Esposito. Above them, the phrase "True Crime Cases" was set inside a puddle splashing like blood.

The main cover image was a fever dream of bedlam. Two huge, blue-colored hands with bulging veins dominate the picture. One is stabbing a knife full through the other, simultaneously piercing the center of a playing card, the ace of spades. A .45 pistol, much too small for either hand, is tumbling in front of them. To the right of the hands, some poker chips fly, and behind them . . . Where to start? One gangster is choking a busty vamp while he shoots another man with a machine gun; two others wrestle as they tumble off a balcony; a fifth one lies dead on the floor; and a sixth is splayed across a bar. Details fill the space between the bodies: a row of tiny, fastidiously drawn liquor bottles and cocktail glasses on the bar; a long mirror behind them, cracked by stray bullets; a ceiling lamp shattered by gunfire. There are six headlines ("Sensational! The Case of the Twisted Cigarettes," "The Mad Musician and His Tunes of Doom," and such), a promotional box ("Be a Detective!"), and the signature of a cover artist worth identifying, Biro.

Gambling, alcohol, sex, shooting, brawling, knifing—Charles Biro packed in nearly everything that mid-century America considered sinful except jazz and homosexuality, although we can guess what kind of music would have been playing in that bar, and what were those two men doing on the balcony, anyway? All that was missing, from Biro's first cover onward through the comic's first several years, was restraint. Unlike most comic books that dealt with outlawry of various sorts, *Crime Does Not Pay* focused almost solely on lawbreakers and their crimes, rather than crime-fighters and law enforcement. Biro—a street thinker with a grandiose streak, unskilled, shameless, and let loose by a social-idealist publisher—became the Bosch of comic books and made *Crime Does Not Pay* an overgrown field of unearthly delights. If the glorification of gangsterism in American popular culture began with Prohibition, it reached an early summit with *Crime Does Not Pay*, in which nothing was prohibited.

The supposed truth of the stories provided Biro and Wood a rationale for depicting acts of violence and improbity that would, in works of the imagination, open them to charges of depravity. *Crime Does Not Pay*, like the true-crime pulps, constructed towers of fiction upon a few stones of fact. To keep Biro and Wood out of trouble, an announcement on the first page of an issue would explain, "In consideration of innocent people involved and relatives of others, the names

of some characters depicted in this true magazine are fictitious."
What of the acts in which those characters were engaged? There
would be no reference to sources. At least two or three stories in each
issue would have a historical or foreign setting—early America, Victorian England, the Old West, the high seas—imparting to them a patina
of historical veracity, or, at least, irrefutability. (Listed as managing editor in the comic's indicia, Bob Wood tended mainly to contracting
and scheduling, in addition to doing some writing and drawing, while
Biro oversaw most of the creative work and made certain that every
cover had his signature, which grew larger and fell higher on the page
over time, despite the fact that Biro's art was sometimes ghosted by
George Tuska.)

Crime Does Not Pay fully exploited crime and criminals, but it
stopped short of glamorizing them. The murderers and thieves in
every issue were invariably painted as pathologically corrupt or lured
into the underworld by malevolent predators. Despite Gleason's leftist politics, social forces such as poverty or inequities of class or race
never forced innocents into crime; nor did broken hearts or loveless
homes. While the comic book wallowed in perfidy, devoting page after page to graphic displays of gunplay, sadism, and bloodspilling, its
moral philosophy was resolutely determinist: Crime was not a relative
or even secular issue, but a simpler matter of the presence of evil. "It
isn't often that parents are directly to blame," wrote Biro or Wood on
the comic's letters page, which offered two dollars for each reader's
letter published. "It is up to the child. It is his will-power and moral
stuff that is challenged. If he is good and clean inside, so he will be
outside." In the hundreds of stories Biro and Wood edited for *Crime
Does Not Pay* and similar comics for Lev Gleason, the criminals never
triumphed in the end. Then again, they never suffered *until* the end of
the stories, facing the penalty for their misdeeds in the final panels,
like Hans and Fritz in prison stripes instead of jammers.

The pages before the obligatory end were hardly so formulaic,
however; to the contrary, they broke ground for comic books through

their close attention to characterization, and that element of dramatic sophistication, more than all the red ink devoted to blood in the panels, was the tyranny of *Crime Does Not Pay*. Few other comic-book makers dedicated so much space and applied such care to the delineation of character as the writers and editors working under Lev Gleason. "The Wild Spree of the Laughing Sadist—Herman Duker" is a typical six-page story. It opens with a three-quarter-page drawing of a man clutching a gorgeous blonde by the hair with his left hand; she has one black eye and blood drooling from her lips onto the smoking revolver the man is holding with his other hand. To their right on the page, we see the head of a dead man on a table; the eyes are rolled back in their sockets, and blood pours from a bullet hole in the middle of the forehead and from a knife slash across the face. The man with the gun is giggling, "Hee, hee, ha, ha, hee, hee!" A preface boxed within the panel tells us, "Some fools commit crimes for money—some because of jealousy or a sudden rage. But Herman Duker was one of those queers who robbed and killed out of sheer pleasure—experiencing delight in others' terror and agony, he laughed his way through crime until fate refused to crack a smile."

Why did he commit the horrors we see? That is the theme, and the story to follow, a psychological inquiry, traces the sadist's life in unnerving detail. In the first few panels, he is a boy, killing the family parakeet and the goldfish. He grows to adolescence, advancing to drowning the dog and setting the cat on fire. We then get two and a half pages of the sadist as a teenager, shooting willy-nilly until he is sent to reform school, where he starts on his fellow delinquents. We do not see him as a young man until the fifth page—after quite some time, by the comic-book clock. Nearly everyone he meets tries to help him or puzzle him out, for as long as they live. There is no plot to speak of, just the jagged outline of a life. In its forty-four panels, the story has almost three thousand words of text and dialogue. The writing is simple but plentiful, and its primary concern is the character of its protagonist, an irredeemable sadist.

As comics historian Maurice Horn noted in *The World Encyclopedia of Comics*, "Not until [Biro] joined the Lev Gleason group in 1941 did his real talent become known . . . Biro proved to be the most innovative and certainly most advanced writer in the comic book field." Biro's transformation is striking, and he never explained how it had come about. While he drew upon his hardscrabble youth to give *Crime Does Not Pay* a coarse authenticity, he also applied the creative technique he learned as a child: He cheated. As several artists who worked closely with Biro would recall, many if not most of the scripts for which Biro took credit were ghostwritten by a woman he had met at MLJ, Virginia Hubbell.

"Biro was an egomaniac," said Pete Morisi. "Look at the covers— his autograph was the biggest type on the cover. He wanted everybody to think that he was the whole show, and he was the whole show, in the sense that he ran everything. He was very good at that. He knew what he wanted. He liked to let on that he wrote everything, but he didn't. Ginny Hubbell wrote just about everything that Charlie Biro took credit for. I didn't think anybody really cared who wrote anything, except Charlie. He cared a lot, and he was the boss."

Hubbell was a bright, earthy woman, fair and smallish, with light brown hair that she wore in a pageboy. She reminded Rudy Palais of Doris Day, in buoyant spirit as much as in appearance. She had grown up in Brooklyn and began writing poetry as a teenager in the late 1920s, then went to college (Boston University and New York University) with the goal of becoming a gym teacher, an idea she abandoned for writing after graduation. She lived with her husband, Carl Hubbell, a minor comics artist with a prosaic style, in Woodstock, where she kept a menagerie of pet woods animals such as possums, snakes, and frogs. To get to Manhattan, the Hubbells sometimes took the train and sometimes worked on a Hudson River barge. Carl Hubbell would usually deliver his artwork and his wife's scripts, lingering around Gleason's office long enough to get the couple's checks, although that could take several hours, during which he would sometimes sketch for pleasure, standing. Morisi once watched him draw a vintage automobile from memory and several months later noticed the same vehicle in a Prohibition-era story Hubbell drew for *Crime Does Not Pay*; Morisi then recognized the car as the jalopy that the Archie character drove, drawn identically in both comics. Both Virginia and Carl Hubbell had done humor for MLJ, as well as some of the adventure and mystery stories that the Archie publisher then slipped between the hormonal goings-on at Riverdale High.

"She was a real smart cookie—college-girl, coed type," said Palais, who came to work for his boyhood competitor in the mid-1940s after stints with Quality, Fiction House, and Harvey. "Bundle of energy, pretty. I didn't see much of her. Charlie tried to keep her out of the picture. But I remember sitting with her someplace, we must have been having coffee at a coffee shop, and she asked me a million questions—never got around to talking about her. She was that kind of person who was really interested in other people, and I think that's why she wrote the way she did. She really wanted to know what made you tick. Charlie didn't give a crap. Charlie couldn't do what she did in a million years."

It was as an editor that Charles Biro distinguished himself. A fervent taskmaster, he imposed exacting and idiosyncratic demands such as the strict prohibition on chiaroscuro. "He insisted that everything had to be outlined—no blacks," said Fred Kida, a Manhattan-born artist, Japanese-American, who had worked at the Eisner and Iger Studio after Eisner's departure, then for Busy Arnold. "I couldn't stand it, because I like to use a lot of blacks, and I think that blacks are just right for the kind of stories he was doing in that magazine of his. What's crime without long shadows and dark skies? Who goes out in the middle of the street and robs people in broad daylight? Biro wanted everything outlined in a thin line, so it could be colored in, and that was it. He said that colors were important, and they are, but not above everything, every time. I always thought that he didn't know how to use blacks—he only knew how to draw with a little thin line, so he decided that was best."

Chief among Biro's requisites was literal realism. "Charlie didn't want to know anything about symbolism or any of that," said Tony DiPreta, who drew for *Crime Does Not Pay* and also tried writing for it, under Biro's encouragement. "He wanted very precise realism, exactly the way things looked. What I learned to do, working for him, was, if there was a machine gun in the story, I went out to find a real machine gun. Now, a lot of people working for other guys, if there was a machine gun, they'd make one up. Well, he didn't want us to do that. I remember, on the guns, there was a gun dealer in New York that Charlie knew, and I went to the place, and I went and got my hands on the guns I was supposed to draw. Cars, I did the same thing, I went out on the street and found the kind of car the story called for, and I'd open the door and look inside—real fast, before I got arrested myself."

To Biro, realism and violence were inextricable. In addition to demonstrating this through the relentless savagery in the stories he produced, he articulated the idea explicitly to his readers in an odd metavignette in the November 1943 issue of *Crime Does Not Pay*. Biro and Bob Wood appear as themselves, discussing the "Who Dunnit" mystery tale in the reader's hand. (Departing from realism on one detail, the drawing did not include Biro's pet monkey.) Wood asks, "Do you think this crime story is too bloody and gory, Charlie?" Biro responds, "It's bloody all right, but it's true! That's the important thing. We want our readers to see all the horror of the crooked path to crime."

His method of showing the horror of crime in whole was to fixate on its minutiae. "Charlie used to yell at me, 'I don't want art—I want detail!'" said Bob Fujitani. "'That's what people look for. That's what impresses them.' He published a cover that had a criminal shoving a woman's face into a lit gas burner on the stove, and he showed it to me. He said, 'Look at that! Look at that detail! See that gas burner?'

A decade later, when he was creating his signature character, Eisner thought of Charteris's pulp hero, The Saint, and the associations that name carried, and he conceived of the Spirit as a character profoundly human, but not secularly so. "The best I can do to explain it is to say that I thought the so-called superheroes, the costumed characters, were ludicrous because they were endowed like gods," Eisner said. "My idea of the Spirit was to make him as human as possible, and I consider our humanity a true expression of the divine. So, in that regard, I was involved in the making of graven images. I learned a respect for the capacity of images to communicate things of deep meaning from my father, and I tried to use that. But in terms of the supernatural, the average comic book was a lot closer to what my father did."

The Catholic Church, steeped in the tradition of employing inspirational imagery to reach the poor and illiterate as well as the educated, was early among twentieth-century cultural institutions to recognize the comic book's effectiveness in appealing to the young masses, and it responded with action on two fronts. One was friendly. During the war years, churches in some two thousand parishes across the country purchased volumes in a series of educational comics, *Picture Stories from the Bible*, for distribution through their Sunday schools. The books, published in New Testament and Old Testament editions, took heroic and episodic accounts from Scripture ("Jonah and the Whale," "The Boy Who Heard the Voice of God," "The Story of Jesus," "Paul's Four Journeys") and adapted them for young readers with tempered wooden drawings and simple wooden language. For the early covers, artist Montgomery Mulford seemed to have heard the voice of Charles Biro: The first shows a brawny Moses in a fistfight by the pyramids; the next, a double for Errol Flynn about to thrust his sword into his prone victim, above the headline "David defeats the Philistines by slaying and beheading Goliath!" Within months, the covers came into accord with the tepid inside pages and presented bloodless, ready-to-frame scenes of Elijah being fed by a raven and the boy Jesus doing chores in Joseph's carpentry shop.

Picture Stories from the Bible is unique in the history of comics as an idea incontestably attributable to M. C. Gaines, the former salesman for Eastern Color Printing who helped put *Famous Funnies* on the newsstands and hence laid claim to inventing the comic book. A pillowy man who resembled a mole, Gaines said he had been a high-school principal before the First World War, although he was never known to mention the name of the school. During Prohibition, he sold "We Want Beer" neckties, which he also claimed to have invented, then drifted about in sales jobs until he landed at Eastern Color. At the time, he, his wife, and their two children, Elaine and Bill, were living with her mother in the Bronx. Gaines's family called him Max; business associates, Charlie; only he referred to himself, in the third person, as M. C. Gaines. A frustrated pedant in a field of Goliathan philistines, he promoted *Picture Stories from the Bible* by writing a historical treatise titled *Narrative Illustration, The Story of the Comics*, which he had published as a pamphlet with a sample of the Bible comics inserted. In 5,600 words of faux-academic verbiage, Gaines traced the history of pictorial storytelling from cave paintings through Sumerian mosaics and Kozanji scrolls to Superman, at one point connecting Little Orphan Annie to Nile women in hieroglyphics. The author's bio, presumably written by Gaines, declared, "Originator of the comic book in its present form, he is also credited with 'discovering' that super-streamlined hero of the young: Superman!"

In a profile of Gaines published in *Forbes* in 1943, he said he had been inspired to adapt the Bible to the comics format upon having heard that half the children in America had received no religious training. Gaines published *Picture Stories from the Bible* through National/All-American, and the first two issues lost considerable sums; with the fourth issue, which was about to be published at the time of the *Forbes* interview, the series was expected to turn a profit, according to Gaines, who said that he had committed the publisher to donating the receipts in full to religious organizations that supported the series. (Gaines followed through at a well-publicized event at the Advertising

Club, where he gave ten clergymen checks of $850 apiece, drawn out of whatever he netted from the sale of a million copies of that issue.) Gaines then set up a new company to publish future editions of the Bible series and other wholesome books for children: Educational Comics, or EC. (In 1944, Gaines sold his share of All-American Comics to his partners, Harry Donenfeld and Jack Liebowitz; he received $500,000 after taxes, mainly for the value of the paper allocations in his name—precious during wartime and worthless a year after he sold them.) "Charlie always wanted to be a teacher, and he claimed to have been a principal somewhere—nobody knew the truth about that, but a lot of us had the impression that something had gone wrong somewhere, and it embittered him," recalled Ivan Klapper, who started working for M. C. Gaines in the late 1930s, initially as an errand boy, later as a clerk, then as a writer. Klapper was the same age as Gaines's son Bill and got to know them both well after the Second World War, when the younger Gaines returned from three years' service in the Army Air Corps. "Charlie was a nasty man, the last person you'd want to have as a teacher or a father. He never said a kind word about his own son. As a matter of fact, he hated him, and he made no bones about it, and Bill felt the same way about him. They kept as far from each other as possible, though, strangely enough, [Bill Gaines] wanted to be a teacher, too—he went [to New York University] to be a science teacher. He didn't want to have anything to do with comic books." In pursuing education, rather than educational comics, the younger Gaines sought a future where his father, somehow in his hazy past, seemed to have failed.

"It was the strangest thing to me that Charlie Gaines was publishing all these Bible stories about love and kindness," said Klapper, "and he was the nastiest son of a bitch on the face of the earth."

As an executive of All-American Comics publishing a line of superhero titles while overseeing the early issues of *Picture Stories from the Bible*, M. C. Gaines found himself on both sides of the Catholic Church's bifurcated response to comic books. *Sensation Comics*, the title that featured Wonder Woman, appeared in 1942 (and for several years to follow) on the list of forbidden books issued by the Church's National Organization for Decent Literature. Founded in February 1939, the NODL was a twentieth-century descendant of Catholic agents for vetting cultural influences dating to the first years of printing, in the mid-sixteenth century, when the Vatican issued the *Index Librorum Prohibitorum*. After four hundred years, the *Index* was still being published, although the global scale of its jurisdiction and the mammoth size of its accretion of books prohibited over the centuries limited its effectiveness in modern American parishes. In 1917, the Vatican established the framework for the NODL in a revised code of canon law, which specified that bishops on the diocesan level, in addition to the pope, had the authority to impose bans on books and other works for defying Catholic doctrine; publications qualifying on these grounds included those depicting atheism, paganism, or heresy; those deemed as obscene or favorable to divorce; and non-Catholic editions of the Bible. Once a bishop declared a publication forbidden, Catholics in his diocese were prohibited by debt of sin from selling, buying, keeping, lending, or reading it.

John Francis Noll, the bishop of Fort Wayne, Indiana, took this charge seriously, and he seized it as a way to help protect American Catholics—especially the young among them—from Communism. Around 1911, when Noll was a parish priest in Huntington, Indiana, and in his mid-thirties, he discovered the wave of newspapers and magazines devoted to the American Socialist movement of the early twentieth century, *The Melting Pot*, *The Appeal to Reason*, *The Menace*, *The Beacon Light*, and others, all of which, to varying degrees, were infused with anti-Catholic sentiment. Noll was alarmed. The next year, when a Socialist candidate for president, *Melting Pot* publisher Eugene V. Debs, won more than 900,000 votes, Noll launched his counterattack, founding the first national Catholic publication, *Our Sunday Visitor*. With this weekly newspaper as his pulpit and a congregation soon to reach three million readers, Noll railed against Communism and the "immoral magazines" that he saw as "part of a Communist plan to destroy the morals of youths." In the early 1930s, he institutionalized this campaign within his diocese by establishing a regional League for Clean Reading to target objectionable works and rally public opinion against them. This was a variation of the Legion of Decency, a national, multidenominational effort led by Catholics (Noll among them) to pressure the Hollywood studios to adhere to the rigidly puritanical content standards of the Hays Office, the Hollywood self-censorship body run by former postmaster general Will H. Hays. By the late 1930s, the liturgy of the Catholic Mass began calling for congregations to recite, after the Gospel reading, "I condemn indecent and immoral pictures and those which glorify crime or criminals. I promise to unite with all who protest against them . . . I promise further to stay away altogether from places of amusement which show pictures that can be an occasion of sin."

In the fall of 1938, Bishop Noll brought his crusade for cleaner reading to the national stage: In a speech at the annual meeting of American bishops, in Washington, Noll made a plea for the institution of an organized, nationwide effort to take on Communism and indecent literature. Within four months, a committee of Catholic bishops, under Noll's leadership, had chartered, manned, funded, and announced the National Organization for Decent Literature. "The traffic in printed obscenity" had "reached gigantic proportions," the bishops reported in *Our Sunday Visitor*. It was "an evil of such magnitude as to threaten the moral, social and national life of our country," the handiwork of publishers with "diabolical intent" to "weaken morality and thereby destroy religion and subvert the social order." The NODL dispatched emissaries to newsstands and drugstores (but not to bookstores or libraries) to evaluate magazines and books sold there. Once a month, the League issued its roster of Publications Disapproved for Youth (or "black list," as Noll called it) through the bishop's second publication, *The Acolyte*, while discouraging parishes from posting the list in public, for fear that it would serve as an adver-tisement to young people looking for something bad to read. The NODL defined its "ultimate purpose" as "not merely to keep Catho-lics from patronizing evil literature, but to keep it out of the commu-nity so that it will not be accessible to any, Catholic or non-Catholic."

To illustrate his intentions, Noll published a one-panel cartoon in *Our Sunday Visitor*. Under the headline "Now Is the Time to Act," it showed a bespectacled, boyish-looking middle-aged man—a dead-on likeness of Noll, labeled "Catholic Organizations"—and in a word bal-loon he said, "We cleaned up the movies—but we've let you parasites exist too long." He was swishing a broom, literally cleaning up a news-stand from which anthropomorphic magazines with tiny legs and feet were scurrying away. They had titles such as *Nasty News*, *Sexy Stuff*, *Photo Philth*, and *Cartoon Dirt*.

When M. C. Gaines found his vehicle for Wonder Woman, *Sensa-tion Comics*, on the NODL's list, he wrote a letter of protest to Noll. "While I am pleased to see that comic magazines as a whole have been eliminated from this N.O.D.L. list," Gaines wrote, "I am, of course, rather concerned that 'Sensation Comics' was included, particularly in view of the fact that I was the originator of the entire comic magazine field." Gaines then listed the membership of his Editorial Advisory Board (identifying the former heavyweight champion as Lieutenant Commander Gene Tunney, U.S.N.R., Executive Board, Boy Scout Foundation and Member, Board of Directors, Catholic Youth Organi-zation) and concluded by requesting details on how the contents of *Sensation Comics* conflicted with the NODL's "Code for Clean Living."

Gaines need not have asked. Created and written by the psychosex-ual provocateur William Moulton Marston (as Charles Moulton, a combination of his and Gaines's names), Wonder Woman was not just barely clothed and extravagantly endowed; she served as the out-let for Marston's obsession with the themes of sexual dominance and submission. His Amazonian heroine's two primary weapons were her "golden lasso" and "bracelets of submission," and almost all her stories had multiple scenes of men or women tied up, chained, manacled, or otherwise trapped in fetishistic paraphernalia. A verifiable fallen academic (from the American University and Tufts, among others), Marston had a gift for dressing sensationally vulgar ideas in pseudo-intellectual jargon, and he exploited it for a few years in Hollywood, advising the studios on how to maneuver around the Hays Office censors and sneak sex in films through symbolism and coded language. Relocated to New York and the publishing industry, he hustled pseudo-science and heterodox titillation through comics and popular magazines (in bylined articles, interviews, and advertisements for Gillette razor blades). Marston talked up a theory that the United States was drifting toward an Amazonian matriarchy that Wonder Woman symbolized. As he explained the thinking behind Wonder Woman in an interview published in *Family Circle* and attributed to one Olive Richard, a pseudonym for Marston's amanuensis, former student, and mistress, Olive Byrne:

> Boys, young and old, satisfy their wish thoughts by reading comics. If they go crazy over Wonder Woman, it means they're longing for a beautiful, exciting girl who's stronger than they are. By their comics tastes ye shall know them! . . . These simple, highly imaginative picture stories satisfy longings that ordinary daily life thwarts and denies. Superman and the army of male comics characters who resemble him satisfy the simple desire to be stronger and more powerful than anybody else. Wonder Woman satisfies the subconscious, elaborately disguised desire of males to be mastered by a woman who loves them.

Bishop Noll replied to M. C. Gaines's inquiry, explaining that the NODL objected only to Wonder Woman's costume. "There is no reason why Wonder Woman should not be better covered, and there is less reason why women who fall under her influence should be running around in bathingsuits," Noll wrote. Yet, he added, "it is very true that 'Sensation Comics' offends less than the average banned magazine because the illustrations are not exactly suggestive."

Costumed (or semicostumed) heroes such as Wonder Woman and Superman, rather than the villains they fought or the outlaws rampant in crime comics, were the main objects of the Catholic Church's early criticism of comic books, censure that began to take the form of a serious campaign against comics. Incendiary articles about comic books began appearing in major Catholic publications; typical among them was "Parents Must Control the Comics," published in *St. Anthony Messenger* in May 1944. It opened with a stark, eerie illustration of a male figure wearing fire-red tights, a long black cape, and an eye mask topped with two high points like horns. He had red dots of stubble, pockmarks, or lesions on his face, and he was playing a flute. Following behind him was a parade of young boys (no girls), and behind them were a couple of parents staring vacantly, with both arms stretched forward, hypnotized by the super pied Satan. The text to follow, by Robert E. Southard, a Jesuit priest and professor at Rockhurst College in Kansas City, Missouri, argued:

> The comic book practice of flourishing half-clad men and women before youth as examples of heroism is a threat both to the appreciation and the attainment of our standard. It is over-emphasizing sex . . . The total effect is to people young imaginations with mental associations that endanger strict sex control. Wisely enough, parents exclude barely clothed individuals such as these, from their homes in real life. On what score can their presence be justified in the medium of loud colored print?

He went on to describe superheroes as exemplars of fascism:

> There is anti-American, dictator propaganda in the glorification of these wrong-righting supermen. If our youth get the notion that it is

heroic for a private person to 'take over' in matters of public order we are ready for a Hitler. Hitler took over Germany when his followers had been persuaded that he was a superman with a mission to right the wrongs of the German state.

Later in 1944, the Catechetical Guild published an eight-page pamphlet expounding on this theme. It was titled *The Case Against the Comics*, and its cover, again, centered upon a devil figure, this one a nude man-beast with fangs and spiked white hair, busy concocting poison in test tubes. Surrounding him was a montage of horribles: bodies falling from a building blasted apart by a rocket, a jagged-nosed thug shooting a nicely attired man in an alley, a superhero with a cowl that resembled an executioner's mask, and the faces of five children (two girls included) sharing a comic book. The kids look drowsy and pained, as if drugged from imbibing the comic pages' satanic brew. As an act of combat with the comics, this cover triumphed over most comic-book art of the time in sheer weirdness. Inside, the text exclaimed:

A large number of comic books depict the heroic adventures of one or more characters whose philosophy may only be described as un-American and in a few instances, anarchistic. The vigilante spirit is rife in the comics: the gestapo method is glorified . . . It is neither Christian nor American to permit the young to be taught in this way the pernicious totalitarian doctrine that the end justifies the means . . . Even juvenile characters in the comic books engage in un-American activities of this nature. Fictitious "junior commando" groups bear a strong resemblance to the bands of child militarists in Nazi Germany.

Conflating paganism with fascism, Catholic writers further indicted superheroes for violations of the second commandment. Answering "What's Wrong with the 'Comics'?" in the February 1943 issue of the monthly *Catholic World*, Rev. Thomas F. Doyle pointed to the otherworldliness, supernaturalism, "weird names and still weirder attributes" of characters such as the Flash, Johnny Thunder, Hawkman, and Yarko (Will Eisner's knockoff of Mandrake the Magician). In their "untold power" to "defy natural laws," superheroes were false cartoon gods—pagan and, again, fascistic, Doyle said. He went on:

> In a vulgar way, [Superman] seems to personify the primitive religion expounded by Nietzsche's *Zarathustra*. "Man alone is and must be our God," says Zarathustra, very much in the style of a Nazi pamphleteer. Like it or not, there are plenty of American children who know more about the man-wonder Superman than they do about Christ or any of the great characters of the Bible.

Even after the war had ended, Catholic leaders continued to link their campaign against comic books to fascism and to fix their criticism on superheroes. In late October 1945, a rumination by Walter J. Ong, a literary scholar who had recently entered the Jesuit seminary, led *Time* magazine to ask, in a headline, "Are Comics Fascist?" The next August, Father Southard, in a speech at Fordham University, called comics "paper incarnations of the devastating Nietzsche Nazi philosophy of force" and denounced superheroes as "a kind of duplicate of the Christian ideal with pagan overtones." He came offering a solution, however: his own "picture presentation of the life of Christ" in the vein of M. C. Gaines's Bible comics, which, he said, would be available to Catholic schools the following year.

In the barrage of criticism of comic books in Catholic circles, one article made a singular charge. In the subheading to the article "Parents Must Control the Comics," Southard (or his editor) wrote, "Every month 25,000,000 comic books are published in this country. Many portray crime, violence, gun-play, sex, and are largely responsible for juvenile delinquency."

After pointing out that crime situations were the common back-drop of superhero comics, Southard noted that "only a special FBI in-vestigation would prove to comic book publishers that any of the current juvenile crimes are connected with what these youths read in comic books. But those who are not in the business can see very good reason to suspect such a connection." That reason? A good Jesuit, Southard concluded his discussion of the topic with a question: If young people inclined to antisocial behavior were to "get ideas" from comics, "what is to prevent them from getting ideas of hijacking, smuggling, gang fighting, train wrecking, robbery, racketeering, and murder?" Southard was making several leaps, none of pure faith: He took the Catholic inquiry into comics from the realm of their nature (moral and political) into that of their effects (individual and social); he ventured from the Church's home terrain of sin onto the state ter-ritory of crime; and, in the gap between the first-page subheading and the text that came three pages after it, he (or his editors) took an enor-mous jump from speculation to declaration. A reader needed only to scan the bold type accompanying that horrifying illustration to learn what bore responsibility for the rising social problem of the day, juve-nile delinquency.

The proposition that comics not only depicted but incited youthful impropriety had roots in the short-lived controversy over Sunday newspaper strips before the First World War, and Sterling North im-plied that idea in 1940, when he raised the specter of "a coming gen-eration even more ferocious than the present one." But to connect comic books directly to juvenile delinquency specifically was to pro-vide them a conduit to the center of debate about the American way of life in the mid-1940s. While the term had circulated in jurispru-dence since the early nineteenth century, it surfaced in journalism dur-ing the Second World War as a way to define a range of phenomena involving young people that, to the prevailing adult authorities, seemed to represent a falling short, a delinquency, in youthful behav-ior. It defined by negation: Like most criticism of the comics, the words "juvenile delinquency" characterized their subject by its failure to meet expectations—not by what it was, but by what a disappointment it was. During the early-twentieth-century outcry over newspaper strips, the language typically used to describe problem youth was a touch lighthearted and rooted in the vernacular; words such as "hooligan," "hoodlum," and "hellion" came from the street and carried with them a sense of grudging familial tolerance. "Juvenile delinquency," with its multisyllabic, legalistic severity, sounded serious and institutional, and brought with it implications of judgment and authority.

Within a year of Pearl Harbor, the American press was probing the effect of the war on home-front families, and reports of uncaged young animals tearing up their neighborhoods began appearing in newspapers and magazines around the country. In the years to follow, there were dozens of prominent stories about young men from fatherless households, roaming the streets in lawless packs, and young women who had absentee working mothers, dropping their morals and whatnot for servicemen at military bases—or worse, for the men in those gangs. Sociologists quoted on the subject classified the coalescing set of antisocial social phenomena as juvenile delinquency, and the subject began to cause public alarm. Earl Warren, the governor of California, instituted a Youth in Wartime Committee and wrote in his letter of appointment, "Normal family life and living conditions have been dislocated, and as a result young problems are greater and more complex than ever before."

J. Edgar Hoover, always on hand to defend the public welfare no matter what the doing might require in additional staffing and funds for his bureau, wrote copiously on juvenile delinquency. "This country is in deadly peril," Hoover warned in an article, "Youth . . . Running Wild," published under his byline in the *Los Angeles Times*.

> For a creeping rot of disintegration is eating into our nation. I am not easily shocked nor easily alarmed. But today, like thousands of others, I am both shocked and alarmed. The arrests of "teen-age" boys

and girls, all over the country are staggering. Some of the crimes youngsters are committing are almost unspeakable. Prostitution, murder, rape . . .

These are not isolated horrors from another world. They are danger signals which every parent—every responsible American should heed. These are symptoms—of a condition which threatens to develop a new "lost generation," more hopelessly lost than any that has gone before.

He was ready with statistics: In the previous year, 17 percent more young men under twenty-one were arrested for assault, 26 percent more for disorderly conduct. For young women, Hoover added, "the figures are even more startling"—increases of 39 percent in arrests for prostitution, 69 percent for disorderly conduct, and 124 percent for vagrancy.

Some challenged Hoover's figures on juvenile crime, arguing that (a) he and officials of his bureau tended to cite arrests, rather than convictions; (b) they failed to take into account the increase in new categories of crime, such as loitering and defying curfews, in many localities; and (c) the growing perception of a juvenile threat focused law-enforcement attention on young people, resulting in a cycle of increased arrests. The Children's Bureau of the Department of Labor, which studied juvenile crime itself, took strong exception to Hoover's data. As the bureau's chief, Katherine Lenroot, wrote in a 1943 pamphlet, *Understanding Juvenile Delinquency*:

We cannot say with certainty whether juvenile delinquency is increasing or decreasing throughout the country as a whole because of the absence of reliable and comprehensive data over a period of years. Such statistics as are available have shown no alarming tendency to increased "juvenile crime" as newspapers perennially claim.

Crime was always just one aspect of juvenile delinquency, anyway. To both the young people labeled as social deviants and their labelers, residence in the subculture called delinquency involved an array of conscious deviations from the conventions of proper society: improper language, attitudes, modes of dress and personal grooming, tastes in music, styles of dance, and reading matter. The complexity of "JD" identity was clear from one of the first incidents to draw national attention to juvenile delinquency: the "Zoot Suit Riots" of June 1943. For about a week that summer, military personnel stationed in Southern California and Nevada clashed in street fights with young civilians in East Los Angeles. The latter, mostly Mexican-Americans, said soldiers were attacking them because of their clothing—those garish, outrageously proportioned uniforms of hipsterdom, tailored for the sole utility of imparting cool. Otherwise impractical, also expensive, and, above all, baffling to outsiders, zoot suits served well as emblems of the hedonism, the self-interest, and the contempt for others that were ascribed to juvenile delinquents. During wartime, news of the Zoot Suit Riots came across as an affront to the ascetic virtue of patriotic citizens. The servicemen caught in the rumbles claimed that the zoot-suiters attacked them, and only civilians were charged with assault. To prevent further incidents of the same kind, the Los Angeles City Council took legislative action and made the wearing of a zoot suit a misdemeanor. Juvenile delinquents of the future would have to find something else to wear.

A Sunday sermon theme, a magazine story subject, a piece of news in the morning paper—juvenile delinquency was an abstraction, out of most Americans' lines of sight in the early 1940s. It became vivid through film. In fall 1943, the *March of Time* series of topical documentary shorts took up delinquency in a film, *Youth in Crisis*. The movie began with shots of eager young men lining up for draft induction, then contrasted them with images of Selective Service rejects and teenagers, too young for military service, running wild—drinking, smoking, jitterbugging, turning over cars and burning them in the streets, rioting, and being led into paddy wagons. The "domestic upheaval and disruption" of the war was spawning "a new spirit of violence and recklessness," announces the narrator in a grim, stentorian monotone. "Freed from parental authority, youngsters are venturing into new and unwholesome worlds," the voice-over tells us, as we watch a teenage boy open a cardboard jewelry box to reveal a marijuana cigarette. An effective piece of film-noirish sensationalism enlaced with wartime piety, *Youth in Crisis* impressed film critics as inexcitable as Bosley Crowther, who gushed, in *The New York Times*, "This is a film which has the character of a searchlight thrown upon a threatening thief. It should be shown in every community and seen by every parent in the land."

Youth in Crisis was still playing in many theaters at the onset of Senate hearings on the welfare of the civilian population during the war, led by Senator Claude Pepper of Florida from November 30 to December 3, 1943. The subject of juvenile delinquency, a minor item on the original agenda, dominated the hearings for several days. Pepper and the members of his committee poked around the issue with witnesses such as Florence Kerr of the Federal Works Agency, but, in the end, reported that they found the available data inconclusive and too contradictory to warrant action. The Senate, like *Youth in Crisis* and all those articles by J. Edgar Hoover, was content to accept juvenile delinquency as a tragic side effect of the war and its disruption of the domestic social structure. There was certainly no viable evidence that comic books could be considered a cause of delinquency.

The Catholic Church, by its own standard of evidence, had a prerogative to find comics culpable of inciting wrongdoing. By the doctrine of the Church, sin could transpire in thought, word, or deed. All a comic book had to do was give a reader bad ideas for the comic to have engendered sin. By the laws of the United States in the 1940s, however, a crime invariably required more than thoughts, and usually more than words: It required deeds.

When the Second World War ended, superhero comics were left with their stock severely diminished. The issue of *Action Comics* on the newsstands on the day Japan surrendered showed a polar bear on a tiny island of Arctic ice, gazing up quizzically at Superman, who is grinning as he flies by, carrying a magic carpet upon which we find the issue's featured characters: a pair of cartoonish Laurel and Hardy look-alikes in bowler hats, sitting with their cute pet, a white rabbit standing on his hind legs. The cover text alerts us to "another adventure featuring those zany magicians by accident—Hocus and Pocus." On the pages inside, the lead stories are "The Adventures of the Stingy Men" and "The Clue of the Crazy Rhyme."

The cover of *Crime Does Not Pay* on the same newsstands that day showed a scene in a barber shop in which two roughnecks in suits and fedoras have busted in on the proprietor and his unsuspecting customer, whose face is covered by a towel in preparation for a shave. A headline announces "All True Crime Stories," three of which are listed under the logo: "The Smile of Death," "The Cocksure Counterfeiter," and "The Slippery Mr. Smith." In the art below this type, we see one thug shoving the barber against a wall as he points a snub-nosed pistol at his mouth. In the foreground, the customer lies prone in the barber chair, relaxed with his hands folded on his belly, while the second hood studies his neck and sharpens a long straight razor on the strop. There is no violence but something more alluring: its imminence. Who could turn their eyes from the fearsome products of Charles Biro's imagination about to make their killing?

The first several issues of *Crime Does Not Pay*, published in 1942, had sold about 200,000 apiece. The following year, a typical issue sold about 300,000 copies. The next year, about 500,000; the next, about 700,000. By 1947, every issue was selling around a million copies, and each one of them was passed to another six to ten readers. Charles Biro was bragging with reason when he inserted a banner across the top of every issue: "More than 5,000,000 Readers Monthly."

One of them was a fourteen-year-old boy named Melvin Hyland Leeland, who lived in a working-class section of Washington, D.C., with his mother, stepfather, and seven younger brothers and sisters.

He attended Our Comforter Catholic School and took odd jobs in the afternoons and on weekends to help support the family. He was a "cheerful boy," according to members of his family quoted in an article in the July 6, 1947, issue of *The Washington Post*. Indeed, the photograph of him in the paper that day shows Leeland grinning, his buckteeth sunk into his lower lip. On the evening of July 5, a Friday, Melvin Leeland was sitting at his dining room table with his best friend, Lloyd "Buzzie" Gregg, explaining the game of Russian roulette. Leeland had a .22-caliber pistol, which he had found at his grandmother's farm in Maryland, sneaked home, and stashed in a shed behind his house. Leeland spun the cylinder and put the barrel of the pistol to his temple. His friend rose from the table and ran, and Leeland blew off his head. When his mother was interviewed by the police, she said the boy had gotten the idea from a comic book.

Two months later, a twelve-year-old named William Becker was found in the basement of his house in Sewickley, Pennsylvania, a suburb of Pittsburgh. He had strung a clothesline over a rafter, wrapped it around his neck, and hanged himself. His mother told the authorities that the boy was an incessant reader of comic books and was reenacting a scene from one of them. "I burned every one I found," she testified at a coroner's inquest, "but Billy always found ways of hiding them." A jury returned a verdict of accidental death but said that it held comic books responsible. A headline in a *New York Times* article reported, "'Comics' Blamed in Death." Shortly thereafter, the Allegheny County coroner, William D. McClelland, announced that, in rage over the Becker case, he was initiating a campaign to "ban" comic books that "glorify crime and weird adventures."

McClelland had law-enforcement support in his state—and beyond. The Pennsylvania Chiefs of Police Association, meeting in Wilkes-Barre that summer, had just passed a resolution denouncing comic books as "the source of inspiration for brutal crimes committed by teen age youths and a major cause of the rapid rise of juvenile delinquency." A few weeks after that, Chief Chris K. Keisling of

Carnegie took the issue to the convention of the Fraternal Order of Police and successfully pressed for a national resolution condemning comic books. "We should act for the nation's mothers," Keisling implored. "They are helpless to protect their children from the lurid booklets through [which] cavort half-nude women" and which "belittle law enforcement and glorify crime." Comic books had crossed the threshold from sin to crime, it seemed, and, just as in that scene on the Pennsylvania state line in *Famous Funnies'* first *War on Crime* story, the police were waiting.

■ ■ ■

Three years after M. C. Gaines sold his stake of All-American comics and left the superhero business, his Educational Comics company was publishing six wholesome titles for very young readers—*Picture Stories from American History*, *Picture Stories from Science*, *Tiny Tot Comics* ("Peter and Pinky in Ice Cream Land"), *Land of the Lost Comics* ("The Picnic in the Dell"), *Animal Fables* ("Bozo the Bowlegged Bull"), and *Dandy Comics* ("Baffy Bill and Molly")—and Gaines's $500,000 in assets had turned into $100,000 in debt. "Charlie Gaines was trying to do something that was supposed to be good for kids, but he didn't really understand kids very well, I don't think, and he was the kind of guy who, you know, always knew better than everybody else, and the whole operation had the smell of castor oil," recalled artist Mort Leav, who picked up a couple of checks drawing Freddy Firefly, Korky Kangaroo, and Hector the Inspector for Gaines between Leav's assignments for *Crime Does Not Pay*. Gaines had made sounder personal investments: a handsome white four-bedroom house in White Plains and a vacation cottage in Lake Placid, the sun-and-ski resort about six hours north of New York City.

In the third week of August 1947, Gaines took his wife, Jessie, their daughter Elaine, then twenty, Helen and Sam Irwin (a pair of friends whom Jessie liked), and the Irwins' young son Billy to the cottage for a few days, primarily to keep Jessie's mind off a family problem. The Gaines's twenty-five-year-old son, Bill, who was about to begin his final year of study at the NYU School of Education in preparation toward becoming a chemistry teacher, had just told his parents that his wife had left him after three years of a marriage that had essentially been arranged by Jessie. (Bill's wife, the former Hazel Grieb, was his second cousin on Jessie's side.) "He said, 'Listen, Ma—Hazel and I are getting divorced,' and his mother's first words were, 'How can you do this to me?' Very sensitive," said Lyle Stuart, who knew Bill Gaines when they were growing up in the same Brooklyn neighborhood and, in later years, became his business manager and confidant. "So Max Gaines took her up to the lake to keep her from having a nervous breakdown, and Bill stayed in New York, out of her sight. For the rest of his life, he blamed himself for what happened up there."

On the afternoon of August 20, Elaine Gaines and a friend of hers from the lake went swimming, and Max Gaines, Sam Irwin, and Sam's son Billy followed the girls in Max's Chris-Craft speedboat. Sam Irwin was at the helm. Somehow, another, larger boat sideswiped the Chris-Craft, capsizing it and killing Gaines and Sam. Billy Irwin found himself clinging to the smashed hull for a short time, until he was rescued. As well as he could parse the flashing blur of his memories, one of the men, probably Gaines, had thrown him to the rear of the boat as the crash came.

Jessie Gaines and her son Bill each inherited 50 percent of Educational Comics, and she implored him to carry on the family business. Bill, reluctant to disappoint his mother after failing in marriage and then killing his father, in his mind, capitulated and started going once a week to the EC offices, a $215-a-month suite of six rooms on the seventh floor of 225 Lafayette Street in Little Italy. He wrote the checks and played with the intercom system while he continued his studies at NYU, a few blocks away. His company was the "smallest, crummiest outfit in the field," as he saw it—"a mess of titles competing with each other to lose the most money." In professional terms, Gaines suddenly found himself in the hull of a small, broken, sinking vessel left capsized by his father.

"If he was losing money," Gaines told his mother, "what do you expect *me* to do?"

5. Puddles of Blood

The debate over comic books hopped from the back of the newspaper to the front, section by section—from the book reviews and religion columns to the "women's" department to the hard-news pages. In the first years after the war, church groups picked up anticomics sentiment from the pulpits and carried it to lay women's clubs, parent-teacher associations, and other civic groups; all of them, in turn, brought it to the police and local government leaders, who began taking vigorous action against comic books in 1948. The charges accreted: Comics were crude, illiterate, badly printed, salacious, addictive, stunting, fascist, Communist, conducive to wrongdoing of all sorts . . . In a radio panel discussion broadcast in New York in early 1948, drama critic John Mason Brown derided comics as "the lowest, most despicable, and most harmful form of trash," because "their word selection is as wretched as their drawing or the paper on which they are printed." Three weeks later, Detroit Police Commissioner Harry S. Toy, calling for a purge of comic books in his city, described them as "loaded with communistic teachings, sex and racial discrimination." The comics offered such a bounty of transgressions that a law-enforcement official had no need to mention crime. "What's wrong with the comics?" countless articles asked, because there were always new answers.

Over the course of 1948, the debate over comic books coalesced on the issue of juvenile delinquency. Unlike the intellectual abstractions of Sterling North, John Mason Brown, and others such as journalist and novelist Marya Mannes (who participated in the radio panel with Brown), the simple, topical notion that comics led kids to commit crimes spoke to adults of all stripes, everywhere. Mannes argued against comic books as detriments to the development of young minds, as she did in *The New Republic*:

Because no thought (unless you can call the "triumph of good over evil" in its most primitive cops-and-robbers sense a "thought") animates them, they demand no thinking. Comic books in their present form are the absence of thought. They are, in fact, the greatest intellectual narcotic on the market . . . Every hour spent in reading comics is an hour in which all inner growth is stopped.

Still, it was headlines such as "'Comics' Blamed in Death" and the talk that spread from them that stirred communities around the country to action against comic books.

Detroit was the first city to crack down on comic books, in April 1948. Under orders from Commissioner Toy, who probably learned about the hazards of comics at a law-enforcement convention, police officers in all precincts of the city seized copies of comics from newsstands and examined them for "objectionable material." Toy reported his findings to Detroit administrators (as well as to the FBI), and they found in them cause to justify an ordinance banning thirty-six comics from Detroit newsstands. As Prosecutor James N. McNally explained, the city classified a comic as objectionable if it met any of four criteria: if (1) it depicted characters "planning or perpetrating a crime"; (2) it had stories "involving a youth in a crime"; (3) the "entire comic [was] dealing with crime or criminal deeds"; (4) it "portray[ed] gruesome or brutal conduct on women, children or race [sic]."

Less than two weeks later, on May 10, the acting police chief of Ann Arbor, Captain Albert E. Housel, announced that the city had "outlawed" thirty comic books (and one nudie magazine) under authority of the county prosecutor, who declared that the publications violated state law prohibiting the sale of publications portraying "crime, bloodshed, and indecency." Four days after that, the mayor of Mt. Prospect, Illinois, persuaded the town board of directors to forbid the display or the sale of any comic book, regardless of its content. By the end of the month, the American Municipal Association reported, two more cities and towns had passed acts to curtail the sale of comics: Indianapolis banned thirty-five titles, and Hillsdale, Michigan, prohibited sale of the same thirty-six as Detroit. Elsewhere, the association said, officials were in the process of pursuing action of various kinds. In the months to follow, more than fifty municipalities, including several of the most populous in the United States, would develop initiatives to curb the sale of comic books.

The Michigan state law had been enacted in 1885 to restrict the distribution of publications devoted to stories of crime and bloodshed. In 1948, there were laws of this sort on the books in twenty states. Most of these statutes were designed to protect minors, the primary readers of comic books, although some applied to adults, too, and they were separate from but tangentially related to the far more widespread legislation on obscenity. Their model was a New York State law of 1884, introduced in response to a controversy of the time over the early ancestors of crime comics, the "story papers" that, in the first decades after the Civil War, printed tawdry, embellished accounts of sensational criminal cases. Written and produced quickly and cheaply for working-class readers, the papers drew the ire of the late nineteenth century's indomitable guardian of American virtue, Anthony Comstock. Secretary of the New York Society for the Suppression of Vice, Comstock denounced the story papers and the "half-dime" novels of the period (predecessors of dime novels by five cents and a couple of decades) in writings, speeches, and letters that provoked Congress, in 1873, to pass a law, "the Comstock Act," that prohibited use of the mail for "things intended for immoral use," such as the story papers, drawings of nudes, or anything else deemed immoral by the newly appointed special agent to the U.S. Post Office, Anthony Comstock.

He railed against the story papers in a book, *Traps for the Young*, published in 1883. "Our youth are in danger; mentally and morally they are cursed by a literature that is a disgrace to the nineteenth century," Comstock wrote. As he described the pages of the story papers,

> Crimes are gilded, and lawlessness is painted to resemble valor, making a bid for bandits, brigands, murderers, thieves, and criminals in general. Who would go to a State prison, the gambling saloon, or the brothel to find a suitable companion for the child? Yet a more insidious foe is selected when these stories are allowed to become associates for the child's mind and to shape and direct the thoughts.

The following year, the New York State Legislature passed a bill outlawing publications made up of "pictures and stories of deeds of bloodshed, lust or crime." Most of the state laws to follow set the same goals and used similar language, while some, such as a Colorado statute of 1885, tied in malign intent by banning "pictures or descriptions, indecent or immoral details of crime, vice or immorality, calculated to corrupt public morals, or to offend common decency, or to make vice and crime, immorality and licentiousness attractive."

On March 29, 1948, sixty-four years after the New York State law was enacted, the United States Supreme Court ruled it unconstitutional, effectively striking down the nineteen comparable acts in other states. The decision was not the impetus for the first municipal actions against comics, each of which represented weeks or months of maneuvering by law-enforcement officials or community leaders. The ruling did, however, blow open the door for future legislation on comic books and other disreputable publications geared for young people—in fact, the majority opinion practically called for it.

In the case that brought the 1884 law to the Supreme Court docket in 1947, a New York City book dealer named Murray Winters had in 1942 been fined $100 for possessing, with intent to sell, copies of a true-crime tabloid called *Headquarters Detective, True Cases from the Police Blotter*. Winters objected on First Amendment grounds. The high court of New York upheld the fine, dismissing the magazine with relish, in its ruling, as "a collection of crime stories which portray in vivid fashion tales of vice, murder and intrigue . . . embellished with pictures of fiendish and gruesome crimes . . . besprinkled with lurid photographs of victims and perpetrators"—*Crime Does Not Pay* without drawings by Charles Biro.

Overturning that decision, the United States Supreme Court saw no special virtue in *Headquarters Detective*; "We can see nothing of any possible value to society in these magazines," noted the opinion by Justice Stanley F. Reed, a centrist Kentuckian appointed ten years earlier by Roosevelt. The high court based its ruling on the vagueness of the 1884 act, which the majority saw as falling short of acceptable "standards of certainty." That is, the court ruled on the language of the legislation, not on the verbal or visual language of the publication involved.

At the same time, the lengthy opinion by Justice Reed explicitly proposed a cause-and-effect relationship between unsavory publications and juvenile delinquency, and it made a point to remind the states, as well as Congress, of their responsibility to act against them. "We recognize the importance of the exercise of a state's police power to minimize all incentives to crime, particularly in the field of sanguinary or salacious publications with their stimulation of juvenile delinquency," he wrote. Further, Reed noted:

To say that a state may not punish by such a vague statute carries no implication that it may not punish circulation of objectionable printed matter, assuming that it is not protected by the principles of the First Amendment . . . Neither the states nor Congress are prevented by the requirement of specificity from carrying out their duty of eliminating evils to which, in their judgment, such publications give rise.

There it was, in the voice of the highest authority in the land: The states and Congress had a *duty* to *punish* those who circulate *objectionable* material and to *eliminate* the *evils* they induce. Translate sanguinary to *bloodthirsty* or *violent*, publications to *comic books*, and we have the standard vocabulary of a thousand diatribes to come, and the marching orders for an odd army assembling around the corner.

■ ■ ■

On the same day the Supreme Court overturned *Winters v. New York*, March 29, 1948, *Time* magazine published an article about comics titled "Puddles of Blood." It reported on a recent symposium on "The Psychopathology of Comic Books," conducted in New York City under the auspices of the Association for the Advancement of Psychotherapy, at which comics were shown to contain an excess of "pictorial beatings, shootings, stranglings, blood puddles and torturings-to-death." These cartoon depictions of violence were escalating "hand in hand" with juvenile delinquency, according to the president of the sponsoring association. The article closed with a paraphrase of his conclusions: "Comic books not only inspire evil but suggest a form for the evil to take." The accompanying photograph showed the association head, psychiatrist Fredric Wertham. A compact middle-aged man with brushed-back gray hair and a high forehead hatched with scowl lines, he peered slightly to one side through opaque horn-rimmed glasses. He was wearing a plain, dark tie and a white lab coat, and his expression suggested puzzlement and displeasure; if one were the photographer of this picture, looking through the camera's viewfinder, one might wonder if one's pants had fallen down. With this image, the emerging crusade against comic books had a face.

Fredric Wertham was hardly the first anticomics crusader. Unlike Sterling North or the Reverend Robert E. Southard, however, Wertham was a man of science (or, at least, scientific-sounding ideas), rather than one of aesthetics or faith. He appeared at the right time, down to the day—such was the precision he seemed to emanate; and he was focused on a resonant proposition: that comic books caused juvenile delinquency, a thesis he came equipped to prove through his own clinical experience.

As a psychiatrist, Wertham was exquisitely credentialed: Born in Munich in 1895, Frederic Wertheimer studied in England and Austria, and received a medical degree from the University of Würzburg; then he moved to the United States to teach at Johns Hopkins and practice at the university's Phipps Psychiatric Clinic. He adopted a somewhat less Germanic-sounding variant on his surname and developed a fascination for the distinctively American elements of his newfound culture, particularly Negro life and popular entertainment. While he was in Baltimore, Wertham later said, he treated black patients sent to him by Clarence Darrow because no other psychiatrist in the city would see them. He became a naturalized citizen (and legally changed his name) in 1929 and, three years later, moved to New York City to head up the new psychiatric clinic connected to the Court of General Sessions, where he conducted evaluations of convicted felons. From that experience, Wertham began to build a career as an expert in criminal behavior.

He had an ear for the headlines and an eye for the spotlight. Testifying on behalf of the defendant at a 1934 murder trial, Wertham said he believed that the accused had been temporarily insane, acting in a psychotic frenzy. While he was on the stand, he took the opportunity to interject that he also believed that virtually all psychiatric testimony in criminal trials was specious. The next day's *New York Times* reported, "Alienists' Testimony Is Usually 'Bunk,' Psychiatrist Swears at Murder Trial." Wertham made himself the story, at the risk of undermining his own testimony and the case of the defendant he had been called upon to help.

A master of his adoptive culture, Wertham strove to be a public figure, a man with a following, and he succeeded by writing prolifically, for a lay readership, on unsavory topics. After his first book, *The Brain as an Organ*, a scholarly treatise on cognitive function published in 1926, Wertham moved on to write a pair of accounts of lurid murders: *Dark Legend*, a story of matricide published in 1941 (and adapted to the Off-Broadway stage in 1952), and *The Show of Violence*, which followed eight sensational murder cases through the New York courts and was published in 1949. Wertham used the narrative form, drawing upon courtroom testimony and transcripts of his interviews with criminals. In *The Show of Violence*, he was his own main character— one who, as *The New York Times Book Review* pointed out, "describes at length his stormy vicissitudes with the authorities, his victories and his defeats. He writes with vigor and no small irritation at the foibles of the law."

Wertham was a nest of contradictions—intelligent and contemplative, yet susceptible to illogic, conjecture, and peculiar leaps of reasoning; temperate in appearance and manner, yet inclined to extravagant, attention-grabbing pontification. He abhorred comics, which were born of the immigrant experience, while he was deeply empathetic to the Negro condition. Through his friendship with Richard Wright, Wertham became acquainted with Ralph Ellison, who, at the time, was vexed by having received draft papers calling him to serve in an army he deplored for its segregation. Wertham met with Ellison, then wrote a letter to the Selective Service Bureau, petitioning for an exemption for Ellison on psychiatric grounds. After the war, Wertham again made news by protesting the federal government's having confined Ezra Pound to a mental hospital under a diagnosis of insanity, instead of incarcerating him on charges of treason.

Devoted to correcting the racial inequity of mental-health care, Wertham tried unsuccessfully for several years to persuade the administration of New York's mayor, Fiorello La Guardia, to fund a psychiatric clinic in Harlem. Undaunted, he mobilized colleagues and leaders in the Negro community (including Wright, Ellison, and writer Earl Brown of *Life* magazine) to help him proceed without government support, and, in March 1946, Wertham opened the Lafargue Clinic in a room in the basement of the parish house of St. Philip's Episcopal Church in Harlem. Named for Paul Lafargue, a Cuban-born Negro physician and political activist in Paris, the clinic was among the first free (or nearly free) psychiatric facilities available to people of any color in the United States. As Ellison wrote of Lafargue, "This clinic (whose staff receives no salary and whose fee is only twenty-five cents—to those who can afford it) is perhaps the most successful attempt in the nation to provide psychotherapy for the underprivileged. Certainly it has become in two years one of Harlem's most important institutions [and] one of the few institutions dedicated to recognizing the total implication of Negro life in the United States."

Wertham said he saw his purpose at Lafargue as providing treatment, not gathering data. "We don't want to come here to do research, although it will be research anyhow," he told an interviewer for *Life* magazine, which published a three-page article on the clinic in 1948, complete with photographs of Wertham, in his lab coat, interviewing a teenage Negro boy, and Wertham playing with blocks with a group of seven small Negro girls. He and his staff of eleven psychiatrists and volunteers decided to conduct research, anyhow, and their subject was the role of comic books in the lives of young people visiting the clinic. The results served as the basis of a five-page feature article written by Judith Crist, published in *Collier's* magazine in March 1948 and titled "Horror in the Nursery."

In 3,800 forceful words, the piece detailed the research that led Wertham to conclude that comic books were corrupting young readers. "His findings, published here for the first time, constitute a warning to the parents of the nine out of ten American homes into which the comic books eventually find their way," Crist wrote. The text had clinical authority—"Lafargue researchers found . . . The Lafargue Clinic also studied . . . Lafargue researchers brush this off . . . Lafargue researchers are not amused . . ."—and drama, through its horrific accounts of young people killing, beating, and stabbing each other, in one case just "to see what it felt like." The opening pages included two large photographs. In one, a young adolescent boy lay on his back, grimacing in pain, while a girl pinned him to the floor and another boy stabbed him in the arm with a fountain pen. To its right, a second photo showed a scene of five adolescents, three boys and two girls, at a rec-room table with a comic book on it. One of the girls was bound in a chair and gagged while the three boys conspired, presumably about her fate.

Wertham was unequivocal about his conclusions: "We found that comic-book reading was a distinct influencing factor in the case of every single delinquent or disturbed child we studied. And that factor must be curbed as it steadily increases." Comic books, he said, echoing the language of Anthony Comstock, were "in intent and effect, demoralizing the morals of youth."

His evidence was slim. He and the Lafargue researchers cited only one instance in which a child was imitating behavior he or she had seen in a comic book—that of the girl being tied, which Crist described in the first paragraph. (The child quoted in the story never mentioned gagging.) In the case of virtually every other act of delinquency recounted in the piece—a twelve-year-old killing a ten-year-old because "he called me a sissy"; the boy and the girl pinning down another kid and stabbing him with a pen; a child breaking into a candy store; and several others— there was no connection to comics. Wertham never even claimed that the young people involved in those events read comics. He noted only that comic books in general, which most children of all sorts read in those days, depicted violence of a comparable nature. Wertham had leapt tall obstructions to his thesis in a single bound.

Strangely, "Horror in the Nursery" never mentioned that the location of Wertham's research site was Harlem. The first sentence of the piece set the scene: "In the basement of St. Philip's Episcopal Church parish house in uptown New York . . . ," evoking associations with WASPy Anglicanism without a hint of how far uptown the Lafargue Clinic was. The text never mentioned Negro culture or, for that matter, race or ethnicity in any context; and all the children in the photographs, which were staged, were white.

Wertham, interviewed for the article prior to the Supreme Court ruling on *Winters v. New York*, anticipated objections to his criticism of comics on First Amendment grounds. Still, he called for legislative action. "The publishers will raise a howl about freedom of speech and of the press," he told Crist:

> Nonsense. We are dealing with the mental health of a generation—the care of which we have left too long in the hands of unscrupulous persons whose only interest is greed and financial gain . . . If those responsible refuse to clean up the comic-book market—and to all appearances most of them do, the time has come to legislate these books off the newsstands and out of the candy stores.

Indeed, in an interview with the New York *Daily News* published in the same month as "Horror in the Nursery," Wertham pointed to the presidential elections coming that November, and he offered to provide his views on comic books to any candidate "who really wants an issue to take directly to the parents of almost every home in this country where there are children."

Many comics artists and writers, engrossed in their work and happy to have it, penciled or inked their panels or typed their scripts with little awareness of the controversy emerging around them. Harry Lampert, who was drawing the Flash for All-American Comics in 1948, noticed one or two stories in the New York papers about "some nonsense" about comic books and juvenile crime, but he never read them. Nor, for that matter, had he read about the Berlin airlift. Lampert's older brother Bernie's wife showed him an "exposé" of comics in "a homemaker book," probably *Collier's* magazine's "Horror in the Nursery," and he only scanned the photographs. "I walked by a lot of newsstands every day, and there were kids mobbed at every one, looking at the comics," said Lampert. "A couple of articles in the paper? There were hundreds of comic books, they made a lot of kids happy." Lampert got a sense of the brewing discontent over comics only once, when he noticed a boy reading a *Flash* comic (on a bus, as he recalled, or perhaps a subway), and told the youngster that he drew the character—and what was going to be on the following month's cover. "Wow! You draw comic books!" said the boy, and someone near them interjected, "I wouldn't brag about it, buddy."

Fred Kida was highly adaptable and busily unconcerned with the comic debate, despite a collegial warning from one of his editors, Ed Cronin at Hillman Comics. Kida was drawing Airboy for Cronin in 1948. "One day, I came in to deliver my assignment," remembered Kida. "I said, 'All right, Ed—I'll see you next time,' and he said, 'Let's hope,' and he gave me the eye. I figured it was just a joke. It wasn't till a while later that I realized he saw the writing on the wall before the rest of most of us did."

In Will Eisner's phrase, "We were too busy to do our own work." Moreover, Eisner said, the people who made comic books "only cared about making comic books. We lived in a bubble, and lived, breathed, and ate comic books. The world could blow up outside the studio, and the average comic-book man wouldn't notice. As a matter of fact, that's exactly what was starting to happen, and none of us was looking out the window to see it."

■　■　■

There was a newsstand about twelve feet long in the lobby of the City Hall building in Hartford, Connecticut, and the proprietor, a burly fellow named James F. O'Brien, found in mid-June 1948 that he was having trouble selling comic books. "We just display them—we don't sell very many," he told a reporter for *The Hartford Courant*. O'Brien would receive bundles of comics from his distributor, and he would send them back, unsold. The next week, he would get new bundles and return them, too. "I think we get the same ones over and over again," he said. O'Brien was missing a windfall; that June, comic books sold between 80 million and 100 million copies per month, nationwide. In Hartford, though, the city council had passed a resolution calling for magazine vendors to "Clean Up the Newsstands" and voluntarily halt the sale of comics with themes of "immorality and crime." The customers in City Hall, apparently reluctant to try differentiating good comics from bad, avoided them all. The city council struggled with the same distinction as it considered passing an ordinance that would ban the sale of "objectionable comic books," loosely defined, for "endangering or possibly contaminating the plastic minds of our children."

Councilman Joseph V. Cronin, a fan of the *Lone Ranger* comic, noted, in session, "There are curvaceous Indian women in it. Is it the intent of this [measure] to prevent the sale only of the worst books to children?" Another council member, Anson T. McCook, added that he had seen a crime comic with "a scene of violence [that] turned my stomach." A third, Milton Nahum, said, "The police ought to be brought in," and the council resolved to act. In the same month, the governing board of New Britain, Connecticut, passed a resolution instructing its police department to "prohibit the display and sales of magazines and comic books pertinent to crime or sex and all other publications of an obscene nature." Bridgeport and Norwalk, Connecticut, were weighing similar moves.

By the end of June, the city of Milwaukee had set up a committee to form a plan to control comics, and the county of Los Angeles was debating the matter. In Los Angeles, an area with a citizenry well at-tuned to the vagaries of creative expression and interpretation, the Board of Supervisors understood the complexity of distinguishing im-ages of depravity from those of shapely squaws. Acting in response to petitions from parent-teacher associations and juvenile-aid groups, County Supervisor Leonard J. Roach proposed an ordinance prohibit-ing the sale to minors of comics the county board would deem objec-tionable. "These so-called comic books are so obviously detrimental to the welfare of children that immediate steps must be taken to pre-vent the continued sale of the literature in the county," Roach said. In debate on the measure, another supervisor, William Smith, asked, "How can we find a formula that will ban objectionable comics with-out also striking a blow against harmless comic characters?" Indeed, the county counsel, Harold Kennedy, warned that the board's under-taking was "like walking a legal tightrope, because the free press prin-ciple is a sacred thing that must be protected. At the same time, it cannot be abused."

Los Angeles commissioned a report on the ramifications of the March Supreme Court ruling, while other cities launched probes into the comics problem or fashioned solutions through jerry-rigged al-liances of police departments, civic groups, PTAs, and other willing par-ties. On July 21 in Chicago, for example, the police and recreation departments together set up a "censorship board," its membership drawn from institutions such as the Juvenile Protection Agency, labor unions, Northwestern and Loyola universities, and the Field Museum of Natural History. The board was granted authority to identify comic books which would then be restricted from sale within the city limits. Police would monitor newsstands for compliance, and, as the *Chicago Tribune* explained, "should the distributors refuse to comply, police would confiscate the books and arrest those selling them." Three days after the plan was approved, the *Tribune* challenged it in an editorial:

Even granting that comic books are frequently moronic and blood-thirsty, their critics should present further evidence before they go about suppressing them. They should prove that they actually cause juvenile delinquency. It is not enough proof to show that juvenile delinquents read the books. So did the marines on their way into Iwo Jima.

A small storm of consternation over the influence of comic books developed almost simultaneously with an eruption of tensions in the political sphere. Relations between the United States and the Soviet Union, strained since American military forces had intervened on behalf of anti-Communist factions in Greece a year earlier, worsened considerably with the Berlin airlift. In cities around the country, civic leaders took action on comic books while Washington politicians worked on Communism. "It was the beginning of a time of uncertainty and trepidation, and there was no mistaking the commonality between what was starting to happen in comic books and what was going on in the rest of the world," said Frank Bourgholtzer, a comic-book editor for Fawcett, who left the business in the mid-1940s to join the staff of *The Wall Street Journal*. "On both levels, some people were saying, 'We're under assault,' and other people were saying, 'Maybe so, but maybe not—let's keep our heads.'"

In July, the Rochester, New York, district attorney, working with distributors in his area, negotiated a voluntary ban of the comics titles forbidden in Indianapolis and Detroit, now a list of fifty (up from thirty-six two months earlier). In August, Bellingham, Washington, passed a binding prohibition of the same fifty, while the mayor of Sacramento, Belle Cooledge, commissioned a study of how the city could restrict the "wicked, wretched" comics. In the first week of September, the national Congress of Correction held its annual meeting in Boston, and the speaker was Fredric Wertham, who pressed for legislation to "ban" the "pollution" of comic books and stop them from spreading "criminal or sexually abnormal ideas" and "creating an atmosphere of deceit, trickery, and cruelty."

As Wertham spoke, the House Un-American Activities Committee was in the midst of its first set of hearings on the Alger Hiss case. "Finger-pointing, paranoia—it was just beginning, and nobody knew quite what to make of it yet," recalled Bourgholtzer. "The comics people were fortunate that HUAC had enough on its hands and didn't go after them."

In fact, HUAC had had a near brush with comic books the previous year, when it investigated sixteen board members of the Joint Anti-Fascist Refugee Committee, a group linked to the Communist Party; the members included the novelist Howard Fast, the theatrical producer Herman Shumlin, and Lev Gleason, publisher of a short-lived leftist variant of the *Reader's Digest* called *Reader's Scope*, as well as *Crime Does Not Pay*. Gleason, along with other members of the Refugee Committee board, was fined $500 for refusing to furnish records to HUAC; he paid the fine and asked to be purged of a contempt charge, escaping the jail sentence given to the Refugee Committee chairman, Edward K. Barsky.

Gleason had delegated the management of his comics operation to Charles Biro and Bob Wood. "Everybody knew he was a Commie," said Pete Morisi, "but I never met him. I didn't know him. I didn't know anybody who knew him. But I think Charlie was getting a little nervous" about the mounting attention to crime comics. In one visit to Biro's office around the summer of 1948, Morisi noticed that Biro had his pet monkey leashed to a leg of a drawing table; "I always looked for that monkey," Morisi said. "If he was sitting there like a nice monkey, that meant Charlie was happy. If he was nervous, that meant there was trouble."

There was trouble: Crime comics were becoming criminal. On September 23, 1948, the County of Los Angeles outlawed the sale of crime comics to minors. People of any age could still *read* the books with impunity, if they already had them or got them from kids; however, it was a misdemeanor, punishable by a $500 fine or up to six months in jail, for any adult "person, firm or corporation to sell, give or in any way furnish to anyone under eighteen a book, magazine or other publication in which there is prominently featured an account of crime and which depicts by the use of drawings or photographs the commission or attempted commission" of any crime on a sizable list, including arson, assault with a deadly weapon or caustic chemicals, burglary, rape, kidnapping, murder, robbery, theft, voluntary manslaughter, and "mayhem." The Board of Supervisors was clearly determined to prevent Angeleno cousins of Murray Winters from crying "vagueness." County counsel Kennedy called his handiwork "pioneering," and it soon appeared successful. Ten days after the measure went into effect, a *New York Times* headline announced, "Objectionable Books of Comics Disappear from Los Angeles Stands After New Law." The move had received such a "flood of approval," counsel Kennedy told the *Times*, that he expected it to lead to "really comprehensive" state legislation.

The next day, the American Municipal Association reported that nearly fifty cities and towns in the United States had so far "banned the sale of certain comic books"—many of them through legislation; some, such as Racine, Wisconsin, and Oneida, New York, through "censorship committees" and pacts with cooperative businesses. In addition, the AMA noted, an effort to take comics regulation to the state level was under way in California. Separately, that day, Los Angeles County Supervisor Roach announced that he was planning to call for a statewide ban on crime comics at the next session of the California assembly, early in 1949. The idea was inspired, he said, by news that a little boy in Pennsylvania had murdered his brother because of a comic book.

That appeared true, according to an Associated Press story published across the country with headlines such as "Boy Shoots Brother to Death in Fight Over Comic Book." According to the county coro-

ner, ten-year-old George Nall, one of two sons of a steelworker and
his wife who lived in Clifton Flats, a suburb of Newcastle, had decided
to trade one of his comic books to a neighbor friend. However, his six-
year-old brother, Samuel, had not yet read the book. The boys fought.
To end the argument, their father sent George to bed in the room the
brothers shared. Samuel sneaked into his parents' room, found his father's shotgun, loaded it with shells kept not-so-hidden in a vase, went
to see George, in bed, and shot him in the head. A tragedy by any measure, it involved comic books only as the object of the boys' passions.
No coverage of the event mentioned the title of the comic book, and
no one ever suggested that Samuel got the idea to shoot his brother
from the pages of comics.

In the months after *Collier's* published "Horror in the Nursery,"
one death was reported to have been inspired directly by a comic-
book story, and at least one serious juvenile crime had some connection to comics. The incidents provided the campaign against comic
books with bits of evidence to support Wertham's conclusions. On
June 2 in Johnstown, Pennsylvania, a fourteen-year-old boy was found
dead, hung from a steam pipe over his bed. Below him lay a Western
comic book open to a page with a drawing of a bandit hung from a
tree. The coroner concluded that the boy had been standing on his
bed, acting out the adventure, and accidentally slipped. Two months
later, in New Albany, Indiana, three boys, seven, eight, and nine, used
a butcher's knife from one of their homes to prod a seven-year-old
friend into the nearby woods. There, the trio stripped him naked,
burned his clothing, bound his arms behind him, tied a rope around
his neck, and hurled it over the branch of a tree. They tried to hoist
him, but did not have the strength, so they tortured him with kitchen
matches. When they interviewed the boys, the juvenile authorities
found that they were "avid readers of comic books dealing with crime
and torture," *The New York Times* reported in a story headlined
"Comic Book Inspires Boys' Torture of Pal," although the children
never said they were imitating a comic book.

The notion that comics instilled lawlessness was becoming so ingrained that the evidential process reversed. Acts of juvenile delinquency were becoming proof of comic-book consumption. In a Brooklyn court in August 1948, four young men were arraigned on charges of holding up a taxi driver and stealing his cab for a thrill ride. The magistrate, David P. McKeen, set bail at $5,000 each and told the suspects, "You look like you come from decent families, and all you have done is brought them pain and suffering. You boys have been reading too many comic books."

Invulnerable in the panels of the comic books, superheroes succumbed to common criminals on the newsstands. In the late 1940s, dozens of costumed characters, including Captain America, the Flash, the Green Lantern, Hawkman, the Human Torch, and the Sub-Mariner, were all discontinued by publishers quick to move on the new trend, crime. In 1946, crime had represented about 3 percent of all comics; in 1947, 9 percent; in 1948, 14 percent. Thirty new crime titles appeared in 1948 alone. A comic-book buyer in New York (or another city where there were not yet prohibitions against crime comics) could choose among *Crime Must Pay the Penalty, Justice Traps the Guilty, Criminals on the Run, Lawbreakers Always Lose, Pay-Off: True Crime Cases, Crime Reporter, Law Against Crime, True Crime Comics, Official True Crime Cases, Crimes By Women, Murder Incorporated, Crime Exposed, Famous Crimes, Manhunt, All-True Crime Cases, Justice, Real Clue Crime Stories, Crime Detective, Wanted, Authentic Police Cases, Gang Busters,* and *Guns Against Gangsters,* among many others. Irked by this swarm of competitors, Gleason ridiculed them in a house ad in *Crime Does Not Pay* that showed mock-ups of parody titles such as *Crime Doesn't Pay Enough, Crime Dares Not Pay, Crime Will Not Pay, Of Course Crime Doesn't Pay, Crime Ain't Payin' Off Lately,* and *Crime Almost Never Wins.* Two months later, Gleason began publishing his own imitation of *Crime Does Not Pay,* called *Crime and Punishment.*

"Wertham and that whole business, it didn't faze us—business was booming," said Rudy Palais. "We didn't even really know very much about it. Not at first—after a while, sure, we did. But that came later." As Palais recalled, Biro was so little threatened by the emerging campaign against crime comics that he and Wood decided to write a story about a juvenile delinquent drawn to a life of crime through comic books. They barely started when they realized that the idea defied their basic tenet that criminals are inherently evil. The prospect that comic books or any other cultural phenomena could influence a person's behavior contradicted their strict determinism. Before Palais left the studio, Biro told him that he had come up with a better plan: He would put Fredric Wertham's face on the body of a bad guy on the cover of *Crime Does Not Pay*. Palais presumed Biro did so, but he could never know for sure, because all the faces Biro drew looked the same.

6. Then Let Us Commit Them

The panic over comic books falls somewhere between the Red Scare and the frenzy over UFO sightings among the pathologies of postwar America. Like Communism, as it looked to much of America during the late 1940s, comics were an old problem that seemed changed, darkened, growing out of control. Like flying saucers, at the same time, comics were wild stuff with the garish aura of pulp fantasy. Comic books were a peril from within, however, rather than one from a foreign country or another planet. The line dividing the comics' advocates and opponents was generational, rather than geographic. While many of the actions to curtail comics were attempts to protect the young, they were also efforts to protect the culture at large *from* the young. Encoded in much of the ranting about comic books and juvenile delinquency were fears not only of what comics readers might become, but of what they already were—that is, a generation of people developing their own interests and tastes, along with a determination to indulge them.

Young readers argued persuasively for comics through their dimes. In 1948, the 80 million to 100 million comic books purchased in America every month generated annual revenue for the industry of at least $72 million. (The usual cover price was ten cents, although some digest-format books sold for five cents apiece.) Hardcover book publishing, by comparison, brought in about $285 million—about seven times more, through books priced more than twenty times higher.

In the same year, a few comics readers began to speak out in protest of the crackdown on the books. The most vocal among them was David Pace Wigransky, who was a fourteen-year-old sophomore at Calvin Coolidge Senior High School in Washington, D.C., when he read Fredric Wertham's essay "The Comics . . . Very Funny" in the May 29, 1948, issue of *The Saturday Review of Literature*. Something of an authority on the subject himself, Wigransky then owned 5,212 comic books. He was a sharp boy and strong-willed; when he was four years old, *The Washington Post* reported how Wigransky, "imbued with something of the pioneer spirit," had climbed up the stairs of his family home in the northwest district and locked himself in his parents' bedroom until police came and forced the door open. Offended by Wertham's article, he countered with a long letter to *The Saturday Review*—one so eloquent that editor Norman Cousins contacted the principal of Wigransky's school to make sure the language of the letter was consistent with the student's usual writing. The July 24 issue of the magazine devoted a page and a third to the letter, and it included a posed studio photograph of Wigransky, a skinny, gravely serious kid with a dark crew cut, wearing a pressed white shirt, poring over an issue of *Funnyman*. A preface from the editor noted, "Although sections of Mr. Wigransky's letter have been omitted for considerations of space, his copy has not been edited." Wigransky wrote, in part:

It is high time that we who are on the defensive become as serious as our attackers. We didn't ask for this fight, but we are in it to the finish. The fate of millions of children hangs in the balance. We owe it to them to continue to give them the reading matter which they have come to know and love.

Dr. Wertham seems to believe that adults should have the perfect right to read anything they please, no matter how vulgar, how vicious, or how depraving, simply because they are adults. Children, on the other hand, should be kept in utter and complete ignorance of anything and everything except the innocuous and sterile world that the Dr. Werthams of the world prefer to keep them prisoner within from birth to maturity. The net result of all this, however, is that when they have to someday grow up, they will be thrust into an entirely different kind of world, a world of violence and cruelty, a world of force and competition, an impersonal world in which they will have to fight their own battles, afraid, insecure, helpless.

The kids know what they want. They are individuals with minds of their own, and very definite tastes in everything. Just because they happen to disagree with him, Dr. Wertham says that they do not know how to discriminate. It is time that society woke up to the fact that children are human beings with opinions of their own, instead of brainless robots to be ordered hither and yon without even so much as asking them their ideas about anything.

The Saturday Review ran pages of responses in issues published through the end of September 1948. Several of the letters discounted Wigransky on the grounds that, as an obviously intelligent boy, he could not be representative of comic-book readers, or that, as a comic-book reader, he could not be intelligent enough to write such a letter by himself. Either way, they tended to support Wigransky's claim that adults did not seem prepared to accept the average young person's capacity for independent thought and discrimination. It was a view that ran deep at the time, even among some parties in the comics-reading generation.

When the town of Spencer, West Virginia, incorporated in 1858, it took the first name of a beloved county judge, Spencer Roane. It was a neighborly place with an acute regard for justice. In the late 1940s, Spencer had about 2,500 residents, most of them farmers or coal miners and their families, and, each Friday, almost everyone would go to the livestock market, the hub of the community's commerce and social life. Sheep and cattle overran the crossroads in the center of the village, an intersection called New California because an enterprising local named Raleigh Butcher once announced that he was heading for the West Coast but got no farther than that spot. "You could almost go from house to house, go into anybody's house without knocking on the door, and if they were having lunch or dinner, whatever it was, you could walk right in, sit right down, and you'd be welcome to eat with them," recalled David Mace, the only son of a couple who ran a small family-style restaurant called the Glass Door (specialty: the one-dollar "plate-lunch dinner"). They lived in a red-shingle house about half a mile from New California, toward Oregon.

"My mother and father worked probably sixteen, eighteen hours a day, and they made sure you were fed and you were clothed," said Mace. "But other than that, I can't honestly say what they thought about anything. They expected you to do the right thing, and it was your responsibility to know good from bad. You were on your own. Of course, most everyone in town agreed with everything that went on in Spencer in those days. It wasn't like things got later on, where you'd have so many different public opinions about everything. We had a nice little tight-knit community. I doubt there was a TV in our community at that time." Television, after all, was just beginning to find an audience. Nine years after RCA brought the technology to the American public, there were only twenty-seven broadcast stations in eighteen cities, most of them on the East Coast and half of them in and around New York City. TV sets—hardwood boxes the size of refrigerators with tiny, roundish, gray screens—were extravagances to be found in only one of every ten American homes, where families could watch rudimentary but high-minded broadcasts of civics debates, lectures, and chamber-music performances for a few hours each day.

Several stores in downtown Spencer sold comic books, and David Mace, like every child he knew, bought them. He thought of them as "thrills and fun," until early in his eighth-grade year at Spencer

Elementary School, in the fall of 1948, when one of his teachers, Mabel Riddel, asked him to stay after class, sat down next to him in a child's desk, and told him that comics had "an evil effect on the minds of young children." Riddel, acting with the support of the PTA, asked Mace to lead his fellow students in an uprising against comics. "She was extremely dedicated—that's the way our school was and the way our teachers were," Mace remembered. "She explained to me about the [harm of] comic books, which I didn't know about. I read 'em, and I never even noticed. The things she had to say made a lot of sense, I could see that, and she told me we could do something about it, and I said, 'Well, let's go!'" Smallish and good-looking, with dark hair (almost black) and blue eyes, Mace was popular and a talker. With Riddel's encouragement and counsel, Mace hit the schoolyard and rallied the upper-class students to join him in a mission to remove all comic books from the homes and stores of Spencer—an elaborate group activity not unlike the games Mace sometimes organized, a scavenger hunt taken out of the playground and into the adult world, ideal for young adolescents beginning to confront the end of childhood and their grade-school years.

For almost a month, Mace led several dozen students in a door-to-door campaign through Spencer. With milk crates in hand or wagons in tow, they urged children and parents to relinquish all the comics in their houses, and implored retailers to stop selling the books. By the last week of October, Mace's brigade had collected more than two thousand comic books of all sorts, from reprints of the *Dick Tracy* strip to crime comics. The kids brought them into school on Tuesday, October 26, a cool, dry, sunny day, and they piled them on the grounds behind the building. The books made a small mountain about six feet high. At the end of the day, the six hundred children who attended the school emptied into the yard and assembled in a semicircle facing the comics. David Mace walked to the far side of the pile and stood before the crowd in his best clothes, a white shirt and black wool pants his mother had ironed fresh that morning for the occasion. He put his left hand on his hip, and, in his right hand, he held a sheet of lined paper with some words he had written, with considerable help from Mrs. Riddel.

"We are met here today to take a step which we believe will bene-fit ourselves, our community, and our country," Mace said. "Believing that comic books are mentally, physically, and morally injurious to boys and girls, we propose to burn those in our possession. We also pledge ourselves to try not to read any more.

"Do you, fellow students, believe that comic books have caused the downfall of many youthful readers?"

The students answered, in unison, "We do."

"Do you believe that you will benefit by refusing to indulge in comic-book reading?" Mace continued.

"We do."

"Then let us commit them," Mace said. He walked a few steps to the pile, took a matchbook from a pants pocket, and lit the cover of a *Superman* comic.

The flames rose to a height of more than twenty-five feet as the children, their teachers, the principal, and a couple of reporters and photographers from the area papers watched for more than an hour. Mrs. Riddel stared with her arms crossed. Several children wept—a signal to those who noticed that not everyone in town agreed with everything that went on in Spencer that day.

When the Associated Press picked up the story from local ac-counts, readers of *The Washington Post*, the *Chicago Tribune*, and dozens of other papers around the country learned how, just three years after the Second World War, American citizens were burning books. Mace would remember receiving letters of support from around the coun-try, which his mother kept in a cigar box in the kitchen. "She was really impressed when we got all that mail," Mace recalled. "What we did was a pretty important thing at that time, and it put our little town in central West Virginia on the map." Indeed, the Spencer paper, *The Times Record*, covered the national coverage of the burning: "Spencer

Graded School Is Famous." Not all the commentary on the event was so prideful, however; as the *Charleston Daily Mail* noted in an editorial:

> The burning of books is too recent in our memories. The Nazis burned them. They went on from there and, in one way or another, burned the authors too. It was the purge by fire of those elements which the Nazi party could not tolerate.
>
> This purge has no place in a democratic educational system. It is not that books as books are sacred. It is just that the idea of burning them is profane. It is a resort to witchcraft when the need is for education, the use of fire when enlightment [*sic*] is called for. Perhaps the point can be clarified by asking how many of the boys and girls who burned 2,000 "bad" books have read 2,000 good ones? Of the two possible tasks, the second deserves priority.

Images of Third Reich soldiers in black uniforms emptying military trucks full of books onto bonfires endured in American memory. Yet most of the German book-burning had been done by students, young people stirred to act against literature that they had been led to think of as corruptive to members of their own generation. Worked up to a nationalist frenzy just three months after Hitler assumed the chancellorship, the German Student Association mobilized university students to burn more than 25,000 books advancing "un-German ideas" in Berlin and other cities throughout Germany in May 1933. In the days and months to follow, the student association organized thirty-four more burnings in university towns across the country, and young people chanted, sang, and gave speeches before the fires. Who better to inspire contempt for the books than members of their intended audience?

In the United States after the war, the incident in Spencer was not singular. A couple of Catholic schools had staged little-noted comic-book protests with ceremonial fires as early as 1945. In November of that year, during Catholic Book Week, nuns teaching at Saints Peter and Paul elementary school in Wisconsin Rapids, Wisconsin, held a competition among students to gather the highest number of "objectionable" comics, as categorized in lists made by the Rev. Robert E. Southard. The boy and girl who brought in the most books were named the king and queen of a bonfire that consumed 1,567 comic books. (King Wayne Provost collected 109; Queen Donna Jean Walloch, 100.) The event was selective, in its way, targeting only comics that Southard listed as Condemned (*Batman*, *Wonder Woman*, *The Spirit*, *Crime Does Not Pay*) or Questionable (*Superman*, *Captain Marvel*, *Archie*). Spared from the pyre were those Southard rated as Harmless (*Mickey Mouse*, *Donald Duck*, and compilations of the Popeye and Katzenjammer Kids newspaper strips, comics that had been condemned in their own day). Two years later, in December 1947, students of St. Gall's School in Chicago collected and burned 3,000 comics (including, again, *Superman*, *Batman*, *The Spirit*, and *Archie*) in a campaign reported to have been suggested by a ten-year-old fourth-grade girl, Marlene Marrello.

Once the Associated Press spread the news from Spencer, the idea of fighting comic books with fire began to catch on in schools and communities across the country, particularly in Catholic parishes already primed to act on the issue. There were two sizable comic-book burnings in the sixty days after David Mace set *Superman* in flames, both at parochial schools: St. Patrick's Academy in Binghamton, New York, and Saints Peter and Paul elementary in Auburn, New York. Many more would be organized at public and parochial schools in the months and years to follow. Easy to mistake from the distance of time as the puppetmastery of reactionary adults exploiting children too sheepish to defend their own enthusiasms, the comic-book burnings of the late 1940s were multilayered demonstrations of the emerging generation's divided loyalties and developing sense of cultural identity. The events exposed the compliance of some young people in the face of adult authority at the same time the incidents fueled the defiance of others.

In Binghamton, the campaign against comics was almost solely the work of a charismatic student named John Farrell. A sixteen-year-old junior at St. Patrick's in the 1948–49 school year, Farrell was the president of his class, as he had been, on and off, since the fifth grade. He was a chunky boy, neither athletic nor conventionally handsome, but a jokester, grand company. He had a broad, toothy grin and a slight underbite that gave him a disarming, comical appearance. In a blue-collar, Irish-Catholic area, where many students' parents (both of them, often) worked in the local factories that manufactured shoes and chemical products, John Farrell was considered well off and cultured; his father was an executive in charge of production at the *Binghamton Press* newspaper, and John dressed and spoke with flair. "He was so damned funny," recalled Paul Plocinski, a classmate who was deeply involved in the comics burning. Tall and sturdy, Plocinski looked like a grown man in his junior year and itched for the freedom of adulthood. "He could imitate every one of those nuns. He was very dignified in his attire, and he knew all about politics, but he used to keep us laughing."

Farrell worked after school as a soda jerk at Crone's pharmacy, a busy, well-regarded store appointed with milled woodwork and a sixteen-foot marble-topped fountain counter. It was a nice environment for good kids to congregate, and it had a magazine rack around the corner from the soda fountain. Part of Farrell's job was to watch the rack to ensure that kids paid for their comics before sitting down at the counter to read them. One of Farrell's friends, Joseph Canny, whose family lived a block away from the Farrells, would sometimes keep John company at Crone's, and even he was granted no free reading privileges. "John was a well-read fellow, and he knew that comic books were controversial," said Canny. A year younger and a grade behind Farrell in school, Canny was a bookish kid, one of three second-generation Irish brothers whose father had died in an odd accident, run over by a driver at his own trucking company, when Joseph Canny was nine. "It started to bother John that Crone's was making every kind of comic book available, with no discrimination, and John was in a position to watch the reading habits of his clientele. He started to notice that the more troublesome kind of kids were more inclined to read comic books, and some of [the books] were pretty rough stuff." Farrell took up the matter with his boss, Ken Crone, but found him unmoved. "That's when John decided to take the initiative, on his own," said Canny. "He was sincere. John was a religious guy, and he was irritated by all these comic books and the content in a lot of them. The thing was all John's idea, and he had the support at the school to make it happen."

St. Patrick's Academy was a spartan Catholic institution housed in a boxy, three-story redbrick building dressed up with a pair of Gothic spires jutting high above the turreted front roof, and an opulent, arched entrance for faculty and guests. Students used the side doors, the left for boys, the right for girls. The cafeteria provided tables and a drinking fountain, but no food, and the basketball team, which was often good, played outdoors, because it had no gym. All the teachers were sisters of the order of St. Joseph. Each class of about thirty students spent thirteen years, from ages five to eighteen, together. Like other smallish private schools of all sorts, St. Patrick's fostered mighty feelings of loyalty, pride, exceptionalism, paranoia, and restiveness. At the end of the school day, so many students lingered together in the halls of St. Patrick's or stayed in classrooms, talking to the nuns, that the Mother Superior, Anna Frances, had to shoo them away.

"It was very intimate—we knew one another personally, and everyone seemed to be involved in whatever was going on, because of the size of the school," recalled James D. Kane, who was a classmate of John Farrell's, took part in the Binghamton comics burning, and went on to enter the priesthood. "It gave us a *good* education," said Kane, emphasizing the word "good" to distinguish it from both "poor" and "excellent." "The others were no better, though the kids in the public schools treated us like second-class citizens. I don't think they liked what we did, most of the time. But we did what we thought was right, regardless of what they thought."

St. Patrick's, the largest of Binghamton's ten Catholic churches in 1948, served about 2,500 residents of the west side, a working-class community of Irish and Slovak families. One neighborhood in the area was essentially owned by Endicott Johnson, the shoe manufacturer, which built solid little A-frame houses for hundreds of its employees and deducted low-interest mortgage payments from their weekly paychecks. (Paul Plocinski grew up in an "Endicott house" and recalled it as "wonderful and beautiful.") Early in the twentieth century, Binghamton had served as the New York State headquarters for the Ku Klux Klan. By 1948, the Klan's legacy was spectral, although the climate of Binghamton remained "fairly judgmental," in the view of Monsignor Kane. "We Catholics were sometimes the target of that," Kane said. "That's one of the reasons we stuck together."

The first phase of Farrell's campaign was a coercion strategy to purge Binghamton stores of objectionable comics. Working under Farrell, students in the four high-school grades of St. Patrick's set out to visit every Binghamton store and newsstand that carried magazines—Murphy's cigar store, Grant's ice-cream shop, Smith's pharmacy—and to urge each of the owners they met to sign a four-by-six index card carrying this pledge: "I will support the drive to end indecent and objectionable literature, comic books and the like, by withdrawing them from my newsstand, and will do all in my power to stop their sale." Dealers who declined were told their stores would be boycotted by the students.

The tactic challenged students as well as the business people they were charged to confront. "We had to go around to all the stores— dime stores, any place they sold magazines—and make sure that they didn't sell comic books anymore, and it was unbearable," said Plocinski. "The storekeepers were shocked—they never heard of such a thing. It was a very difficult thing, but we did it because we were expected to, and we thought we were doing a good thing. But, to tell you the truth, I wasn't completely sure about that." Once, Plocinski picked up a comic to show a dealer an example of the kind of books the students were protesting, and he purchased it, thereby removing it from the shelf. He then took it home and tried to hide it, only to find that the spot under the living-room sofa cushions was already taken: His father was keeping his detective magazines there.

News vendors, riled and unsure how to handle this unusual pressure from youthful ranks, complained to their local magazine distributor, Abraham M. Pierson, who reported their distress to the *Binghamton Sun*, the competition to Farrell's father's paper. "I know a lot of dealers around here were getting worried about the kids asking them to sign cards [and] one fellow told me that he was really sore about the thing," said Pierson. "One fellow was going to throw the boys out." (There were as many teenage girls as boys involved in the campaign.) Still, Farrell and his troops elicited pledges from thirty-five Binghamton retailers.

St. Patrick's students boycotted the rest, including the students' favorite after-school hangout, Smith's, which was across the street from the school on Oak Street. "We were very serious," explained Vincent Hawley, a freshman at the time. A quiet, earnest boy, Hawley entered St. Patrick's in the fourth grade, when his family moved eighteen miles north from rural Silver Lake Township, Pennsylvania, where he had attended a one-room schoolhouse. "We were determined to boycott all these places that were selling these things until they took the comic books off the shelves, and one of the places was the most popular place where we used to go. We were so serious we even made periodic checks to make sure our own students were upholding the boycott, and one day after school, we went over to Smith's—we just stood outside to remind the owner of all the business he was losing, and while we were there, one of our students walked out of the place. Three hundred ninety-nine of us were boycotting the place, and only one kid defied the boycott. When he came out, one of the kids jumped him, and it turned into a huge, big fistfight. We were serious."

For several weeks, St. Patrick's students barnstormed the sidewalks of Binghamton's west side, collecting the materials for the climax of their campaign, a public burning. "We were crusaders," said Hawley. "We all read the comics—the comics were huge! But I separated the good ones and the bad ones in my mind. The hero comics were good, and then there were the other ones. The ones that we were trying to eliminate were the bad ones. We weren't against comics per se, but how some of them were being used." Hawley and his fellow crusaders so embraced superhero comics' ethos of eradicating evil that they employed it against other comics.

To Paul Plocinski and some others he knew, however, the distinctions between differing comics or between the comics' form and content were vexing to parse. "I had been trading comics for years," said Plocinski. "I had stacks of them. The drawings were really artful, very much so—the artwork was wonderful. We thought we were doing a good thing by collecting the comics and conducting this protest, but it gave me a pain in my stomach. I was torn up inside, and I wasn't the only one."

The day of the burning, Friday, December 10, was cold and gray. Mother Anna Frances ended classes early, at 11:00 a.m., and released the entire student body of about 560 onto the playground behind the school. To document the occasion, someone set up a stepladder and took a photograph from the top, moments before the fire was set. Published in the 1949 St. Patrick's yearbook, the picture shows a group of eight students—Plocinski, in the center, dressed nattily in a dark wool coat and a white scarf, flanked by three other boys and four girls (none of them Farrell, who was standing on the photographer's side of the scene). The kids have shipping cartons for Rice Krispies and Ivory Snow full of comic books, and they are emptying them into a deep stone kiln meant for the school trash. Behind them, we see a mass of children, many of them early grade-schoolers, bundled in coats with hoods, zippered tight, or wool caps, in gloves or mittens. One boy on the far right is shoving another to make sure he gets in the picture. A small fellow in the front row, wearing a one-piece snowsuit, has his legs spread wide apart, planted to hold his position. In the second row, a boy too short for his face to be photographed waves a cross in the air with his right hand. Most of the faces are smiling; a few brows are furrowed; only two or three young children look afraid.

With a few hundred comics in the kiln, a Sister Lucia, Farrell's chief ally among the nuns, lit the books. Then, as the fire began to rage, she led the students in singing the St. Patrick's alma mater and "The Catholic Action Song":

> *An army of youth flying the standards of truth*
> *We're fighting for Christ, the Lord*
> *Heads lifted high, Catholic Action our cry*
> *And the Cross our only sword.*
> *On earth's battlefield, never a vantage we'll yield*
> *As dauntlessly on we swing*
> *Comrades true, dare and do, 'neath the Queen's white and blue*
> *For our flag, for our faith, for Christ the King*

Farrell and his compatriots kept the fire stoked for four hours, tossing in more boxes of comics while the students of St. Patrick's watched. The flames stretched as high as thirty feet. By three o'clock, when the children were released, the group of onlookers had multiplied to include many parents, neighbors, reporters, and members of the parish command.

"I remember it very vividly," said Joseph Canny. "I watched them burn it all up, and I thought, This is really something! I thought it was good—I thought it was a good thing, and I was impressed that John had been able to pull it off." Through the Associated Press, again, news of the comics burning at St. Patrick's made newspapers around the country. "I had no idea at the beginning that it would turn out to be such a big thing," said Canny. "I was really proud of John."

The *Catholic Sun*, a daily Church paper published in Syracuse, commended the St. Patrick's students for bringing their song of "Catholic action" to life:

The action of the St. Patrick's pupils earned deserved national recognition. It was a public protest. It was a dramatization of a very present problem. It does call for a sincere and sustained response from responsible leaders in the publication business. It does declare that the menace of the comics is not mere theory . . . The students of St. Patrick's are to be congratulated for they have earned the respect and regard of every good American.

The only public dissent came from magazine sellers watching the dime bins of their cash registers. As the *Binghamton Sun* paraphrased distributor Abraham Pierson, "Banning books should not be left up to a group of high school students," because authority on the matter "should be given only to those acquainted with the problem." In essence, the complaint was consistent with much of the criticism of young comic-book readers, faulting the St. Patrick's students not for their views, but for daring to have any, one way or the other. Pierson made no claim that John Farrell and his group acted unfairly, illegally, or unethically; he never challenged them for being wrong, but only for being young.

The Sunday after the St. Patrick's bonfire, the bishop of Albany, Edmund F. Gibbons, called for a diocese-wide boycott much like the one the students had imposed in Binghamton, dispensing with the gesture of first calling for pledges by the businesses involved. Bishop Gibbons issued a letter to be read at all masses that day, which said, in part:

Another evil of our times is found in the pictorial magazine and comic book which portray indecent pictures and sensational details of crime. This evil is particularly devastating to the young, and I call upon our people to boycott establishments which sell such literature.

Less than two weeks later, three days before Christmas, *The Citizen-Advertiser* of Auburn, New York, a small city about sixty miles northwest of Binghamton, reported that the students of a local Catholic school, Saints Peter and Paul, took "quick action" and made a "huge bonfire" of comic books collected by students acting under the direction of the principal, Sister Boniface. Praising the action in an editorial, the paper noted, "This action follows that taken elsewhere in many parts of the country by other irritated parents and authorities," reinforcing that the event was not necessarily an expression of all the students' points of view.

"The holidays came, and everything was wonderful," said Paul Plocinski, "except every time I saw a fireplace burning with the Christmas stockings hung, I thought about that bonfire and all those comic books, and it made me sick. I started to get angry, and really wished we hadn't done that. Burning things! I said to myself, I'm never going to do that again, and went out and bought myself some comic books." Plocinski would always remember the day during Christmas vacation when he walked alone to Smith's shop, ventured tentatively back into the forbidden place, and picked out a comic from the rack. (The title would escape him with time.) "I put my dime on the counter," Plocinski said, "and I don't know what I said—probably, 'Thank you very much, sir.' But I know what I was thinking—Take that, John Farrell!" Plocinski walked home with the comic book rolled tight in his back pocket and tucked under his coat, so no one would see if he bumped into anyone from school.

■　■　■

The history of censorship in twentieth-century America is largely a story of self-regulation in the name of self-preservation—voluntary restraint enacted on the assumption that governmental restriction would be worse. In the film industry, the comic-book business's older cousin, moviemakers had long dealt with controversies over content much like those comics publishers confronted in the 1940s; as early as 1896, Edison's spicy Vitascope short, *Dolorita's Passion Dance*, was banned from the Atlantic City boardwalk. During the first decade of the silent era, the city of Chicago called upon its police department to censor films, and states began passing laws to control what appeared on movie screens. When, in 1915, the Supreme Court upheld the legitimacy of an Ohio state film-censorship body (*Mutual Film Corp. v. Industrial Commission of Ohio*), the movie industry acted to halt the proliferation of similar groups, which were free to edit films as they saw fit; within a year, the studios formed the National Association of the Motion Picture Industry and imposed production guidelines for its members. The effort floundered but set a footing for the later, better-organized Motion Picture Producers and Distributors of America, through which, in 1930, Hollywood defused efforts in Congress to regulate movie content, introducing its own Production Code and setting up Will H. Hays, a backlot J. Edgar Hoover, to enforce it. The Hays Office prevented Jane from further skinny-dipping in Tarzan's lagoon and cleansed scripts of movies such as Bing Crosby's *Going My Way* of such offensive language as "pig dust," while training a generation of screenwriters, film actors, and moviegoers to tease multiple levels of meaning from half-glances, sly gestures, and coded language. The movies lost their freedom, while they gained in subtext.

Using the Hollywood consortium and its Production Code as models, a small group of comic-book publishers—Phil Keenan of Hillman Periodicals (publishers of *Pageant* magazine as well as *Real Clue Crime Stories* and *Airboy* comics), Lev Gleason of *Crime Does Not Pay*, Bill Gaines of EC, Harold Moore of *Famous Funnies*, and Rae Herman of Orbit Periodicals—along with two distributors, Frank Armer and Irving Manheimer, put together a comics trade organization, the Association of Comics Magazine Publishers, and, through it, fashioned a code of "minimum editorial standards." Founding president Keenan, in announcing the plan on July 1, 1948, said he had enlisted twelve members out of the thirty-four comics publishers then issuing some 270 titles per month. Their Comics Code, adapted from language in the film Production Code (expanded on the subject of crime), urged (but did not oblige) its members (and other publishers, over whom the group had little influence) to honor six principles:

- Sexy, wanton comics should not be published. No drawing should show a female indecently or unduly exposed, and in no event more nude than in a bathing suit commonly worn in the U.S.A.
- Crime should not be presented in such a way as to throw sympathy against law and justice or to inspire others with the desire for imitation. No comics shall show the details and methods of a crime committed by a youth. Policemen, judges, government officials and respected institutions should not be portrayed as stupid or ineffective, or represented in such a way as to weaken respect for established authority.
- No scenes of sadistic torture should be shown.
- Vulgar and obscene language should never be used. Slang should be kept to a minimum and used only when essential to the story.
- Divorce should not be treated humorously or represented as glamorous or alluring.
- Ridicule of or attack on any religious or racial group is never permissible.

The association planned to have a committee review comic-book pages before publication and approve them or return them for modifications, if necessary. Acceptable titles would be permitted to bear the phrases "Authorized A.C.M.P." and "Conforms to the Comics Code" on their covers.

Soon after the group was formed, it hired as its executive director Henry E. Schultz, a Manhattan attorney, president of the board of Queens College, and member of the New York City Board of Higher Education. He was well chosen to front an effort designed to convey an image of sturdy American wholesomeness. Solid and broad-shouldered, Schultz had an oversized head, like a screen actor, steely chiseled features, no lips, and slightly receding straight black hair. He looked exactly like Captain Marvel. In December 1948, *Newsweek* covered what it described as "a full-fledged fight" between the comics industry and its critics, and described Schultz as "a strapping, darkly handsome attorney" serving as "comic-book czar" from his "cavernous, swank" Manhattan office.

Schultz served loyally. In a debate on comics and juvenile delinquency at a conference in Washington, D.C., sponsored by the General Federation of Women's Clubs, Schultz oozed indignation. He scolded his opponent, James V. Bennett, director of the Federal Bureau of Prisons, warning that the growing consternation over comics was "beginning to develop into a wild kind of hysteria." As for comics and delinquency, Schultz huffed, "The publisher of the leading crime comic [Lev Gleason, cofounder of the ACMP] would be purple with rage at the charge that his books cause crime. He has sixty thousand letters praising them as crime prevention, and he has been honored by the Sheriffs of New Jersey for his part in elimination of crime."

By the end of 1948, the ACMP had only fourteen members out of the thirty-five publishers now producing some three hundred titles per month; the twenty-one companies not participating included not only the producers of the most violent crime comics (Fox, Harvey), but the publishers of some of the most popular superhero titles: National/DC (*Superman, Batman*), Timely/Atlas/Marvel (*Captain America*), and Fawcett (*Captain Marvel*), as well as MLJ (*Archie*) and Gilberton (*Classics Illustrated*). As an executive with Fox explained his philosophy, "There are more morons than people, you know." National, Timely, MLJ, and other absentees held their own editorial guidelines to be adequate, declined affiliation with small-timers such as EC and Orbit or easy targets such as Gleason's operation, or feared bogging down their production schedule by accommodating a review process. The last item proved of no concern; the ACMP soon aban-

doned its plan to screen pages before publication as unwieldy. Under-
manned and underarmed, much like the motion-picture industry's
first organization, the Association of Comics Magazine Publishers
never had much chance to fulfill its charter, and its code went little noticed by comic-book makers, their readers, and the authorities hover-
ing over them both.

7. Woofer and Tweeter

What was it about the field of chemistry that appealed to the young Bill Gaines? The precision of hard science? Obsessed with measurements and order, he used a ruler and a T square to position every item on his desk at Educational Comics for optimum efficiency (stapler two inches back from the blotter on the left side, letter opener one inch to its right), and he checked all the trash cans and ashtrays in the office to make sure they were empty before he left at the end of each day. Was it the subject matter of chemistry—the elemental nature of things, what induces them to change, and how they react and interact? Gaines was an internal creature, quiet and enigmatic, but he relished stimulating company and inspired others; rarely one to volunteer an idea or make a joke, he was a listener, a dream audience with a true and easy laugh. What of the laboratory process? Gaines tinkered with the rudimentary office equipment at EC and put an attachment on the receiver of his telephone so he could talk and, at the same time, putter with both hands. When he first assumed control of his late father's company, the business did not provide enough interaction with peers, nor enough opportunity for meaningful experimentation—enough creative chemistry—to keep him engaged. Soon, however, he and EC were transformed, mainly through the effect of a new element in their environment, Al Feldstein.

"In the beginning, I hated the business," Gaines later recalled. He concentrated on finishing the course work for his undergraduate degree and left most of the publishing decisions to the financial director, Frank Lee, and the circulation manager, Sol Cohen, a pair of aging jobbers Gaines had inherited along with *Tiny Tot Comics*, the rest of M. C. Gaines's tiny tot of a company, and its debt. Cohen thought it might be good for the firm to try branching out of the realm of early childhood—at least a few years, into adolescence. He took note of MLJ's success with *Archie*, which several other publishers were already imitating (National/DC with *Buzzy*, Timely with *Patsy Walker*, Fox with *Junior* and *Sunny*, transients such as Humor Publishing with *The Adventures of Homer Cobb* and *Hap Hazard*), and, in a circuitous recruitment effort, Cohen mentioned to the owner of Wroten Lettering (the service EC employed to ink the words on its pages) that EC was in the market for artists to work on a new comic for teenagers. James Wroten passed the information to the stable at Fox, where the artists and writers were notoriously underpaid and overtaxed.

On a morning in the first week of February 1948, an artist who had worked on no fewer than four teen comics titles, Al Feldstein, brought his portfolio to 225 Lafayette Street, an outwardly imposing Greek Revival building with a gilded, high-ceilinged bank on the ground floor and, above it, ten floors of low-rent office suites accessible through a small side entrance. (All the money was downstairs.) Feldstein took the elevator to the seventh floor, walked down a long hall that seemed gloomy at ten o'clock, and entered the suite at the far end. He was dressed sharply, as usual, in a gray suit, a white shirt, and a jaunty tie. Then twenty-two, Feldstein was a compact man with tight-cropped, wavy hair and the elegant pug looks and manner of John Garfield. He asked for Cohen, and Cohen greeted him, exchanged unpleasantries about Feldstein's main client, Victor Fox, and led Feldstein in to meet Bill Gaines. Cohen left the room. Feldstein stood in front of Gaines's desk, which had no papers on it. Gaines, a thick man who wore black horn-rimmed glasses and a crew cut as flat as his standard expression, was in his shirtsleeves and had a plain, dark tie loosened at the neck. He stayed seated, and he said, "Let me see the work." Although Feldstein knew virtually nothing about Gaines at the time, Feldstein thought he looked like a high-school science teacher (or so he would later claim). The two said little as Gaines began to flip through Feldstein's portfolio.

Apart from a few pages from *Science Comics* ("How Tunnels Are Constructed") and other oddities such as the sleeves for a series of children's storybook records, most of what Gaines saw were tearsheets from *Junior* and *Sunny*. The drawings were stiff and boxy; the ink lines heavy, like the art in a technical manual for toolmakers; the anatomy, baldly but exactingly preposterous. Gaines found panel after panel of outrageously proportioned teenage girls, their waists thinner than their legs, their breasts larger than their heads. The trade term for this bosom-centric style was "headlight" art, although Feldstein's was more of a klieg-light approach, and Bill Gaines loved it. Feldstein looked on as Gaines removed his glasses, placed them neatly in a case in his desk drawer, and lowered his face to study Feldstein's art, his nose almost touching the paper. Gaines chuckled quietly as Feldstein watched the back of his head rattle. Without glancing up from the pages, Gaines asked Feldstein if he had used models for the drawings. Bill Gaines had made a joke. For the next hour or so, the men chatted—about Feldstein, about their fathers, about their mutual dissatisfaction with the comics business, and more about Feldstein.

An artist with a keen business sense, like Will Eisner, Albert G. Feldstein was the younger of two sons of parents with creative streaks; they had met in a small, private music school in Brooklyn, where his mother, Beatrice, was studying violin, and his father, Max, voice. Abandoning the arts for commerce, Max Feldstein set up a laboratory that molded false teeth, and it thrived until the late Depression years, when the Feldsteins went bankrupt and lost their nice redbrick and stucco home in Flatbush, Brooklyn, and moved to a two-bedroom, fourth-floor walk-up apartment eleven blocks in the wrong direction. Al Feldstein was twelve, and the family upheaval accelerated his emerging doubts about parental wisdom. "I loved them, but I didn't respect them," said Feldstein. "They were so wrapped up in themselves that I developed an attitude that parents were self-indulgent and parental authority was a lot of crap. My dad was hard to reach. I never knew him well. I had a need for his attention, his encouragement, and his participation in my life. But he was not interested in my interests— he was only involved with trying to make a living and failing at it, and my mother was so involved in her own problems, whatever they were, financial and otherwise, whatever problems there were in her marriage as a result of my father's failures, that she took out a lot of her frustrations on her children, me and my brother. My parents molded me, and they made me antiparent. They also made me aware of the importance of money in terms of well-being in a marriage, and so I grew up rather opportunistic, wanting to make a good living."

Quick-witted and ambitious, Feldstein would gather children from his neighborhood, charge them two cents apiece, and put on puppet shows, improvising the stories and doing all the characters' voices. He liked to draw, and, with the encouragement of an elementary-school teacher, Mrs. Kingsland, entered a couple of juvenile art contests (one sponsored by the Wanamaker department store, another connected to the upcoming 1939 World's Fair) and did fairly well (third prize and an honorable mention, respectively). Talented enough to pass the admissions exam for New York's selective High School of Music and Art, a test that included drawing under observation, Feldstein was admitted in 1938 and soon walked the halls with a handful of teenage artists who would gather a decade later at 225 Lafayette Street: Will Elder, Harvey Kurtzman, Al Jaffee, and John Severin. Feldstein, a few years younger than those four, socialized with none of them, nor many others, in school. "I was a bit of a loner, and it was hard to get too close to anybody there, because the students were scattered all over the city, and I had a hard time scraping up a nickel to go to somebody's house after school," said Feldstein. Still, he said, "My years at Music and Art were invaluable. They developed me as a person in terms of my social conscience. I was exposed to wonderful teachers, enthusiastic teachers, socially conscious teachers who were talking about the problems of the day and philosophy and things. They were probably Communists, and they shaped my social and political thinking." The same ideas would not escape Elder, Kurtzman, or Jaffee. (Severin grew to be less radically inclined.)

Feldstein was taking courses at Brooklyn College by day and painting at the Art Students League at night, when he heard that an old classmate from high school, Norman Maurer, was earning riches, $25 per page, by drawing comic books. Feldstein looked up Jerry Iger. "He checked out my work and said, 'Okay, I can give you a job as a runner. Come in after school. I'll pay you three dollars a week, and you sit and you erase the pencil lines on pages, and when I got an errand for you, you run the errand, and you'll learn from what passes in front of your face.' That was how I did my apprenticeship. I just kind of walked in and said, 'Here I am,' you know, like a farm girl walking into the house of prostitution and saying, 'Look at me. I want to work.' And that's how I felt about comics. I felt like a talented prostitute, making a buck selling my talent.

"But, you know, I learned, and I changed my mind. I sat next to Bob Webb, who was doing *Sheena, Queen of the Jungle*, and he let me do the background—I started to do palm trees and vegetation, and then he let me do the leopard spots on Sheena's breasts and crotch, on her costume, which was added after the fact. Webb drew her stark naked. Pretty soon, I started to notice that some of the guys there were really artists—Webb and Lou Fine and Reed Crandall and Alex Blum. I finally realized that these guys were damn good. It's just that they were just applying their abilities to a rather unrespected form that the kids loved but their parents didn't understand, and that really clicked with me, because I didn't understand parents."

During the war, Feldstein served under Special Services in the Army Air Corps, working on the art for posters and slide presentations while running a lucrative side venture painting his specialty, anatomically outlandish women, on flight jackets. He returned to comics after his discharge, married his girlfriend "because everybody was getting married," and scuffled. At the time he followed a lettering company's lead for work at a prospective start-up by a tenuous company in Little Italy, Feldstein, his (first) wife Claire, who was pregnant, and their almost-two-year-old daughter Leslie were living in a three-room apartment on the same floor as Claire's parents on Ocean Parkway, across the street from the Parkside Skating Rink, in Brooklyn. Feldstein was working mainly for Victor Fox, the slipperiest of publishers in an unstable field, squeezing a few extra dollars from him by writing as well as drawing and using his wife as a front for the scripts. He had a table set up in the only available space in his apartment, a narrow foyer, and worked there mainly during the night while his family slept.

When Feldstein met Bill Gaines and chatted him up, he was a desperate man in a nice suit (from a bottom rack of Ripley's of Fifth Avenue). By the time he left Lafayette Street that morning, Feldstein had a commission from Gaines to create an original comic, and he returned a week later with the pencil sketches for the cover and the first story of *Going Steady with Peggy*, a sexed-up twist on his own earlier variations on *Archie*. Gaines contracted Feldstein to produce the book, at $31 per page of art and text, plus $25 for each cover. (Although Gaines gave Feldstein the impression that he had agreed to share the book's profits with Feldstein, the paperwork they signed, on February 13, 1948, failed to mention any such arrangement.) The deal was moot: While Feldstein was working on the first story for *Going Steady with Peggy*, Victor Fox announced that he was canceling *Sunny* and *Junior*, and Gaines telephoned Feldstein. " 'Come in,' he says," as Feldstein recalled. " 'We have to talk.' So I go in and he says, 'Look,' he says, 'the fad for funny-teenager comics is dying out. I know about the fact that you haven't got *Junior* anymore, but I can't do *Peggy*, because I'll lose my shirt. So you and I are finished.'

"I was pushy and a little bit obnoxious, I guess—I was very ambitious, and I took advantage of any opportunity that came upon me. So I said, 'All right, Bill, tear up the contract, and let me work on your other books.' And he said, 'Okay.' So I started to work for Bill on his existing comics, but I wanted more money, so I said, 'Look, I write my own stories. This stuff, these scripts you're buying, are junk. I can write just as good as any of them, and I need the income.' So he said, 'Okay, write—write your own stuff,' and so from the very outset with Bill, I was writing my own stories and illustrating them, and that's the way we worked for a while."

Feldstein's influence on Gaines and EC expanded as the men grew closer. Noticing more free space in suite 706 than in his foyer, Feldstein persuaded Gaines to allow him to work full-time in the office, while still being paid by the job. "What happened was, because of our proximity in the office, he and I would go out to lunch together," usually at a homey pasta house, Patrissy's, on nearby Kenmare Street. Feldstein put on about fifteen pounds by the end of 1948. Gaines, meantime, sold the family's house in White Plains and moved with his mother into a spacious three-bedroom apartment on Fort Hamilton Parkway in Brooklyn. Since Feldstein lived on his route home, Gaines would give him a lift each evening in his blue 1947 Chrysler Town and Country, a woody wagon with varnished mahogany on the sides, enough chrome on the interior to make another small vehicle, and one of the new "hydromatic" transmissions that changed gears automatically. It was a car that, like many of the grown-up toys Gaines collected, conveyed both boyish playfulness and manly prosperity in conspicuous extremes. In the living room of the new family apartment, Gaines had an RCA Berkshire television, an $800 model with an enormous twenty-one-inch picture (rear-projected, by way of a mirror system, onto a flat screen) and a cabinet of mahogany that matched his car, and Gaines had it wired up to a complicated new "hi-fi" system with an enormous Sunn amplifier and separate woofers and tweeters. "I never heard of using two different speakers to play one record," Feldstein said. "I thought it was the most fantastic thing." To demonstrate the sound system, Gaines liked to play one of the records in his London FFRR ("full frequency-range recording") collection, a 78-rpm novelty disc that reproduced the sounds of a locomotive approaching, an airplane taking off, barnyard animals, and such, and he would stand in the center of the room miming all the actions.

"He was playing at being a publisher, and this was fine with me, because I was getting paid, he was giving me a lot of opportunities—to express myself and develop ideas and make money," Feldstein said. "We spent a lot of time together, and we became very close friends. It might not have been a really deep friendship. He needed me for his purposes, and I needed him for my purposes, and we kind of developed a relationship that would solve this, satisfy that."

Gaines experimented, mostly by imitation, as Feldstein helped him try to develop a formula potent enough to bring them both artistic satisfaction and financial reward, the former something unfamiliar and exciting to the publisher, the latter much the same to the artist. Gaines relished brainstorming with Feldstein, and Feldstein wanted to buy a hi-fi set. "We took our work very seriously in those days," Gaines later recalled. "We busied ourselves copying trends for a year or so." Having picked up the rights to a comics series about the magician Blackstone prior to Feldstein's arrival, Gaines had published a comic called *Blackstone the Magician Detective Fights Crime!* Evoking its confusion exquisitely, the cover showed a curvy redheaded woman in a red bra and underpants trapped by an octopus while a bald, Germanic-looking heavy aims a .45 at her. Blackstone stood in the background, manacled to a stone wall, and a box of type announced, "And introducing the

Happy Houlihans, America's Craziest and Most Lovable Family!" The Houlihans were then spun into their own title, which was soon after revamped as a crime Western called *Saddle Justice*; it, in turn, became a Western love-story comic, *Saddle Romances*. *Fat and Slat*, one of M. C. Gaines's kiddie titles, became another Western, *Gunfighter*, which included some fine atmospheric art by Johnny Craig and Graham Ingels, as well as contributions by Feldstein. An early attempt to produce a comic with appeal to the overseas market, *International Comics*, morphed into *International Crime Patrol*, which proceeded to drop the global angle to become *Crime Patrol*, a standard-issue Lev Gleason knock-off, subtitled "Real Stories from Police Files." Sheldon Moldoff, an inventive artist-writer originally hired by the elder Gaines, had created a science-fantasy feature about a sexy young "Princess of the Moon" and her beau, Prince Mengu, which appeared in *Animal Fables*. Bill Gaines gave it its own title, *Moon Girl and the Prince*, which he promptly shortened to *Moon Girl*. With Feldstein's help, that turned into *Moon Girl Fights Crime* and then to *A Moon . . . A Girl . . . A Romance*.

"We were feeling our way and trying to do something good, but it was never good enough for Al Feldstein," said Ivan Klapper, who served as editor of *International Crime Patrol* and wrote a few stories for its successor, *Crime Patrol*. "I felt I was being pushed aside by Al Feldstein. He somehow or other ingratiated himself with Bill, and he could *produce*—he was very good at producing the product—and he convinced Bill Gaines that he and Bill had all the best ideas. There were others there at the time—[the writer] Gardner Fox and I and others—and we had one or two good ideas that we came up with by ourselves, without Al Feldstein."

Indeed, several months before Feldstein came to EC, Sheldon Moldoff had gone to Bill Gaines with a proposal to create an original comic of eerie horror stories. The notion, like many in comic books, had its roots in the pulps, where narratives of young women assaulted by "weird menaces" (that is, those with otherworldly methods of removing their victims' garments) had filled magazines such as *Terror*

Tales and *Horror Stories* for years. Variations on gothic fright had also appeared in several comics—*Suspense Comics* (which began in 1943), *Yellowjacket* (which included eight horror stories, billed as "Tales of Terror," in its run of ten issues, beginning in 1944), and *Eerie* (which had one issue published in 1947). Still, Moldoff believed his idea to be fresh and capable of distinguishing EC by tapping an underexploited market, and so did Bill Gaines. "I met with him," remembered Moldoff, "and he said sales were bad, but he was trying to make a go of it. I said, 'Bill, I have an idea. Let me work up an issue for you. If you like it, you can have it, but I expect a piece of the business, a percentage.' And he said, 'No problem—go ahead.'" Over the next month or so, Moldoff prepared two full, ready-to-print magazines, subcontracting some of the writing to Gardner Fox and Dick Kraus, and some art to Johnny Craig and Howard Larsen: *Tales of the Supernatural* and *This Magazine Is Haunted*.

"Bill said, 'Great—I love them,'" said Moldoff. "He got his lawyer to draw up a contract. It gave me a percentage, and I signed it." Gaines put the pages for the two magazines in the top drawer of his desk, where they stayed. (Later, Gaines published two of the stories for *Tales of the Supernatural* that had been written and drawn by Kraus and Larsen without notifying Moldoff.)

At some point after that, Gaines and Feldstein were riding home, listening to music in the car, and their conversation drifted to the scary radio dramas they had both enjoyed in childhood, *Inner Sanctum* and *Lights Out*. They were breezing along Ocean Parkway when Feldstein said that the horror genre might well be worth trying at EC. "I was thinking about how we could get out of this terrible pattern prevalent in the comic-book industry of imitating successful magazines," Feldstein said. "I was terribly ambitious, you know, and I wanted us to try other things and do things that had never been done before, because I thought that was the route to success—why should we be copying other people? Why shouldn't we be the one they're copying? But I had never thought of horror until that point. So I said to Bill, 'That's what we should do—we both love the stuff, and nobody else is doing it.' There were little things out there, but nothing major and nothing really good and really scary, and he said, 'You're right—let's do it.'" For decades to come, Feldstein would describe this conversation, more than once recounting it with Gaines present, and Gaines never saw fit to dispute Feldstein's account, nor did he ever mention the signed contract with Moldoff that lay in his desk.

Neither Gaines nor Feldstein was concerned with meeting the standards of the Association of Comics Magazine Publishers. Gaines had practice tyrannizing the ACMP administrator, Henry E. Schultz, whom Gaines dismissed as a factotum. "I used to go up to Schultz and yell and scream and pull my hair and talk him out of almost anything," Gaines explained. "And if you look at my [early EC] books with the seal on them, you'll see what we could publish with the association's approval, because Schultz was just getting a salary." (The last four issues of both of EC's cops-and-robbers titles, *Crime Patrol* and *War Against Crime*, were published with the ACMP seal of approval and with no diminishment in their quantity of gunplay and bloodshed.) Neither were Gaines and Feldstein fearful of aggravating the civic groups and legislators focusing on comic-book content. "We thought we'd be pretty safe, because we'd be doing something different, and they were going after crime," Feldstein said. After all, weird menaces functioned outside the laws of nature. Who on earth had authority over them?

■   ■   ■

Of the two printing salesmen for Eastern Color who had both laid claim to inventing the comic book, only Harry Wildenberg survived to watch what marched forth on the looping trail of *Famous Funnies*, and he did so at some distance, with remorse. Semiretired at age sixty-two, Wildenberg was selling cigars in Key West when a journalist for *The Commonweal*, the Catholic weekly, located him early in 1949 for an article, "How the Comic Book Started—and How the Originator Looks on It Now." He wished he had never gotten the notion to fold those sheets of Sunday newspaper strips in four, and he would prefer to see the whole comic-book medium abolished, he said. He was "highly pleased" to hear about the Los Angeles County ordinance outlawing the sale of controversial comic books, and he was "happiest" when he read about schoolchildren burning comics, according to the article. "I don't feel proud that I started the comic books. If I had an inkling of the harm they would do, I would never have gone through with the idea," Wildenberg said. "I'm glad parents and educators are waking up to the menace of the comic books."

A professor in the School of Education at New York University, Francis J. Kafka, responded with a letter to the editor defending the higher potential of the comic-book medium. "The comics can be inspired and informative, imaginative, interesting and funny, all at once," Kafka argued.

Wildenberg's reply was a cynical acknowledgment of young readers' fascination with blood and guts. "The primary appeal of comics to the juvenile mind lies in their goriness and violence," Wildenberg wrote. "The more violent the greater their fascination for the young. Publishers of comic books are aware of this fact and vie with each other in making their pages drip with blood and murder plots. Tame the comics, harness them to good works and children will have nothing to do with them." His old rival's son, Bill Gaines, could not have gotten better marketing advice.

The progressing crusade against comics on multiple levels provided Harry Wildenberg the opportunity to light many a cigar in satisfaction by 1949. In the final weeks of the preceding year, the National Parent-Teachers Association had issued a directive for a "national housecleaning" of comic books and had distributed a tutorial to help its local chapters spur municipal and state legislation to regulate the sale of comics, and thousands of PTAs around the country began following the plan. Around the same time, the National Institute of

Municipal Law Officers distributed a set of guidelines for enacting comic-book controls. "The criminal and sexual theme of these tales have [sic] been the direct contributing cause of many incidents of juvenile delinquency and to the imbedding of immoral and unhealthy ideas in the minds of our youngsters," wrote the general counsel for the institute. "It is inconceivable that a workable plan cannot be evolved. The police power can and must be exercised so as to eliminate the vice of objectionable comic books." Shortly thereafter, the United States Conference of Mayors published a ten-page handbook, *Municipal Control of Objectionable Comic Books*, and the municipal government trade journal, *American City*, reported, "Comic Book Control Can Be a Success."

Some actions came only after considerable study and debate. In New Orleans, for instance, the mayor and the city council commissioned a report on the comics controversy, which, within its forty-nine pages, noted that comics "rank with jazz music as being one of the few truly American art forms." In its conclusion, the report argued, "The wholesale condemnation of all comics magazines is one of the worst mistakes of some of the critics. The fact is both sides are right. The books are not all bad, as the more extreme critics say; nor all good, as some of their publishers and defenders contend. Like all other creative products, they must be judged individually. And that is what most critics, parents, and public officials have failed to do." Still, the city council found a third of published comics to be "offensive, objectionable, and undesirable," and, on February 2, 1949, it appointed a board to monitor news dealers' compliance with a blacklist of titles.

In Cleveland, early in May, two council members objected to a prospective ordinance to ban crime comics, one of them arguing that it would "throw Sherlock Holmes and Shakespeare out of the window." A week later, the council voted unanimously to outlaw the sale of comics depicting the "commission or attempted commission of the crimes of arson, assault, burglary, kidnapping, mayhem, larceny, manslaughter, murder, rape, prostitution, sodomy or extortion." Conviction would result in a fine of $50 to $500 and/or up to six months' incarceration in the city workhouse. To enforce the law, the police department established a permanent detail of two officers dedicated to the comic-book beat. Cleveland's model was Los Angeles County, where, on April 23, William D. Dickey, the proprietor of a drugstore on Florence Avenue in Walnut Park, was arraigned for his arrest on charges of selling a copy of *Crime Does Not Pay* to a teenager. Around the same time, actions to ban controversial comics were introduced in cities including Baltimore, Cleveland, Milwaukee, Sacramento, and St. Louis, as well as in numerous smaller towns such as Falls Church, Virginia; Nashua, New Hampshire; and Coral Gables, Florida. (As *The Sacramento Union* reported in its lead page-one story, "Crime Comic Book Ban Voted By City Council—$500 Fines, Term in Jail for Violators.")

In Falls Church, a young Ted White was attending Madison Elementary School, where some friends passed along a small handful of comics for him to read on his walk home. One was an issue of *Sensation Comics* featuring Wonder Woman, whom White had never seen before. The sight of the character and her sadomasochistic heroics so slowed the boy's legs that he was nearly an hour late home for dinner when he looked up from the book to see his mother marching toward him on the sidewalk. She yanked the comics out of his hands and tugged him home. "She was furious, and she told me that comic books were the cause of all sorts of horrible things," recalled White. When he and his mother reached their house, she told him to go to his room, gather his comics—about two dozen books he had taken several years to collect—and bring them to the backyard. The family had an incinerator to burn their garbage. As White watched, his mother dropped his comics down the chute. "I was enormously upset about the fact that she would do this to me. It was a violation. It was akin to rape from my point of view—I mean, something that had been mine ceased to be mine. From that point on, I had much more interest in comics than I had before, because they had become forbidden fruit. As a direct consequence of that, I began seriously collecting comic books."

A few voices of youthful dissent wafted through the din of comic-book criticism during the first months of 1949. When eighth-graders and ninth-graders participated in a youth forum on comic books on January 4, *The New York Times* reported "700 Students See Hopes for Comic Books." Held in the auditorium of Herman Ridder Junior High School in the Bronx, the event presented a panel of six students in a spirited debate about comics. The kids began critically, voicing some of the same complaints that Sterling North had in 1940—comics were "badly printed" and "harmful because they contain dirt and use-less material." Before long, however, the kids shifted into a united de-fense of comics, at one point describing the books as "literature put into picture form." One panelist, Jane Alexander, said, "They take you away from a normal child's life. Fantasy is a part of a normal child's life." Another spoke against comics censorship on First Amendment grounds, adding that films and newspapers had more lurid content than comics. The students denounced the proposition that comic books were responsible for criminal behavior, arguing "environment, not the comics, induce crime" and that "juvenile delinquency was prevalent even before the invention of the printing press." When asked, "Should comic books be banned?" one of the students, Merton Rothman, called legislation restricting comics "an abuse of freedom of the press," and the assembly erupted into applause.

Rothman, a small, shy, round-faced thirteen-year-old eighth-grader, later recalled the forum as a "precious chance to have our voices heard" on a subject "of profound concern" to the students. "All of my friends read comic books, and we traded them. They were important to us," said Rothman, whose favorite character was Jack Cole's out-landish Plastic Man. "One remark I remember saying had to do with feminine immodesty in comics, but I didn't mean it." (Rothman said, at the forum, "The girls are scantily clothed, and these should be improved," according to an account published in the *New York World-Telegram and Sun*.) "It's important to understand that we were kids in public, in front of our teachers, and there was a certain pressure to be good and say the right thing. I assure you, Wonder Woman was more appealing to me for her cleavage than for her bullet-repellent bracelets." To understand the mixed signals young people sent in public comments about comics in the postwar years, Rothman said, "you need to discount most of the criticism from the kids as trying to be good kids" and "amplify the rest."

While most young people no doubt saw the editorial pages as adult territory, off limits to them, some were so distressed by the crusade against comics that they wrote letters to newspaper editors. One group of high-school students pooled their literary resources for a letter published in the *Syracuse Herald-American* on February 23 in response to the city's ordinance banning crime comics:

> Sale of some types of comic books to the young people of our community has been forbidden. This, in most cases, is a very good measure, but why stop there? How about the so-called best sellers that are so freely circulated among the parents of these same children? These adults, who were directly responsible for the enactment of this curb on the funnies, read this type of book constantly and don't consider it good unless it is full of the vile language and corrupt thoughts which thoroughly disgust any decent person. The reading matter in comic books may not be of the highest caliber but it is mild in comparison with that found in adult books.
>
> In our estimation these actions by our elders are of no constructive use and stimulate only disrespect in their children's minds. We ask you, is it a fair procedure to ban the children's books and to continue to read this type of maladjusted literature yourselves?
>
> (Signed) Disgusted High School Students

A protest half hidden by a thin veil of piety, the letter challenged adult reading habits as a means of asserting young people's fitness to determine their own.

Still, groups of students continued to burn comic books in school yards around the country, some under the sway of their parents and teachers, some in concord with them, some unsure of their own points of view and doubtful of the propriety of disagreeing with their elders, some emboldened to defiance through the burnings themselves. In one case—a grand public protest organized in Rumson, New Jersey, an affluent town near the seashore—the young people involved were exceptionally young, Cub Scouts, and they were only part of an elaborate plan arranged by a Cubmaster, Louis Cooke, a scout committeeman, Ralph Walter, and the mayor, Edward Wilson. As it was announced on January 6 at a "fathers' night" meeting of the Rumson High School PTA, the event was to involve a two-day drive to collect comic books "portraying murderers and criminals," a journalist at the meeting reported. A group of forty Cubs would tour the borough in a fire truck, "with siren screaming, and collect objectionable books at homes along the way." Then the mayor would lead the boys in a procession from Borough Hall to Rumson's Victory Park, where Wilson would present awards to the scouts and lead them in burning the comic books. The Cub who had gathered the most comics would have the honor of applying the torch to the books. When the national office of the Cub Scouts of America declined to support the bonfire, and newspapers as far-flung as Michigan's *Ironwood Daily Globe* questioned it, the Rumson event was revised to conclude with the scouts donating the comics to the Salvation Army for scrap.

A few weeks later, a Girl Scout leader in the farm-country town of Cape Girardeau, Missouri, Mrs. Thomas Mullen, guided her troop and local students in a comic-book burning, unencumbered. (The event had not been widely publicized in advance.) The scouts, fourteen-to-eighteen-year-old members of Senior Troop 29, began gathering crime comics, as well as Western and romance titles (because of their shootings and sexual innuendo, respectively), then turned the burning over to students at St. Mary's, a Catholic high school of about 275 housed in an austere redbrick building, a refurbished old hospital. Following a script by the parish pastor, Rev. Theon Schoen, the students conducted a mock trial of four comic-book characters, portrayed by upperclassmen who pleaded guilty to "leading young people astray and building up false conceptions in the minds of youth." The trial, held on the school grounds after classes, concluded with a "great big bonfire," as one of the students, Bonnie Wulfers, would remember it. As the books burned, Schoen led the assembled group of more than four hundred students from St. Mary's elementary and high schools in a version of the now-standard pledge to "neither read nor purchase objectionable publications and to stay away from retail establishments where such are sold."

The student who played Superman in the trial, fourteen-year-old Donald Heisserer, had never owned nor read a comic book, anyway. The second oldest of five children and the only boy, Heisserer had had primary responsibility for running the family wheat and dairy farm since his father died, when he was nine. There was a radio but no television in the house, and the telephone was on an eight-family party line; it rang only once every few days. Heisserer's mother had no driver's license. For fun and the money his family always needed, Donald Heisserer hunted mushrats and sold their hides for $3.75 apiece.

"We were more or less in an isolated area, and as far as comic books were concerned, I would not even have known where to go get them," recalled Heisserer. "I just did that because everybody at school was collecting them and tearing them up. As far as our actual feelings were, not many of us ever did have the opportunity really to go out and get comic books and read them. After I got my work done, I was tired and went to sleep, and a lot of the students were rural kids. The Girl Scouts and the Parent-Teacher Association got this crusade going.

The same kind of groups got together and got the nightclubs to close at ten. There was enough sentiment against stuff like that there that you could get a group together and make a big bonfire.

"The thing about it is that I didn't give the comic books much thought until that time, and when we did that bonfire, I started to think something really just wasn't right about it," Heisserer said. "I thought they were trying to use us, and I didn't think that was right. It got me pretty mad. I never did think about the teachers in the same way after that."

As the students collected comics for the bonfire, some of the boys kept them categorized by genre, as Heisserer recalled. Crime comics went in one box, superhero titles in another, and jungle books, with their covers of heroines swinging from vines in leopard-skin bikinis, went in a pile that several of the young crusaders hid under a step in the boys' lavatory.

The political debate over crime comics bubbled up from the city halls to the statehouses, where the legislative process is somewhat less susceptible to regional vagaries and where its results have broader sweep. By March 1949, laws to regulate comic books, most of them designed to prohibit the sale of crime comics to minors, were pending in fourteen states. A bill in New York State, comics publishers' home base, posed a unique threat to the industry in that it directly targeted the makers, rather than the sellers or the readers, of the material, and its objective was something close to a priori censorship. Its sponsor, Republican Benjamin F. Feinberg, was a sixty-one-year-old former high-school principal best known for his authorship of the "Feinberg law," which made membership in the Communist Party grounds for dismissal from the public school system. The comic-book legislation he proposed went beyond the usual strictures; it would establish a new comic-book division of the State Department of Education, which would have the authority to approve or reject comics on the basis of their content before the books were distributed; makers of acceptable comics would be granted a permit to publish. Any company choosing to publish a rejected comic without a permit would be required to submit a copy of the unaccepted book to the county district attorney no less than thirty days in advance of its proposed date of sale. On February 23, the bill passed the State Senate in a vote of forty-nine to six, the dissenters all Democrats.

Editorials protested the act as stifling free speech, though uniformly on those grounds alone. The core idea that comic books were insidious seemed beyond dispute. As *The New York Times* decreed:

> Many people are deeply concerned over the moral and social effect of this flood of pulp paper that has been loosed on the newsstands in the last decade or so. Its publishers are now reaping the whirlwind of indignation that is the result of their own failure of self-restraint. That official censorship should be proposed or effectuated, as it has in many cities, was inevitable.
>
> We think the comic books have, on the whole, had an injurious effect on children and in various ways . . . But in time, and before they have done too much harm to morals or taste, public opinion will succeed in making the reforms needed. To wait for that to happen is far less dangerous than to abridge freedom of the right to publish.

The Nation noted:

> We would be the first to acknowledge that a generation of Americans has been driven several degrees toward illiteracy by the "comic" book. And it is appalling that 60,000,000 comic books are sold in this country every month. This being granted, however, we must put ourselves on record against the current nationwide drive to liquidate the comic book through censorship . . . Comic books are an opening wedge. If they can be "purified"—that is, controlled—newspapers, periodicals, books, films, and everything else will follow.

On April 19, Thomas E. Dewey, the Republican governor of New York (and famously almost president the previous year), vetoed the legislation, declaring it too vague in the manner of *Winters v. New York*. "The bill before me makes little change in the language already held invalid by the highest court in the land," Dewey explained. Feinberg, unyielding, said the defeated bill was not "the last thing." The legislature set up a joint committee to study comics further (and would return to the subject, with greater zeal and a stronger footing, in time).

North of the state, meanwhile, Canadian legislators had more success at regulating crime comics, which had been pouring across the border from New York. Some five million crime comics were estimated to circulate through Canada annually, both through imports from the United States and in reprints produced in Toronto from plates made in America. The Canadian bill, introduced by a popular Tory, Edmund Davie Fulton, passed in both houses of Parliament on December 7, 1949, amending the country's penal law to provide for a maximum sentence of two years' imprisonment for anyone who "prints, publishes, sells, or distributes any magazine, periodical, or book which exclusively or substantially comprises matter depicting the commission of crimes, real or fictitious, thereby tending or likely to induce or influence youthful persons to violate the law or to corrupt the morals of such persons."

Fulton, a thirty-three-year-old former Rhodes Scholar and infantry officer in the Second World War, had been moved to campaign for a law against crime comics upon learning of the murder of a Yukon man by two boys, ages eleven and thirteen, who were avid comic-book readers. "There was no other explanation why the boys should have shot and killed the man driving past in this car," Fulton later said, explaining his advocacy of the law. "They probably didn't intend to kill him. They were imitating what they had seen portrayed day after day in crime comics to which they were exposed."

Then again, Fulton added, "I also have to confess that many experts and impartial experts in the field of psychiatry were found on the side of those who held that crime comics and similar publications were not harmful to children, but merely provided a useful outlet for what they called their natural violent instincts and tendencies."

8. Love . . . LOVE . . . LOVE!!

Then the frenzy over crime comics began to subside. Under the siege of the headlines, the legislation, the public burnings, the sermons, and the speeches in town halls and school auditoriums across the country, comics publishers toned down many of their crime titles and dropped others, and the genre began to seem less sanguinary. By 1950, *Crime Does Not Pay* was a largely reformed magazine, nearly bloodless, its focus shifted from the inner lives of criminals to the consequences of their acts and the valiance of their captors. The first word in the logo shrank by half an inch in height, and the last three words more than doubled in height to a full inch. (*Crime* was still twice as tall as *Does Not Pay*, but no longer eight times the size.) A banner across the top of each issue promoted the book as "A force for good in the community!" Beneath its old slogan, "The Magazine with the Widest Range of Appeal," another line now added, "Dedicated to the Eradication of Crime," and a box in a corner of the main cover drawing had a black-and-white photo of a taut-lipped policewoman identified as Mary Sullivan, "former chief of the New York City Police Department Women's Bureau now 'Crime Does Not Pay' Editorial Consultant." Below her picture was an endorsement: "I approve of this magazine as a good moral influence on our youth. I recommend it to parents as a powerful lesson for good behavior."

Other publishers, such as Victor Fox, kept pumping blood onto the panels while attempting to insulate themselves from charges of corrupting youth, by labeling their crime comics as "Not Intended for Children" and "For Adults Only." Since there were few reliable statistics on comic-book readership at the time, however, no one in the field ever knew how many grown-ups were reading comics. Nor did anyone—not even Will Eisner, the first to talk openly about comic books as a medium with the potential to warrant adult attention—ever mistake comics for something other than a form of entertainment geared mainly for and consumed mostly by young people. "Victor Fox was blowing smoke," said Pete Morisi, whose work for Fox included a four-page adaptation of Longfellow titled "Skipper Hoy and That Wreck, the Hesperus." According to Morisi, "He never really meant any comics for adults. He never meant a word he said. That shows you how nervous the people in the business were—if Victor Fox is bothering to cover his behind, it had to be getting serious out there, and it was." Fox was so unscrupulous that he routinely made contributors grovel for payment only to issue them bad checks. Morisi, stung repeatedly, married, and often desperate for payment long overdue, once resorted to barging into Fox's office unannounced. He climbed over the top of Fox's desk and began to strangle him until Fox agreed to write Morisi a check; Fox paid Morisi for the full sum due him—nearly a thousand dollars for pages billed at $20 apiece. Morisi decided to stop working for Fox when the check bounced.

"The crime trend was losing steam, and it showed all the way around," said Morisi. "It was getting boring to basically do pretty much the same kind of story every time, and if it was running its course for me, for us, I have to assume the kids were getting bored, too. Everybody was always looking for the new thing—'What's the new thing?' Crime wasn't the new thing anymore, and it wasn't as exciting as it used to be. It was getting tamed down." Morisi recalled taking an assignment for *Crime Does Not Pay* in or around 1950, only to get a surprising lecture from Charles Biro. "'Listen, Pete,' he says. 'We've got a good thing going here, and we don't want to lose it. I don't want to see any blood and guts. I don't want any violence. Just give me detail, lots of detail!'

"'Detail of *what*?' I say. 'What am I supposed to show?'

"Charlie says, 'Tits!'

"Crime was going out. Sex was in," said Morisi.

Although about thirty crime titles were still being published in 1950, more than ten had disappeared since 1948. Meanwhile, romance was blooming on the newsstands. The first comic book devoted to love stories, Crestwood's *Young Romance*, had not appeared until the summer of 1947 (cover dated September–October), and at the end of that year, it was still alone (poor thing, solitude being the worst fate in the world of romance comics). In 1948, there were only three new love titles: *Sweethearts*, *My Romance*, and *My Life*. By the end of 1949, there were some 125 romance comics, and, a year later, 148 from twenty-six publishers. Fox alone published *My Story*, *My Love Story*, *My Love Life*, *My Love Affair*, *My Love Secret*, *My Secret Affair*, *My Secret Life*, *My Private Life*, *My Life*, and more than a dozen other titles of their ilk. This was the binge-and-purge policy of product development, transferred from one skittish, predatory trade, the garment industry, to another.

In a self-parody of comics publishers' readiness to leap from crime to love, Al Feldstein and Bill Gaines wrote and Feldstein illustrated a love story, "The Love Story to End *All* Love Stories," for their own *Modern Love*. It depicted Feldstein and Gaines themselves as sycophantic editors for a fictional publisher called T. Tot. "Gentlemen," the white-haired, mustached, WASPy Tot announces, tugging on his lapels with both hands, "*Modern Love* is a complete sell-out! Change all the titles! T. Tot Publishing Company is dropping its crime!"

The Gaines character, incredulous, points to a wall of comic-book covers as he asks, "No more 'Crime Might Pay'? No more 'Crime

Could Pay'? No more 'Crime Ought to Pay'? No more 'Crime Used to Pay'? No more 'Crime Does So Pay'? No more CRIME, T.T.?"

"No," explains Tot, wagging his right index finger. "I want . . . 'LOVE Might Pay,' 'LOVE Could Pay,' 'LOVE Ought to Pay,' 'LOVE Should Pay,' and 'LOVE Does So Pay'! It will PAY!"

In the following panel, we see a rival publisher, V.W. of Wolf Comics (a canid stand-in for Fox), sitting near a wall of covers for his comics, *Crimes by Criminals*, *Crimes by Dogs*, and *Crimes by Cats*. "T. Tot has made a killing!" Wolf tells two of his own sycophants. "Change our comic book line! From now on . . . it's love . . . LOVE . . . LOVE!!"

Thus it was in 1950, when nearly a fifth of the more than 650 comics published were now romances, in some cases grafted with other genres (Fawcett's *Cowboy Love*, ACG's *Romantic Adventures*, Star's *School-Day Romances*). Their success points to the appeal of comic books across gender lines in the late forties and early fifties, confuting the image of comics as a domain restricted to adolescent males. (This perception, common at the time, would become more deeply ingrained in later years.) While teenage girls were understood to be the primary audience of romance comics, boys surely relished them; in fact, many romance titles exploited the license that came with a presumption of being for girls' eyes only by featuring women characters who just loved to chat about their love lives while they dressed and undressed.

Comic books had had heroines intended to appeal to young women and men alike since the war years, when the quotient of females in the home-front marketplace expanded at the same time that military readership increased the demand for drawings of shapely young female characters suitable for pinning up. With many male artists drafted, moreover, women artists found more work and were frequently assigned to do the female-oriented comics. There were jungle girls to outnumber the African population: Camilia (drawn by Fran Hopper and the supremely talented Marcia Snyder), Judy of the Jungle (by the versatile Alex Schomberg), Tiger Girl (by Matt Baker),

Sheena (perpetuated by innumerable artists under Jerry Iger), and countless others. There were costumed heroines and quasi-military heroines: Phantom Lady (by Matt Baker), Yankee Girl (by Ann Brewster), the Blond Bomber, and the Girl Commandos (both of the latter drawn by Jill Elgin and Barbara Hall). There were science-fiction heroines—Gale Allen and Her All-Girl Squadron and Mysta of the Moon (both by Fran Hopper)—and there was a wondrous assortment of strong, smart, and sexy proto-post-feminists: the nurse-turned-aviatrix Jane Martin (by Fran Hopper and Ann Brewster), "girl detective" Glory Forbes (by Jean Levander), and the crime-solving fashion model Toni Gayle (by Janice Valleau, who sometimes signed her married name, Winkleman). "We always had a love angle, even though the stories were adventure stories, really, but the girls in the stories, like Toni Gayle, who I loved to do, had it all over the men," said Janice Valleau Winkleman. "Even in the love stories, where the girls were always chasing the men, the girls were smarter and sexier."

The artist and writer credited with co-creating romance comics, Joe Simon, thought of the effort as an attempt to elevate the medium as well as an opportunity to mine a new market. "Comic books were supposed to be very juvenile, that's what the publishers thought," said Simon, who, with his partner Jack Kirby, produced the first love comic, *Young Romance*, and subtitled it "For the more ADULT readers of comics!" The son of a tailor (as was his partner), Simon grew up in Rochester, New York, and did some sports cartooning in Syracuse, where he attended college, before moving to Manhattan and entering the comics trade in 1940, at the age of twenty-five. With Jack Kirby, whom he met while both men were working for Fox, Simon created Captain America, the superstrong patriot that gave Timely its first comic-book hit, during the war. Simon was good at business and claimed to have negotiated a deal with Crestwood for 50 percent of the profits of *Young Romance* and its 1949 follow-up, *Young Love*; during the books' prime, in 1950, he and Kirby were each earning $1,000 per week, according to Simon.

"It was supposedly very risky to put out love stories for children, but we knew that a lot of comic-book readers were high-school age and, as a result, they wanted to read about people a few years older, so that's how we approached *Young Romance*. We never talked down, and we were very realistic and adult. Nobody else knew how good we were doing for a couple of years, and then they caught on, and everybody started copying us. The kids really liked what we were trying to do, I think because we didn't treat them like kids. We were practically kids ourselves, you know, so we didn't look down on them."

The boom in romance comics cannot be attributed solely to Simon and Kirby's foresight and sensitivity, however. Two years earlier, the biologist and zoologist Alfred Kinsey had published the results of his study *Sexual Behavior in the Human Male*. The book, 800 pages of turgid, academic writing about things most readers no doubt knew but seemed stunned to find in print (homosexuality existed; men reached their sexual peak in their teens), sold half a million copies at $6.50 apiece. At the time, the early years of the atomic age, the very intractability of the Kinsey Report was key to its impact; all the statistics and technical terms gave postwar America a way to open up the discourse on sex without shame. The subject of mating habits became something respectably, even chicly scientific. The following year, in Canada, a former mayor of Winnipeg named Richard H. G. Bonnycastle started a small publishing company, Harlequin Books, catering to the emerging paperback trade. Among its first releases were two romance novels, *The Manatee: Strange Loves of a Seaman* and *Honeymoon Mountain: Deborah Loses Her Innocence*. Lust was in the air.

Produced in the same Manhattan sweatshops that generated every other type of comic book, romance comics were written and drawn by hungry, nimble young writers and artists—most of them, but not all, male—who might do a superhero comic one week, a crime book the next, then a Western. With romance comics came a rare opportunity not only to release their anima but to tap personal experience and apply their common frame of reference to their work. The characters were their creators' ages, for the most part; they wore the same baggy, cuffed trousers and sweaters with padded shoulders, and they met in the same chromed sandwich shops and knotty-pined roadhouses. Romance comics lacked the wild abandon of early superhero comics, but they had an air of normalcy and familiarity rare among comic books in their day.

As in all genre fiction, the plots tended toward the formulaic. Some romance comics were essentially *Wuthering Heights* with new costumes. The protagonists, invariably young women, found themselves torn between two suitors: one disreputable, a Heathcliff driving a white-walled coupe or playing in a swing band, who promised thrills and threatened heartbreak; the other stolid but dull, an Edgar Linton from the neighborhood, carrying the prospect of long-term security and social acceptability. In eight-page morality plays, romance comics gave girls of the postwar years the materials to indulge enduring adolescent fantasies while touching upon an issue with timely resonance. "The girls were always attracted to the boy from the other side of the tracks—that was an old cliché, but it had a different kind of meaning at the time we were doing the romance comics," recalled Kimball Aamodt, whom the artist Alex Toth called "the greatest of the romance writers" for the gentle naturalism of his stories. A native of North Dakota, Aamodt had come to New York after the war to study English at NYU on the GI Bill and write a novel based on his experiences as a Navy pilot. Following the lead of his college friend Walter Geier, Aamodt started writing comics in 1949, contributing to Simon and Kirby's romance books.

"Juvenile delinquency was the big thing then [that] everybody was talking about," Aamodt said. "The wild kind of boys in the love stories were the delinquent types, so when a girl went in that direction in one of our stories, she was really making a statement. We didn't try to get political, but we didn't go in for the idea that the boy from the wrong side of town was wrong in every way. We tried to be a little more democratic. It was boy meets girl, but we took the writing very seriously—

I was a frustrated novelist. We knew that a whole lot of kids were reading the comics and taking them very seriously, so we tried to do the same thing."

Some romance comics defied formula and cliché, portraying young women struggling to break free of the social conventions of the day. Writers such as Aamodt, his partner Walter Geier, and Dana Dutch (a prolific writer of neatly crafted scripts, full of surprise, for the St. John publishing company), told stories of free-spirited, willful girls who thought and acted independently, challenging not only their parents, but their boyfriends—adults and males, the two major forces of authority at the time. No other genre of comic books was as overt in its depiction of youthful rebellion as romance comics, in which stories such as "I Joined a Teen-Age Sex Club" and "My Mother Was My Rival" were not uncommon. That the romance books were, at first, seen as harmless—just love stories, only girl stuff—allowed them to flourish in an era when other comics were held in suspicion.

In a typical story by Dana Dutch, "Thrill Seekers' Weekend," published in St. John's *Teen-Age Romances*, two young women trick their parents and skip off to another town to spend the weekend in a hotel with their boyfriends, who check into the adjacent room. They hide their ages to sneak into a bar, and no one finds them out. When the adventure is over and the four kids return home, they face no consequences for breaking all the rules (or most of the rules, since the couples never couple up for long). To the contrary, the last panel shows one of the girls dancing blissfully with her beau; unrepentant, she and the boy were enriched, rewarded for their defiance and experimentation.

Another Dutch script, in St. John's *Blue Ribbon Comics*, opens with the heroine addressing the reader: "How many times have you been tempted to pursue a dangerous romance? I guess there's a wild streak in every girl and I gave full vent to mine by throwing myself into the arms of a boy to whom every good looking girl was 'whistle-bait.'" Titled "I Set a Trap for a Wolf," the story follows the girl in a scheme to outdo a would-be lothario. She dares to call him for a date (a scandalously aggressive act in 1948), persuades him to crash a party with her, leads him on a moonlight walk, and makes all the sexual advances. "We girls should demand equal rights with boys," she tells her sister. "Isn't this a free country? Why shouldn't we be allowed to do everything boys do?" The ending, again, is a happy one: The girl, through self-assertion, brings the boy to maturity.

"We tried to avoid the usual, expected thing," said Walter Geier, a versatile writer who had done some scripts for radio and early television, as well as a bit of acting Off-Off-Broadway, before answering a classified ad to write for Simon and Kirby. Geier planned the characters and the story lines for his comics so thoroughly that he would submit a one-thousand-word synopsis of each script to the editor in advance. This was almost solely for his own benefit, since few editors responded with substantive comments. In one of Geier's romances, "Just Good Friends," written for *Young Love*, the narrator and central character is a man caught unknowingly between two women who are more emotionally sophisticated than he. The script (which Geier retained and filed, with all his comics work, alongside his radio and television scripts) shows an effort to toe into subtext by creating tension between the text and the accompanying imagery:

CAPTION: Ellie kissed me . . . in a very sisterly fashion, of course.
ART: Ellie really plants one on Will . . . it's anything but sisterly.

"I wrote just about every kind of comic—romance, Westerns, crime, weird adventure, he-man stuff, everything but superheroes and teen-age humor, not because I thought [those genres] were dumb, although I did, but simply because the superhero market was dead and the editor at *Archie* wouldn't hire me," said Geier. "I thought romance is a complicated subject, and young girls are pretty smart, probably smarter than boys. So I tried to give them something worthy of their attention." In a rare instance when he received a response to one of his story-length synopses, an editor told Geier, "Don't overdo it—remember, you're writing for the chambermaid in the hotel." Geier ignored him.

"That really bothered me," Geier said. "I don't know about chambermaids, but I was still pretty young then, and the young girls I knew weren't stupid."

Some of the most original and important visual artists in comics worked in romance: Wally Wood, Johnny Craig, and Jack Kamen for Fox; Alex Toth for Standard; Mort Leav for Orbit; Everett Raymond Kinstler for National/DC; and Lily Renée and Matt Baker for St. John. They had in common styles that were naturalistic, fitting the intimate, domestic story content, though their approaches varied: Wood had a fixation on visual minutiae; Craig, a swiftness of pace; Kamen, a stark clarity; Toth, a keen sense of design and composition; Leav, a casualness; Kinstler, warmth and beauty; Renée, an airy grace; and Baker, a masterly command of the female form. "When we think of romance comics today, we think of Lichtenstein and his mannered close-ups of tears dripping down a cheek," said Kinstler. "No comics publisher would have hired Lichtenstein—he wasn't good enough. Romance comics dealt with a range of emotions, some of them quite subtle and sophisticated, and they called for real storytelling ability, and I consider that of paramount importance. The stories were emotional, and a great deal had to be implied through facial expressions and body language. The stories had heart and passion, and they were sexy. They weren't kid stuff, and that's why they required the skills of some very good artists. [Romance comics] were the closest thing to illustration and real books in subtlety and sophistication."

To a pair of young aspiring novelists, Arnold Drake and Leslie Waller, the gap between romance comics and conventional literature seemed narrow enough to attempt bridging. Drake, one of four artistically inclined siblings who grew up on Manhattan's Riverside Drive, was taking a writing course at NYU on the GI Bill and working on one of his estimated seven hundred unfinished novels when he was introduced to Waller by Drake's brother-in-law, who told the fellows he saw them as compatibly unconventional. (Drake's older brothers Milton and Irvin were both popular songwriters, their sister Beatrice a serious-minded poet who contributed to the deft nonsense lyrics of Milton's hit, "Mairzy Doats.") Waller, a Chicagoan, had studied at the University of Chicago and worked as a crime reporter for the city's daily *Sun* before the war. He served in the Army Air Corps, assigned to intelligence, then moved to New York for graduate study in literature at Columbia, also on the GI Bill. Waller did his thesis, in 1950, on Dashiell Hammett. He and Drake started collaborating, at first for fun, writing a series of topical songs and skits called "The Living Newspaper," which they performed as a duo at parties, and then for intended profit, hacking out Western comics for Fawcett. "We heard there was money to be made in comic books," remembered Drake, "and we devoted about a year to proving that wrong." At some point prior to 1950, they came up with the notion of writing a full-length book in comics format, designed for young adults; they wrote a four-page outline of the plot and pitched it to the publisher Archer St. John, who gave them an okay but no contract or advance.

"We had been doing comic books of various kinds, and they were kind of primitive, and neither of us wanted to continue that way, so we decided we would try and do something a little more adult," recalled Waller, who went on to write several dozen literate, pulpy novels under the pseudonyms D. S. Cody and Patrick Mann, as well as his own name. (Waller wrote the books upon which the films *Dog Day Afternoon* and *Hide in Plain Sight* were based.) "In those days, comics were considered pretty low in adult value, which is, of course, why kids loved them. We hadn't worked all of this out in our minds. We just ventured ahead."

Drake and Waller thought of the book as a "picture novel"—a full-length work of fiction in graphic form. (The next time anyone would try anything comparable, twenty-five years later, it would be called a "graphic novel.") As Drake remembered, "The attitude about comics then was, because you started reading them as a child, they were a thing you were supposed to outgrow. The attitude was, for an adult to read a comic book was a mark of ignorance. A lot of people thought that way, including a lot of people within the craft. But Les and I knew we were geniuses, so we thought we would simply change the world. Our goal was to create a kind of Warner Brothers low-budget film-noir action-romance on paper, in words and pictures."

Titled *It Rhymes with Lust*, the book was a potboiler centered around a busty redheaded widow in her thirties, named Rust Masson—an antiheroine modeled on Joan Crawford—who runs an oppressive, politically entangled mining operation. When angry workers stage a strike and the local political bosses decide to bust it (providing a third option for the title's rhyme), the woman's stepdaughter takes sides against the company and falls in love with a handsome newspaperman. A pulpy mix of leftist social realism and melodrama, peppered with romance, the book was distinguished by some nicely staged scenes (Rust seduces the reporter under a portrait of her late husband), bits of punchy dialogue ("All you do is play the cards Rust Masson has dealt you, until we're ready to switch decks"), and the extraordinary novelty of its mode of presentation.

For the illustrations, St. John retained one of its best artists, Matt Baker. Raised in Homestead, Pennsylvania, a blue-collar suburb of Pittsburgh, he had a gift for drawing anything well and women extraordinarily, which helped him avoid the steel mills that awaited other young Negro men of his time and place. Little is known of Baker's private life beyond the fact that he had a younger brother, John, who had some talent as an artist and, through Matt, got occasional assignments from Fox but made his living in a dry-cleaning shop in Homestead. Matt Baker was a tall, sturdy, vigorous, handsome man with a gentle, closed-mouth smile, a deep gaze, and a dark-coffee complexion. "He could have been a movie star or a model," recalled Bob Lubbers, who worked with Baker at Fiction House. In a rough and casual business, Baker was always dressed impeccably in broad-shouldered, double-breasted suits and stylish silk ties. He had at least four fedoras, in brown, black, green, and maroon, which he wore to match his suits. He lived in Harlem, probably alone, presumably well, and he drove a yellow convertible coupe.

"All the women, white and black, went crazy for him, and I know he had a bunch of gals on the hook," Lubbers said. "You know how he drew women perfectly? The anatomy was magnificent, down to every muscle. Everyone who knew him knew that could only come from exhaustive personal research. He was the envy of everybody." As highly as Baker and his work were held by his peers, a trace of stereotyping remained in the talk of Baker's presumed sexual prowess. Al Feldstein was also good-looking, dapper, and adept at drawing curvaceous women; yet, for all the objectification in Feldstein's art, no one was so ready to sexualize its artist.

Baker worked prolifically to support his fine living, though he never rushed his work. His skills were such that once, when Baker was working with Lee Ames at Fiction House, Ames watched Baker put his pencil down on a sheet of art board and carefully, steadily render an entire page without making a correction, like Lou Fine. "He wasn't that fast—he was that good," said Ames. He had heart trouble (which would take his life before long) and would occasionally be laid up for a few days, ailing or recuperating. If he submitted an assignment a bit after deadline, white colleagues were known to whisper cracks about sloth. "You know that, oh that lazy so-and-so," recalled Ames. "It was a crime, and you'd think the guys in comics would know better." After all, Baker was not alone among African-American artists in comic books; in addition to his brother, the comics artists of color in the 1940s and early '50s included Andre LeBlanc, a veteran of the Eisner and Iger shop; Alvin C. Hollingsworth, a meticulous penciller who worked extensively in romance comics before establishing a reputation as a painter and art professor at the City University of New York; and Warren Broderick, a solid journeyman who worked with Harry Harrison and Wally Wood.

"Matt was working for Iger when I came in the shop after the war," recalled the artist Jack Kamen, "and he was really the idol of the shop. I think he really looked down on some of what he had to do—how couldn't he, with that kind of talent? I think that Matt, like myself, also had the feeling that he could go on and do something on a more elevated scale. We had a conversation one time that gave me this distinct impression, and I don't remember every word, but he said he didn't think he could go anywhere else, and he might have been right. I had a hard enough time trying to make the jump into the advertising field, and I wasn't black."

Baker was the authors' first choice to draw *It Rhymes with Lust*, and also Archer St. John's, though for different reasons, according to Drake. "Matt Baker was one of the first important artists in comics," said Drake. "Not one of the first important black artists, one of the first important artists, period. We were extremely fortunate to have him, and St. John is to be admired for having hired him in the prejudiced climate of the time, but it should be recognized also that St. John got him for less money than would have been paid to a white artist. So that was involved in St. John's decision to use him, because it was such an exceptionally huge job, and it would have cost St. John a lot of money at the going rates. But no decisions are pure."

It Rhymes with Lust was printed in black and white, to impart a sense of gravitas and save money, too. "We told St. John that, because we wanted this to be a link between a comic book and a *book* book, it should be in black and white, so the reading public would recognize it as being closer to '*lit-er-a-ture*,'" Drake said with an effete flourish. The text was credited to "Drake Waller," the art jointly to Matt Baker, who did the principal drawing, in pencil, and Ray Osrin, his frequent collaborator at St. John, who inked Baker's work. "Frankly, we were afraid to expose ourselves with our real names," Drake explained. "Les was writing novels, and I was trying my hand at writing plays and short stories. We wanted to be pioneers, but we watched our backs.

We weren't about to ruin our prospects in the literary establishment, where comic books were looked upon as garbage."

The cover promoted the book as both "An Original Full-Length Novel" and one in a would-be series of "Picture Novels," the latter idea reinforced by a logo in the top left corner, designed and rendered by Drake, that showed a writer's pen and an artist's brush crossed like swords. Below the main art, a full-color montage of Rust Masson in a low-cut black dress, a ballot box, factory smokestacks, and a .45, the "sell lines" taunted: "She was greedy, heartless and calculating. She knew what she wanted and was ready to sacrifice anything to get it." This was fairly temperate language in a field in which the cover of the paperback of *The Sun Also Rises* asked, "Could he live without the power to love?" Priced at twenty-five cents, like pulp novels at the time, *It Rhymes with Lust* sold only a few hundred copies, at most, according to Drake. "Our publisher loved it, but he didn't love it enough to promote it, and it needed promotion," he said. "The newsstands didn't know where to put it, so they didn't put it anywhere, and it died in boxes in a back room at St. John's." Twenty-five years before its time, the first "picture novel" was, true to its title, a bust.

■ ■ ■

As the thugs packed up their tommy guns and drifted out of the comic-book panels, and the ingenues and the wolves moved in, the campaign to legislate the comics lost its primary target and its legal rationale. The books grew less absorbed with criminal activity, the purview of the state, and more concerned with social and personal behavior, matters of the heart and mind. Arrests of minors started to level off after the war, diminishing the urgency of the whole issue of juvenile delinquency. At the same time, growing scrutiny increased doubts about the core charge that comics incited juvenile crime.

Headlines began to suggest that perhaps the ten-cent creatures were not so monstrous, after all. In the second week of January 1950,

Love . . . LOVE . . . LOVE!!

Newsweek published a story titled "Comfort for Comics," about a year-long study of 2,881 children in central Massachusetts. Presented at a conference of the American Association for the Advancement of Science in New York, the report concluded (in the magazine's paraphrase) that comic-book readers had a "tendency toward normal hero worship" and "hardly warranted criticism that comic books appealed to readers with 'the brain of a child, the sexual drive of a satyr, and the spiritual delicacy of a gorilla,'" as Fredric Wertham had charged. Further, the study found "no statistically significant effect of the comics upon the personalities of their young devotees."

Two weeks later, *The New York Times* ran a long piece largely vindicating comics, under the headline "Anti-Comics Drive Reported Waning" and the subhead "'Love' Type Found Replacing 'Crime'— Medium Gains as Educational Aid." Reporting that a Los Angeles court had ruled the county ordinance against crime comics to be unconstitutional, the article noted, "Last year's hysteria has died down." (Under appeal, the California decision would soon advance to a higher court.) "Sanity is creeping into the entire picture on comics," Henry E. Schultz of the comics association announced. "Parents are beginning to realize the problem is not solved by quick, easy panaceas like legislation, banning or burning of the comic books." Still, the legislative news was conflicting, and not everyone observing comics shared Schultz's rosy vision. In the month since the Canadian Parliament had banned crime comics in that country, sales of romance comics were soaring in Canada. In time, predicted Dr. Harvey Zorbaugh, chairman of the NYU School of Education's Department of Educational Sociology and director of the university's workshop on "The Cartoon Narrative as a Medium of Communication," the same parties who railed against crime comics would attack the romance genre with equal zeal.

The crusaders against comics were unbowed. Three days after Zorbaugh's comments, Fredric Wertham's lieutenant at the Lafargue Clinic, Dr. Hilde Mosse, gave a talk on "The Destructive Effect of Comics on Children" at the elite Emerson School on East Ninety-sixth

Street in Manhattan. Identified as "acting physician in charge" of La-fargue, Mosse criticized romance comics for presenting a "distorted picture of love," and she noted, accurately, that "there are still many comic books devoted exclusively to crime." Although most of those books had been tamed considerably, Mosse argued, "the jungle comic books and the crime comic books continue to propagate race hatred and sadism." She chastised the New York State Legislature for failing to introduce a new bill restricting comics sales, and she dismissed arti-cles in a recent issue of the *Journal of Educational Sociology* that had challenged Wertham's claims, by noting—accurately, again—that two of the authors (Henry E. Schultz of the ACMP and Josette Frank of Child Study Association) had served as paid consultants to comic-book publishers. Mosse served her boss as well as Schultz had just served his employers, without mentioning why she was standing in for Wertham in such a high-profile forum: He was on leave from La-fargue, writing a book on the subject of comic books.

That spring, a new study presented at a conference on youth in Chicago reaffirmed the conclusions reported earlier in *Newsweek*. Dr. Sophie Schroeder-Sloman, superintendent of the Chicago-based Insti-tute for Juvenile Research, presented a paper on well-adjusted children that showed that all of the psychologically healthy subjects studied read comic books, challenging the idea of a causal link between comic-book reading and maladjustment. Later at the conference, Dr. Martin L. Reymert, director of the laboratory for child research at Mooseheart school, near Chicago, told the group of some two thou-sand social workers, "We should be less speedy in laying the blame for acts of juvenile delinquency at the doorstep of these media of mass communications," including radio and television, as well as comics. Within two years, TV broadcasting had expanded from 27 to 103 sta-tions, and more than five million American homes now had antennas on their roofs. The programming, moreover, was beginning to shift away from the public-service content that impressed the politicians who granted broadcast licenses to the burlesques, popular songfests, and puppet shows that sold TV sets.

In Washington on the same day as the conference in Chicago, May 18, Estes Kefauver, a first-term senator from Tennessee, announced that a new committee to investigate interstate crime would probe the allegations of a relationship between comic books and juvenile delinquency. An owlish, courtly Democrat, forty-seven, Kefauver had served eight years in the House of Representatives before winning election to the Senate in 1948. He seemed an unlikely politician, to the benefit of his image as a man of the people: Soft-spoken and homely, he had a hangdog face drooping behind large horn-rimmed glasses. Kefauver came across as shy; a family friend who watched Kefauver grow up in Madisonville, Tennessee, a small town in the Great Smoky foothills, called him "a sort of by-himself boy." Yet he had a hardy ego and ambition; in eighth grade, he wrote, as many virtuous and confident eighth-grade boys used to do, that his goal was to become president. In the House, Kefauver built a reputation as a principled Southern moderate. He led a subcommittee that investigated charges of judicial corruption, which led to the resignation of a Pennsylvania judge, but he stood with the Southern bloc in an effort to prevent President Truman from pulling the first bricks out of the tower of segregation. While campaigning in his state, Kefauver liked to wear a coonskin cap, an artifact of his defining early electoral triumph over the pawn of a Memphis-based political boss, Edward Crump, who had tried to smear Kefauver by likening him to a stealthy, pilfering raccoon. "I may be a coon," Kefauver countered, "but I'm not Mr. Crump's pet coon." From his entry into politics, Kefauver had a knack for disarming opponents with folksy charm.

After his election to the Senate, *The Washington Post* published a series of articles on organized crime, an evergreen journalistic subject rendered timely in the postwar years by rises in interstate travel and commerce. The publisher of the *Post*, Philip Graham, was fishing for a senator to take up the issue, and he turned to Kefauver, because he had an image of integrity and a home state unlikely to be damaged by the Senate's findings. As Graham later recalled, Kefauver was not interested in the idea until Graham brought up the 1952 elections and asked him, "Estes, don't you want to be vice president?"

Approved on May 3, 1950, the Special Committee to Investigate Crime in Interstate Commerce was chartered to study the nature and effects of racketeering across state lines. Kefauver was chairman, joined by the Democrats Lester C. Hunt of Wyoming and Herbert R. O'Conor of Maryland, and the Republicans Charles W. Tobey of New Hampshire and Alexander Wiley of Wisconsin. The committee began its work quietly. The first hearings, conducted in Miami during the last week of May, were done behind closed doors. On June 22, the committee held public hearings in Washington, and they were followed over a year's time with hearings in more than a dozen major cities. In Washington, the committee devoted several days to the issue of juvenile delinquency and comic books, calling nearly a hundred witnesses, among them sixty-five public officials (including FBI Director Hoover), eight psychologists and experts on child development (excluding Wertham, who was invited but declined to participate on grounds that he had inadequate time to prepare), ten comics publishers (including Lev Gleason of *Crime Does Not Pay* and Monroe Froehlich, Jr., of Timely / Atlas / Marvel), and others such as the comic-strip artist Milton Caniff. "Any overall study of crime in present-day America would be incomplete if it did not include adequate consideration of the problem of juvenile delinquency," noted the committee in a statement explaining its interest in the "frequently heard charges that juvenile delinquency has increased considerably during the past five years and that this increase has been stimulated by the publication of the so-called crime comic books."

As the testimony unraveled, so did the case to incriminate crime comics. A few witnesses, such as A. H. Conner, acting director of the Federal Bureau of Prisons, spoke vigorously against comics. "No one can state with certainty that juvenile delinquency would decrease if crime comics were not available to juveniles," testified Conner. "Nevertheless, it is clear that many such publications serve as sources of contamination of impressionable minds, provide explicit instruction in the methods by which criminals operate, and contribute to a weakening of the ethical values of the community." Most of those who testified, however, offered mild, qualified criticism of certain comics or defended the bulk of them.

Even J. Edgar Hoover abandoned his early objection to crime comics. While acknowledging that arrests of juveniles had leveled off, rather than increased, during the postwar years, he added that he thought "the incidence of crime among young people is still abnormally high." As for comic books, Hoover said, the "lurid and macabre" variety "may influence the susceptible boy or girl who already possesses definite anti-social tendencies. It is doubtful, however, that an appreciable decrease in juvenile delinquency would result if crime comic books of all types were not readily available to children."

Among the judicial authorities who testified, Louis Goldstein, chairman of the Board of County Judges of Kings County, New York, said, "My own experience with comic books has been favorable. In the many years of close and intimate contact which I have had with thousands of defendants, both in the capacity of prosecuting assistant district attorney and judge of the County Court, I never came across a single case where the delinquent or criminal act would be attributed to the reading of comic books."

The most eloquent defense of comic books and their readers came from the artist Milton Caniff, creator of the influential newspaper adventure strip *Terry and the Pirates*. By showing evil at its most vivid, Caniff explained, comics called attention to what was good. "Practitioners of the inexact science of psychiatry have long served as apologists for the present parental generation by attributing every childhood ill from measles to shyness to the reading of comic books," Caniff said. "Children are natural critics. No lobby can reach them.

They will follow only the line of behavior which is their natural tendency. The portrayal of the blackness of evil which makes virtue white by contrast, and, as in all folk tales, the desire to emulate the St. George of the moment slaying the current dragon, is a healthy and desirable instinct to arouse."

When Kefauver's committee issued its report on juvenile delinquency and comics, on November 11, 1950, the news made the front pages of the *Daily News* and *The New York Times*. Monroe Froehlich, Jr., the executive of Timely who had testified on behalf of comics in Washington, brought a pile of the New York dailies into work that day and read all the reports on the Kefauver committee's findings until he found one that mentioned his name. (The UPI story on the committee report noted that Froehlich "suggested some officials may have made the comics a scapegoat to obscure their own failures as law-enforcement agents.") Froehlich kept copies of one or two papers and left all the others on the floor in a mess for his editor, Stan Lee, to clean up. "Well, that puts *them* out of business!" Froehlich announced.

The Kefauver committee continued its investigation into organized crime. In fact, its work would go on to take an expected turn in 1951, when the New York hearings were televised in a potent demonstration of the young medium's ability to meld politics and entertainment. Through television, Estes Kefauver would soon become a political celebrity, and he would move past juvenile delinquency and comic books, temporarily.

9. New Trend

Shirley Norris, the receptionist at EC, liked to take her coffee break by the window overlooking the intersection of Lafayette and Spring Streets, so she could watch the old Italian men who sat in chairs on the sidewalk and the women who darted around them with their groceries in cloth sacks. From time to time, she would notice a police car approaching from the west on Spring Street, and she would watch it turn left and head uptown. Never once did she see the cops cross Lafayette Street and enter Little Italy. When she thought about that, she would smile or laugh out loud or sigh, happy to be working where she was. Did the patrolmen consider their presence unnecessary on turf already protected by institutions of its own? Did they think of the territory as outside their jurisdiction—or beyond their capacity for enforcement? Two things were certain: The enterprises on Spring Street flourished in the absence of law enforcement, and so did the outré goings-on in the corner suite seven stories up.

Bill Gaines and Al Feldstein started what they called "A New Trend in Comic Books" just as the movement to legislate comics was fading. Early in 1950, they introduced two titles, the products of their decision the previous year to stake a claim to originality in the pathologically imitative comic-book business by emulating *Lights Out* and other scary radio programs of the 1940s. Both of their new comics, *The Crypt of Terror* and *The Vault of Horror*, made slow, taunting entrances through the creaky comic-book marketing means of the day. First, EC's *Crime Patrol* signaled an imminent shift in tone with the title of the first story in its October–November issue, "Three Clues to TERROR," although the tale itself was a fairly conventional police procedural. The cover of the next issue of *Crime Patrol* announced, "Complete in this issue! An illustrated TERROR-TALE from THE CRYPT OF TERROR!" referring to the last story in that magazine, a suspense yarn about a murderous businessman, titled "Return from the Grave," written and drawn by Feldstein. By the next issue, all four stories in *Crime Patrol* were centered on horror: "The Corpse in the Crematorium," "Trapped in the Tomb," "The Graveyard Feet," and "The Spectre in the Castle." Several steps ahead of the postal inspectors this time, Gaines and Feldstein changed the contents of the magazine before switching the title to *The Crypt of Terror* with the April–May issue. (They duplicated this process with their other crime title, *War Against Crime*, morphing it into *The Vault of Horror* during the same period.) "We were test-marketing, to see how the crime magazines did with the introduction of horror, and we heard from the spot-checkers we hired to report on newsstand sales that they sold better than usual, so we knew we were onto something," said Feldstein. "We were experimenting, because nobody had ever tried to do horror in the comic-book format, that Bill and I knew of."

Their knowledge was limited. Recalling the venture several years later, Gaines said, flatly, "I was the first publisher in the United States to publish horror comics. I am responsible. I started them." The fact remains that others had published comics with horror stories of various sorts as early as 1940, when Bill Gaines was an eighteen-year-old science buff who never read comic books, and *Prize Comics* was running a regular feature about Frankenstein. (During the war, the monster turned on Mary Shelley and became a Nazi-fighting hero.)

Citizens of a derivative society, comic-book creators took ideas from all the popular arts, as well as each other's work, and horror had been a staple of the pulps and Hollywood films since the 1930s, although the genre tended to drift in and out of vogue. The first comic book devoted entirely to fright, *Spook Comics*, was published in 1946 (with a cover portrait of Lucifer himself leering through a monocle at a young brunette clutching a long drapery to her torso), and a similar book, *Eerie Comics,* appeared the following year. By fall 1949, when EC started to try out horror within the pages of its crime comics, Timely/Atlas/Marvel was well into the process of replacing super-hero titles such as *Sub-Mariner Comics* with horror-oriented books such as *Amazing Mysteries*; by the end of that year, Timely virtually abandoned costumed heroes for ghouls and vampires, the one constant being the preponderance of capes. In 1950, EC was not the first to publish horror comics, just the most adventurous and serious-minded of several publishers to have turned to the macabre.

Their timing was apt. On September 3, 1949, U.S. government intelligence discovered that the Soviet Union had tested an atomic bomb. Suddenly, for most Americans, young people among them, the Cold War was no longer a political abstraction, a jumble of foreign maps with dotted borders or debates over economic theory, but a palpable threat of vast and gruesome devastation. The zombies with hollow eye sockets and skin peeling off their bones who haunted the boneyards in the panels of *The Crypt of Terror* could not have been far removed from the readers' mental pictures of their own fate in the wake of the nuclear holocaust now possible at any moment.

Traditional campfire fright was just one element in EC's horror comics, and horror was but one of several genres comprising the "New Trend" as it took form in 1950. A month after Gaines and Feldstein published the first issues of *The Crypt of Terror* and *The Vault of Horror*, they introduced two unusual science-oriented titles: *Weird Science* (formerly titled *Saddle Romances*), which had off-beat, sometimes frightful science-fiction stories, and *Weird Fantasy* (formerly *A Moon . . .*

177

A Girl . . . A Romance), which mingled science and the supernatural. That fall, they returned to crime, but with a focus on *crime passionnel* rather than gangsterism, in *Crime SuspenStories* (and its 1952 follow-up, *Shock SuspenStories*). The interchangeable magazine names and slogans at EC were always confusing and essentially irrelevant; in the absence of recurring characters (apart from the cameo narrators of the horror comics, the Crypt-Keeper, the Vault-Keeper, and the Old Witch, who were virtually indistinguishable), the anthology comics of the "New Trend" developed a group identity rooted in their creators' cynicism, readiness to defy convention, and willingness to shock. Six months after its first issue, *The Crypt of Terror* was renamed *Tales from the Crypt*; and a third EC horror title, *The Haunt of Fear* (formerly *Gunfighter*) was replaced with a war comic, *Two-Fisted Tales*, by the end of 1950. Discriminating comics readers learned to look for the EC logo, an effective twist on the ACMP's inconsequential seal of approval.

"I was about to stop reading comics—I said, 'Well, it's time to move on,'" recalled Bhob Stewart, who was thirteen in 1950, when he came upon an early issue of *The Vault of Horror* in the drugstore in Greenwood, Mississippi. "I said, 'What is this?' I read a couple of EC comics, and I said, 'Well, obviously, this changes everything. I can't stop reading comics,' because those comics were so different from everything I had been reading, and I began to buy every one of them. The stories were like radio stories rather than comic-book stories, and they had a point of view that seemed original and provocative to me. They had an attitude that connected with me at the age of thirteen." Although Stewart traded comics with his friends, none of them shared his interest in EC, a fact that helped establish the line's stature as something elite—and its readers' status as comic-book connoisseurs—in Stewart's mind. (Stewart would soon grow so absorbed with EC that, in 1953, he would produce one of the first comic-book fanzines, *The EC Fan Bulletin*, with a rudimentary home printing kit called a hectograph. Bill Gaines would be so impressed by the venture that he would co-opt it with a promotional variation called *The EC Fan-Addicts Bulletin.*)

EC made a specialty of intimate, domestic terror from the first story in the debut issue of *The Haunt of Fear*, a slow-moving narrative of marital disintegration and guilt called "The Wall" and subtitled "A Psychological Study." Written and drawn by Johnny Craig, it combined two Poe tales, "The Tell-Tale Heart" and "The Cask of Amontillado," to tell of a milquetoast husband maddened by his shrewish wife's devotion to her cat, Snooky. When the fellow accidentally kills the woman with a blow meant for the pet, he hides her body behind a wall in the basement, only to be so racked by his conscience that he imagines the cat tearing him apart in vengeance. The monster in the piece was the wife, the brick wall a neat metaphor for the predicating conception of marriage as deadly entrapment. The pages of nearly all the EC comics (including the science-fiction titles, excluding only the war books) swelled with similar portrayals of marriage and family life as sources of unbearable torment. Married people, especially wives, were invariably duplicitous, conniving, abusive, and often murderous. "We got a lot of mileage out of scheming wives and vengeful husbands," Gaines said. In EC's horror paradigm, the true graveyard was the living room of the American home.

"I don't know if Al and Bill had trouble with the ladies, but the guys and gals in the stories were always trying to bump each other off," said Jack Kamen, an EC artist who had worked with Al Feldstein in the Iger studio. Raised in Brooklyn, Kamen had some home art lessons and critical early encouragement from his father, a Russian-born clothier with a knack for sketching. When his father died, Kamen quit high school to help support the family of five by drawing comics. At sixteen, he was bringing home ninety dollars per week from the Chesler shop and studying painting at night at the Art Students League on a work scholarship. Kamen harbored ambitions in fine art but never seemed to have the time to pursue them. A roundish, ebullient man with wild eyes and a manner of speech that sounded like giggling with words, Kamen had a crisp, tightly controlled drawing style well suited to EC's contemporary domestic stories. He had a special facility for drawing steely glamour girls, nearly all of whom resembled his wife, Evelyn. Gaines and Feldstein called the scripts they wrote for Kamen "Buster stories," because the women either called the men "Buster" or looked ready to do so.

"I would dress the women well in elegant clothes, and the men would have beautifully tailored suits, and they would be living in a nice house somewhere, and they would go out for a nice walk, and she would push him in front of a truck," said Kamen. "There were no happy couples, except for the girl and the truck driver in the end, and something terrible would happen to them, probably. There was no such thing as a happy household in EC." To young people of the postwar years, when the mainstream culture glorified suburban domesticity as the modern American ideal—the life that made the Cold War worth fighting—nothing else in the panels of EC comics, not the giant alien cockroach that ate earthlings, not the baseball game played with human body parts, was so subversive as the idea that the exits of the Long Island Expressway emptied onto levels of Hell.

Gaines and Feldstein laced the pages of EC comics with coded challenges to the prevailing standards of normalcy. Working allegorically through genre stories, they sought to engender sympathy for misfits, underdogs, and exiles of every breed—human, animal, fish, alien, living, dead, undead, and combinations thereof. Some of the characters were no doubt close to their creators' self-images or fantasy ideals: the unrecognized artist in "Portrait in Wax!" (*The Vault of Horror*), who created magnificent etchings in his garret until he was assaulted by an envious rival. Some were clichés: the little boy in "Horror of the School Room" (*The Haunt of Fear*), who was punished as a liar because he said he had a secret friend, an invisible giant (who, in the end, proved his existence to the boy's punisher). Many were gloriously weird: the man with the basket on his shoulder whom the townspeople set out to lynch when they learned that he was hiding a second head ("The Basket!," *The Haunt of Fear*); the colony of mutant victims of an atomic blast, every one different from the next—one with a single eye, one with a pointy bald head, one with his nose under his mouth ("Child of Tomorrow," *Weird Fantasy*). EC's monsters, like Frankenstein's, were never quite what the mob presumed them to be.

According to Gaines, the writing always had priority over the artwork at EC. "The EC approach in all these books is to offer better stories than can be found in other comics," he explained in an article published in 1954. "At EC the copy itself—both caption and dialogue—has taken the number one position. This is a switch from the old days of comics when the art was most important and the story second. We take our stories very seriously."

Gaines could be forgiven his bias, speaking not only as EC's publisher but as one of its main writers. For Gaines, the "New Trend" marked a significant shift of his own course, into the creative realm for the first time in his life (and for the last). "Those were the happiest days," Gaines recalled in the late 1960s. "I was about 95 percent creative and probably 5 percent business. Of course, it's a lot more fun to be creative. Al and I wrote practically all of the material, so there was no problem with control over writers, because we were the writers."

Generally, Gaines would contribute the story ideas, and Feldstein would work them up. Gaines's process was to stay up till dawn, aided by the Dexedrine he had been prescribed as a diet medication, reading stacks of magazines and short-story anthologies, trolling for characters, situations, and plots for Feldstein to flesh out and adapt to the EC style. Gaines called these appropriations "springboards," and he relished finding them and pitching them to Feldstein. "I read like a maniac," Gaines said. "I would read every science fiction and horror story I could get my hands on. They couldn't possibly publish them fast enough.

"I'd get this idea and I'd write it down on a piece of paper. I had this gigantic batch of plots, thousands of pieces of paper, each with a springboard on it. The big thing in my life in those days was to sell Al Feldstein a story.

"Al and I would sit there, and I'd try to sell him on a springboard," Gaines said. "After he had rejected the first thirty-three on general principles, he *might* show a little interest in number thirty-four. Then I'd give him the hard sell and he'd run into the next room and start breaking down the plot into story form. He'd normally write a story in three hours, but during those three hours I'd have a nervous stomach, wondering if Al was going to come in screaming, 'I can't write that goddamn plot!' When that happened, it would already be afternoon, and we'd have to start all over again, because we simply *had* to have a complete story by five o'clock."

Feldstein, who was paid by the project rather than on salary, wrote one complete story per day, at least four days per week. In addition, he served as the editor of four EC comics, working with the occasional freelance writer and commissioning all the art for those four titles, and he also drew some complete stories and did many of the books' covers. To save precious minutes, he composed the dialogue in pencil directly onto the artboards on which the artists would produce the finished work. (The Wroten service would erase Feldstein's writing and ink in the words with a lettering machine.) He never made an outline or drafted a script. "I amazed myself," said Feldstein, who had no writing experience before coming to EC. "I had an innate sense of dramatic pacing. Somehow, the story would always have just the right number of words and wrap up at exactly the right point." (Actually, many of Feldstein's EC stories are overstuffed with verbiage; some panels are so packed with text that the artists had space left to draw nothing but eyes peering under the word balloons, and the endings often came abruptly, with a dense paragraph of explanation necessary to explain or complete the tale.) Feldstein would almost always finish by five and bring the boards to Gaines, who would read the text aloud to Feldstein and whoever else happened to be nearby at the time.

"This was the fun part," Gaines remembered. "We always thought of our work as being theatrical, and it had to read right. We suggested to our readers that they do this, and a lot of them did."

Since the volume of EC's output required more "springboards" than Gaines's supply of nighttime reading and amphetamines could fulfill, Gaines put a call for contributions in *Writer's Digest*, and the criteria he listed for EC content indicate his nearly radical eagerness to defy the conventions not only of comic books, but of all popular culture in the early 1950s. He wrote:

> You should know this about our horror books. We have no ghosts, devils, goblins or the like. We tolerate vampires and werewolves, if they follow tradition and behave the way respectable vampires and werewolves should.
>
> We love walking corpse stories.
>
> We'll accept an occasional zombie or mummy.
>
> And we relish the *contes cruels* story.
>
> *Shock SuspenStories* do not contain supernaturalism. *Crime Suspen-Stories* contain no shock. These are logical stories in which the villain tries to get away with murder—and probably does. No cops and robbers stories.
>
> Virtue doesn't have to triumph over evil.

Outside of the pulp novels of Mickey Spillane and the films of Sam Fuller, there were few places in the arts, high or low, where sadism, unpunished murder, and the triumph of evil were so welcome.

Gaines and Feldstein said they tried to mold the content of each story to fit—or to work in contrast with—the style of a particular artist, as they did with their homey tales of devilment for Jack Kamen. "We tried to have an artist in mind when we were planning a story— it helped us picture the story and gave us a better result," said Feldstein. "For instance, we would start out and say, 'Hey, what about something for Jack Davis?' He had a very strange, very cluttered, rural or rustic style that wasn't really like comic-book art. That would tell us how the story should go—'Okay, we're in a swamp . . .' And we had to have a weird, hairy creature for Jack to draw, with big feet and [opportunities for] all that hatchwork Jack loved to do."

This account belies Gaines's contention that the text had primacy at EC, and so did the published pages. Feldstein's stories, each done in a few hours' time by a production-oriented writer of limited imagination, grew repetitive, despite the boldness and shock value of their content. Emulating the O. Henry short stories he remembered from elementary school, Feldstein gave every EC story a "twist" ending: The big-game hunter ends up as human prey, his head hung as a trophy; the man who loves to watch live lobsters die in the pot ends up boiling to death. The reader, expecting the twist, knows the ending from the first page. Among the cheapest of literary tricks, the surprise ending works best in the hands of a writer who anticipates the reader's anticipation and respects it while he toys with it, understanding that the thrill lies not in the surprise but in the earning of it. Such was an approach to writing for which Al Feldstein had no capacity, no interest, or, perhaps, simply no time.

Most of the EC art, by contrast, was fresh and exuberant. As comics historian Mike Benton wrote in his critical overview of the field, *The Comic Book in America*, "Although the EC stories . . . were literate and oftentimes provocative, it was the EC artwork that elevated the comic books far beyond their forebears, imitators, and successors." Gaines seemed to have the extraordinary fortune of employing many of the most creative people in comics: Johnny Craig, Reed Crandall, Will Elder, Graham Ingels, Bernard Krigstein, Harvey Kurtzman, Jack Kamen, John Severin, Al Williamson, and Wally Wood, among others. Of course, what appeared to be an ability to attract exceptional artists was in part a gift for inspiring the artists he hired. Gaines wanted art of high quality to do justice to the writing he prized. He paid well, typically $25 per page, a bit more than the industry norm of

$15 to $20 per page; he made the payments promptly, upon acceptance (at the urging of Feldstein, who had done his share of begging from Victor Fox); he encouraged artists to use their own styles, rather than adapt their work to a "house look"; he had them ink their own pencil drawings, to retain their personality; and he allowed them to sign their work prominently, while most publishers enforced anonymity to keep the help in their place.

"Of course, Bill Gaines's books were superior, in the sense that he attempted and encouraged and accepted a lot more honesty in story and in art," said Bernard Krigstein. "He surrounded himself with people that could satisfy his feeling for these things, so that consistently he was able to put out a lot of good work—and, along with that, I thought, a lot of work that was really . . . that had an unacceptable level, too. In other words, I'm glad I did not get assigned some of the stories that were published. But I couldn't really fault him on that, because he balanced it off with some really mature, truthful, honest storytelling."

A gifted painter trained at Brooklyn College, Krigstein first drew comics, for the money, in the early 1940s, but soon became one of the medium's most devout champions. He saw parity not only among comic books and historical modes of visual storytelling, but among comics and all the arts, high, low, and otherwise. "I belong to low culture," he said. "Not only do I belong to low culture, I don't think low culture is low culture. It's all culture." Krigstein's dedication to comic books as an art form led him, in the early 1950s, to organize the Society of Comic Book Illustrators, a malformed hybrid of a trade group and a union, dedicated to raising comics artists' esteem and page rates. "I took the position that comics was a great art, that we were in fact fine artists and illustrators," Krigstein said. Prior to his arrival at EC, Krigstein had proven his seriousness with incisively composed and deftly rendered art for stories barely worth the effort, such as "Conning the Confidence Man" in *Justice Traps the Guilty* and "The Huckster's Castle" in *Crime Detective*. Krigstein flourished at EC, where his assignments came with freedom and some good text. His special strength was composition. Krigstein had an expansive, dimensional approach to panel design, less indebted to the camera than that of most comics artists, and he understood composition as content, not merely context. He deepened EC stories such as "More Blessed to Give . . ." (in *Crime SuspenStories*) and "The Catacombs" (another variation on Poe's "Cask of Amontillado," published in *The Vault of Horror*), shifting point of view through the placement of his characters and their body language, compressing time or distending it by varying the size and the shape of his panels.

The opening art of one story, "Monotony," in *Crime SuspenStories*, is an elegant example of what Krigstein could do. He devoted a full page of six panels to presenting the main character, an office clerk, as he: (panel one) enters his cubicle; (panel two) hangs his coat, hat, and umbrella; (panel three) removes the page for the previous day from his desk calendar; (panel four) dusts his chair with his handkerchief; (panel five) sharpens his pencils; (panel six) takes his seat at his desk. Krigstein presents this action, accentuating that it is scarcely action at all, in a sequence of flat, spare images. The main character is shown in full body, and there is no change in perspective from panel to panel. Our attention is drawn to minor subtleties of movement: the slight, stiff tilt of the fellow's back as he hangs his garments, the way he presses one hand against the small of his back as he snaps off the calendar page with his other hand. There are no word balloons, only captions, and they are unnecessary; Krigstein's images do all the work, through their compositional restraint, and make the monotony hypnotic.

Gaines nurtured a familial atmosphere at EC, a company he took over from his father, co-owned with his mother, and operated in a residential neighborhood on the periphery of Little Italy, where family and business were often conjoined. Frustrated in his youth by M. C. Gaines's severity and detachment, Bill Gaines adopted a paternalistic attitude toward the EC artists and writers, most of whom were around his age or just a few years younger. "I knew Bill as well as anybody, and I can tell you, he was dedicated to being everything his father wasn't," said Feldstein. "His father was a dominant tyrant who told Bill he was a useless nothing, so Bill made himself the most supportive, encouraging, understanding, loving father figure in the world."

Al Williamson, the youngest of the EC artists, was twenty-one and insecure about his work when he took his first assignment for EC, early in 1952. Still living with his mother in Manhattan, Williamson was a comics artist who drew with little interest in the money; he sought artistic satisfaction and rarely found it. "EC was more like a family than other companies, and I needed that," said Williamson, who, in the early 1950s, had the appearance of a sensitive theater student in an audition for a role as a juvenile delinquent. He wore blue jeans everywhere and had a long, duck's-ass haircut, and he spoke little to anyone. Williamson was so devoted to his craft that he would spend days on a single panel, rendering fine details that would be obliterated by the comics' cheap printing. "For me, the fifties were not a very good time—they weren't good for a guy like me, because I didn't fit in anywhere I looked. I was a mess. I had no confidence in myself. I went into Bill one day, and I said, 'Bill, I need to talk to you. I need help.' He said, 'What's wrong?' 'I don't know. I need help.' And he talked to me, and he got me to start seeing a shrink—his own shrink, and the guy was a big help. I went to Bill because I didn't think of him as a boss. We cared for each other.

"It was very inspirational working there. But I was never happy with my work, no matter what. I was pretty screwed up."

If the artists and writers at EC functioned like a family, they were the March sisters of comic books, a brood of fearsome competitors mutually stimulated by affection and envy. As Gaines explained, "They had a tremendous admiration for one another. Wally Wood would come in with a story and three artists would crowd around him and *faint*, just poring over every brushstroke and every panel, and, of course, Wally, who's getting this adulation, sits there and loves it. Next time around it's his turn to adulate someone—Williamson comes in with his story and Wally Wood faints. And everybody tried to outdo each other, which is one of the reasons we got such incredibly good art. They were all in a friendly competition to see who could make everybody faint more than the other guy."

Most of the people under him thought of Gaines as exceptionally generous, despite the fact that he bought all the rights to their work in perpetuity and kept the original art. When an artist delivered a set of finished pages, Gaines wrote a check on the spot, then stamped the back with a sine qua non, making the assignment of rights a condition of endorsement. He wiggled out of his commitments (one verbal, one in writing) to share profits with Al Feldstein and Sheldon Mayer, but he threw parties every Christmas and presented an expensive gift—a home-movie set-up or a 35mm camera—to every artist who had contributed a specified number of pieces that year. Those who fell short by a single story received nothing. "Bill was incredibly kind, and generous to a fault," said Jack Davis, a Georgia-born artist who was knocking around New York, doing some work for a five-cent Western comic called *Lucky Star*, when, in 1950, he walked into the EC office, cold, and Feldstein gave him an assignment to do a mummy story for *The Haunt of Fear*. A sweet, lumbering man, Davis came to be known for the rough-hewn fury of his horror comics work and the speed of its execution. "No other publisher I knew in those days ever gave gifts to anybody," Davis said. "You felt like you were respected with Bill, and that went a long way in those days, if you were in comic books."

A few others saw Gaines's conditional benevolence as manipulation. The late Harvey Kurtzman, the editor of EC's pair of war comics, *Two-Fisted Tales* and *Frontline Combat*, objected strongly to his publisher's claim to familial privilege and made the point by declining one of Gaines's gifts. "Bill wanted to be Big Daddy, and Harvey resented it," according to his widow, Adele Kurtzman. "He gave the Christmas party, and he gave everybody a movie camera and a screen, and Harvey said, 'I want to be paid for what I do, I don't want a gift. I have a father. I don't need that.'"

Malevolent or benign, Bill Gaines honored the tradition of Major Malcolm Wheeler-Nicholson, Harry "A" Chesler, and Busy Arnold, and made EC feel fraternal, even clannish. "Everybody there was brilliant and a little dopey," said Marie Severin, who took up the task of coloring the pages of EC comics in 1951, at age twenty-two. The younger sister of EC artist John Severin, she was skilled at draftsmanship as well as coloring, and she played a key role at EC, embellishing the original black-and-white art without overwhelming it, often softening the gruesome scenes with muted tones. "You have to be a little dopey to be an artist, and Bill was just like the rest of us. He believed in us. He made us feel like we were great, and we could do what we wanted to, and he was right there with us. Even the violence—I thought it was good that we were telling stories about killers. That's good—that's good stuff! It's a healthy thing to know that there are bad things out there. Otherwise, [the readers] wouldn't know what not to do, and Bill had discerning taste, so we knew that what we did had to be up to a certain level."

To the majority of comic-book publishers, the new trend, horror, meant no more than a new market to exploit and called only for refitting the editorial machinery to churn out vampires as well as vamps. By the end of 1952, nearly one-third of all the comics on the newsstands were devoted to the macabre. (Many of the rest were romance, which remained a popular comics category, although it declined as horror grew.) More than a dozen publishers were producing about 150 horror-oriented titles: *Chamber of Chills, Witches Tales, Tomb of Terror, Out of the Night, Weird Thrillers, Nightmare,* and a thesaurus's worth of others. Timely, the first major comics publisher to focus on horror, was putting out twenty-five horror books, each of which had six stories. "There was a hell of a lot of editing to do, but I could handle it without any problem," recalled Stan Lee, who said he single-handedly processed all the text for the whole line—and, he said, wrote "hundreds" of stories and, he said, commissioned all the art, he said, and designed characters, he said, and . . .

"The horror craze was a challenge for the average publisher, because you had to come up with new ideas for every story. That was easy for me. Not everybody could do it," said Lee, whose editorial stewardship helped make Timely the most successful publisher in comics by 1952, with sales half again as great as that of its closest competitor, Dell, and twice that of National/DC. "Books came and went, because they petered out. The editors couldn't sustain the interest, so they used a lot of tricks to get the reader's attention."

With their generic titles and lack of heroes, horror comics, EC's excepted, offered little to keep readers loyal. The only recurring character in most books was Satan. Publishers, unable to establish a following for a given title, had to compete for the attention of the same readers, month after month, and the game in this competition was shock. Horror comics were soon caught in an upward spiral of gruesomeness. One month's issue would depict a man's neck being slashed, and the next would have a decapitation. The one to follow would show a human head used as a bowling ball or a woman roasting her husband's body parts (head, a leg, hands, feet) on a barbecue grill. "You did what you had to do—what moved 'em off the racks," said publisher Stanley P. Morse, who produced several acutely vile horror comics under various corporate names. One of Morse's books, *Weird Mysteries*, featured a cover picture of a human brain being ripped out of a skull; another, *Weird Chills*, had stories with pithily evocative titles such as "Hate" and "Violence." Unrepentant half a century after his shameless tenure in comics, Morse said, "I don't know what the hell I published. I never knew. I never read the things. I never cared."

■ ■ ■

New Trend

The debate over comics smoldered. Several towns and cities as well as one key state continued to poke at the comics issue, drawing upon information predating or contradicting the findings of the Kefauver Crime Committee, which had largely exonerated crime comics from the charge of inciting juvenile delinquency. On February 14, 1952, Walden, New York, a small river town in the Hudson Valley, commemorated national Crime Prevention Week by announcing a voluntary ban on a dozen crime comics, and before the end of that week, the New York State Legislature returned to the subject of comics. Assemblyman Joseph F. Carlino, the chairman of a joint legislative subcommittee chartered to study comics, introduced a package of six new acts to regulate the books. A second-term Republican from Nassau County, Carlino took the action after his committee came to several damning conclusions about comics and their publishers. Among them:

> The entire industry is remiss in its failure to institute effective measures to police and restrain the undesirable minority.
>
> The reading of crime "comics" stimulate [*sic*] sadistic and masochistic attitudes and interfere [*sic*] with the normal development of sexual habits in children and produce [*sic*] abnormal sexual tendencies in adolescence.
>
> Instead of reforming their bad practices, the publishers of bad crime "comics" have banded together, employed resourceful legal and public relations counsel, so-called "educators," and experts in a deliberate effort to continue such harmful practices and to fight any and every effort to arrest or control such practices.

As with the legislation vetoed by Governor Dewey three years earlier, one of Carlino's measures would establish a state-run body to regulate the content of comic books produced in New York—that is, virtually all comic books—prior to publication, through the Department of Education. Several of the remaining acts were designed to modify the state penal code and to grant the state courts jurisdiction over violations of the proposed regulations. On March 12, the Assembly passed one of the bills, which would make it a misdemeanor "to publish or sell comic books dealing with fictional crime, bloodshed or lust that might incite minors to violence or immorality." It went through on a vote of 141 to 4 but was vetoed a month later by Governor Dewey, again on the grounds of vagueness. By then, however, the legislature had already sanctioned a new committee, to be led by Carlino, for further study of "the effect on minors" of not only comic books, but also television, radio, "picture magazines," and "so-called 'pocket books.'" Set back (temporarily) for vagueness, Carlino took his efforts into four more broad areas.

In Maryland, meanwhile, a jurist and an attorney for the state tried striking against crime comics through an existing statute prohibiting the sale to minors of publications featuring portrayals of criminal acts—a Comstock-era law of questionable legality after the Supreme Court decision of 1948. Assistant State's Attorney Woodrow A. Shriver, acting on a complaint by juvenile court judge Theodore L. Miazga that children brought before him had been inspired by crime comics, made a personal survey of ten newsstands in Prince George's County and purchased a dozen comics that he considered illegal. Shriver and Miazga both asked the county police to begin enforcing the standing law, and on July 7, 1952, three news dealers were arrested for selling crime comics. They faced a penalty of a $200 fine and up to a year in jail. One of the dealers, Warren Tremaine, manager of Albrecht's Pharmacy in the College Park area, was stunned by what he considered a gross injustice. "They didn't like one of the books I was selling," Tremaine recalled, "but there were worse ones." What came to mind, in particular, were the "monster things."

10. Humor in a Jugular Vein

Comic-book editors, anonymous and largely unsupervised, made of their jobs what they wished. Some, such as Al Vigoda, an editor at Fox (whose younger brother Abe would later go into movie acting), were in it for a fast buck; Vigoda paid $20 per page of comic art, $30 for those who kicked back $2 per page to Vigoda without mentioning the terms to Victor Fox. Other editors clung to a view of employment in comics as a provisional stage in literary careers with grander prospects ahead, a parallel to the common perception of comic-book reading as a passing phase in children's lives—a diversion that may serve a purpose for a time but is best abandoned before too long. At Fawcett, for instance, editor Stanley Kauffmann worked on Captain Marvel scripts by day in order to buy the hours to do the literary writing that would soon liberate him from comics. "I did the [comics] work for the paycheck, so I could do my own writing and provide future historians the grounds for my canonization, or such was my plan," said Kauffmann, who would go on to be an important film critic, as well as a novelist and playwright. "As I wrote [comic-book] scripts and edited things, I began to see how much relation there was to film, and then I began to see the moving from box to box as camera shots, and this was somewhat interesting to me. But in no way did I take comic books seriously, except to do [them] well enough to earn my pay. There were others who took the work more seriously—one of my colleagues, in particular, treated comics as if they were fine art, and discretion prevents me from providing his name, because he was a fool." (When Kauffmann left Fawcett, in the mid-1940s, he was replaced by another young literary aspirant, Patricia Highsmith, who edited the stories about Billy Batson and his family while she worked on a book that would become *Strangers on a Train*. "My work [in comics] had nothing to do with literature," Highsmith later said of her tenure in comics, "but it did stimulate my imagination.")

At EC, Al Feldstein and his fellow editor Harvey Kurtzman performed a set of elliptical variations on the debate over comics as commerce or art. Feldstein, a workhorse under the reins of a publisher with esteem for the muse, profited enormously by producing comics pages by the ton, paid for by the pound, and much of his stuff—particularly his eerily ossified cover art—turned out well. Even his hurried writing had an affecting, corny charm. By 1952, Feldstein had gained creative authority over all but three of Bill Gaines's publications, and the work proved so lucrative that Feldstein moved his wife and their two children to a three-bedroom ranch house in Merrick, Long Island, within walking distance of the train station. (A third child was born in Merrick.) He took up golf and boating, and he bought a hi-fi set with a mammoth, ten-watt Sunn amplifier and separate woofers and tweeters, a system newer and fancier than Bill Gaines's. Feldstein was living the suburban ideal he subverted in the pages of EC comics.

Kurtzman found Feldstein's success maddening. He had come to EC in 1949 after a stint at Timely, where he had written and drawn a couple of nutty one-page filler cartoons called *Hey Look* and *Sheldon*. Like Feldstein, Kurtzman had grown up in Brooklyn; a poor kid, he created his first original cartoon strip, *Ikey and Mikey*, on the sidewalks of his neighborhood, using shards of plaster from hunks of walls in abandoned lots as chalk. He was the middle child of three sons, all artistically inclined. Their father, David Kurtzman, a restless sort who made a modest living as an assistant to a jeweler, setting stones and sizing rings he could never afford to own, died of a bleeding ulcer at age thirty-six, when Harvey was four years old. "Even though I was young, I guess I was aware of the fact that making a living was hard work," Kurtzman wrote in a memoir, *My Life as a Cartoonist*. "Coming to terms with the world was not easy for me, which was why I drew. I drew to get attention from the people around me." Kurtzman's mother, Edith, a firebrand who took her family's hardships as evidence of the inequity of capitalism, subscribed to the *Daily Worker* and sent her sons to the red-diaper Camp Kinderland in the Catskills for at least one summer.

Kurtzman's first assignment for EC was the art for an educational pamphlet packaged by the late M. C. Gaines's brother David and published out of the Lafayette Street office. Titled *Lucky Fights It Through*, the booklet was a Western story about venereal disease—as Kurtzman later described it, "a comic on how to cure syphilis or spot the sores and recognize them, and it came with a little record, 'The Lonesome Cowboy' or 'The Diseased Cowboy,' something like that. I did such a good job, think of all the people out there who became cured through my comic strip. I don't know whether it helped cure or helped the sickness, because it showed this guy running around with hookers. It showed how to do it." (The song on the thin plastic 78-rpm record that accompanied the book was titled "The Story of That Ignorant, Ignorant Cowboy.")

Once Kurtzman proved his ability to handle straight realism, Bill Gaines assigned him the editorship of *Two-Fisted Tales*, which had been conceived as a "he-man" comic about adventurers, swashbucklers, and other fighting men, but which became a war comic after American forces landed in Korea in June 1950. "The war books, of course, were inspired by the Korean War," Kurtzman recalled. "So whoever started that war, it was his fault that we did the war books."

A war book by subject, but not by sympathy, *Two-Fisted Tales* and its follow-up, *Frontline Combat*, both of which Kurtzman edited, were close to antiwar in their refusal to glamorize combat or romanticize the combatants on any side. Kurtzman wrote most of the scripts, penciled and inked a full story in virtually every issue (for the first couple of years), and provided rough sketches of the remaining pages for his corps of favored artists: Wally Wood, John Severin, Will Elder, and Jack Davis. On Kurtzman's battlefields, the gallant American knights who marched through most war comics gave way to jittery, ambivalent GIs, sympathetic enemies who felt pain when they were shot, devastating losses, and pointless victories. The second issue of *Two-Fisted Tales*, for example, included a sweeping allegory called "War Story!" (written by Kurtzman and drawn by Severin and Wood), set during the Second World War and centered on a sadistic American infantryman. "Watch me get that @*!!?#@*!@*!?" he says as he defies a cease-fire order and shoots a Japanese soldier waving a white flag of surrender. "Heh, heh! Got 'im in the gut! Look at 'im wriggle!" When his platoon liberates a group of Americans, the POWs report having received fair treatment under a Japanese commander, now gravely wounded. "That's him over there!" one of the men says. "He treated us O.K.! We ought to get him to the hospital tent." In the end, the American sadist sneaks into the tent and stabs the Japanese officer, who is covered by a blanket, only to find that he has inadvertently murdered his own twin brother. While heavy-handed in the we-are-all-brothers symbolism, the story, like dozens in the Kurtzman issues to follow, was so dubious of the rightness of the American side that it would have made the author's mother proud. Other parents no doubt watched their children reading *Two-Fisted Tales* and *Frontline Combat* and figured that the kids were being spoon-fed jingoism, unaware of the books' diet of cynicism toward the American military and sensitivity to the impartial cruelty of war.

"In my war comics, I avoided the usual glamorous stuff of the big good-looking GI beating up the ugly little yellow man," Kurtzman later explained. "I was reading the news of the Korean War along with everybody else. It struck me that war is not a very nice business, and the comic-book companies dealing in the subject matter of war tended to make war glamorous. That offended me.

"I felt that people should know the truth about war and everything else. As a matter of fact, I finally came to the conclusion that it's the truth that one should be interested in, that if you aim your thinking toward telling the truth, then you'd be doing something worthwhile."

Kurtzman often spent hours in the New York Public Library, researching military uniforms, equipment, and historical settings. For a story about missions to rescue pilots shot down over the sea, he wanted firsthand experience flying above the Atlantic in a small craft, so he arranged to ride in a test flight conducted at the Grumman aircraft plant in Bethpage, Long Island. "He drove us pretty crazy," said Jack Davis. "Every gun had to be exactly the right make and model of firearm for the story, and the hat and the shoes and the buttons had to be exactly correct—everything. Realism was like a crusade [for Kurtzman]." When Davis submitted the art for one story, "Combat Medic," Kurtzman admonished him for drawing an Army medic's kit with the gauze pads on the wrong side of the sulfa.

Because of the research he conducted and the fastidiousness he applied, Kurtzman believed that he was outperforming Feldstein for significantly less compensation, and he went to Gaines for a raise. "Harvey felt that he was doing a better job than Al, which he was, intrinsically," Gaines later said. "On the other hand, I kept pointing out that Al's books were selling better than his, which they were. So it was a kind of stand-off." Gaines recommended that Kurtzman simply improve his productivity and edit a third title, thereby increasing his income half again. Kurtzman agreed to Gaines's plan and suggested something he thought he could do easily, without research: a comic book devoted to his first passion, humor. For the book's title, Gaines or Feldstein or Kurtzman (we'll never know, since all three took credit for the idea) thought of adapting a catchphrase that Feldstein had been using in the letters pages of the horror books: "EC's Mad Mag," which Kurtzman reduced to the perfect single syllable in the middle. "That's the real, stupid reason why there's a *Mad*," Gaines recalled. "Because [Kurtzman] was discontented with Feldstein working three and a half times as fast as he did . . . I didn't want to publish a humor magazine."

Decades later, when *Mad* had become a cultural institution, Kurtzman would embellish the story of its origin, claiming that he came up with the idea for a humorous comic book and began working up drawings for it while he was hospitalized for jaundice that he had contracted from overwork on the war comics. Kurtzman did indeed come down with jaundice while working at EC, as Gaines reported in an editor's note in the July–August 1953 issue of *Two-Fisted Tales*; however, that was about nine months after the debut of *Mad*. (The same edition of *Two-Fisted Tales* included a house ad for *Mad* issue number five.) His account presented Kurtzman as he would portray himself in half a dozen other contexts, as a martyr to his own genius, and it neatly links him personally to the character who would come to symbolize the publication he created, Alfred E. Neuman. "It was a face from an old high school biology book, used as an example of a person who lacked iodine," Kurtzman said. At the same time, his story evokes the jaundiced point of view that would distinguish *Mad*'s humor, rooting it literally in Kurtzman's bloodstream.

There had always been comical comics, of course—books with silly big-foot characters and talking animals, geared for young children, as well as books in the *Archie* school of teen-oriented humor, read mainly by preteens. Yet, in comics publishing, humor had been relegated almost exclusively to juvenilia. Few people in comics made much effort to tailor comedy to the young adults who read things such as *The Spirit*, St. John's romance comics, or EC's line. Indeed, prideful comics artists and writers tended to resist humor for fear that it would make their work seem even more lightweight than it was already taken to be. "The average person thought of comic books as joke books," said Will

Eisner. "The first step to overcome that would be to not make jokes. But that's an immature approach. I always tried to inject humor in *The Spirit*, and I think that's one of the things that made it more sophisticated—more serious, if you will. But the humor itself had to be sophisticated, and that's not easy to accomplish. What Harvey did was very brave, because he chose to produce a whole book full of humor for the older reader. I wouldn't have known how to do that."

Neither did Kurtzman, at first. "In the beginning," Kurtzman said, "I have to admit that we didn't really know just where we were going with *Mad*." His only idea, he said, "was to do parodies."

Fueled at first by his enmity toward Feldstein, Kurtzman chose the subject of comic books, including the sort Feldstein made, to be the object of his new title's satire. The first issue of *Mad*, which appeared on newsstands in August 1952, was, in large part, a parody of his publisher's own goods, a blitz of spitballs down the hall of 225 Lafayette Street. Subtitled "Humor in a Jugular Vein," the book had four stories in comics format: one horror ("Hoohah!"), one science fiction ("Blobs!" inspired by E. M. Forster's parable of a future overtaken by technology, "The Machine Stops"), one crime ("Ganefs!"), and one Western ("Varmint!"), along with a pair of one-page all-text stories to satisfy postal requirements. All four were written by Kurtzman, and they were drawn by his war-comics stalwarts Jack Davis, Wally Wood, Will Elder, and John Severin.

From the beginning, *Mad* was giddy adolescent fun. The stories seemed written for the pleasure of the writing, with no fear of being too silly or obvious or odd. "Beg pardon, gents," says the block-jawed cowboy hero of the Western story as he sashays into the saloon. "Bartender! Lemme have a glass of . . . milk!" Most of the humor was visual and more clever than the text. At the end of the horror tale, in a take-off on Feldstein's twist endings, a young couple drives away from the spooky house as the sweet old man living there removes his head and tucks it under his arm. In the sci-fi spoof, a vending machine dispenses ice-cream sodas and sexy young female robots for drooling boys of tomorrow; and in the Western, the hero is so stoic that he stands in the saloon motionless, expressionless, for six pages. The first *Mad* was a gleeful, unassuming surprise, like a funny cartoon drawn on a sidewalk.

On only one page of "Blobs!" did Kurtzman break away from the comic-book theme to parody contemporary society, poking fun at the emerging big targets of the 1950s: electric appliances, highway congestion, and television. Two men of the future, looking back at "the ancient year of 1952," puzzle over the behavior of their ancestors: "Friends would drive over to other friends' houses in automobiles . . . and instead of talking to the friends, they would look at television machines for a few hours, and then they would ride home!" Tame by the standards *Mad* would later set, this was social satire uncommon in its time for squarely, overtly ridiculing the adult world in a milieu for young people.

The art below that block of text, by Wally Wood from a layout by Kurtzman, shows a suburban living room with moderne chairs and lamps and a console TV set. A group of balding, dim-looking middle-aged men in suits roar in laughter as they watch the screen, which shows a grim slapstick comedian smacking a pie in someone's face. On top of the TV, a few books are stacked between bookends of "Thinker" statuettes slouched in boredom. In the middle of the room, a little boy yanks at his mother's skirt, trying to pull her away from the TV; he is screaming, and, though there is no balloon to give us his words, the expression of exasperation on his face suggests nothing other than "Get me outta here!" The woman hushes the kid with a finger to her lips, and one of the men scowls down at him. The child, the only engaged intelligence in sight, is unheard, disdained, and desperate to escape the mesmerizing idiocy around him.

■ ■ ■

Emboldened by delusions of immunity, comic-book makers allowed the horror and suspense comics of the early 1950s to grow ever more gruesome and lurid, and the blood overflowing the pages drew the decency hounds back to their trail. As the publisher Stanley P. Morse described the escalation of graphic violence in comics such as his *Weird Chills*, "Nobody complained, so we gave the people what they wanted until they started complaining about it." Morse's fiercest critic, Fredric Wertham, saw the darkening of comics much the same way. "When the decision of Governor Dewey and the lack of decision of Senator Kefauver had given the green light to the comic-book industry, they went ahead full steam," Wertham charged, writing about a 1952 issue of Harvey's *Black Cat Mystery*. "Now no holds are barred," Wertham continued. "Horror, crime, sadism, monsters, ghouls, corpses dead and alive—in short, real freedom of expression. All this in comic books addressed to and sold to children."

The debate over comics rekindled, with the horror and romance genres providing the books' critics with rich new sources of fuel for complaint. On December 1, 1952, a special committee of the House of Representatives led by E. C. Gathings, a Democrat from Arkansas then in his seventh term, initiated hearings on the subject of "immoral, obscene and otherwise offensive" publications, including comic books that could be considered sexually provocative or "too gory." Gathings argued persuasively against the public display of lewdness by performing a hootchy-kootchy dance on the House floor. His Select Committee on Current Pornographic Materials focused primarily on pulp novels, with their leering cover art, and nudie magazines such as *Stag*. (Hugh Hefner was still working on the prototype for *Playboy*, which would be published the following year.) Since every state except New Mexico had long-standing laws covering obscenity, and since federal regulations already prohibited transportation of indecent materials by common carrier (railroads, trucks, or airlines), Gathings initiated the hearings with little hint of his committee's legislative objectives beyond the possibility of extending the ban on interstate carriage of obscene goods to apply to personal vehicles and pedestrians.

Meanwhile, the issue of delinquency was coming alive again, with reports of crimes by young people mounting once more. In 1952, the United States Children's Bureau announced an increase of 10 percent in juvenile delinquency nationally and 20 percent in New York City during the previous year, compared with 1950. The New York State Youth Commission, much the same, reported a 17.8 percent rise in arrests of persons under sixteen during 1951; the number of such arrests in 1950, by contrast, had been the lowest in fourteen years. Most analysts blamed the Korean War, applying the long-held theory that disruption of family life, combined with wartime factors such as the atmosphere of violence and anxiety in the news, led to delinquency, although the issues were open to debate, as always. Indeed, a major study of delinquency conducted by *The New York Times* in 1952 concluded that uncertainty about the causes of juvenile delinquency was itself a cause of juvenile delinquency. In a front-page story, "Youth Delinquency Growing Rapidly Over the Country," the *Times* reported, "The public gets alarmed in sporadic cycles, perhaps first about sex offenders, then about narcotic addicts, but lacks convictions about the causes of delinquency. This makes it difficult to set up treatment facilities to help seriously troubled children or to prevent delinquency."

After a week of hearings, the Gathings committee came to no conclusions and recommended no legislation, but made news with an updated version of the charge that comic books inspired juvenile crime. The final person to provide testimony was the mother of a minor accused of murder, who said comics and "girlie" magazines had poisoned her son. Robert Hearn, then sixteen, was one of four underage young men from the Detroit area accused of stabbing a gas station attendant to death during a robbery attempt in Pontiac, Michigan. "We definitely feel that these books were a contributing factor—if not more than that," Mrs. Dwight Hearn told Gathings's committee as she wept. "He was always a good boy. He never got into trouble. But a few months before this he started reading these things. He would just lie on the bed and read his comic books . . . He started talking like the hoodlums in the stories. He said his father was silly for going to work." Next thing, young Hearn quit Sunday school and his barbering class, broke up with his girlfriend, and started smoking marijuana and drinking. Papers across the country picked up the story without reference to the Kefauver crime committee report which had cast doubts on the claims of a causal link between comics and delinquency. At 225 Lafayette Street, artist Al Williamson recalled, Bill Gaines read about the recent hearings and briefly considered suing E. C. Gathings for infringing upon the company trademark with his initials.

Barry Gray, the host of a popular radio talk show in New York, picked up the issue of comic books in the last months of 1952 and went on to make comics a pet subject of his caustic topical monologues and feisty interviews. A transplant from radio stations around Southern California, Gray broadcast from a dining table on a platform in the back of Chandler's, a steak house on East Fifty-fourth Street, from midnight to 3:00 a.m. The idea was to deliver the talk of the town, live and on location, heavily filtered through Gray's vivid personality. Gray was an enormous man who wore a broad-brimmed fedora cocked over his eyes, or so he sounded on the radio. Theatergoers would stop in Chandler's after the opening of a play or a movie, and Gray would quiz them on the performance, invariably ending the discussion with a lecture on an essential aspect of a show he had not seen. His opinions were strong but unpredictable, ideal for stirring listeners to come back night after night. When Gathings started making noise about obscenity, pocket books, and comic books in early November 1952, Gray began arguing on the air for legislation to regulate the sale of comics.

Marv Levy, a former schoolmate of *Mad* artists Kurtzman, Elder, Jaffee, and Severin at New York's High School of Music and Art, was then doing commercial art and some comics, such as adaptations of Hans Christian Andersen tales for Ziff-Davis, one of the cleanest of comics publishers. Through a publicity agent who rented a desk in his studio, Levy arranged to go on the air with Gray to defend comic books and his friends in the field. However, on the night Levy appeared, November 8, 1952, Gray was out of town, and the actor and comedian Steve Allen filled in for him. "Where's Marv Levy?" Allen asked early in the broadcast (recorded by a transcription service that sold disposable floppy plastic records of radio programs by mail order). "Want to come up here, Marv, and draw a picture on my forehead?"

Allen prodded him: "I suppose the sales in comic books come primarily from the blood-and-guts kind of books. Do you work on that sort of book?"

"No," Levy replied in a voice flattened by nerves, "my work has been mainly in the humorous and decorative kind of books. Those are the books that don't hurt anybody and may even help out a little bit. [But] I have nothing against the blood-and-guts type.

"I personally don't think it will have too detrimental an effect on children to read comic books," Levy said. "In the nursery rhymes, you find rather macabre little tales of farmers' wives who cut off rodents' tails with butchers' knives and men who jump into bramble bushes and scratch their eyes out and people putting cats in wells. Women putting children in ovens like gingerbread men."

When Gray returned to his show, he invited Levy back, but gave him considerably less airtime. Gray opened the program, broadcast on December 12, 1952, with a plug for one of his sponsors, Michaels Brothers department store: "If you want to buy a steam shovel or pots and pans or a new stove or linoleum or any kind of toy or furnishings or drapes, Michaels Brothers." Levy, speaking more confidently this time, began the conversation by explaining the broad age range of comics readers. "In the last decade, since the Second World War, the rise in comic books has been very high," Levy said. "The books that you see on the newsstands that might appear somewhat lewd or a little too strong to take, which, in your estimation, might not fit in line with what you'd like children to read, those are produced for older readers but are distributed along regular newsstands."

"In other words," Gray responded, "you feel that if they'd gone through their proper channels, there would be nothing wrong with a GI reading this comic book, because he's old enough to understand that it's just a comic book. But you feel that the youngsters should not be allowed to read them."

"Well," Levy said, "the matter of allowance brings up the point of censorship."

"I'm sure you'll agree that we would hate to see the United States government censor comic books, because that would lead to other censorship," Gray added, and he was off and running. "I've been following this to-do down in Washington with a great deal of interest. I'm afraid that however authoritative the committee might feel, and however righteous they may feel in attempting to stop the kind of traffic that is currently going on in comic books, I'm afraid that censorship wouldn't stop just in comic books. It would transcend that field and go into other fields, and the first thing you'd know, we'd have censorship throughout our life.

"No one man should be told what he is allowed to see," Gray continued. "He should be able to decide for himself. Of course, I can't make an opinion for a twelve- or thirteen-year-old. I'd like to make a recommendation, though. We have a law in New York that forbids a tobacco salesman from selling to a twelve-year-old a package of cigarettes. And, as a result, most youngsters don't smoke. In other words, if they're old enough to make up their own minds, they're old enough to smoke.

"Now, along the same lines, why is it not possible for the candy store operator to refuse to sell a certain kind of comic book to a youngster under penalty of law? Certain books should be stamped for adults only, and if the youngster happens to get them, it's going to be an isolated case, just like cigarette smoking. But at least make an attempt. The storekeeper . . . must cooperate, because if you tack a $50 fine at the end of it, as they do with cigarette sales. But the moment you put it in the hands of the government, you're stepping on dangerous ground."

Gray's commentary, like much of the talk about comics at the time, expressed fears that transcended comics, in language that was righteous, impassioned, and confused. (After all, only the hands of government can apply the force of law.) Recalling the period years later, Marv Levy said, "I think he had a point—the crime and horror comics were going too far. I thought the whole thing [the controversy over comics] had passed, and it started getting worse."

A colleague of Levy's at Ziff-Davis, the artist Howard Post, appeared on Barry Gray's program not long after Levy. Post had been driving home from a late night's work, listening to the car radio, when he heard one of Gray's speeches on comics—a harsh one chastising comic-book artists, as Post recalled—and he backtracked to Chandler's and double-parked. (Recordings of this broadcast have not survived.) Post found a place to stand by the bar and hollered something like, "You don't know what you're talking about!" Gray, as attuned as any comics artist to the entertainment value of a brawl, waved Post to his table and put him on the air. Although this discussion is lost to the ether, Post would recall Gray as driven to incoherence by rising indignation. "He was desperate to blame comics for all the ills of youth," Post remembered. "He was doing a terrible injustice. He didn't make any sense. He thought of himself as a hero, like a superhero, the champion of the people. It was obvious that he had had enough of comic books, and he wanted something done about [them], but he really didn't know the right thing to do."

The call for comics legislation echoed in the statehouses of New York and Pennsylvania, where, in 1953, lawmakers returned to the issue of comics with bills to regulate the books on broadening grounds for their absorption not only with crime, but also with sex and horror.

206

On February 17, the unflagging Joseph F. Carlino submitted a set of new bills focused on comic books, including one aimed to prevent distributors from strong-arming news dealers to accept comics by the lot, rather than by the title (a practice then common, called "tie-in sales"); one to raise the fine for violation of an existing statute prohibiting the sale or display of "lewd, lascivious, filthy, indecent, or disgusting" literature from $50 to $250; and one that would grant local police chiefs and sheriffs the authority to seize from newsstands any comic or pocket book dealing with "lust, bloodshed, violence or crime . . . so massed as to incite" minors. The same bill would empower the same local officials, as well as mayors, to seek injunctions against anyone selling, distributing, or possessing books of the same sort. Governor Dewey declined to sign them, but with tempered dissent. Indeed, an AP story published throughout the state mistakenly reported that Dewey approved the legislation that March. (He would eventually approve all three bills, but not until they were resubmitted a year later.)

In Harrisburg, meanwhile, two bipartisan teams and one Republican legislator introduced three bills to regulate comics in Pennsylvania for reasons entwining morality and law. A broad measure, designed to cut off crime, horror, and the saucier romance comics at their supply, would make it illegal to sell, publish, or print a comic depicting "fictional deeds of crime, bloodshed, lust, or immorality, which tend to incite minors to violent or depraved or immoral acts." Violation would call for penalties of up to $1,000 or one year in jail, or both. A second act, fixed on crime comics, prohibited adults from giving, selling, or "in any way" furnishing to anyone under age fifteen a comic book that portrayed any crime on a detailed list (including arson, "assault with caustic chemicals, robbery, mayhem, and rape"). A third bill outlawed "obscene comic books" specifically. In calling for a resolution to study the feasibility of the measures, a Democratic representative, J. P. Moran, assailed horror comics as "lurid, gruesome, fear-inspiring and morbid, to say the least," and he urged the assembly, "This is really serious in Pennsylvania, and we should do something about it." When Moran began describing the content of some horror comic books he had seen, another representative interrupted him after twenty minutes. "The gentleman has a right to talk us to death," said Albert S. Readinger, a fellow Democrat, "but I doubt if he has a right to scare us to death."

11. Panic

Comics were getting worse at the worst possible time. In the same weeks that legislators such as Carlino, Moran, and others were making speeches on their statehouse floors, urging action to protect young people from the insidious effects of comics—and, in turn, to safeguard parents from their own children—Joseph McCarthy was railing in Congress against the Communist subversion he imagined in the heart of the United States government. When McCarthy called the first witnesses in the hearings of his Committee on Government Operations, in January 1953, some people working in comic books began to feel that the Gathings hearings a few weeks earlier, the rising pitch of public commentary on comics, and McCarthy's paranoia were of a piece. "The witch-hunt psychology was starting to spread, and comics were right there in it," recalled Howard Post, whose dedication to freedom of expression and civil liberties outweighed his antipathy for Communism. "McCarthy had the nugget of a good thing, and so did a lot of people criticizing comics, including Wertham—the guys over there [in the Soviet Union] were butchers, and there were comics that were going crazy. There was some nasty stuff out there. But McCarthy was a maniac, and he did nothing but harm, and

Wertham was no better. He condemned all of comics in a blanket way, and we all started to feel it. I remember really starting to feel the heat just around the same time as McCarthy. It started to be, if you said you were a comic-book artist, people would look at you funny and move away, [as if] you said you were a Communist."

The controversy over comic books was neither a subset of the Red Scare nor a direct parallel to it, however. McCarthyism, a movement out of the heartland to purge the country of modes of thinking associated with the Northeastern intelligentsia and the New Deal, was a form of anti-elitism as well as anti-Communism. The sentiment against comics was the near opposite, despite the urban New York origin of its target; it was a kind of anti-anti-elitism, a campaign by protectors of rarefied ideals of literacy, sophistication, and virtue to rein in the practitioners of a wild, homegrown form of vernacular American expression. Artists such as Marv Levy and Howard Post, who drew unassailable kiddie cartoons for Ziff-Davis, were not the main quarry of most comic-book critics; nor was Janice Valleau Winkleman, who went from Archie to do Toni Gayle, the fashion model/detective; nor Al Jaffee, who did the goofy Inferior Man and teenage funnies; nor Jay Scott Pike, who wrote tepid romance comics; nor Ken Bald, who illustrated Pike's stories; nor Nick Cardy or David Gantz or Don Perlin . . . Yet all of them, and a great many others among the hundreds of artists and writers working in comics in 1953, began to sense a growing distance between their studios and the outside world, partly because the work on their tables was done in drawings and word balloons, partly because their whole field was tainted by the reckless extremism of horror comics, and partly because of the mounting resistance to all forms of heterodoxy in the sociopolitical climate.

"It was a bad time to be weird," said the artist Al Williamson. "You were either a Communist or a juvenile delinquent." Williamson, who spoke with a hint of Spanish inflection left from his childhood in Bogotá and who dressed almost exclusively in blue jeans and T-shirts, felt particularly susceptible to both charges. Once, while working on a memorable EC story, a time-travel parable with allusions to Genesis ("A New Beginning," published in the November–December 1953 issue of *Weird Science*), Williamson decided to redesign a critical element in the art, an elaborate piece of machinery, after he had finished most of the drawing. He wanted to stick a patch onto the illustration board but had run out of rubber cement. When he went to a Midtown Manhattan stationery store, the salesman looked him over, slowly, and refused to sell him glue and be party to some illicit delinquent snorting rite.

In 1953, public anxiety over juvenile delinquency was deepening, though not as a result of any significant new statistical data. Early in the year, movie houses around the country ran a trailer for a new film. It opened with a shot of a motorcycle gang racing down a highway, filling both lanes, heading straight toward the audience. As the bikers loomed closer, superimposed titles announced:

Columbia Pictures presents . . .
a challenging, outspoken drama in the bold STANLEY KRAMER tradition . . .
the story of a gang of hot-riding hot-heads who ride into, terrorize, and take
    over a town . . .

The trailer cut to a close-up of the lead rider: Marlon Brando, sleekly impassive in dark shades and black leather.

. . . led by that "Streetcar" man
MARLON BRANDO
as
THE WILD ONE

Snippets from a few of the movie's scenes reeled past: A young woman in a tight sweater threw herself at Brando, purring "Remember the night . . ." Brando handed her his empty beer bottle and turned away. Brando rode his cycle alone down a road, then stopped alongside a woman, and she slapped him. Brando walked up to a fellow sitting on a motorcycle and pushed him off. A gang fight raged. An old man pleaded, "You'd better send somebody for the militia." Superimposed titles quoted dialogue from the film and closed the trailer with a taunt:

"After a while you got to have fun . . .
"And if someone gets hurt . . .
"That's just tough!"
You'll thrill to the shock-studded adventures of this hot-blood and his
jazzed-up hoodlums

Stanley Kramer, who made a specialty of packaging sensationalism as social realism, understood the sex appeal of bad behavior, particularly to young people. By romanticizing the thrill-seeking and nihilism of gang life, Kramer and his director, Laszlo Benedek, gave juvenile delinquency an unruly glamour; they made it something not just timely but modish; and by casting Marlon Brando, the hotshot exemplar of brutish American sangfroid, Kramer and Benedek gave delinquents-to-be a Hollywood hero (or antihero) to emulate. For members of the generation old enough to remember how Clark Gable had removed his shirt to reveal his bare chest in *It Happened One Night* and nearly destroyed the undershirt industry, the image of Gable's successor terrorizing towns for kicks cut deep. *The Wild One* evoked a hoodlumism acutely threatening to the prevailing culture: one that was jazzed-up—that is, blacked up, literally in leather from cap to boots, and figuratively in the gangs' alienation from mainstream (white) society and frustration with it. Roaring along, two lanes at a time, Brando and his pack commandeered the very symbol of postwar prosperity and suburban expansion, the highways—the prewar generation's conduit of escape from the cities and their messy complexities of race and class.

Panic

In the spring of 1953, juvenile crime showed no signs of worsening; to the contrary, on April 16, a headline in *The New York Times* announced "Youth Delinquency Down," citing new figures marking a decline in crimes by minors in New York State. Eleven days later, the United States Senate approved a resolution to launch an investigation into the causes and the effects of juvenile delinquency. The cosponsors of the initiative were Senators Estes Kefauver of Tennessee and Robert C. Hendrickson, a first-term Republican from New Jersey. In statements issued shortly before the resolution was passed, Kefauver and Hendrickson called delinquency the "fifth horseman of doom." Hendrickson, claiming that juvenile crime was "at its highest peak since World War II" (without citing statistics or their sources), emphasized that "the crimes being committed by the young of our Nation are harder, fiercer, more shocking than ever before in our Nation's history." Kefauver, neatly tying in the Soviet problem, urged, "If we are preparing our armed strength for the long pull of the cold war, it becomes imperative that we find the right answers for appropriate local and Federal action." In August, a subcommittee of the Committee of the Judiciary was organized to conduct hearings investigating delinquency. Hendrickson was named the chairman, joined by Kefauver and two other senators: Thomas C. Hennings, a Democrat from Missouri, and William Langer, a Republican from North Dakota.

No one needed statistics to prove the susceptibility of American youth to subversion in 1953. That summer, the Korean War ended with the governments of the North and the South consenting to a cease-fire, and when American prisoners were released from North Korean camps operated with the help of Communist China, the GIs behaved strangely: They spoke in flat tones, followed orders literally, and showed no emotion, not even when they met their loved ones from home. Word spread that the Communists, employing a mysterious formula of drugs, torture, and psychiatric science, had "washed" the Americans' brains. A public grappling with fears that its youth could be contaminated by unwanted influences saw the evidence in

213

the news, and the popular lexicon gained a word for the workings of every threat from Communism to television to comic books.

"It was getting a little scary—there were some really nasty comics then, and they were giving us all a bad name," said Janice Valleau Winkleman, whose father hatched a plan to liberate her from comics, late in 1953. From time to time, when her husband, Ed, was away on business, her father would drive her from her house in suburban New Jersey to Manhattan so she could deliver her artwork to Busy Arnold. One morning, he drove her to Wall Street, held her by the arm, and brought her to a finance company, where he had set up a job interview without her knowledge. She was furious, and not only because she was wearing slacks, flats, and no make-up. "He practically kidnapped me," Winkleman said. "He said, 'No daughter of mine has to do that such and such—that crap.'

"I said, 'But I like it. What's wrong with it?' He never saw a thing I ever did. He just heard something about how terrible . . . comics [were]. He thought he was saving my life." Winkleman went through with the interview, with her father standing behind her. She was offered the job and said, as she recalled, "Thank you very much. It sounds great. I'm sure my father would be happy to take the job." Declining a ride uptown to Arnold's office at Quality Comics, Winkleman walked to the subway with her artwork in hand and picked up a couple of magazines to occupy her during the ride. As she flipped through one, she realized why her father decided suddenly to enact his intervention. The November 1953 issue of *Ladies' Home Journal*, a magazine her mother read devoutly, had an article titled "What Parents Don't Know About Comic Books," an excerpt from an upcoming book by Dr. Fredric Wertham.

■ ■ ■

Rabbits leave their young on their own, expecting the creatures to sustain themselves or die, about thirty days after birth, and so did comic-book

Top left: Cartoon noir: Will Eisner's Spirit (right, facing Police Commissioner Dolan).

Above left: The "Laughing Sadist": *Crime Does Not Pay*'s Herman Duker at work.

Above right: It Rhymes with Lust: the first "picture novel," with art by Matt Baker.

Below: Banned in Boston: the last panel of Will Elder's interpretation of "A Visit from St. Nicholas," from the first issue of *Panic*, EC's imitation of its own *Mad*.

Above left: Future comic-art pranksters Al Jaffee and Billy Eisenberg (Elder) as prodigies at New York's High School of Music and Art.

Above right: Will Eisner—as he liked to be thought of, a writer in a graphic medium—composes a *Spirit* story in his studio office.

Below: EC writer-publisher Bill Gaines reviews the story of the day, prepared by his partner, writer-artist-editor Al Feldstein.

Top: Sterling North, defender of wholesome children's literature, at the typewriter on which he wrote his own.

Above: Fredric Wertham, psychiatrist and crusader, as he posed for the author photo for *Seduction of the Innocent.*

Right: A cartoon stand-in for Bishop John Francis Noll, founder of the National Organization for Decent Literature, sweeps the newsstands clean.

A boy of the early fifties keeps his fascination with comic-book fright under covers.

Comics on fire at St. Patrick's Academy in Binghamton, New York, 1949.

Stores Tagged by Reading Group

Above left: Kids swap "bad" books for "good" at the Stark County Fair in Canton, Ohio.

Above right: In downtown Canton, a member of a mayoral committee clamps down on Konkel's Drugstore.

Below: Confidential File: In staged documentary-style footage, comic-book reading leads a group of boys to torture a child in the woods.

Above and right: Two sets of Senate hearings: at one, only hands; at the other, just a head.

Wertham testifies at the Senate subcommittee hearings on comic books and juvenile delinquency in the Federal Courthouse in Manhattan.

Above: The Comics Code Authority enacts a makeover under former New York City magistrate Charles F. Murphy.

Below: Gaines, ripping up one of his comics for the camera, announces the end of EC's New Trend line.

This was fifties life: Costello, Kefauver, and a hundred more in a full-page drawing by Will Elder from the first issue of *Mad* in magazine format.

publishers. Their version of test marketing was to create a new product and drop it onto the newsstands to compete with hundreds of
other titles, old and new. If the book made money—that is, by the
standard model, if it sold at least 60 percent of its print order—the
publisher would produce another issue and continue doing so as long
as the title remained profitable. *Mad* was an exception, as it was in
many ways, sustained by its makers' enthusiasms through losses for at
least three issues, perhaps four. "The first three issues weren't too
good," Gaines later told an interviewer. "We were feeling our way
along. We lost several thousand dollars. We fell pretty short of a
break-even point on our first sales. But in our fourth issue . . . sales
picked up tremendously." (The print run for the first three issues of
Mad was 350,000 copies.) In the article he wrote for *Writer's Digest*,
Gaines explained, colorfully, "*Mad* #1 lost money. My editor, Harvey
Kurtzman, looked at me mournfully. I looked at him mournfully. *Mad*
#2 lost money. *Mad* #3 lost money. *Mad* #4 lost money. Kurtzman and
I were not looking at each other at all when the sales reports began to
come in on *Mad* #5. With a bang, we had done it." Whether the turn-
around came with the fourth issue, which included a scalding parody
of Superman, or the fifth, which had a deliriously gruesome and sexy
cover illustration by Will Elder, instead of one by the magazine's
founding editor, Harvey Kurtzman, *Mad* had found its voice and its
public.

   Branching out from lampoons of EC's own comics, *Mad* became a
forum to mock all of American culture; still a comic book and still
meant for young readers, it took aim at adult society with the
weaponry of the schoolyard: funny faces, cat-calls, relentless silliness,
rudeness, and cruelty. As Kurtzman remembered, "We began . . . by
doing parodies of every comic book in sight. And when we ran out of
comics, we started to do parodies of everything else." In the fourth
and fifth issues, *Mad* was satirizing the movies ("Robin Hood!"), radio
("Outer Sanctum!"), and dating habits ("Flob Was a Slob!"), as well as
comics ("Superduperman!") and the reignited crusade against them. A

legitimate-looking house ad on the inside cover of the fifth issue paid seeming tribute to its publisher with a black-and-white portrait (by Feldstein) of Gaines, beaming and crowned by a halo, above a dense block of biographical text. It read, in part:

> [Gaines] began selling "cartoon books" [you know the kind!] on dark street corners outside burlesque houses. When he had read them all, he turned to peddling dope near nursery schools . . . took the cure . . . opened an establishment in a district of scarlet illumination . . . took the cure . . . and finally, seeking the ultimate in depravity and debasement, quite naturally turned to the comic magazine industry . . . Bill introduced to the American public the notorious E.C. line . . . E.C. standing for Evil Comics. His editorial policy is a reflection of his highly developed sense of immoral obligation . . . "All I care is get inta every story *sadism, snakes, masochism, pyromania, snakes, fetishes, snakes, necrophilia, phallic symbols, snakes,* and all the rest of that *esoterica* what I can't think of this minute."

Mad's visual style coalesced at the same time, largely through the influence of Kurtzman's high-school friend Will Elder. (Wolf William Eisenberg, born in 1921, began his career working as Will Elder, signed his first name Bill on and off for a while, then settled on Will for the long term.) He could render anything he could see with the precision of a photograph—or mimic virtually any fine-art style, including various modes of impressionism and early abstract art—yet he had no inclination to waste his time on anything other than his overriding interest, pranksterism. The sound of his name, to those who knew him well, such as his former schoolmates and fellow cartoonists Al Jaffee (who met Elder in eighth grade, when they were both being tested for admission to the High School of Music and Art), John Severin, and David Gantz, was a cue for a grin and a round of "Crazy Willy" stories: the time, when he was a kid in the Bronx, when Elder took discarded pieces of beef carcasses from a meat-processing plant, arranged them in old clothes on the railroad tracks, and started screaming that his friend Moishe had been killed; or the time, when he was in high school, that he smeared chalk dust on his face and pretended to be hanging dead in the coat closet; or, when he went to lunch with some friends from EC and tried to pay the cashier with leaves of lettuce that he had in his wallet. His humor was almost aggressively madcap, startling, often dark, and silly.

Kurtzman set his old friend loose at *Mad*, and Elder overran the pages with bits of lunatic business—unscripted little stories within stories, visual non sequiturs, kooky details. In the opening panel of Elder's one contribution to the premiere issue of *Mad* ("Ganefs!"), Elder added no fewer than three dozen sight gags not in the script. (The number increases each time one counts.) The table between the boss thief and his henchman has fifteen or so items on it, including an empty malt-shop mug with two straws, as if the hoods had just shared a milkshake. A bottle on the table is half filled with blood, and it, too, has a pair of straws in it. Elder called the element he brought to *Mad* "chicken fat," so named, he said, for "the part of the soup that is bad for you, yet gives the soup its delicious flavor," and Gaines contended that Elder, more than any other artist, writer, or editor, defined *Mad*'s approach to humor: "pure mayhem." Idiosyncratic, indulgent, digressive, and uneven but uniquely potent in its accretive effect, Elder's work was wholly American art, a rough counterpart to the majestic, overstuffed improvisations of Walt Whitman or Charlie Parker, transferred to the literature of the playground.

"Will was the one who gave *Mad* magazine its look and style, which were different from [those of] any comic book that had been created before," Kurtzman wrote in his memoirs. "He was the one who started filling the margins of every page with hundreds of tiny cartoons. They had nothing to do with the story on the page. They were just crazy little cartoons that ran around the larger cartoons. And they gave each page something extra for the readers. It was crazy, and it took a lot of work, but Will enjoyed doing it."

As Elder himself recalled, "Harvey let me go. Harvey said, 'I'm going to leave you alone,' because we were old friends, a couple of crazy poor kids from the same school and the same streets, and we understood each other. 'All those nutty things you do, now you can do them on paper,' and I went ahead, and I threw everything I had in there. I just did a lot of crazy things, everything I could think of off the top of my head, and the kids liked it."

Within a year of its first issue, *Mad* had spawned no fewer than six imitations from other publishers: *Madhouse*, *Bughouse*, *Crazy*, *Eh!*, *Nuts!*, *Unsane*, and *Whack*. Al Feldstein, less than sanguine about the success of a magazine that had begun as a parody of his work, brought a proposition to Gaines bold even by Feldstein's standards. "I took Bill out to lunch and, actually, rather, I asked him to take me out—he paid," Feldstein remembered, "and I said, 'You know how everybody's imitating *Mad*? Well, why don't we put out our own imitation of *Mad*? The market will bear it, obviously.'" Feldstein argued that the publication would not increase EC's expenses, since Gaines had already decided to consolidate two of the titles Feldstein had been editing, *Weird Science* and *Weird Fantasy*, into one, *Weird Science-Fantasy*. Failure to publish the new book, however, would have represented a cut in pay for Feldstein. Gaines consented, as usual with Feldstein, and assigned him the editorship of a new comic called *Panic*. It was no more than an impersonation of *Mad*, from its slogan, "Humor in a Varicose Vein" (*Mad*'s was "Humor in a Jugular Vein"), to the editor's new semi-rebus signature, "A. Feld," followed by a drawing of a beer stein (Kurtzman signed his name "H. Kurtz," plus a stick-figure of a man). Both titles used several of the same artists, including Elder, Wally Wood, and Jack Davis; the main difference between the books was the story content, since *Panic* was written solely by Feldstein, who was not funny. "I used to say, '*Panic* is not anything like *Mad*—it's much funnier.'" That was Feldstein's idea of a joke.

To disguise its second-class status, Gaines and Feldstein claimed, in the comic's first issue, that *Panic* had preceded *Mad* in concept. "*Mad* is an imitation of *Panic!*" exclaimed a note on the letters page. "Yes, *Panic* was created many months before the first issue of *Mad* ever appeared. It was all ready to go. It was locked in the 'New Book' file, safe from the prying eyes of our competitors . . . Why then, you ask, did we wait? We'll tell you why! Frankly, we didn't think it would sell!" The story, neither believable nor humorous, left open the question of why Gaines and Feldstein thought *Mad* would sell better than *Panic*. The implicit answer was their faith in Kurtzman. He, of course, was furious to see his own publisher undermining *Mad*'s uniqueness. Feldstein "plundered all my techniques and artists," Kurtzman said. "For me, there was a real conflict of interest."

When *Panic* first appeared on the newsstands, in December 1953, EC receptionist Shirley Norris finally saw the police cross Lafayette Street into Little Italy.

The premiere issue, published under M. C. Gaines's old *Tiny Tot* imprint, as an inside gag, was cover-dated March 1954 and distributed shortly before Christmas 1953, in an effort to capitalize on the holiday market of school kids with time and pocket change to spare. The cover, by Feldstein, showed a nasty-looking boy peering from the side of a festively decorated fireplace, from which Santa's left leg was about to drop into a glistening bear trap. The inside pages had a *Mad*-style mix of parodies: "My Gun Is the Jury," a lampoon of Mickey Spillane pulp (with art by Davis); "This Is Your Strife," a television spoof (with art by Joe Orlando); "Little Red Riding Hood," an odd, gloomy story (with art by Kamen) that looked like an outtake from a horror comic recycled with new captions; and one piece of inspiration: "The Night Before Christmas," which presented the text to the Clement Clarke Moore poem, unchanged but accompanied, over eight pages, by thirty-two panels of outlandishly incongruous, hyperkinetic illustrations by Will Elder. (Shortly before the issue was prepared, Kurtzman had set Elder loose on Poe's "The Raven" for an upcoming issue of *Mad*, and Feldstein liked what he saw.) The piece opened with images of various creatures—a mouse, some pigs, a donkey, a lion, and an elephant, among them—not stirring because they were dead, dangling from hooks in a meat cooler. One animal was living: a "stewed lamb" cradling a bottle of moonshine between its paws. There were boxes of (presumably literal) "lady fingers" and, below one pig carcass, a sign reading, "Fresh ground meat . . . was in the ground this morning." From juvenile gore, the illustrations whizzed along to juvenile lust (children nestle with visions of the "sugarplums" Marilyn Monroe and Jane Russell), lawlessness (Santa's toy sack carried treats such as a Junior Counterfeit Printing Press and a Poison Dart Game), irreverence (Santa's sleigh, a red Cadillac convertible on skis, had a "Just Divorced" sign on the trunk and, dangling from the rear fender, a meat cleaver and a couple of knives), and self-deprecation (when Santa turned "with a jerk," he had an arm around a cartoon Will Elder).

"I had a good time thinking of every kind of wild way to interpret all the words of the poem," recalled Elder. "I thought [the art] was funny, but it happened that some other people didn't agree. That was the beginning of the whole hullabaloo for EC. It didn't take very much. There were people out there who really didn't like the idea that we were doing something for kids . . . [that] made fun of things that were supposed to be sacred, like Santa Claus. We never saw it coming."

On December 18, a few days after *Panic* hit the newsstands, the Governor's Council of Massachusetts called for a ban of the comic within the state on the grounds that it "desecrated Christmas" and depicted the holiday in a "pagan" manner. A councilor, Patrick J. "Sonny" McDonough, specified the portrayal of Santa Claus as recently divorced, as well as the images of cutlery adorning his vehicle, as evidence of the book's transgressions. (He need not have reached so, since every story about Santa Claus is pagan.) Under orders of the council, the state attorney general, George Fingold, and the head of the State Police, Captain Joseph Crescio, acted to cut off distribution of *Panic* throughout Massachusetts, and by December 21, the book had been pulled from newsstands in the Greater Boston area. Fingold warned distributors who resisted compliance that they would be susceptible to criminal prosecution. The possible charges were unclear.

Gaines retaliated by withdrawing *Panic* from the state of Massachusetts, an apparent capitulation which he saw as punitive to distributors and news dealers who had submitted to an overstepping interdiction. "The idea was, 'If you don't want us, we don't want you,'" explained Feldstein, who said he had felt a "certain literary pride" in having a book of his banned, offset by a fear that Gaines would somehow justify shutting down *Panic* altogether on principle. For the moment, Gaines announced that EC would no longer offer *Panic*, nor its line of *Picture Stories from the Bible* comics, in Massachusetts. As *The Boston Daily Globe* reported, "State Bans 'Night Before'; Publisher Yanks Bible Tales." Gaines never mentioned, and the newspaper did not realize, that M. C. Gaines's Bible comics had been out of print for more than five years.

On Monday, December 28, *The New York Times* published a report on the ban of *Panic* in Massachusetts. Before lunchtime the following day, two policemen entered the EC offices and asked the receptionist, Shirley Norris, if they could buy a copy of *Panic*. "After it hit the newspapers, there was a public outcry, and somebody must have told the police chief 'Something has to be done about this,'" recalled Lyle Stuart, EC's business manager at the time. A former juvenile delinquent from Gaines's boyhood neighborhood, presumably reformed, Stuart had recently assumed EC's financial stewardship from M. C. Gaines's very old friend Frank Lee, who had left the company in protest over the tenor of its horror comics. Stuart, who had been well educated in the street, smelled a set-up. While Norris handed the police the comic book, Stuart slipped into Gaines's office, locked him in there, and strolled up to the officers.

"They wanted to know who the president of the company was—they were about to make an arrest," Stuart remembered. "Bill was very frightened, very nervous—I mean, he was *scared*, and I was concerned. I said to the cops, 'You can't take him. It'll kill him if you take that man.' I said, 'I'm the business manager. How about you take me?'

And they called the precinct headquarters in Little Italy, where they had arrested some of the big gangsters, and they told the sergeant, 'We have the business manager,' and he told them, 'Yeah, bring him— he's okay.' So we drove down to the police station, and then when we got there, they suddenly realized I wasn't the one who had sold them the magazine. Shirley, the receptionist, had sold it to them."

One of the arresting officers kept Stuart under custody while the other one returned to 225 Lafayette Street to retrieve Norris. When she entered the station, she was smiling. "The cop came back to the office, and he said, 'Excuse me, miss, we had to go down to see your boss,'" recalled Shirley Norris. "I thought I was going down to pick up Lyle or—I didn't know what to think—maybe he needed me to help him with something. Lyle always needed me for something." She and the officer walked the eight blocks to the Fifth Precinct station on Elizabeth Street, chatting and joking. "I thought it was funny—the police had Lyle—until I was in the room down there," said Norris.

"Do you know why you're here, Shirley?" said Stuart, who was resting on a bench, half reclining, stone-faced, and Norris quickly sobered. One of the policemen asked her if she had sold him a copy of *Panic*. Norris turned to Stuart for a cue, and he gave her none. "Well, yes . . . ," she answered.

"You're under arrest, ma'am," said the officer, as Norris began to cry. A few minutes later, when she had calmed, Stuart left the station, and the police processed Norris's arrest for violation of a New York statute prohibiting the sale of indecent literature. The charge carried a penalty of up to a year in prison, if Norris was convicted.

When the case was arraigned, early in January 1954, Gaines's attorney, Martin Sheiman, represented Norris, and Stuart accompanied them. (Gaines, still unnerved, stayed in his office.) The judge asked to see evidence of the offense in question, and the prosecuting attorney handed him a copy of *Panic*, pointing out a drawing in the story "My Gun Is the Jury." It showed a curvy blond gangster's moll sitting cross-legged in the front seat of a car. She was wearing a blue cocktail dress, and a sliver of the lace trim of her slip poked out below the hem, which fell an inch or two above the knee. The prosecutor called the image "disgusting." (He never brought up the fact that, later in the story, when the moll was murdered by a pistol blast in the stomach, her blouse flew open to reveal that she was really a hairy-chested man in drag.) The judge asked the prosecutor if he had seen the lingerie ads in the subways, and he called for the next case on the docket.

"I couldn't believe this was happening to me—I thought, I could go to jail," said Norris. "The cops—on the cop side, those men were serious. They were really serious. It was a very strange situation, and I was scared about it."

As Al Feldstein recalled the incident, "That was the thing that made us realize that things were getting really sticky in this great, free country of ours."

Some who followed Lyle Stuart's adventures wondered if the to-do over *Panic*, from the ban in Massachusetts to Shirley Norris's arrest, might have been a plot by Walter Winchell to punish Stuart for a damaging exposé of Winchell that Stuart had published several years earlier. Stuart never himself considered Winchell culpable in the *Panic* mess. "Winchell didn't have that kind of pull, even in his heyday, and he had very little influence at that stage," said Stuart. "Walter Winchell could not make the Attorney General of the state of Massachusetts ignore the law of the land, and Walter Winchell could not make a police chief in Little Italy order unwarranted arrests. But I can tell you who could." Through their passion for the brash unorthodoxy that *Panic* and its model, *Mad*, represented, one group had the power to drive the forces of postwar authority to petty, desperate action, as Stuart (among others) saw it in the early fifties: "their kids."

The way *Panic* treated Christmas was still in the news on Valentine's Day. For the Sunday edition of *The Hartford Courant* published on February 14, 1954, the editor decided to lower the title of the paper on the front page and publish a story above the logotype, a step unprecedented in the *Courant*'s 190-year history. A banner headline read,

"Depravity for Children—10 Cents a Copy!" and a photograph showed an array of recent comic books: EC's *Tales from the Crypt* and *The Vault of Horror*; Stanley P. Morse's *Weird Mysteries*; a few other horror titles; Fox's *My Secret Marriage*; *Mad* and one of its imitators, *Crazy*; and, in the center of them all, *Panic*. The story was the first in a four-part series of reports on the comic-book controversy that the *Courant* initiated shortly after its editorial-page columnist, Thomas E. Murphy, discovered horror comics and lacerated them in a piece titled "Design for Murder." Murphy, who later adapted several of his columns on the subject for the *Reader's Digest*, detailed his revulsion at the sight of some comics left at his house by a neighbor's child. "This morning I want to talk about murder and how the children of Connecticut are being served a poison diet," Murphy wrote in his *Courant* column. "Nobody's more in favor of freedom of the press than I am. But I don't think anybody has the right to poison the minds of my children. Indeed, when I came across these depraved, degenerate bits of scatology, I wished strongly that I had my hands on the human scum that conceived them and published them to make money." Murphy was especially repelled by a few stories in books published by Morse, including "I Killed Mary," from *Weird Mysteries*, in which an effete country boy mustered the nerve to make advances to a girl reclining on a haystack, only to have her reject him as a "sissy." The boy, accordingly, killed her with an ax, chopped her into pieces, then hanged himself by the rafters of the barn.

The *Courant* promoted its investigation into comics as a "series of articles on the illustrated courses in murder, crime and sex on sale at 10 cents a copy under the guise of comic books for children." For the first entry, the series writer, Irving M. Kravsow, ventured to the newsstands in a section of Hartford "where juvenile delinquents traveling singly and in gangs have troubled the area in recent years." The comics he found, both on display and hidden under the counter, available by request, were rife with "murder, mayhem, robbery, rape, cannibalism, carnage, sex, sadism, and worse," Kravsow wrote. What,

224

exactly, could be worse than all that he left to his readers' alliterative imagination. Kravsow relayed his shock at the contents not only of the horror comics he discovered (one issue of which had depictions of twenty violent deaths, by the writer's count), but also of the romance and the humor books. In the comics devoted to the "love story in pictures," Kravsow was outraged to find rebellious, carnal young women in stories that "all have the same theme of young girls defying their parents and running off with men." In the Christmas issue of *Panic*, still on sale then, Kravsow discovered Will Elder's art, which he described as "gross and obscene drawings that defy description"; and he found special offense in the presence of such images in a product from a company that called itself Tiny Tot Comics.

From the back streets of Hartford, Kravsow traveled to Manhattan to meet the people he held responsible for the comics he had encountered—that is, two publishers, Morse and Gaines, as well as the spokesman for the Association of Comics Magazine Publishers, Henry E. Schultz. Armed with his copies of the comic books shown on the front page of the *Courant*, Kravsow found all three men, different as they were, equally defensive. "No decent person would ever try to defend these books," Schultz said, "but they are only a part of the whole industry. There are enough good comics around to replace this filth." The best Schultz could do, as the reporter quoted him, was to note that comics publishers were generating indecent, filthy, indefensible work and good comics in equal measure.

Kravsow opened a copy of *Weird Mysteries* to the story "I Killed Mary" and handed it to Morse. "I don't see anything wrong with this story," said Morse, as Kravsow quoted him in the *Courant*. "This story has a moral. It shows that crime doesn't pay."

Kravsow pressed, "Is that the moral in the story?"

"Well," Morse replied, "the boy kills the girl to gain recognition for a daring deed and nobody believes him. The crime was in vain. It didn't pay." (Morse, asked about this conversation years later, said, "The guy was a troublemaker, and I was trying to get rid of him.")

Gaines dipped behind his father's *Picture Stories from the Bible* for cover. "You see, the profits from books some people have termed objectionable allow us to produce educational comics," he told Kravsow. Gaines claimed, not quite inaccurately, that EC was still selling the Bible comics at fifty to sixty-five cents apiece, which were the prices at which the company made available what was left of the old stock, by special order. Presented with a copy of *Panic*, Gaines flipped through the pages and rose to defend his efforts at EC—cogently, at first. "This issue has been banned in Boston," he said. "I don't see why. There's nothing wrong with it. It's a satire on various aspects of modern life, such as radio and television programs, books, and life in general.

"We try to entertain and educate," said Gaines, starting to backslide. "That's all there is to it. A lot of people have the idea we're a bunch of monsters who sit around drooling and dreaming up horror and filth. That's not true, as you can see. We have our story conferences here [in his EC office]. We discuss horror stories and ideas, but when the conference is over, so are the thoughts and discussion. We don't take our work home with us." At least, Gaines argued, he and the members of the EC staff were not *literally* the flesh-eating walking dead.

For the third part of the series, Kravsow brought his load of comics around to Hartford city leaders and offered them a forum to express their disgust with what they saw. In the series' fourth part and in an additional article by Kravsow published shortly after the series ran, the *Courant* reported on the city's response to the paper's self-proclaimed crusade against objectionable comics. Late in February 1954, one of the two major wholesalers in Hartford temporarily suspended the distribution of comic books of every kind, and it issued a statement of commitment to discontinue the sale of controversial titles from that point on. The East Hartford Board of Education, at the same time, urged the mayor, John W. Torpey, to advance legislation and, if necessary, police action to purge the city newsstands of crime, horror, and "sex" comics. In a letter to Torpey, the board wrote:

It is our sincere belief that these publications are one of the most insidious forces affecting our youth today. [The comics] tend to destroy all respect for authority, incite to [*sic*] all forms of delinquency and ridicule everything decent and good. They are a menace to the right thinking of our American youth and should be banned throughout the country.

It was further voted [by the board] to support every effort to bring about state and national legislation to rid the country of their vile and hateful influence.

Nowhere in the articles published on the ten-cent menace in *The Hartford Courant* was a single comics artist or writer quoted. "I thought that their work spoke for itself," Kravsow later explained. Nor did Kravsow interview any of the young people who had chosen to buy and read the comic books targeted by the paper. "That was because I thought it was a parental problem, not a kid problem," he explained. "I remember, when I was a kid, I read comic books all the time, and my parents didn't have the slightest idea of what comic books I was reading. I thought that parents should be paying more attention to what their kids were reading—this was up to the parents, not the kids."

The *Courant* reprinted the series as a pamphlet, in magazine format, under the same title, *Depravity for Children—10 Cents a Copy!*, and gave copies away upon request. Demand by schools and civic groups was such that the paper needed to have three printings. Some people mistook the title for a price listing and taped dimes onto their orders. As a result of the series, Kravsow got a job offer from a Connecticut magazine distributor who wanted him to serve as an in-house censor, screening objectionable comics. Kravsow declined. "I wanted to move on," he said, "and I was leery about censorship and things like that."

12. The Triumph of Dr. Payn

Around the winter holidays late in 1953, Will Eisner was at a cocktail party in Manhattan, chatting with a tweedy fellow about Saul Bellow's *Adventures of Augie March*, which had recently been published. The men's drinks were low, and a hostess came along to refill their glasses just as Eisner's new friend asked him what he did for a living. "I write comic books," Eisner said, and the other man responded, "How dreadful for you" and walked away before he got his drink.

"I had had it," Eisner said. "It was very dispiriting. You were held in disdain if somebody knew what you did.

"During all the years I was putting my heart and soul into the Spirit, I got very little attention," Eisner recalled. "I got very little fan mail. There was no such thing as intellectual criticism of comic books. Nobody was writing anything about them except to say how terrible they were, and I wasn't the only one trying to do something good—there was Harvey [Kurtzman], and a lot of the people at EC and some others were very creative and serious about what they were doing. But nobody cared outside of comics. I felt that nobody was paying attention, except the readers, and they were mostly kids, so nobody took them seriously."

The Triumph of Dr. Payn

The *Spirit* Sunday newspaper supplement, always more successful creatively than commercially, had begun to fail in both ways during the first years of the 1950s, a victim of the mood swings in the comics readership, cutbacks at newspapers facing rising paper costs, and Eisner's diminished enthusiasm for the venture. By the summer of 1952, Eisner had handed off much of the responsibility for the Spirit to Jules Feiffer and Wally Wood, working as Eisner's ghostwriter and artist, and they moved the Spirit stories from the city streets to the surface of the moon in a desperate, if cleverly scripted, attempt to capitalize on the atomic-era craze for science fiction. In October 1952, Eisner suspended production of the Spirit and shifted his attention to producing commercial art for industrial and military clients, remunerative work that promised ongoing financial security for his family, which now included two young children. By the end of the following year, Eisner had decided not to bother coming up with another new comic-book idea. He essentially stopped trying to fulfill his father's aspiration to make a name in art and took up his mother's ambition to run a nice storefront business.

The decision unsettled him—"I was torn for a while"—until, on a Saturday afternoon in the spring of 1954, he saw Fredric Wertham promoting his new book, a critique of comics, on television. "When Dr. Wertham came out with his book [and] he started plugging it on TV and in the papers, everywhere, I felt like I was hearing the voice of every comic-book hater I had ever met, and I knew that I could no longer function in that atmosphere. I was certain that I had made the right decision to get out, and I got out just in time, although I was equipped to survive, because I had a good head for business. I knew I was smart to get out when I did, because the walls were starting to fall down."

Fredric Wertham's book, *Seduction of the Innocent* (subtitled *The Influence of Comic Books on Today's Youth*), rumbled out on a convoy of publicity unusual in its time for a work of social science and psychiatry. Nearly six months before *Seduction of the Innocent* was published, teaser ads to promote the excerpt in *Ladies' Home Journal* peppered the "women's pages" of newspapers around the country. If you lived in Walla Walla, Washington, for instance, and if you were reading the city's morning daily, the *Union Bulletin*, on October 21, 1953, you would have found, among the ads for Kitchen Kraft prefluffed flour and nylon-trimmed ladies' slips, a comic-book drawing of a buxom, vaguely exotic woman lurching forward at you. She was wearing a low-cut, strapless ruffled dress, and the image was cropped below the bust in a way that made the ruffles look like the fingers of hands gripping her breasts. "What parents don't know about the comic books," announced the ad. "Read the shocking facts, based on a 7-year investigation. Dr. Fredric Wertham gives his findings in the November *Ladies' Home Journal*." The next day you would have seen, above and to the right of the ad for Western Thrift Drug Stores' letters from Santa, a drawing of an attractive blond woman in a low-cut gown dancing with a handsome man in a white evening jacket. Above this: "The truth about comic books!" Five days later, you would have found, above the ad displaying Bell Laboratories' experimental new product, the transistor ("Now used mostly for military purposes . . ."), a cartoon of a man about to use a hypodermic needle to pierce the eyeball of a girl. The headline: "What are comic books doing to your children?" Around this time, *Ladies' Home Journal* sent advance copies of its excerpt of Wertham's book to newspaper editors, prompting articles such as the one in a November 1953 issue of the *Los Angeles Times* titled "Sex and Sadism Rampant: It's Time Parents Awakened to Danger in Comic Books." The piece asked, "How many [parents] have stopped to read the kind [of comics] that Junior has in his back pocket? Are they full of sadism, torture and lust? Probably, from the ratio given by Dr. Wertham, they have a good chance of being the builders of violence and tough-talking gangsters."

Wertham was not the only author to put incendiary thoughts about comics between hard covers; he was the first to get a whole book out of them. In the five years prior to the publication of *Seduc-*

tion of the Innocent, three other writers had published books with chapters devoted to critical analyses of comics. Gershon Legman, a professional eccentric who, under a pseudonym, had previously written a cunnilingus handbook (*Oragenitalism: An Encyclopaedic Outline of Oral Technique in Genital Excitation*), spat purple venom upon comic books in his self-published *Love and Death*:

> Garishly presented in clashing colors, and cheaply printed in forty-eight pages of paper-bound pulp with even more garish covers, what recourse there is in comic-books to the printed word is, totally, language violence.

Gilbert Seldes, in *The Great Audience*, decided that comic books were a betrayal of the promise of George Herriman's *Krazy Kat*, the newspaper strip that Seldes had celebrated, twenty-six years earlier, in *The Seven Lively Arts*:

> Unlike the other mass media, comic books have almost no aesthetic interest . . . [Theirs] is an atmosphere of violence, of contempt for the processes of law; not only is the criminal central to action, but the hero is himself lawless.

Albert E. Kahn, a specialist in political sensationalism, focused, too, on comics violence, which he portrayed as a tool for breeding militants, in *The Game of Death: Effects of the Cold War on Our Children*:

> The influence of comic books has fitted the needs of the Cold War, since they have been accustoming millions upon millions of young Americans to concepts of violence, savagery, and sudden death.

Seduction of the Innocent brought these arguments to the coffee table. The book not only fed the campaign against comics, but dressed it up well. Its cover was stark—all type, with the title set in lean, pure-red capital letters on a white background, and with the subtitle and the author's name below, in white, inside a band of black, a design scheme evocative of early-twentieth-century constructivist art and Soviet propaganda posters. The back cover had a lengthy biography of Wertham, beginning with references to his research work at Johns Hopkins three decades earlier and a research fellowship he had been awarded in 1929. The author photo, by Gordon Parks, presented Wertham in a stylish, broad-lapelled pinstripe suit, with a white handkerchief popping just-so from his breast pocket. As he often was in photographs, Wertham was staring intently to one side, at something out of view; we cannot share in what he sees, but only in his palpable displeasure. "He was very serious and almost frightening in his intensity," recalled Parks, the *Life* photographer, who had met Wertham through Ralph Ellison and admired Wertham's work at the Lafargue Clinic in Harlem.

The book's title was a parallel to its nineteenth-century antecedent, Anthony Comstock's polemic on the hazards of half-dime novels and story papers, *Traps for the Young*, with a nod to the comic books' first prominent critic, Sterling North, whose prototypal critique, published in 1940, concluded by portraying comics publishers as engaged in the "cultural slaughter of the innocents." In its evocation of sexual conquest and youth (the latter referenced explicitly in the subtitle on the cover), the title of Wertham's book outdid Comstock by suggesting pedophilia, as if to say that comic books represented the intellectual rape of American children. The phrase also had the ring and punch of hard-boiled fiction (*Street of the Lost*, *Dagger of the Mind*), the adult counterpart to the comic books Wertham saw as destructive to young readers.

One type of book the title did not suggest was a scholarly work of scientific research, and *Seduction of the Innocent* was no such thing, despite the attempts by Wertham and his publisher to claim it was. If, to many readers, the book appeared to be a serious treatment of a popular subject, it was elementally a popular treatment of a serious subject. Apart from the issue of comics' value as art, their significance as a cultural phenomenon would never be more apparent than it was in 1954. Wertham chose to release his findings not in one of the peer-review publications in his field, such as *The American Journal of Psychiatry*, but, rather, in *Ladies' Home Journal*, where the text of his book fit companionably among articles such as "Revolution in Mothballs" and "Can This Marriage Be Saved?"

Seduction of the Innocent's opening words, an explanation of Wertham's methods presented as a "publisher's note" (likely drafted by and no doubt approved by the author), describe the book as "the result of seven years of scientific investigation conducted by" Wertham, who, the text reminds us, "has had long experience in technical research." After a paragraph of biography, the note picks up its discussion of the book: "Thoroughly documented by facts and cases, [it] gives the substance of Dr. Wertham's expert opinion on the effects that comic books have on the minds and behavior of children who come in contact with them." On the first page, the foundation of the book gave way. Which was it: a work of "scientific investigation" or "expert opinion"? One based upon "technical research" or "cases"?

Fredric Wertham was a physician, not a social scientist. As he described his working methods in the text of *Seduction of the Innocent*:

> If I find a child with a fever I do not ask him, "What is the cause of your fever? Do you have measles?" I examine him and make my own diagnosis. It is our clinical judgment, in all kinds of behavior disorders and personality difficulties of children, that comic books do play a part. Of course they are not in the textbooks. But once alerted to the possibility, we unexpectedly found, in case after case, that comic books were a contributing factor not to be neglected.

Wertham conducted no scientific investigation—that is, no study applying the scientific method; he employed no formal measures to test anything, and he had no control groups. His book provided no endnotes and no corroborative support for his conclusions, which were derived mainly through his psychiatric diagnoses of his patients (and his staff's diagnoses of their patients) at three treatment centers in New York City: the Lafargue Clinic, the Quaker Emergency Service Readjustment Center, and the Mental Hygiene Clinic at Bellevue Hospital. Wertham looked no further, drawing solely upon the cases that came before him and his colleagues, and he extrapolated from their evaluations of those cases the judgment that all comic books—not merely crime or horror or romance comics, but all—were harmful to the development of young minds.

Wertham used malleable terms, defining virtually all comic books—including romances, Westerns, science fiction, parodies, and jungle stories—as "crime comics," on the grounds that all of them, in his view, portrayed some violation of legal, moral, or religious codes. Wertham had other problems with the remaining genres of books, such as teen humor and talking-animal books—mainly that they were vulgar, ungrammatical, poorly drawn, and cheaply printed, stunting children's intellectual growth and bad for children's eyes, recapitulations of the turn-of-the-century criticism of newspaper funnies. Free on his terms to insert the word "crime" to characterize any comic that any of his patients read, Wertham was able to make persuasive-sounding correlations between the behavior of the troubled youths he treated and their reading habits, between juvenile crime and "crime comics." Wertham had served in various facilities open to young people with problems, and he found that most of the children he encountered, like virtually all kids at the time, read comic books—or "crime comics," by Wertham's use of the term. "Our researches have proved that there is a significant correlation between crime-comics reading and the more serious forms of juvenile delinquency," Wertham wrote. Moreover, Wertham decided,

> the role of comic books in delinquency is not the whole nor by any means the worst harm they do to children. It is just one part of it.

Many children who never become delinquent or conspicuously disturbed have been adversely affected by them.

In the essence of its thesis, *Seduction of the Innocent* had an antecedent in the work of the French magistrate, writer, and lecturer Louis Proal, who was respected at the turn of the twentieth century as an authority on criminal behavior. Proal, like Wertham, used the testimony of criminals on their reading habits to demonstrate parallels between the acts they committed and fictional events they had encountered in books—in their cases, in the novels of Dostoyevsky, George Sand, Flaubert, Zola, and other authors. Impressed by his own findings, Proal tested his approach on history, drawing on documentary evidence, and he concluded that works by Shakespeare and Goethe had inspired their readers to commit various crimes, including murder. Proal believed that all such literature should be banned.

Unlike many critics of crime, horror, and romance comics in the newspaper columns and state assemblies, Wertham considered superhero comics as dangerous as any others. In fact, he reserved a specially toxic venom for National/DC's popular trio of heroes, Superman, Batman, and Wonder Woman, whom Wertham saw, respectively, as exemplars of fascism, homoeroticism, and sadomasochism. It was only in the case of Wonder Woman that Wertham came close to the intentions of the character's creator (Wertham's rival in pop head-shrinking, the sexual provocateur William Moulton Marston), although one of the uncredited contributors to Batman, Jerry Robinson, said decades after the fact that there was a "tinge" of the homoerotic in the comics' portrayal of Batman and his boy sidekick, Robin. "What they did between the panels was their own business," Robinson joked.

"We established the basic ingredients of the most numerous and widely read comic books: violence; sadism and cruelty; the superman philosophy, an offshoot of Nietzsche's superman who said, 'When you go to women, don't forget the whip,'" Wertham wrote. Resuscitating the early-wartime interpretation of Superman as a symbol of Hitler's despotic fantasies of master-race supremacy, Wertham cracked, "With the big S on his uniform—we should, I suppose, be thankful that it is not an S.S."

One of Wertham's main objections to superheroes, and indeed to all comic books, was the cynicism toward authority elemental to the comics' nature as an outlet of expression for artists and writers who saw themselves as cultural outcasts and viewed their medium as undervalued or misunderstood. This sensibility lay at the heart of the comics' appeal to young people struggling to establish their generational identity, and Wertham abhorred it. "The contempt for law and police and the brutality of punishment in comic books is subconsciously translated by children into conflict with authority, and they develop a special indifference to it," Wertham wrote.

> The very children for whose unruly behavior I would want to prescribe psychotherapy in an anti-superman direction have been nourished (or rather poisoned) by the endless repetition of Superman stories. How can they respect the hard-working mother, father or teacher who is so pedestrian, trying to teach common rules of conduct, wanting you to keep your feet on the ground and unable even figuratively speaking to fly through the air? Psychologically Superman undermines the authority and the dignity of the ordinary man and woman in the minds of children.

Unceasing in its determination to relate the contents of comic books to the psyches of their readers, *Seduction of the Innocent* virtually ignored the relationship between comics and their creators. Wertham was unwilling or unable to see comics as works of creative expression, products of the minds and the hearts of their writers and artists. This would have been odd enough in a book by any psychiatrist; it was unaccountable from Wertham, who, a decade earlier, had been one of the first psychiatrists to attempt to dust a work of literature for its author's psychological fingerprints. In 1944, Wertham analyzed Richard Wright, seeking to find the inspirations for the events, the characters, and the themes in his novel *Native Son*, and Wertham presented his findings to the American Psychological Association in a paper titled "How Bigger Was Born" (for the novel's protagonist, Bigger Thomas). Through his analysis of Wright for this inquiry, Wertham elicited a memory from the author that, according to Wertham, explained Wright's unconscious reasons for choosing Dalton as the name for the white family by whom Thomas was employed; early in his adult life, Wright had briefly worked at a research institute studying color-blindness, a condition then sometimes called "Daltonism." As a report on Wertham's paper in *The New York Times* paraphrased its conclusions, "The dream runs through the whole creative process." In comic books, however, Wertham saw not a ripple of dreams—indeed, no creativity, but only the artless factory output of avaricious publishers.

> The writers of comic books rarely want to be professional crime comic book writers . . . They want to get their ten dollars a page and pay the rent. They do not write comic book stories for artistic or emotional self-expression . . . Crime comic book writers should not be blamed for comic books. They are not free men. They are told what to do and they do it—or else . . . But of course, like comic book vendors, they have to be afraid of the ruthless economic power of the comic book industry.
>
> When we extended our studies to include artists who make draw-ings for crime comic books, far from blaming them we found that they are victims too. I doubt whether there are any artists doing this work whose life ambition was to draw for crime comic books . . . Whenever the question of control of crime comics is raised, the in-dustry starts to fuss about freedom of expression . . . [But the] text and drawings of crime comics are concocted, not created. And there is no freedom of concoction.

By portraying comic-book creators as hapless victims of Dickensian overlords, Wertham hid a refusal to consider their legitimacy as artists behind a defense of their honor as artists. In the same stroke, he exempted himself from the responsibility of assessing how the contents of comic books might relate to the inner lives of their makers. Could it have been that superheroes, in their alien omnipotence, were fantasy outlets for artists who felt powerless, by virtue of their class, race, education, or personality factors only a psychiatrist could explain? Was it possible that the lawbreaking and violence in comics were, to some degree, projections of their creators' frustrations? Could the heroes' victories in the final panels tell us something about their makers' sense of self-worth? What about the outré sexuality of Wonder Woman and the comics' many jungle queens? Could they have been protests against prevailing standards of normalcy by outsiders of all sorts trying to come to terms with their own identities? Were comic-book writers and artists speaking cogently, through their work, to young people seeking affirmation of their own discontent with the status quo? These were questions for a psychiatrist, but not for Fredric Wertham, and if there was a book in them, it was not *Seduction of the Innocent*.

Equally patronizing in his treatment of those who created comics and those who bought them, Wertham never wavered from the promise of his title; he portrayed comic-book readers exclusively as innocents, describing virtually all readers of titles of all kinds as "children." Wertham was correct to note that the very young had access to every type of comic book on the newsstand, and he pointed out, usefully, that warnings such as the "For Adults Only" label that Fox used on its most lurid comics were likely an enticement to the wrong readers. If *Seduction of the Innocent* encouraged some parents to keep copies of Stanley P. Morse's *Weird Chills* out of third-graders' hands, Wertham performed a worthy service. At the same time, his obdurate infantilization of the comics readership was inaccurate and tactical, rather than scientific. It diminished the adolescents and young adults who turned to comics in part because the books represented an escape from childhood, a way to begin dealing with the mysteries, the titillations, and the dangers of adulthood while reading safely in their bedrooms, under the covers.

"To me, the most offensive thing about that book was that [Wertham] presumed that everybody who read comics was a child or an idiot," said Al Feldstein. "We [at EC] functioned out of a presumption that our readers were at least fourteen, maybe thirteen, and older—up to adulthood, through adulthood. Mature readers, in terms of comic books. That never occurred to [Wertham]. That never occurred to a lot of people who didn't understand comics. Our readers were more mature. They were almost adults, or on their way there, that's why they were reading us."

Wertham's book was a solicitation, not an inquiry—a kind of seduction itself; accordingly, it concluded with an inducement to act. The final chapter, "The Triumph of Dr. Payn," alluded to the body-chopping sadist who had appeared in *Black Cat Mystery* two years earlier; but Wertham used the notion of the character's triumph—that is, the conquest of youth culture by the forces of depravity that, in Wertham's eyes, Dr. Payn represented—as a threat. Without unified action against the comic-book industry, America's youth could be lost, Wertham warned. Still, he held hope:

> I am convinced that in some way or other the democratic process will assert itself and crime comic books will go, and with them all they stand for and all that sustains them. But before they can tackle Superman, Dr. Payn, and all their myriad incarnations, people will have to learn that it is a distorted idea to think that democracy means giving good and evil an equal chance at expression. We must learn that freedom is not something that one can have, but is something that one must do.

Spirited and idealistic, if vague, the message left readers with a loaded choice of doctors: Wertham or Payn.

In the middle of its 397 pages, *Seduction of the Innocent* included a sixteen-page insert of illustrations, reproduced (in black and white) from comic-book pages and covers. Wertham selected acutely provocative images, of course, and he amplified their impact with eyebrow-raising descriptions; ten out of the book's thirty-one captions used the word "children." One page showed the cover art from an issue of EC's *Crime SuspenStories*: a drawing by Johnny Craig of a man hanging in a noose, his eyes rolled back in his head; and the caption read, "Cover of a children's comic book." (For *Seduction of the Innocent*, Craig's signature had been whited-out of the artwork, perhaps at the recommendation of Rinehart and Company, since Wertham did not acquire permission to reprint any comic-book art.) One page showed a tight close-up of a small section of a drawing of a male character's bare shoulder, with the caption, "In ordinary comic books, there are pictures within pictures for children who know how to look." With a bit of imagination, the hatch marks at the intersection of the shoulder muscles resembled a rough sketch of a woman's pubic area. Other pages in the insert presented a cover of Matt Baker's busty heroine Phantom Lady, tied by ropes to a post; a cover of *Crime Detective Comics* with a psychiatrist resembling Wertham, bound and gagged; two panels from the EC story "Foul Play!" from *The Haunt of Fear*, about a baseball game played with human body parts, with art by Jack Davis; and other samples of comics art at its extremes.

Davis, a genteel fellow, was humiliated to find his work included in Wertham's book. "That business with that book, that was awful," Davis recalled. "Bill and Al wrote the story, and I thought it was all kind of funny and no big deal, and then, when it came out in that book, I wanted to bury my head. I wished I never did it. Bill said, 'Jack, Jack—don't worry about it. It was just a joke. This'll blow over—don't you worry about it.' But I wasn't so sure."

Gaines, recalling his first response to *Seduction of the Innocent* (in an interview conducted in 1969), affirmed that he considered the book funny at first. "I read [Wertham's] book and found it full of the worst kind of mistakes, blunders," Gaines said. "He completely missed the point of a number of our stories. We found his book humorous. It was amazing how a man could be so far off base on this sort of thing. The things he read into our motives, they were completely fallacious because his understanding of the stories was screwed up." Although Gaines could not recall an example on the spot at the time, the bulk of references to comic-book story content in *Seduction of the Innocent* ignored or distorted their context. For instance, Wertham referred to "a horrible picture of a man shot in the stomach, with a face of agonized pain, and such dialogue as: 'You know as well as I do that any water he'd drink'd pour right out of his gut! It'd be MURDER!'" He described the Mickey Spillane parody in *Panic* without mentioning that the comic's intent was to ridicule the vulgar excesses of pulp fiction. Naturally, Wertham could not leave unmentioned the fact that the publisher was listed as Tiny Tot Comics, Inc.

With the notable exceptions of Tiny Tot's brain trust (Feldstein, Gaines, their business manager, Lyle Stuart), most people working in comics seemed to know Wertham's book no better than Wertham knew theirs. Many read the reviews or the articles and editorials about *Seduction of the Innocent*, or parts of them; or they caught Wertham's immobile face on television, as Will Eisner had, or heard him lecturing solemnly, on the radio. It seems fair to assume that many comics professionals would have been interested in reading the book, although scarcely any would ever affirm as much. (No fewer than seventy comic-book artists, writers, editors, and others who were working in comics around 1954 would say they never read *Seduction of the Innocent*, read only snippets or excerpts, or just scanned the illustrations.) Still, when the book was published, Wertham and his claims, or the gist of them, dominated the talk of the comic-book studios. Everyone seemed to know all they needed or wanted to know: that a book—a "real" book, published with hard covers and written by a doctor—said terrible things about them and the kind of books they made.

"The whole idea was driving us crazy, and it was all we talked about," said Bob Fujitani, who was drawing for *Crime Does Not Pay* at the time. "'That Wertham—the guy's crazy!' The only thought I had was, this goddamn guy is ruining comics. He's trying to put us out of business, and this is our livelihood! And there was a matter of pride. We were artists—we were proud people, and here was this guy leading this crusade against something we really cared about. All the guys—we were scared to death, and I mean really scared to death." Fujitani would recall his editor, Bob Wood, announcing that he was going to "go find Wertham and kill him with his bare hands." Wood may well have done so, Fujitani thought, if Wood had had the where-withal to look outside the local bars.

Tony DiPreta, Fujitani's colleague among the freelance artists working for Charles Biro and Bob Wood, read a newspaper article about *Seduction of the Innocent* and began to wonder if Wertham was right and he was hurting young readers by drawing for *Crime Does Not Pay*. A practicing Catholic, DiPreta took his concern to the confession booth and told his priest about his work. "I said, 'Father, I draw for comic books,'" recalled DiPreta. "I said, 'I'm drawing all these violent things, and people get shot, there's blood and guts and—Father, I didn't realize it was wrong, and now I realize it, and I'm so sorry. But I need to work, and I like what I'm doing.'" His priest granted DiPreta absolution, without comment, and DiPreta took that as tacit permission to stay on the job.

Outside of the comic-book business, *Seduction of the Innocent* was taken seriously and was well received by nearly every major critic. Among the exceptions was Reuel Denney, who, in *The New Republic*, found sizable holes in Wertham's methods and thinking. "[Wertham's] theory of how people get meanings out of what they read and see in pictures is psychologically over-simplified," Denney wrote. "It assumes that the messages received by comic-book readers are unambiguous. It assumes that children themselves are unaware of the questionable quality of the 'messages' that the author himself finds in some of the comic books. This study overworks, as well, the same fallacy that other psychiatrists have deluded themselves with—the notion that fiction is quite directly responsible for the fantasies and emulations of readers."

Leading the chorus of acclamation for Wertham's book, Sterling North reveled in its validation of his own thesis and said that *Seduction of the Innocent* "may well be the most important book of the year." (Rinehart and Company included this comment in its ads for the book, attributing it to North's review of *Seduction of the Innocent* in the *New York World-Telegram and Sun*; however, that review did not include the phrase, a fact that suggests that North supplied it separately to Rinehart or Wertham.) Deriding comic books as "graphic inanity and boring trash turned out by . . . cultural hoodlums," North argued, in his review, that comics reading should be forbidden in "literate households."

In *The New York Times Book Review*, the sociologist C. Wright Mills lauded Wertham for his outrage in the name of public service. "Dr. Wertham has read these ugly pamphlets with the eye of the psychiatrist; it has made him an angry man, who has good reasons for anger," wrote Mills. "Dr. Wertham's cases, his careful observations and his sober reflections about the American child in a world of comic violence and unfunny filth testify to a most commendable use of the professional mind in the service of the public." In *The New Yorker*, much the same, the critic Wolcott Gibbs was willing to indulge Wertham's excesses because his conclusions seemed so consequential. "Altogether, [the book] is a formidable indictment, and if some of the charges appear to be only partly substantiated and if the language in which they are made is often extravagant, it still seems clear that something more pernicious than simple witlessness and monumental vulgarity is involved," wrote Gibbs. He found much to offend in the comics Wertham brought to bear, particularly what Gibbs described as the books' "incitement to rebellion against constituted authority," which Gibbs derided as an inclination to Communism.

"At the moment, the comics are under attack again, and *Seduction of the Innocent* has provided their enemies with some of their most potent ammunition," Gibbs concluded. "The evidence that the Doctor has assembled is overpowering . . . The concrete evidence it offers of a real crime against the children seems to be practically unanswerable. I like to think that Superman and his pals are up against the battle of their perverse, fantastic, and foolish lives."

13. What Are We Afraid Of?

Much as the movies shaped the public perception of juvenile delinquency in the early 1950s, television molded the political response. The Senate hearings on delinquency, led by Robert C. Hendrickson of New Jersey with help from the cosponsor of his committee, Tennessee senator Estes Kefauver, followed the model of Kefauver's previous hearings on organized crime, which had had a sensational impact when they had been televised a few years earlier. The crime hearings Kefauver conducted in 1950 and early 1951 had, through the phenomenon of their broadcasts, left such an impression on the American consciousness that they haunted the delinquency hearings of 1953 and 1954, the way the TV picture tubes of the day left the ghost impression of one scene superimposed on the scene to follow.

In January 1951, two months after Kefauver's committee on organized crime announced the results of its own sessions on comics and delinquency (largely exonerating the former of responsibility for the latter), Kefauver took his traveling crime committee to New Orleans, where a local television station decided to broadcast the hearings on crime. As legislative inquiries, rather than judicial proceedings, the hearings were exempt from the rules prohibiting broadcasts from courtrooms on the grounds that they would unfairly subject defendants and witnesses to public display. Viewers in New Orleans had never seen the likes of the crime hearings—real-life drama starring the underworld kingpins of the region and their cohorts in local politics. Talk of the hearings dominated the city's papers and quickly spread across the country through the wire services and the newsmagazines. The broadcasting station in New Orleans received 1,300 letters about the hearings within three days. When Kefauver and his committee moved on to Detroit, St. Louis, and cities on the West Coast, TV cameras followed. By the time he arrived in New York, the national headquarters of organized crime, Estes Kefauver was on the cover of *Time*.

Cynics could have questioned the editorial purity of the cover choice, since Time Inc. had chosen to launch a circulation drive by sponsoring commercial telecasts of the New York crime hearings, which began on Monday, March 12, 1951, the date on the Kefauver cover. Thanks to the publisher's sponsorship and an intricate, unprecedented pooling arrangement involving the local broadcaster (WPIX), the three TV networks, and several independent stations, the New York hearings reached viewers within signal range of stations in twenty cities on the East Coast and in the Midwest. Although a few Senate hearings prior to Kefauver's (including some of the 1948 House Un-American Activities Committee sessions on Alger Hiss) had been televised locally, the New York crime hearings were the first to be broadcast nationally (by the definition of a national broadcast in 1951), and they aired at a pivotal moment in America's venture into the television era—more than half the homes in the country now had TV sets.

Broadcast live during the day from the federal courthouse in Foley Square in Lower Manhattan, the hearings were ideal for TV. Here was a crime story packed with spicy illicit business—gambling and bootlegging and murder and extortion and graft—and the characters were neatly delineated good guys and bad guys. On one side, sitting in a row behind the courthouse bench, were the four Senate committee members, their counsel, and their leader, Kefauver, who emanated the same sort of languorous, down-home authority as the silent-movie cowboy Harry Carey in his role as the president of the Senate in *Mr. Smith Goes to Washington*. On the other side, seated across from the bench at a plain oak table, came some fifty witnesses, among them several of the most notorious figures in organized crime: Frank Costello (Francisco Castaglia), a former lieutenant of Lucky Luciano who replaced his boss as the head of the top New York crime syndicate when Luciano was deported by Governor Dewey in 1946; Anthony "Tony Tough" Anastasio, understood to be the director of the "Murder Inc." hit squad; and Anastasio's colleague Joe Adonis (Joseph Doto); as well as Virginia Hill, a Mob hostess and former mistress of Luciano's protégé, Bugsy Siegel. The star witnesses fit their parts as well as Kefauver did his. Fastidiously attired and groomed in dark suits, they exuded wealth, privilege, and resentment, as they protested ("I didn't do a damn thing"), dodged questions ("I gotta refreshen my memory on dese tings"), suffered sudden bouts of laryngitis and other maladies, and pleaded the Fifth.

Costello, attuned to the presence of power and unwilling to capitulate to it, objected to the cameras at Foley Square. Shortly after Costello was sworn in and began his testimony, on March 13, 1951, one of his attorneys asked that the proceedings be stopped. "Mr. Costello doesn't care to submit himself as a spectacle," the lawyer argued, and, after a brief consultation, the members of the committee agreed to order the TV crew to keep Costello's face out of view. Costello proceeded to testify, and the cameras had to show *something*. Resourcefully, someone at WPIX decided to have one camera focus tight on Costello's hands. What the witness said no longer mattered. As Costello blathered on about the legitimacy of his investments in the production of kewpie dolls and the innocence of his friendship with City Hall bosses and the inconsequence of the large sums of cash that social acquaintances had given him for no reason, his hands spoke more cogently. TV screens in living rooms around the country filled with images of Costello's manicured fingers twitching, sweating, clutching a handkerchief, drumming on the table, and tearing sheets of notepaper into shreds and rolling them into tiny balls.

The broadcasts of the Kefauver committee hearings on organized crime were so popular that the New York City electric company, Con Edison, had to add an additional generator to handle the power demand during the broadcasts. Some 70 percent of New Yorkers with TV sets tuned in for the hearings—seventeen times the number of people who usually watched daytime television. Those without sets filled bars and restaurants in the morning or watched through appliance-store windows. Two theaters in Manhattan, finding their seats vacant during the "Kefauver hours," set up systems to project the broadcasts on their screens and welcomed the public for free. (Popcorn and drinks were available at the usual prices.) Homemakers had "Kefauver parties" and formed shopping clubs to limit their time away from their TV sets. Several schools dismissed students early so they could watch the hearings at home. Sales of Pops-Rite corn for home popping more than doubled during the eight days of the New York hearings.

"The effect was unbelievable," recalled Kefauver in *Crime in America*, the book he produced (with considerable assistance from *Saturday Evening Post* writer Sidney Shalett) about the hearings. "In New York City, some merchants wrote us, their businesses were paralyzed . . . We became a national crusade, a great debating forum, an arouser of public opinion on the state of the nation's morals."

As *Life* reported shortly after the hearings, "The week of March 12, 1951, will occupy a special place in history. The U.S. and the world had never experienced anything like it . . . Never before had the attention of the nation been so completely riveted on a single matter. The Senate investigation into interstate crime was almost the sole subject of national conversation." Beyond the fact that *Life*'s parent company had a stake in the hearings, there was something to the magazine's hyperbole. An estimated twenty million to thirty million people tuned in to see Frank Costello, more than had watched the World Series broadcast in fall 1950. President Truman received thousands of letters praising the crime committee's work and calling for action to reduce collusion between local politicians and organized crime. (Jerry Siegel, co-creator of *Superman*, wrote one of those letters.) Truman, a product of the infamous political machine of Kansas City, Missouri, boss Tom Pendergast, resented Kefauver for challenging a system he accepted, for the independence Truman considered arrogant, if not traitorous, and for tarnishing local Democratic leaders before the presidential campaign season. Kefauver had already redefined that season, however; he had been campaigning without candidacy through the crime hearings, building a national reputation on television without mediation by traditional power brokers.

On January 23, 1952, four months after the crime committee submitted its final report, Kefauver announced that he was running for president. *Life* noted, in a profile of the candidate published that March, "Senator Estes Kefauver is the nation's first serious dabbler in a new brand of political magic—the awesome power of TV. When he announced his candidacy . . . his one asset, thanks to his Senate Crime Inquiry, was a name as well advertised as the most popular soap chips—and with an aroma equally antiseptic." Kefauver won the New Hampshire primary and other key contests leading up to the nomination, but never earned the support of the party establishment or its retiring president. When the first ballot at the Democratic convention showed Kefauver ahead of the party favorite, Illinois governor Adlai Stevenson, Truman interceded, through intermediaries, to ensure that Stevenson got the votes to win. Such was the party's antipathy toward Kefauver that he was rejected for the vice presidential nomination in favor of John Sparkman, a virtually unknown senator from Alabama.

"The boss-run convention machinery had me stopped," Kefauver later recalled in an article for *Collier's* titled "Why Not Let the People Elect Our President?"

> I had aroused the implacable enmity of certain politicians, including some defeated hacks and various political yeomen who were taking orders implicitly from the outgoing Truman administration . . . Being thus committed to "stop Kefauver" these "machine stalwarts," who were all-powerful behind the convention scenes, disregarded what the people and the largest bloc of delegates said they wanted.

Not long after his loss, Kefauver was asked if he had given up the idea of being president, and he said, "Oh, no."

Tracing the pattern of Estes Kefauver's committee on organized crime, Robert C. Hendrickson's committee on juvenile delinquency began its work in November 1953 with several weeks of hearings in Washington, followed by sessions in Boston, Denver, and Philadelphia. The hearings took up a variety of topics in each location: gangs, narcotics, pornography, juvenile access to firearms, child prostitution. Formally sanctioned to explore the need for legislation on matters related to interstate commerce, postal delivery, and other areas of federal jurisdiction, the committee also sought to raise public awareness of delinquency and to exert influence through the inquiry's visibility. After all, the Kefauver committee, which was generally viewed as a success, resulted in no legislation; at the same time, the light it cast on organized crime led to state raceway regulations and the prosecution of gangsters in several cities, and it prompted the Treasury Department to set up a program to examine the income-tax returns of suspected racketeers. Among Hendrickson's main interests were the causes of delinquency, and he suspected from the outset that popular entertainment might be the most potent. On the eve of his first hearings, in Washington, Hendrickson told reporters that his committee had received some 7,500 unsolicited letters from voters concerned about delinquency; among them, Hendrickson said, 90 percent believed that the "chief reason" for juvenile crime was "the increasing emphasis on sex and crime in public entertainment."

Hendrickson conducted his work with confidence that he and his committee had deep and broad support, from the electorate to the president. Eisenhower, who generally resisted government intervention in the exchange of ideas, had, just a few months earlier, told students at the Dartmouth College commencement, "Don't join the book burners . . . Don't be afraid to go in your library and read every book, as long as any document does not offend our own ideas of decency. That should be the only censorship." In a letter released to the press the day before Thanksgiving 1953, he called delinquency "a problem filled with heartbreak" and told Hendrickson, "I know you share with me the fervent hope that your deliberations will result in suggestions for action which will reduce substantially the incalculable unhappiness which juvenile delinquency now causes our children, their parents, pastors, educators, and all who are concerned with the problem. It is a problem of national importance and one in which the federal government properly takes a keen interest."

Within three months of the first hearings on delinquency, Hendrickson's mail pile had grown to some twenty thousand letters, with 65 to 75 percent targeting comic books and "crime shows" on television as likely causes of juvenile crime. Hendrickson, citing "significant public concern over the possible harmful effects of comic books on the young mind," announced on February 20, 1954, that his committee would soon conduct a set of hearings devoted to comics. This was three days after *The Hartford Courant* ran the last entry in Irving Kravsow's four-part series, "Depravity for Children." The sessions would take place, on a date as yet undecided, in New York, in the chambers of the federal courthouse at Foley Square, and they would be televised.

Bill Gaines read about the pending hearings and fumed. "He was not about to let that happen to him . . . what happened to those gangsters, with Kefauver," recalled Lyle Stuart. "Bill believed in his heart that he was on the side of freedom and right and had nothing to fear." In a fit of prankish fury, Gaines dug out his file of oddball newspaper clips about comics, and he used a couple of items as the basis of a house ad intended both to parody comic-book critics and to mobilize EC readers against them. It was one of a small handful of pieces of writing that Gaines ever did by himself, according to Feldstein, Stuart, and artist Jack Davis, who illustrated Gaines's text. The headline on the top of the page asked, in tall block letters, "ARE YOU A RED DUPE?" Below it, a sequence of three comic drawings showed (a) a Soviet citizen printing a comic book (*Panicsky*); (b) a KGB officer stomping apart the printing press; (c) the citizen hanging from a noose, dead, while the officer warms his hands at a bonfire of comics. The text below read:

> Here in America, we can STILL publish comic magazines, newspapers, slicks, books and the Bible. We don't HAVE to send them to a censor first. Not YET . . .
>
> But there are some people in America who would LIKE to censor . . . who would LIKE to suppress comics. It isn't that they don't like comics for THEM! They don't like them for YOU!

After a bit more along these lines, the ad proclaimed, in a second headline: THE GROUP MOST ANXIOUS TO DESTROY COMICS ARE THE COMMUNISTS! As evidence, Gaines submitted an excerpt from an item in the July 13, 1953, issue of the *Daily Worker*, which condemned "so-called 'comics' [for] brutalizing American youth, the better to prepare them for military service in implementing [their] government's aims of world domination." At the bottom, the ad concluded:

> So the NEXT time some joker gets up at a P.T.A. meeting, or starts jabbering about the "naughty comic books" at your local candy store,

give him the ONCE-OVER. We're not saying he IS a Communist! He may be innocent of the whole thing! He may be a DUPE! He may not even READ the "Daily Worker"! It's just that he's SWALLOWED the RED BAIT . . . HOOK, LINE, and SINKER!

Before the ad was published, Gaines sent a copy to the office of Robert C. Hendrickson, who did not see the humor in being associated with a murderous, book-burning agent of the KGB. On April 9, Hendrickson carried the ad onto the Senate floor, and he gave a speech denouncing Gaines and defending the plans of his committee. "The American people have a right to know the facts," Hendrickson said. "Yet, Mr. President, some would attempt to tie this problem to freedom of the press. In fact, it has even been suggested to our investigative staff that anyone interested in the question of comic books is tied up with some dark plot to promote a police state . . . Mr. President, there are evidently vested interests throwing up smoke screens about their activities which would prevent us from even raising a question concerning the impact of crime and horror comics on the young mind. It seems to this subcommittee that you do not have to be a fellow traveler to raise questions . . .

"If some groups are trying to indict as Communists the thousands of concerned Americans who have been writing this subcommittee apprehensive about horror comics, then the FBI had better get busy, because I would fancy that there are literally millions of 'Reds' in this nation of ours whom we thought all along were either just plain Democrats or Republicans. And I make that statement in all sarcasm." As much as Hendrickson disapproved of Gaines's wise-ass humor, he seemed to find its spirit infectious.

Hendrickson scheduled two days of Senate hearings on comic books to begin on Wednesday, April 21, 1954. The executive director of the committee, Richard Clendenen, a social worker who had served for seven years as head of the juvenile delinquency division of the United States Children's Bureau, recommended the witnesses: a group of fourteen including a few comic-book publishers (Monroe Froehlich, Jr., of Timely / Atlas / Marvel, Helen Meyer of Dell); psychiatrists and experts on juvenile delinquency (Fredric Wertham, Lauretta Bender of Bellevue Hospital, Gunnar Dybwad of the Child Study Association of America); distributors and news dealers; newspaper comic-strip artists (Milton Caniff, Walt Kelly); and miscellaneous others such as Henry E. Schultz, director of the Association of Comics Magazine Publishers. No comic-book artists or writers were called; nor were the publishers of the most controversial comics: Lev Gleason, Victor Fox, Bill Gaines, and Stanley P. Morse. "Somebody came and asked me a few questions, but I got rid of them," recalled Morse, referring to an exploratory inquiry conducted by a member of Clendenen's staff. "I didn't want anything to do with that business. What do you think I was, a suicide case?"

Bill Gaines volunteered to testify, against Feldstein's advice, and Hendrickson welcomed him. For a week before the hearings, Gaines handed off nearly all his EC duties to Stuart and Feldstein so he could concentrate on preparing his testimony. He worked alone in his office for hours every day, typing drafts of an opening statement, and he discarded each one. At least once, he stayed at Lafayette Street late into the night, aided by the Dexedrine that he had been taking as a diet medication; Stuart would recall getting a call from Gaines, who wanted to test a draft of a statement on him, at around eleven, three or four nights before the hearings. A few days later, on the evening of April 20, Gaines phoned Stuart after dinner and asked him to come to the office and help. Stuart arrived at around ten to find Gaines at his desk, shuffling through pages of typescript, which he had crumpled into balls and thrown away, then reclaimed from the trash and patted flat. There was a blank sheet of paper in his typewriter. When Gaines hopped up from his chair and started pacing, Stuart sat down at Gaines's desk, behind the keyboard. "Look at me, Bill," Stuart said, as he later recalled. "I'm a United States Senator, and I'm wondering if I should pass a law to put you out of business. Is there anything you'd like to say to me?"

Gaines extemporized, Stuart typed; they read the results and tried again; Stuart made suggestions, and Gaines liked some and rejected others that struck him as too theoretical or legalistic—Gaines said he mainly wanted to tell the story of his own life and work; Stuart typed another draft, Gaines read it and marked it in pencil; Stuart added flourishes; they wrote and rewrote. To stay awake, Stuart sipped coffee, and Gaines popped tablets of No-Doz on top of the Dexedrine. Around five or six in the morning, Stuart handed Gaines a clean version of their final draft, typed on EC letterhead. Gaines asked Stuart to meet him at Foley Square at nine, an hour before the hearings were scheduled to begin.

"He was eager to go down there and say his piece," recalled Stuart. "He thought he was doing a good thing. He was appearing as a friendly witness, and he believed that if he went there and just told the good senators what he was doing and why he was doing it, they would understand, and everything would be fine."

When Stuart arrived at Foley Square, a few minutes early, he found Gaines waiting near the side of the courthouse. A dozen or so people—most of them men in jackets and ties, a few with cameras, one or two taking notes—loitered around the columns flanking the front doors. It was a cool spring morning, a bit overcast. Gaines was wearing a loose-fitting pale gray suit, and he was perspiring. Irving Kravsow, the reporter from *The Hartford Courant*, had come from Connecticut to cover the event and saw Gaines but did not recognize him at first; Gaines looked heavier—an illusion of his bulky, light-colored clothing, perhaps—and also older than he had seemed when Kravsow had met him in his EC office two months earlier.

The Hendrickson committee hearings on comic books took place in room 110, where the Kefauver crime hearings had begun before they had been relocated to larger quarters on the third floor to accommodate the crowds. Like the chambers in many such courthouses, these had been designed, in the early 1930s, to uphold the citizenry's confidence in American jurisprudence through an atmosphere of dignified neutrality. (The architect of the Foley Square courthouse, Cass Gilbert, happened also to have designed 225 Lafayette Street.) The walls, the floors, and the furnishings were all of burnished oak— a blur of earth tones disrupted for the occasion by a large display of full-color comic-book covers. There were twenty-four of them arranged in three rows under the heading "Representative Comic Book Covers/ Crime, Horror & Weird Variety," and the titles included *Crime Does Not Pay*, *Justice Traps the Guilty*, *Marvel Tales*, *Tales from the Crypt*, *The Haunt of Fear*, and *Crime SuspenStories*. On one side of the room, the members of the committee—Hendrickson roughly in the center, flanked on his left by Senator William Langer and on his right by Kefauver and Thomas C. Hennings—sat behind a long bench, almost exactly as Kefauver and his own committee had sat at the crime hearings. Eight to ten rows of seats, enough to accommodate about 150 spectators, were set up along the wall perpendicular to the bench, on its right side; they were filled, and more people waited outside the chambers. A broad table for the witnesses to present their testimony was situated in the middle of the room at a forty-five-degree angle, so the committee and the public would each have a three-quarter view of the witnesses but the witnesses would have no direct eye contact with anyone. Arrays of enormous microphones were arranged on the bench and on the table, with heavy cables leading to an area behind the spectators, where camera crews for both television and movie newsreels were set up. Three stenographers—two young women taking shorthand and one man using a stenographic machine—sat near the witness table. "Crowded, busy, tense—like a movie set," remembered Stuart.

At 10:00 a.m., Robert C. Hendrickson leaned close to the microphone and called the hearings to order. "Today and tomorrow the United States Subcommittee on Investigating Juvenile Delinquency, of which I am the chairman, is going into the problem of horror and crime comic books," Hendrickson announced, speaking quickly in a pinched monotone. "By comic books, we mean pamphlets illustrating stories depicting crimes or dealing with horror and sadism."

Hendrickson, fifty-six, had thin, silvery hair, brushed straight back, and a small mustache, and he wore two-tone glasses; he embodied clichés of Northeastern austerity as Kefauver did those of Southern grace. He started the proceedings on notes of restraint and open-mindedness. "We are not a committee of blue-nosed censors," said Hendrickson. "We have no preconceived notions as to the possible need for new legislation. We want to find out what damage, if any, is being done to our children's minds by certain types of publications which contain a substantial degree of sadism, crime, and horror . . .

"It would be wrong to assume that crime and horror comic books are the major cause of juvenile delinquency. It would be just as erroneous to state categorically that they have no effect whatsoever in aggravating the problem. We are here to determine what effect on the whole problem of causation crime and horror comic books do have."

The hearings began with a slide show, prepared and presented by the committee's executive director, Richard Clendenen, a lean, square-jawed man in early middle age. As an aide dimmed the lights, Clendenen explained that the committee was "almost exclusively" concerned with crime and horror comics, which he described as typically portraying "almost all types of crime . . . committed through extremely cruel, sadistic, and punitive kinds of acts." To put the slide pictures in perspective, as he saw them, Clendenen said, "Now, in presenting these I would like to say that while it is not a random sampling, actually it is a deliberate sampling in trying to present the various types of stories and pictures . . . They are quite typical of the stories and pictures which appear in this type of publication." Clendenen proceeded to show pages from six stories from the most gruesome horror comics. He ended with a pair of stories from EC.

"The final comic is one entitled *Shock SuspenStories*," Clendenen said. "It contains four stories in which six persons die violently. One particular story in this issue is called 'Orphan.' This is the story of a small, golden-haired girl named Lucy, of perhaps eight or ten years of age, and the story is told in her own words.

"Lucy hates both her parents. Her father is an alcoholic who beats her when drunk. Her mother, who never wanted Lucy, has a secret boyfriend . . . Snatching a gun from the night table, Lucy shoots her father from the window. She then runs out into the yard and presses the gun into the hands of her mother who has fainted and lies unconscious on the ground. Then, through Lucy's perjured testimony at the trial, both the mother and the boyfriend are convicted of murdering the father and are electrocuted."

Clicking to a slide, Clendenen said, "This picture shows, first, 'Mommie' and then 'Stevie' as they die in the electric chair."

Click. "The latter two pictures show Lucy's joyous contentment that it all has worked out as she planned . . . The last two comic books I mentioned are published by the Entertaining Comic group, and I mention it because the publisher of the Entertaining Comic group will be appearing here later this morning."

Clendenen proceeded to submit as exhibits a stack of documents pertinent to the inquiry: a report to the committee from the Department of Health, Education and Welfare; a compendium of publications about comics and delinquency assembled by the Library of Congress; material from the Gathings hearings two years earlier; and a variety of articles from newspapers, popular magazines, and scholarly journals. To spare the committee the burden of reading the materials, Clendenen summarized them briefly. "I do feel that it is eminently accurate and fair to say that there is substantial, although not always unanimous, agreement on the following three points," he said.

"One, that the reading of a crime comic will not cause a well-adjusted and well-socialized boy or girl to go out and commit crime.

"Two, there may be a detrimental and delinquency-producing effect upon some emotionally disturbed children who may gain suggestion, support, and sanction for acting out his own hostile and aggressive feeling.

"Three, there is reason to believe that as among youngsters, the most avid and extensive consumers of comics are the very boys and girls less able to tolerate this type of material. As a matter of fact, many experts feel that excessive reading of materials of this kind in itself is symptomatic of some emotional maladjustment in a youngster."

Actually, in all the materials Clendenen submitted as exhibits, only one expert made any such claim—Wertham, who was quoted and paraphrased repeatedly. Several documents included significant challenges to Wertham, although Clendenen pointed out none of them in his presentation. One was an article titled "The Comics and Delinquency: Cause or Scapegoat?" written by Frederic M. Thrasher, a professor at New York University, and published in the *Journal of Educational Sociology*. Thrasher analyzed Wertham's methods and found them indefensible:

> We may criticize Wertham's conclusions on many grounds, but the major weakness of his position is that it is not supported by research data . . . He introduces extraneous facts and statements which by implication he links with his thesis that the comics are a major factor in causing delinquency and emotional disturbance in children . . . Wertham . . . cites a series of sensational child crimes headlined in the press (not his own cases), which he imputes to the comics without any evidence that the juvenile offenders involved ever read or were interested in comic books.
>
> Of the millions of comic books which Wertham claims deal with crime and brutality, he is content to rest his case on the selection of a few extreme and offensive examples which he makes no attempt to prove are typical. No systematic inventory of comic-book content is presented . . . Without such an inventory these conjectures are prejudiced and worthless.

In conclusion, it may be said that no acceptable evidence has been produced by Wertham or anyone else for the conclusion that the reading of comic magazines has, or has not a significant relation to delinquent behavior.

Among the documents Clendenen did point out to the committee was the copy of the "Are You a Red Dupe?" ad Gaines had sent to Hendrickson's office. Citing Gaines as the source of the material, Clendenen described the allegorical little cartoon on the top of the page, read the statement at the bottom, and told the committee, "Some people would make out anyone who raised any question whatsoever about the comics was also giving out Red-inspired propaganda."

Senator Hennings interjected, "They do not seem to care what they do or what they purvey or what they dish out to these youngsters as long as it sells and brings in the money. This seems to be an effort, this 'Are You a Red Dupe?' business, to forestall or bring such pressure to bear as can be against any attempt to even look into or to examine this and see what they may be doing."

Clendenen replied, "I would interpret it as such," and Kefauver concurred. "This is very interesting," Kefauver added solemnly. "They attempt to quote the *Daily Worker* to show that anyone who questions comics is a Communist." Hendrickson chimed in that he agreed with Kefauver, Hennings repeated his initial objection to the ad, and Clendenen reaffirmed his assent with them all.

The opening witness was Dr. Harris Peck, director of the Bureau of Mental Health Services for the New York City Court of Domestic Relations, which, Peck explained, included the city's "family court" as well as its "children's court." His testimony was circumspect and brief. Generally speaking, he said, "some caution must be observed in attributing to the comic books a major impetus for delinquency." Peck acknowledged, at the same time, that some of his colleagues found reasons to justify stronger criticism of comics. Then again, he added, others considered the books essentially harmless.

Kefauver asked, "So you think you are in the middle of the road in appraising the matter?" and Peck said, "I think that would be a fair estimate of my position."

The second witness, Henry E. Schultz of the Association of Comics Magazine Publishers, followed Peck down that road. Abandoning the fiery advocacy that had distinguished his early tenure with the comics trade group, Schultz bemoaned the decrepit state of the organization and admitted that its content code was ineffectual—indeed, unenforceable, because of inadequate participation by comics publishers. At the time of the hearings, Schultz explained, the ACMP had only twelve members, and most of them were distributors, printers, and engravers. Of more than thirty publishers in the comic-book industry in April 1954, only three belonged to the ACMP (Timely/Atlas/ Marvel, Gleason Publications, and Eastern Color, publisher of *Famous Funnies*). "I say that our experience in continuing this organization has been a study in frustration," Schultz told the committee. "When I came into the picture some six or seven years ago, we had one-third of the industry. Since that time there have been defections from that very substantially so that today, unfortunately, our association represents a very insignificant, small fraction of the industry—those few diehards who still believe that by some miracle the organization of their original premise, which was a program of self-regulation of comics, might yet come true. Unfortunately, it has not happened."

Sounding much like the comic-book critics he used to debate, Schultz implored the committee: "I would hope, if I may make one plea in conclusion, that this committee, in the face of the larger scope of this problem—it is a serious, important, difficult problem—could do a great service, in my judgment, if it would, while excoriating the bad taste and the vulgarity sometimes bordering on obscenity that occurs in these publications, I think many of the comic-book publishers have failed in their duty to mothers to take this great medium, which was seven years ago a wonderful, vital thing, and they have debased it in many ways. I think they should be criticized for that.

"But I think the whole problem of comic books and their impact must be put in proper focus," Schultz said, mustering a plea for mercy upon comics on grounds not of their harmlessness, but of their inconsequence. "How much of an impact all of the mass media can make on this problem and what little corner of it the comic book occupies is a very difficult measurement to make."

Schultz said a few final words, a fumbling attempt to explain the value of the ACMP seal of approval, which the association's three member publishers printed on the covers of their comics. "I really don't know," Schultz said. "The seal has lost its imprint and its value in many ways . . . except for somebody who takes the trouble to look very closely at that little legend that might have some meaning to it. Other than that, I think it has no value." With that, at 12:20 p.m., Hendrickson called a recess for lunch.

Gaines, who kept popping Dexedrine and No-Doz to fight exhaustion, had no appetite. He and Stuart shuffled around the halls of the courthouse, grousing about Clendenen's early fixation on EC stories and the "Red Dupe" ad. "Bill felt like he was being made a target, because he was the one who had the guts to volunteer to come in and take a stand and defend the business," recalled Stuart. "He couldn't wait to get in there and give that speech we spent all night writing." Before the end of the recess, Gaines spotted Irving Kravsow outside the chamber room, and he confronted him.

"This is all your fault, you know," Gaines barked, with Stuart at his side. Kravsow, a reporter in the presence of a hot interview prospect, chatted up Gaines on his impressions of the hearings. Gaines treated the conversation like a dry run of his testimony, ridiculing Wertham and defending comic-book readers as citizens whose rights were being threatened. Kravsow never got to ask him a question. "He was really on a rampage," recalled Kravsow. "I thought he was a little scary, to tell you the truth."

As Gaines walked away, he told Stuart, "See that? I set him straight.

All I have to do is show these guys the error of their ways, and they'll come around."

"Bill," Stuart said, "how can you be so naive? And why don't we eat something?" They went to a nearby deli, and Stuart had a sandwich, Gaines a bottle of Coca-Cola, before the hearings reconvened at two.

The first witness of the afternoon was Fredric Wertham. As he took his seat, he turned his chair a bit to the right so he could face the committee directly. Wertham was wearing a white jacket over a white shirt and a plain black tie; he looked as if he had come straight from doing scientific work, still in his lab clothes. He spoke in piercing tones sharpened by his German accent; and what he said was an amalgam of science, self-promotion, outrage, and sarcasm as biting as anything in *Mad*. He introduced himself with a recitation of his impressive credentials, noting almost immediately that, in 1929, he had been awarded a fellowship to conduct research on the brain. "Some part of my research at that time was on paresis and brain syphilis," Wertham noted. "It came in good stead when I came to study comic books."

His testimony was essentially a recapitulation of the core arguments in *Seduction of the Innocent*, which had just been published and was beginning to garner attention. (C. Wright Mills's review of the book appeared three days after the hearings.) Wertham described the work that provided him with the material for *Seduction of the Innocent* as "a sober, painstaking, laborious clinical study," adding that he and his associates had "read all that we could get hold of that was written in defense of comic books, which is almost a more trying task than reading the comic books themselves."

Speaking to the cameras, Wertham made a simple, direct statement of his position, phrased slowly and spoken in a clear, ringing voice temporarily absent of his accent: "It is my opinion," Wertham said—then he took a long pause—"without any reasonable doubt"—another long pause—"and without any reservation"—long pause—"that comic

books"—pause—"are an important"—pause—"contributing factor"—
short pause—"in many cases"—shorter pause—"of juvenile delinquency."

Bringing this threat home to every parent in his audience, he continued, "There arises the question: What kind of child is affected? I
say again without any reasonable doubt and based on hundreds and
hundreds of cases of all kinds, that it is primarily the normal child. As
a matter of fact, the most morbid children that we have seen are the
ones who are less affected by comic books because they are wrapped
up in their own fantasies."

As always, Wertham referred to virtually all comic books as "crime
comics," and he aimed his most pointed criticism not at cops-and-
robbers, horror, or romance books, but at superhero comics. "I would
like to point out to you one other crime comic book which we have
found to be particularly injurious to the ethical development of children and those are the Superman comic books," he told the committee. "They arouse in children fantasies of sadistic joy in seeing other
people punished over and over again while you yourself remain im-
mune. We have called it the Superman complex."

Gaines sat with Stuart and studied Wertham, whom he had never
before seen at work. As Wertham spoke, Gaines's right leg rattled violently. At one point, Wertham took a dig at one of EC's tamer stories,
a morality tale intended to protest bigotry toward Mexican immigrants. Wertham lambasted the story's use of the word "Spic," which
the writers, Gaines and Feldstein, had put in the mouths of the story's
heavies. "I think Hitler was a beginner compared to the comic-book
industry," Wertham said. "They get the children much younger. They
teach them race hatred at the age of four, before they can read."

Speaking to Stuart or, perhaps, just to himself, Gaines said, in a full
voice, "That's it—I'm going to get that bastard."

Before closing his testimony, Wertham noted that *Seduction of the
Innocent* had been chosen to be a Book of the Month Club selection,
and he followed the point with a question: "Will this book be distrib-

uted, or will the sinister hand of these corrupters of children, of this comic-book industry, will they prevent distribution?"

As Wertham stepped down, Gaines was called to give his testimony. He put his briefcase on the witness table, took out his prepared statement, and sat, clutching the papers. When he began to speak, Hendrickson scribbled notes, and Kefauver leaned back in his chair, taking Gaines in. If a television camera had zoomed in on Kefauver's left hand, it would have shown his thumb slowly rubbing his fingertips. "Gentlemen, I would like to make a short statement," Gaines said. He gave his name and cited his credentials, including his certification to teach in New York City public high schools, and he began to read. "I am here as a voluntary witness. I asked for and was given this chance to be heard.

"Two decades ago my late father was instrumental in starting the comic magazine industry. He edited the first few issues of the first modern comic magazine, *Famous Funnies*."

Kefauver interrupted. "*Famous* what?"

"*Funnies*," Gaines answered.

"Go ahead," Kefauver said.

"My father was proud of the industry he helped found," Gaines continued. "He was bringing enjoyment to millions of people. The heritage he left is the vast comic-book industry, which employs thousands of writers, artists, engravers, and printers. It has weaned hundreds of thousands of children from pictures to the printed word. It has stirred their imagination, given them an outlet for their problems and frustrations, but most important, given them millions of hours of entertainment. But it is nothing more nor nothing less than a comic magazine."

Once again, Gaines sought to employ his father's legacy to underlay his own claim to legitimacy, despite the fact that the story of EC's origins under M. C. Gaines and its radical turn of course under his son dramatized the very essence of parents' fears about comic books: that they represented a generational divide; that their kids might grow up and go their own way, undoing everything their parents had believed in and worked to build. "I publish comic magazines in addition to *Picture Stories from the Bible*," Gaines explained. "For example, I publish horror comics. I was the first publisher in these United States to publish horror comics. I am responsible, I started them.

"Some may not like them," Gaines pointed out, and he paused without lifting his eyes from his statement. "That's a matter of personal taste." Gaines paused again, and he rolled his tongue in his mouth and chewed it for a moment. "It would be just as difficult to explain the harmless thrill of a horror story to a Dr. Wertham as it would be to explain the sublimity of love to a frigid old maid.

"My father was proud of the comics he published, and I am proud of the comics I publish. We use the best writers, the finest artists, we spare nothing to make each magazine, each story, each page, a work of art."

Gaines never looked up from his statement, but his voice rose. "The comic magazine is one of the few remaining pleasures that a person may buy for a dime today. Pleasure is what we sell, entertainment, reading enjoyment. Entertaining reading has never harmed anyone. Men of good will, free men, should be very grateful for one sentence in the statement made by Federal Judge John M. Woolsey when he lifted the ban on *Ulysses*. Judge Woolsey said, 'It is only with the normal person that the law is concerned. May I repeat,' he said; 'it is only with the normal person that the law is concerned.'

"Our American children are for the most part normal children. They are bright children, but those who want to prohibit comic magazines seem to see dirty, sneaky, perverted monsters who use the comics as a blueprint for action. Perverted little monsters are few and far between. They don't read comics. The chances are most of them are in schools for retarded children.

"What are we afraid of? Are we afraid of our own children? Do we forget that they are citizens, too, and entitled to select what to read or do? We think our children are so evil, simpleminded, that it takes a story of murder to set them to murder"—Gaines's voice grew stronger—"a story of robbery to set them to robbery?"

Stuart, who was especially proud of his help with that passage, cheered Gaines on silently and sensed him beginning to overcome his nerves, though he wished Gaines would look up from the page and stop rattling his leg. A few minutes later, at the conclusion of his prepared remarks, Gaines lay his papers on the desk and addressed the committee off the cuff, though he still tended to stare down, now at the tabletop. "I would like to discuss, if you bear with me a moment more, something which Dr. Wertham provoked me into," Gaines said. "Dr. Wertham, I am happy to say, I have just caught in a half-truth, and I am very indignant about it. He said there is a magazine now on the stands preaching racial intolerance. The magazine he is referring to is my magazine. What he said, as much as he said, was true. There do appear in this magazine such materials as 'Spic,' 'Dirty Mexican,' but Dr. Wertham did not tell you what the plot of the story was. This is one of the series of stories designed to show the evils of race prejudice and mob violence, in this case against Mexican Catholics. Previous stories in this same magazine have dealt with anti-Semitism, and anti-Negro feelings, evils of dope addiction and development of juvenile delinquents. This is one of the most brilliantly written stories that I have ever had the pleasure to publish. I was very proud of it, and to find it being used in such a nefarious way made me quite angry."

Junior counsel Herbert Beaser, ignoring the substance of Gaines's charge against Wertham, picked up that its premise suggested a contradiction in Gaines's portrayal of the comic medium's potential. Were comics "nothing more nor nothing less" than a vehicle for "entertainment," "enjoyment," and "harmless thrills," as Gaines had claimed in his prepared remarks; or were they capable of affecting their readers' attitudes about serious matters such as racial and ethnic prejudice, as he implied in his impromptu comments? "Why do you say you cannot at the same time and in the same manner use the pages of your magazine to get a message which would affect children adversely—that is, to have an effect upon their doing these deeds of violence or sadism, whatever is depicted?" Beaser asked.

"Because no message is being given to them," Gaines replied. Lowering his head and his voice, he tried to explain how EC varied its story treatment to signal distinctions of intent. In the case of "a story with a message," Gaines explained, the "preaching" was "spelled out carefully in the captions." He was backing onto shaky ground, and he began to stumble. In truth, all of EC's stories used the narrative mode almost exclusively, and none was polemical in its word balloons or captions.

After several minutes of foundering debate with Beaser on the fine points of comic-book captioning, Gaines changed tactics. Echoing Wertham, intentionally or not, Gaines emphasized his years of experience with the material in question, and he noted that EC conducted tests of its stories with sample readers. The existence of such tests surprised the committee, as it did Lyle Stuart and others from EC who were watching the hearings at home. "It has been my experience in writing these stories for the last six or seven years that whenever we have tested them out on kids, or teenagers, or adults, no one ever associates himself with someone who is going to be put upon," Gaines said. "They always associate themselves with the one who is doing the putting upon."

Hendrickson interjected, "You do test them out on children, do you?"

"Yes," Gaines answered.

Beaser followed up, "How do you do that?"

Fortunately for Gaines, Hennings interrupted, recognizing an opportune time to bring up the story of Lucy, the child murderess. "Is that one of your series, the pictures of the two in the electric chair, the little girl down in the corner?"

"Yes."

"As we understood from what we heard of that story," Hennings said, "the little girl is not being put upon there, is she? She is triumphant apparently, that is insofar as we heard the relation of the story this morning."

"If I may explain," Gaines replied, "the reader does not know that until the last panel, which is one of the things we try to do in our stories, is have an O. Henry ending for each story . . . You will see that a child leads a miserable life in the six or seven pages. It is only on the last page she emerges triumphant."

"As a result of murder and perjury, she emerges as triumphant?" Hennings asked.

"That is right."

The committee's chief counsel, Herbert Hannoch, interjected: "Is that the O. Henry finish?"

"Yes," Gaines answered.

"In other words," Hannoch said, "everybody reading that would think this girl would go to jail. So the O. Henry finish changes that, makes her a wonderful-looking girl?"

"No one knows she did it until the last panel," Gaines said.

"You think it does them a lot of good to read these things?" Hannoch asked.

"I don't think it does them a bit of good," Gaines replied, "but I don't think it does them a bit of harm, either." From his opening defense of comic books as a creative mechanism for airing problems, venting frustrations, and stirring imaginations, Gaines had resorted to dismissing comics as inert, neither harmful nor of any notable benefit.

As the committee continued its questioning, parrying with Gaines over details and abstractions, he weakened. His head slumped down to eight or ten inches from the witness table, and his leg no longer rattled. Stuart, who knew Gaines as well as anyone (other than Gaines's mother and, perhaps, Feldstein), could tell Gaines was fighting to remain not only lucid, but awake. "He was losing it," said Stuart.

Recalling this point in his testimony, Gaines later explained,

"Dexedrine keeps you hyper, but when it wears off, it leaves you like a limp rag. Halfway through, it wore off, and I sat there like a punch-drunk fighter, getting pummeled."

A few minutes later, counsel Beaser pressed Gaines on the connected matters of comics' potential influence on their readers and Gaines's sense of responsibility as a publisher. "Let me get the limits as far as what you put into your magazine," Beaser said. "Is the sole test of what you would put into your magazine whether it sells? Is there any limit you can think of that you would not put in a magazine because you thought a child should not see or read about it?"

"No," Gaines answered. "I wouldn't say that there is any limit for the reason you outlined. My only limits are bounds of good taste, what I consider good taste."

"Then you think a child cannot in any way, in any way, shape, or manner, be hurt by anything that a child reads or sees?"

"I don't believe so."

"There would be no limit actually to what you put in the magazines?" Beaser asked.

"Only within the bounds of good taste," Gaines said.

"Your own good taste and salability?"

"Yes."

Kefauver interrupted from the bench, holding up a copy of a recent issue of *Crime SuspenStories*. The cover, by Johnny Craig, showed the severed head of an attractive blond woman, dangling by the hair in the hand grip of the killer. "Here is your May 22 issue," Kefauver said. "This seems to be a man with a bloody ax holding a woman's head up, which has been severed from her body. Do you think that is in good taste?"

"Yes, sir, I do, for the cover of a horror comic," Gaines said. "A cover in bad taste, for example, might be defined as holding the head a little higher so that the neck could be seen dripping blood from it and moving the body over a little further so that the neck of the body could be seen to be bloody."

"You have blood coming out of her mouth," Kefauver noted.

"A little."

"Here is blood on the ax," Kefauver said. "I think most adults are shocked by that." Holding up another issue of *Crime SuspenStories*, Kefauver continued, "This is the July one. It seems to be a man with a woman in a boat, and he is choking her to death here with a crowbar. Is that in good taste?"

"I think so," Gaines said.

Hannoch asked, "How could it be worse?"

Hennings interrupted. "I don't think it is really the function of our committee to argue with this gentleman. I believe that he has given us about the sum and substance of his philosophy . . ."

Joe Simon and Jack Kirby were watching the hearings with their friend and collaborator, the comics writer Jack Oleck, at Simon's apartment in Midtown Manhattan. At this moment in Gaines's testimony, Kirby groaned and Simon chided Gaines through the TV screen: "Stupid, stupid, stupid!"

What a pair of disembodied hands were to the organized-crime hearings, a severed head was to the delinquency sessions. Among the many who watched the hearings of April 21, 1954, on television, the memory of record was that of Estes Kefauver holding up the cover of *Crime SuspenStories*, only to be told by a wan, bespectacled comic-book publisher that the drawing of an ax murder was in good taste by his standards. On April 22, the second day of the hearings, *The New York Times* ran a page-one story centered on Gaines: "No Harm in Horror, Comics Issuer Says." (Of the piece's twenty-one paragraphs, thirteen dealt with Gaines and his testimony, and one concerned Wertham.) In the *New York Post*, columnist Max Lerner wrote:

> The high point of the day was William M. Gaines . . . When Gaines defended as "good taste" a particularly gory comic book cover, showing the severed head of a woman held aloft by a man with an ax, he was saying that every publisher of comic books is a moral as well as

an aesthetic law unto himself. This means that society is a jungle—a proposition we cannot accept.

Newspapers in places as far from Foley Square as Lima, Ohio, published editorials decrying Gaines's testimony, and *Time* and *Newsweek* both recounted the "good taste" incident in detail.

Bill Gaines, in a few brief sentences about a horror-comic cover, had crystallized the whole controversy over comic books. Nothing in more than a decade and a half of debate over comics had the impact of Gaines's statement that a certain amount of blood, shown a particular way, was in good taste for a horror comic. The issue at stake, Gaines and his inquisitors made clear, was not really juvenile crime or mental health or literacy or the effect of comic-book printing on the eyes, but the idea of *taste*—the proposition that aesthetic values are relative. The threat implicit in Gaines's terse, cryptic comments about taste lay not in whether any amount of blood was good or bad, but in the fact that he claimed the prerogative to decide the matter on his own terms. What was right for one book or one reader might be wrong for another of a different orientation or of a different age, Gaines suggested. In fact, he made the point explicit in the "Are You a Red Dupe?" ad that had incited Hendrickson to rage on the Senate floor. "It isn't that they don't like comics for THEM!" Gaines wrote. "They don't like them for YOU!" To the parents of comic-book readers during the postwar years, crime and horror comics seemed vivid evidence of a generation going wild through its tastes not only in reading material, but also in dress, language, and music. Indeed, within a year of the Hendrickson committee hearings, a new, musical threat to the cultural status quo, rock and roll, would emerge, and it would come to replace comics as a target of public enmity.

The hearings on comic books and juvenile delinquency, like the earlier sessions on organized crime, came across as judicial proceedings rather than legislative inquiries. (At the 1951 crime sessions, one senator, Herbert R. O'Conor of Maryland, had accidentally referred to one witness as "the defendant.") Not just Bill Gaines, but the whole of comic books appeared to be on trial, and the phantoms of the crime hearings seemed to incriminate them by association. Foley Square, Estes Kefauver, cameras and lights, talk of murder and bloodshed and vice. Gaines soon realized what had happened. "It was a difficult experience, because all of a sudden you find that everyone you know kind of regards you as a criminal," he recalled. "There had been the famous Kefauver hearings before this, with criminals and the Mafia, and they were very big. So all of a sudden we comic publishers, and me in particular, find ourselves classed in with Frank Costello and all the other crooks dragged up before Kefauver. Kefauver technically was not the head of the comics committee, but Kefauver was pretty rough on *me*."

Gaines, bedridden with stomach pains for days after the hearings, did not return to work until Monday, April 26. Having lost a good ten pounds during the previous week, he invited Feldstein to lunch and found an unexpected benefit of his Foley Square ordeal. The waiters at Patrissy's seemed especially attentive, and they brought a full plate of biscotti for dessert, on the house. Feldstein supposed that word of the hearings had spread around Little Italy, and Gaines was now presumed to be in with the Mob.

14. We've Had It!

Two flashpoints of postwar paranoia coincided on April 22, 1954. Both took the form of U.S. Senate hearings, and both were front-page news across the country that day. As Robert C. Hendrickson concluded his inquiry into comic books and juvenile delinquency, in New York, Joseph McCarthy began his probe into alleged Communist infiltration of the Army, in Washington. Both sessions were decisive, but in contrary ways. The comic-book hearings boosted a crusade on the ascent, setting into motion a whirl of events that would soon prove devastating to the comics industry, while the Army hearings eroded a movement in decline, discrediting McCarthy and his school of vitriolic Red-baiting. Within a year of the dual hearings, McCarthy's political career would essentially be over, and so would be the creative careers of a great many of the people who made comic books.

Soon after the Hendrickson hearings and the nearly simultaneous publication of *Seduction of the Innocent*, comics artists and writers began to feel their effects. Bob Oksner, a specialist in humor and light comic art, was doing public-service features for National/DC ("Get a Box Seat to Nature's Wonders," "How Safe Is Your Driving?") that spring. He and his wife had recently moved to Teaneck, New Jersey, and visited a local rabbi to discuss the prospect of joining his synagogue. When Oksner mentioned that he drew comic books, the rabbi froze and began to lecture him—"How can you do that? Look what you're doing to the children!" as Oksner recalled. He and his wife left the temple without joining.

Dick Ayers, an inker who was working on Western and science-fiction comics (as well as some horror titles), mostly for Timely, had a daughter then in the third grade, and she asked her parents for books to donate to a school fund drive. Her father offered a box of comics, including some he had autographed specially for the cause. The school returned the books with a message that they should not be sold but be burned. Shortly thereafter, a son of Ayers had to give an oral report about his family, and he lied about his father's occupation, saying he worked in a factory, to avoid embarrassment.

Weeks after the hearings, the comic-book controversy remained on the lead pages of newspapers around the country. In upstate New York, on May 10, the *Buffalo Evening News* began a five-part public-service series, "Horror for Young Readers—All for the Price of a Dime" (likely inspired by *The Hartford Courant*'s "Depravity for Children—10 Cents a Copy!"). Written by the paper's Washington-bureau reporter, Arthur L. Davis, it essentially reprinted selections from the testimony of the major witnesses at the Hendrickson hearings, apparently drawn from a transcript provided to Davis in the capital. Hendrickson, delighted with the series, read from it on the Senate floor and had it entered into the *Congressional Record*.

In Ohio, two weeks later, the *Cleveland Press* launched a four-part series on "blood, violence and sex" in comic books. Fixing on the local angle, reporter Bud Weidenthal purchased a selection of horror, romance, and crime comics at area after-school hangouts, and he described the most lurid contents in luxurious detail. (The first entry of the series was illustrated by word balloons with dialogue such as "First we'll get rid of this pop gun and then I'm going to beat you within an inch of your life" and "Tom . . . Dick . . . Harry . . . They came and went. I had my laughs and my good times. Men were a dime-a-dozen to me . . .") Prodded by the series, the Cleveland police prosecutor, Bernard J. Conway, conducted his own study of comics on sale in the city, reading some three hundred books confiscated from news dealers. Conway made a "purge list" of twenty-three titles (among them, *Crime and Punishment, Chamber of Thrills, Web of Evil*, and *Teen-Age Romance*) and instructed the police force to remove any copies of them found in Cleveland stores. News dealers who persisted in displaying the comics were subject to arrest for violation of a standing city ordinance that prohibited the display of "literature unfit for juveniles," Conway said. The statute called for penalties of up to $500 for first offenses and for second violations up to six months in the city workhouse. "Arrests are Ordered in Sex Comic Sales—Objectionable Books Will Be Listed for 'Get-Tough' Campaign," warned the *Press* in a banner headline across the top of page one.

The *Press* ran only one letter of dissent from a reader, John M. Mosberger:

> I think the editor will remember that the Jesse James books, those on the Dalton gang, the Nick Carter series, and others too numerous to mention were the equal of the comic books of today in horror—in fact, surpassed them . . . Furthermore, editor, the horror movies of the silent days . . . would make the comic books of today look like ordinary stuff by comparison.
>
> The major contributor toward child delinquency is not the comic book, books on sex and crime, horror movies, but it is the modern trend of husbands and wives both working . . . Delinquency soars as more and more married women take jobs or positions in factory or office.

Robert C. Hendrickson's committee continued to investigate delinquency (and received its own share of letters advancing Mosberger's theory). Encouraged by the public response to the April hearings, Hendrickson decided to schedule an additional session on comic books, to be held in New York that June. Gaines, wounded but still defiant, wrote Hendrickson a letter of protest, in which he groused about his treatment at the April hearings and charged that the committee's undeclared objective was to damage not only Gaines, but the whole comic-book business. Rationalizing his exhaustion at the hearings, Gaines pointed out that the time of his testimony had been pushed back several hours to accommodate Wertham:

> I need not tell you that this was far from the kid-glove patience accorded Dr. Wertham—who spoke for hours on end—much of his contribution being obvious gush designed solely to increase the sale of his book . . . The headline-seeking carnival staged by your committee has given fuel to those in our society who want to tar with the censor's brush. As a result, my business together with the entire comics industry has been severely damaged. Since this was so obviously an objective of your committee, I trust it will give you some satisfaction.

Gaines also initiated a retaliatory campaign against Hendrickson's efforts: a new house ad calling for EC fans to rally in the comics' defense. Published in the fall issues of five EC comics, which appeared on the newsstands during the summer, and also printed in the bulletin mailed to the five thousand members of EC's house-run "Fan-Addicts Club," it said, in part:

A Special Editorial: This Is an Appeal for Action!

THE PROBLEM: Comics are under fire . . . horror and crime comics in particular. Due to the efforts of various "do-gooders" and "do-gooder" groups, a large segment of the public is being led to believe that certain comic magazines cause juvenile delinquency, warp the minds of America's youth, and affect the development of the personalities of those who read them . . . Eventually, everyone gets frightened. The newsdealer gets frightened. He removes the books from display. The wholesaler gets frightened. He refuses shipments. The congressmen get frightened . . . November is coming! They start an investigation. This wave of hysteria has seriously threatened the very existence of the whole comic magazine industry.

WE BELIEVE: Your editors sincerely believe that the claim of these crusaders . . . that comics are bad for children . . . is *nonsense* . . . We [also] believe that those who oppose comics are a small minority. Yet this minority is causing the hysteria. The voice of the *majority* . . . you who buy comics, read them, enjoy them, and are not harmed by them . . . has not been heard!

IT'S TIME THAT THE MAJORITY'S VOICE BE HEARD! It is time that the Senate Subcommittee hears from YOU . . . *each and every one of you!*

Of course, if you or your parents *disagree* with us, and believe that comics ARE bad, let your sentiments be known on that too! The important thing is that the Subcommittee hear from actual comic book readers and/or their parents, rather than from people who never read a comic magazine in their lives, but simply want to destroy them.

Hendrickson responded with an appeal to his own fan base, the Senate. He wrote an incendiary speech denouncing Gaines and defending his committee's ongoing study of comic books. "Recently, I received a vicious letter from one of the so-called comic-book publishers, who attacked the integrity of this subcommittee," Hendrickson noted. "The warped thinking as manifested by this letter, I believe, deserves reply on the floor of the Senate." After identifying Gaines and his company, Hendrickson quoted choice bits from Gaines's correspondence: "He said, with a certain degree of temerity, that the subcommittee is staging a 'headline-seeking carnival' with the express purpose of 'destroying the comic-book industry.' In one phase of his diatribe, this man charged that 'public blacklists' of comics have been set up in certain cities as a result of our hearings." Recounting in detail Gaines's testimony about taste, Hendrickson derided Gaines's "calm appraisal of his handiwork to the shocked incredulity of the subcommittee and spectators."

As for Gaines's "Appeal for Action," Hendrickson dismissed it as an attempt "to pressure us by getting hundreds of youngsters to write in protesting our inquiry. I have here a copy of a special bulletin which he has sent to thousands of American youngsters urging such action. Now, I do not object to youngsters writing to their Congressmen. In fact, I welcome it. But I do object to his inferring in this bulletin to thousands of young people that Congressional investigations are conducted because 'November is coming.' It's malicious, Mr. President, to attempt to discredit the integrity of the Senate in the eyes of American youth. And I deeply resent it."

To illustrate the benefit of his inquiry, Hendrickson pointed out, "Some thirty titles have been discontinued as a direct result of our hearings." He concluded, "No attack upon this subcommittee by a publisher whose own product evoked consternation and revulsion at our hearings can deter us from shedding additional light upon any fact of mass communications media that may even remotely be contributing to the present, frightening juvenile delinquency scourge."

The second hearings on comic books by the Hendrickson committee on juvenile delinquency were held on Friday, June 4, in familiar quarters, room 110 of the Foley Square courthouse. Unlike the previous sessions and the Kefauver committee crime hearings before them, however, these were largely technical in their orientation and not televised. Only half the committee members were present: Hendrickson and Thomas C. Hennings, along with Richard Clendenen, the committee director, Herbert Beaser, who had replaced Herbert Hannoch as chief counsel, and a few members of their staffs. Five of the

eight witnesses (three distributors, the chair of a news dealers association, and a drugstore owner) were involved in the hearings' principal
area of the inquiry, comic-book distribution and sales; one was a colleague of Hendrickson in the New Jersey Bar Association; the other,
New York State Assemblyman James A. FitzPatrick, a champion of
legislation on comics who had wanted to participate in the April probe
but had had another commitment at the time. Calling the hearings to
order, Hendrickson established the function of the sessions as a contin-
uation of the delinquency committee's investigation into "lascivious
and lustful crime and horror" comics. "The response to our earlier
hearings into horror comic books has been extremely gratifying to the
chairman," Hendrickson said. "Today we are going to look into the
matter of selling and distribution practices, and into certain proposals
which have been advanced as helpful in combating the detrimental influence upon youth of certain types of publications." That some
comics influenced young people and that, further, their influence was
one of detriment was now a given, no longer open for discussion.

Much of the day's testimony was devoted to the subject of "tie-in"
sales, wherein distributors supplied magazines to news sellers in bulk
shipments, choosing the publications for the sellers. This system, in
some instances, imposed pressure upon news dealers to carry whatever publications the distributors, for whatever reasons, might promote. At the June 4 hearings, all eight witnesses assented on the need
for both news dealers and distributors to select their merchandise
with greater discrimination, to purge the newsstands of objectionable
comic books. The only disagreement involved the delicate matter of
standards: Who would define objectionableness, and how would ad-
herence to standards, once established, be enforced? Those in the
news industry argued for voluntary self-restraint; FitzPatrick called
for more governmental intervention.

The first witness of the day, FitzPatrick came with a lengthy prepared statement in which he retold the first story in the infamous premiere issue of *Panic*, "My Gun Is the Jury," describing the drawings

and reciting the dialogue, virtually panel by panel. Clearly unaware that the work was a parody intended to ridicule Mickey Spillane and the readers of his sadomasochistic pulp, FitzPatrick quoted the word balloons as evidence of the comic's own aesthetic. "'I make myself sick . . . But those idiots out there buy this stuff. They eat it up. They love it! The gorier, the better! This . . . and sex.' Now, if there ever was a complete and utter demonstration of the reason for the publication of this book, I respectfully submit, Senator, that there it is, and there it is in print," FitzPatrick said. He moved on through the same issue of *Panic*—"skipping over this rot, and I call it rot without any reservation whatsoever"—FitzPatrick stopped and lingered on Will Elder's dizzy take-off on "The Night Before Christmas," the original text of which he called "one of the most wonderful poems that we have ever had in our entire history," the new visual treatment of which he depicted as "complete and utter rot." Stressing, repeatedly, that this work was published by Tiny Tot Comics, FitzPatrick claimed that the publisher, Gaines, "himself [said] . . . the sole purpose of this publication" was "sex and horror."

The best salve for such rot, FitzPatrick concluded, was law. "Community programs to curb sales are springing up . . . People are waking up at last, but there is still much to be done," he said. "I feel that it is high time for our people, the Congress and the courts, to awaken to the realization that the framers of the Constitution could not have intended the great guarantees of the freedom of the press as license for irresponsible publishers to contaminate the minds and morals of our children for profit. We need much more effective legislation both on the state and federal level."

In the weeks to follow, FitzPatrick's hopes began to be realized. Civic groups took further action against controversial comic books, and appeals for new legislation on comics mounted. On June 23, Massachusetts Attorney General George Fingold announced that he had negotiated an agreement among news distributors in the Greater Boston area to "halt circulation" of objectionable comics; in addition,

Fingold said, he planned to meet the following week with additional distributors to discuss a statewide curb on the books. Four days later, the National Sheriffs' Association voted, at its annual meeting in Washington, D.C., for a resolution "condemning" horror comics and urging that their sale be curtailed by regulation. Five days after that, the National Council of Juvenile Court judges, at its convention in Colorado Springs, called for legislation "outlawing" those "comic books and horror magazines depicting crime, sadism, vulgar sex, and horror scenes"; such materials, the judges decreed, "contribute toward the moral breakdown of our children today." After another five days, Mrs. Theodore S. Chapman, president of the General Federation of Women's Clubs, announced at a press conference that she was initiating a "war" on "lurid" comic books; through the organization's eleven million members, the federation would implore publishers to discontinue "gruesome" comics and solicit state and municipal leaders to enact legislation "to prevent the distribution of offending comics," Chapman said. Two days later, on July 10, the California Congress of Parents and Teachers agreed, at its annual meeting, to lobby the California board of managers for "legislative action to outlaw" comic books "that depict sadistic crime, perversion and vulgar sex and horror themes"; meanwhile, the group would petition the national organization of Parent-Teacher Associations to mobilize its chapters across the country to act against objectionable comics. Before summer's end, more organizations, from the Ladies Auxiliary of the Military Order of the Purple Heart to the criminal law division of the American Bar Association, would join the crescendo of condemnations of lurid comics and calls for government intervention to protect American youth from them.

"There was a sense of desperation in the air, and it was contagious," remembered Dr. Rocco Motto, a Southern California psychiatrist, who had been called as an expert witness in a suit over the Los Angeles County law restricting the sale of crime comics. "Parents had a genuine concern about the behavior of adolescents and young adults, because they were not meeting their parents' expectations. Of course, these parents had forgotten that it was perfectly appropriate for adolescents to rebel against their parents. All parents forget that . . . but, in this period, the situation was intensified by the fact that there were these new modes of popular culture—comic books and television, and, of course, the movies, still, although they weren't new—[which] glamorized rebels, and young people were emulating these rebels in the comic books and elsewhere. As a result, parents and others—not only parents—were desperate for a solution, and comic books were the perfect target . . . [because] they had no credible defenders.

"When I decided to say some of these things [in court], people were shocked, because all they had heard was that comic books were doing dreadful things and something had to be done about them." In the case at which Motto testified on behalf of a news dealer arrested for selling crime comics, the opposing attorneys called as its expert witness Dr. Hilde Mosse, Wertham's associate at the Lafargue Clinic.

Artists and writers felt the pressure mounting against comics. Many, such as Joe Simon, John Severin, Carmine Infantino, and Jim Mooney, saw their friends shrinking in numbers. Mooney, for instance, kept a cabin in the Catskill Mountains, near Woodstock, but rarely discussed with the local folks how he made his living. In the summer of 1954, Stan Lee, Mooney's editor at Timely, came to visit the artist for a weekend, and one of Mooney's area friends dropped by. The fellow, a dealer in hunting equipment, engaged Mooney in conversation about antique rifles, and Lee interrupted, noting that, as a comic-book editor, he had expertise in weapons. "The guy blew his stack," remembered Mooney. "He said, 'You do comic books? That is absolutely criminal—totally reprehensible. You should go to jail for the crime you're committing,' and on and on." The man left Mooney's cabin and never returned. Some years later, Mooney learned that the dealer had been shipping arms to soldiers of fortune in South America. "The guy was helping who-knows-who to kill how many people, and [he thought] we were worse for making comic books."

Mike Esposito, who was running a small comics-production shop with a fellow artist, Ross Andru, found his wife harassed by her friends about his work. "Get out of that business—do anything, join the post office," she told him, as Esposito recalled.

Bill Gaines, still as proud of EC's comics as he had said in his opening testimony on April 21 and still confident that he was serving the legitimate interests of his young readers, found the atmosphere of discontent with crime and horror comics debilitating, economically as well as intellectually and emotionally. Comic-book wholesalers and news dealers, having been the focus of state legislation and a Senate subcommittee hearing, now faced the ire of a horde of civic groups. EC, which used a relatively small and weak distributor, Leader News, was losing sales to dealers increasingly reluctant to carry comics that might antagonize customers or provoke local authorities. "We were getting bundles of comics sent back unopened," Al Feldstein recalled. "Bill was worried—this was his livelihood, his baby. He had to do something, but he didn't know what, and he was a little gun-shy after what happened to him at the hearings."

Lyle Stuart, who was shy in the sight of no gun, as he had demonstrated by taking on Walter Winchell, encouraged Gaines to fight the polemical battle over comics with more and better polemics. Stuart suggested that Gaines try to build a coalition of comics publishers; it could fund authoritative research to disprove Wertham's charges and conduct a public-relations campaign to restore confidence in all comic books, including EC's. One of Stuart's ideas was to commission a study on comics by Eleanor and Sheldon Gluek, Harvard researchers who had published extensively on juvenile delinquency and who attributed the phenomenon primarily to upbringing and the home environment.

"I said, 'Bill, we both know that something has to be done, or we're dead. We don't want government censorship, and that's around the corner. Let's get together with other publishers and see if we can put together a plan,'" Stuart remembered. "Bill was interested, but he was nervous about it. I said, 'You pay for the lunches, and I'll set it up.'"

Stuart proceeded to arrange a series of intimate, exploratory luncheons with several publishers, at Toots Shor's restaurant, the show-business hang-out in the theater district. They went well enough to encourage Gaines to invite all the comics publishers in New York to meet at once. He reserved a hotel room and mailed an open invitation. It began:

Dear Fellow Comic Book Publisher:

If fools rush in where angels fear to tread, then I suppose EC is being pretty foolish. We may get our fingers burned and our toes stepped on. Be that as it may, it seems to me that someone has to take the initiative.

As Gaines later recalled, "To everybody's surprise, nine publishers showed up at the first meeting. Thirteen at the second. By the fourth meeting, the organization was an industry-wide movement and was ready for formal incorporation." Thirty-eight publishers, distributors, printers, and engravers attended that fourth session, held at the Biltmore Hotel in Manhattan on August 17, 1954. Elliot Caplan, a writer and editor at Toby Press (and brother of *Li'l Abner* artist Al Capp) served as chairman, with John Goldwater, publisher of *Archie* comics, in charge of the organizational committee. The assembly had evolved into a comics-industry trade group, a replacement for the ineffectual Association of Comics Magazine Publishers; the charter members decided to call themselves the Comics Magazine Association of America, and they decided, as one of their first orders of business, to establish a new code of standards for comic-book content, along with a system of enforcement to be directed by an unimpeachable independent overseer. The officers of the group agreed to offer the position to Fredric Wertham, and they began hammering out the terms of their content code. Among the early recommendations were prohibitions on the words "horror" and "terror" in comic-book titles.

Bill Gaines, the publisher of *The Vault of Horror* and *The Crypt of Terror*, rose from his seat. He said, "This is not what I had in mind," and he walked out.

"It was always an ironic thing to me that I was the guy who started the damn association, and they turned around, and the first thing they did was ban the words "weird," "horror," and "terror" from any comic magazine . . . Those were my three big words." (In fact, the group never limited the use of the word "weird" in comics.) When the CMAA incorporated, on September 7, 1954, its members included twenty-six publishers (among them, National/DC, Timely/Atlas/ Marvel, Archie, Harvey, Gleason, Quality, and St. John) and nineteen companies involved in technical operations and distribution. Only three major comics publishers had declined to join: Dell, whose juvenile humor books were well established as wholesome; Gilberton, publishers of *Classics Illustrated*, whose link to serious literature imparted respectability (and whose editors might have realized that the high quotient of bloodshed in its adaptations of Shakespeare could pose a challenge to the CMAA); and EC, which could not function in an environment inhospitable to horror and terror. Gaines and Stuart both despised John Goldwater, who was elected charter president of the association, and Goldwater was understood to resent Gaines for *Mad*'s portrayal of his star character as a juvenile delinquent in the comic's parody, "Starchie."

By the second week of September, the CMAA had drafted and ratified a "code of ethics," had retained a full-time director to enforce it, and had allocated an annual budget of $100,000 for a staff, facilities, and equipment to support the code. The CMAA declined to hire Wertham (or Wertham rejected the offer; the facts are not clear) and instead retained Charles F. Murphy, a forty-four-year-old New York City municipal-court judge, as code administrator. Stolid and handsome, Murphy could have passed for a cousin of Henry E. Schultz (whom the CMAA employed as chief counsel). Murphy's résumé showed a fitting interest in young people: He had created and produced a weekly radio program, "Youth Talks It Over," and ran a private organization, Teen Plan, Inc., to help high-schoolers find work. "He was as clean as they come," said Dick Giordano, an artist for Charlton, who came to work closely with Murphy after the Comics Code went into effect. To introduce the new face of the comics industry with appropriate panache, the CMAA hired the Ruder & Finn public-relations agency to stage a press conference on September 16.

Bill Gaines, knowing the CMAA's plans, announced a press conference of his own for September 14. It was held in the reception area of the EC offices, rearranged for the occasion with Gaines's desk moved from his office into the center of the room. Gaines sat at the desk and gazed straight ahead as he fidgeted with a few comic books in a pile before him. He was wearing his usual horn-rimmed glasses, a plain gray suit, a white shirt, and a dark bow tie, looking very much like the chemistry teacher he might have become, had he not inherited his father's business. Hanging directly behind him was a framed oil painting of a science-fiction scene done by Al Feldstein—a bleak image of the barren, crater-pocked surface of the moon, occupied only by a small party of astronauts and a rocket ship poised to blast off. If you stood a few feet in front of Gaines's desk and looked at him, Gaines would appear to be sitting on the moon with the ship behind him. To his left, on his desktop, was a rack displaying the covers of twelve EC comics—all his titles except the war and the humor books. Gaines's lips were curled in a pouty frown. "In January of 1950, I published the first horror comic magazine ever published in America," he said. "The magazines were quite successful. Reader enthusiasm was reflected in high sales. At one time there were over a hundred imitations on the newsstands.

"I have decided now to discontinue all horror and crime comics. This decision will be put into immediate effect." Gaines took a couple of the EC comics from the rack on his desk and tore them apart.

"In recent months," he continued, "there has been much clamor against horror and crime comics based on a premise that horror and crime comics stimulate juvenile delinquency, a premise that has never been proved, and which in fact has been refuted by prominent psychiatrists and other experts.

"In many cities wholesalers and dealers are reluctant to distribute or display horror and crime comics . . . Although print orders have been cut, our line is still a profitable one and our horror and crime comics are still making money . . . But EC has always been the leader. And so once again we are taking the lead, this time in discontinuing crime and horror. We are doing it not for business reasons so much as because this seems to be what the American parents want—and the American parents should be served.

"We hope that, as they always have, other publishers will follow our lead and discontinue crime and horror. If this happens, our own financial sacrifice in taking this step will be justified by the renewed good public feelings toward comics." Gaines shifted into an attack of the new comics association, which had not yet been announced, charging the group with hypocrisy for allowing horror stories to be published in comics with benign titles and cover art. "In other words, if comic publishers are to police their own industry, we must be, like Caesar's wife, above suspicion," he said. "The public doesn't want horror and crime comics and so we should not fool parents by putting innocuous titles and pictures of clowns on the covers of the magazines and then telling them that things have been cleaned up."

Gaines went on to announce that EC, without participation in the new association, was developing a "new line" of comics, "which will hit the newsstands early in 1955 [and] will, we believe, meet favor with comics' most angry critics. We are striving to put out comics which will offend no one—which will without losing entertainment value— be known as a clean, clean line." The decision represented $40,000 in lost revenue on combined circulation of two million copies per year,

Gaines said, adding that he was planning to invest $250,000 in development of new comics.

It was a scene with everything EC always delivered: shocks, suspense, flights of creative fancy, death, and a twist ending. Just five months after Gaines had faced down the U.S. Senate, defending not only his comics but the privilege of their creators and their readers to defy prevailing opinion, he capitulated on the very grounds upon which he had fought: taste. He surrendered to the parental authority he had defied ever since he had taken over his father's company, killing the comics he had always held dear as his own creation. The decision, which had come only a day or two before he made it public, struck those closest to Gaines, Feldstein and Stuart, as both startling and inevitable. "It came as a shock at first, when he broke the news to us, before he made his statement," recalled Feldstein. "But I knew that he was doing the right thing. He was so completely hurt that he had been vilified so—he fought back and held on for a while, but nothing he did made any difference—things just got worse, and it hurt him terribly."

Gaines had few other options, perhaps no other, according to Feldstein. "He couldn't carry on, because he was losing money—every month, more boxes of books came back to us, unopened—and the comics authority was about to put him out of business, because they outlawed everything we were doing," Feldstein continued. "His only choice, really, was to give up—throw in the towel and try to start over. He was about to be killed, and what he did, really, was say, 'You can't kill me. I'm going to commit hari-kari.'"

Stuart, in rare agreement with Feldstein, thought Gaines had "made the ultimate sacrifice" of the work he treasured as "the best strategy to survive" as a comics publisher. "If the comics association had worked out as we had intended and John Goldwater hadn't steamrolled the thing and squeezed Bill out," said Stuart, "he might have stood a chance, but that was never going to happen. He was the enemy. He had to go. He was the human sacrifice." As Stuart remembered the days leading up to Gaines's press conference, "He had two plans, and he couldn't make up his mind. He was either going to drop the whole EC line, which is what he did, and start a new line, which is what he tried to do, or he was going to get out of the business altogether and open a wine shop."

In his public statement, Gaines disguised his desperation with noble talk and misrepresented his financial position. In the more intimate surroundings of his comic-book pages, Gaines laid bare his plight. The final issues of EC's horror and suspense titles included an editorial note under the headline "In Memoriam":

As a result of the hysterical, injudicious, and unfounded charges leveled at crime and horror comics, many retailers and wholesalers throughout the country have been intimidated into refusing to handle this type of magazine.

Although we at EC still believe, as we have in the past, that the charges against horror and crime comics are utter nonsense, there's no point in going into a defense of this kind of literature at the present time. Economically, our situation is acute. Magazines that do not get onto the newsstand do not sell. We are forced to capitulate. We give up. WE'VE HAD IT!

Naturally, with comic magazine censorship now a fact, we at EC look forward to an immediate drop in the crime and juvenile delinquency rate of the United States. We trust there will be fewer robberies, fewer murders, and fewer rapes!

Two days after Gaines's announcement, the Comics Magazine Association of America made its debut at a press conference in the organization's new offices on East Forty-second Street, off Fifth Avenue. "It will take a little time to set up the machinery to do this properly," said Charles F. Murphy, the Code administrator, "but I am confident that within a few months all books which do not pass our standards will not find their way into the homes of America." The process took very little time. About five weeks after Murphy's statement, on October 27, Goldwater, with Murphy at his side, announced that the Comics Code had been drafted and enacted. In fact, Murphy said that day, "It is not only ready but as of this very moment it is working . . . I can promise you now that it will be enforced." A staff of five censors was working full-time, screening comic-book layouts after the inking stage. The Comics Code, Murphy said proudly, "compares favorably with similar codes prepared for the radio, television and motion-picture industries."

In truth, the CMAA Comics Code was far more rigid and puritanical than the earlier ACMP comics code, FCC guidelines, or the Hays Office standards for motion pictures. Bill Gaines could never have participated in the CMAA, because it banned everything EC was publishing at that point, including *Mad* and *Panic*. The preamble for the Comics Code described its aspiration to be "a landmark in the history of self-regulation for the entire communications industry," and it succeeded: The Code was an unprecedented (and never surpassed) monument of self-imposed repression and prudery. A few highlights from the document's abundant stipulations:

- Policemen, judges, government officials and respected institutions shall never be presented in such a way as to create disrespect for established authority.
- No comics shall explicitly present the unique details and methods of a crime.
- No magazine shall use the word horror or terror in its title.
- All scenes of horror, excessive bloodshed, gory or gruesome crimes, depravity, lust, sadism, masochism shall not be permitted.
- All lurid, unsavory, gruesome illustrations shall be eliminated.
- Scenes dealing with, or instruments associated with walking dead, torture, vampires and vampirism, ghouls, cannibalism and werewolfism are prohibited.
- Profanity, obscenity, smut, vulgarity, or words or symbols which have acquired undesirable meanings are forbidden.

- Passion or romantic interest shall never be treated in such a way as to stimulate the lower and baser emotions.
- Suggestive and salacious illustration or suggestive posture is unacceptable.
- Females shall be drawn realistically without exaggeration of any physical qualities.
- Respect for parents, the moral code, and for honorable behavior shall be fostered.
- The treatment of love-romance stories shall emphasize the value of the home and the sanctity of marriage.

These are twelve of the Code's forty-one requirements for comic-book imagery, text, covers, titles, and advertisements. Anything the remaining twenty-nine items failed to note was essentially covered anyway, in Part C of the Code's General Standards, which stated, sweepingly, "All elements or techniques not specifically mentioned herein, but which are contrary to the spirit and intent of the Code, and are considered violations of good taste or decency, shall be prohibited."

Comics artists and writers accustomed to working in an environment with little or no creative oversight were unsure what to make of the Comics Code, at first. Was it essentially inconsequential—a political gimmick, like the ACMP code? If not, those who bothered to read it realized, the CMAA Code had the potential to transform their medium and make their lives miserable. The severity of its rules was a matter no more and no less serious than its administrator's interest in compliance. "One of the reasons I liked to do comic books was the freedom," said Walter Geier. "When the industry decided to reform—quote, unquote—they put out the Code, and we all got a copy of it. I read it over. Now, I had some experience with censorship in television, but I never saw anything like this. I said, 'Well, this is well and good, unless we're supposed to follow it. Then we may as well do coloring books, because the comic book as we know it is now dead.'"

The rule of most concern to Geier, as a writer and free-speech advocate, was the restriction on "disrespect for established authority" (item number five under "General Standards: Part A"), which cut to a source of the comics' appeal to young people. Geier thought of the prohibition as "insidious" and "fascist" and something worse in the eyes of 1950s America, "the kind of thing you'd expect in Russia." Still, he reserved judgment on the relevance of the Code until he could see it tested.

Created in the wake of the Senate hearings to discourage government action on comic books, the CMAA could not impede the march for comics legislation led by judges, sheriffs, PTAs, and civic groups in 1954. As *Time* pointed out on September 27, the "nationwide campaign against the books" was "running so strong" that Oklahoma City and Houston passed ordinances banning the sale of crime and horror comics around the same time that Bill Gaines canceled the EC line and John Goldwater announced the formation of CMAA. (Cheering on the action in Texas, an editorial in the *Houston Chronicle* praised the "banning [of] filthy comics which are a stench in the nose of every decent person.") Reiterating the scene of the severed head from Gaines's April testimony, *Time* described the new comics association as a society of "publishers of 'good' comics" who "hope to police themselves and avoid being put out of business." Cities and states were clearly reluctant to relinquish that police power. From autumn 1954 to the following summer, bills outlawing or limiting the sale of controversial comics progressed through the lawmaking bodies of two of the country's three largest cities, Los Angeles and Chicago, and more than a dozen states.

In Los Angeles, calls to replace the failed comics legislation of 1948 came from the zealous comic-book committee of the California Congress of Parents and Teachers, soon joined by the Los Angeles Board of Education. By mid-November 1954, the Los Angeles County Board of Supervisors moved to draw up an ordinance banning certain comics;

as defined by county supervisor Kenneth Hahn, such comics would be "those which belittle American institutions or traditions, those which depict details of methods of crime commission, those which incite prejudice against classes, races or creed and those which tend to emphasize vulgarity, obscenity or the glamorizing of crime and immoral behavior." The ordinance, which stipulated penalties of up to $500 and six months in the county jail, was submitted as an "emergency measure" and made law in February 1955. The following month, through further efforts of the California PTA group, the state senate approved legislation modeled on the New York State law prohibiting comic-book "tie-in" sales of crime and horror comics. Governor Goodwin Knight signed the bill on April 21, while the state legislature continued working on drafts of additional bills to restrict the sale of comics to minors.

Like most of the comics legislation in the works around the country at the time, the Los Angeles County measures and the California state bill advanced with little public debate; talks on comic books at meetings of PTAs and community groups ("By Knowing Worthy Publications," "Do You Know What Your Children Are Reading?") were essentially anticomic rallies; and newspaper columns on the subject ("Impoverishing the Youthful Mind," "Are Comic Books Menace or Nuisance?") tended to be severely critical, especially of horror and crime comics. As a Gallup Poll of the period showed, some 70 percent of American adults said they believed that comic books deserved to be blamed for juvenile delinquency. (Among those polled, 26 percent said comics deserved a "great deal" of blame; 31 percent, "some" blame; 12 percent, a little blame.) The pollster noted dryly in his interpretation of the results, "Older people are much more inclined to brand both comic books and TV-radio crime programs as factors contributing to juvenile delinquency than are young people." Those young people had few outlets for expression, outside of the schoolyard.

In an uncommon gesture of equanimity, the coauthors of the *Los Angeles Times'* family-advice column, Frances L. Ilg and Louise B.

Ames, reprinted a lengthy defense of comics by a seventeen-year-old boy who had read one of their recent pieces on comics. (They withheld his name.) He argued, "When one is not able to study, enjoy and appreciate a comic book with the same gusto as a Beethoven symphony, a Verdi opera, or a Hemingway novel, then one has regressed, rather than progressed on the road of life." Referring to other young people whom the columnists had praised for outgrowing comics, the teenage writer decried the kids as "well on their way to becoming narrow-minded, snobbish, dull, pseudo-intellectuals, with the stuffy, somewhat negligible ability to discuss Proust or Freud, but without the ability to enjoy sharing with their children in their first trips into the literary jungles, on the dark safaris of the comic books." Ilg and Ames devoted their next column to refuting the boy.

■　■　■

The farm country around Stone Bank, a mill town in southeastern Wisconsin, is spotted with lakes, and one of them used to have a roadhouse called Weisling's Breezy Point along a cove. On the weekends, the place would fill with day-trippers from Milwaukee. Adults could have drinks and snacks at the bar inside while the kids played on the bank or took a swim. There was no lifeguard. There was, however, a local resident named Ruth Lutwitzi, who would spend the weekend afternoons standing on a pier about fifty yards to the left side of the Breezy Point. In the late 1940s and early '50s, she saved the lives of three children who had started to drown in the lake. In 1955, she decided to devote the weekdays to patrolling the cultural waters, running a campaign against comic books.

The mother of five (one boy and four girls), Lutwitzi was a bright, resourceful woman committed to the heartland values of hard work and self-sacrifice. She kept a vegetable garden nearly half an acre square and raised a few chickens, to save grocery money, and used a pressure cooker to reduce her time in the kitchen. "She was always running from one good deed to the next," recalled one of her daughters, Ruth Schlicher. "She wasn't political—I don't know what party she belonged to—but she was very moral. She felt extremely strong about what was right and what was wrong." A happy woman, easy to like, Lutwitzi was a natural leader; when she walked from her house to the lake, ducks would trail her, and they would follow her back when she went home.

Lutwitzi's husband, Walter, an electrician, was a Navy veteran, and one of the couple's sons had served in the Second World War on a submarine that had been silent for eight months and presumed lost (but had really been on a secret mission). After the war, both parents became active in the American Legion. Ruth Lutwitzi was co-chair of the Child Welfare department of the Legion Auxiliary unit for her district in 1954, when the national leadership of the Auxiliary introduced an initiative to combat lurid comic books. As her fellow chair, Vanita Marlow, recalled, "She picked that up and ran like a bear." Lutwitzi had been wholly unfamiliar with comics until she learned about them through the Auxiliary, according to Marlow. "She was appalled, and she worked hard to make sure those things didn't infest our children."

Begun the previous fall as "Operation Book Swap," the Auxiliary's campaign was inspired by a program of the same name that had begun that September in Canton, Ohio, wherein a committee under the town's mayor had enticed young people to relinquish their crime and horror comic books; for every ten comics each child handed over at a booth at the county fair, he or she could claim a hardcover book from a stock of more than a thousand copies of two hundred titles, such as *Swiss Family Robinson* and *Heidi*. The initial targets of the Ohio effort were crime and horror comics, although distinctions proved difficult for the youngsters manning the county-fair booth to make; any comic was accepted. Kids in and around Canton turned in some thirty thousand comics, which were hauled by trucks to the local dump. Announcing the American Legion's adaptation of the Canton project, the national chair, Mrs. Carl W. Zeller of Ohio, acknowledged the new Comics Code as "a stab in the right direction," while pointing out that publishers generating one-fourth of all comic-book sales had not joined the CMAA. The Auxiliary's Book Swap, Zeller said, could be an antidote to the "literary diet of crime, horror, and sex comics fed systematically to millions of our children."

To prepare for the Stone Bank Book Swap, Ruth Lutwitzi purchased a batch of comic books, some from area shops, others from stores in Oconomowoc (the nearest mid-sized town), and she laid them out on the kitchen table for examination. "She had 'em marked up and everything," recalled her daughter Helen Miller, who was a high-school senior at the time. "I thought that was really fascinating, because I didn't know very much about life or sex or whatever, and all these pages were marked, and I thought, Hmmm . . . this ought to be some good reading." Ruth Lutwitzi cut out panels from the comics as visual aids in a lecture that she wrote and presented to area PTAs and church groups. "She was violently against the comic books," said Miller.

Under Lutwitzi's leadership, the Book Swap took place at the Stone Bank elementary school on Friday, March 14. A rural school converted to a "state-graded" school, Stone Bank had about a hundred students in grades one through eight, taught by four teachers in four classrooms. That day, the students brought in 546 comic books and received forty-six books in return. A prize of three dollars went to twelve-year-old Sharon Knoll, from Oconomowoc, for bringing in 127 comics. "I don't know where they got them all," recalled Milton Babinec, who taught fourth and fifth grades in the Stone Bank School at the time. "But I have a pretty good idea why the town of Stone Bank was so riled up about comics. After the war, people started moving here and integrating here, and they brought their ideas from the city [of Milwaukee], and that's what comic books meant to the people of Stone Bank. The rural people were scared."

In each of the hardbound books the students received, there was a letter from Lutwitzi:

Dear Young Reader,

    You have performed a great service to your country today, by getting rid of those ten crime and horror comic books. Those ten books were like ten enemies who were trying to destroy good American boys and girls . . .

    America is not a land of crime, horror, murder, hatred and bloodshed. America is a land of good, strong, law-abiding people who read good books, think good thoughts, do great work, love God and their neighbor. That's America.

The awards ceremony was conducted in the yard behind the Stone Bank School. At its conclusion, Lutwitzi led the children in making a grand pile of comic books, and she set them to flames. The fire raged to a height of twelve or fifteen feet and burned for more than half an hour. A photo of the event published in the *Waukesha Daily Freeman* showed the three prizewinners, two of them holding the books they had won, the third playing with the ashes of the burned comics. "I thought it was terribly wrong. [But] I was a young teacher, and you have to kind of—I was new, and I just got the job, and I had a wife," said Babinec. "I don't think many of the kids liked it very much, either. In fact, I know a lot of them didn't. I think a lot of them were bribed by the free book."

During the first six months of 1955, American Legion Auxiliary units across the country took part in Operation Book Swap, and many but not all of the events climaxed with book burning. The national headquarters estimated that "hundreds of thousands of objectionable comic books" had been gathered and destroyed in dozens of locations. Most but not all of the ceremonies took place in rural areas like Stone Bank, where the American Legion was an important community institution: Fulton, New York; Palatine, Illinois; Wakeman, Ohio, where about two hundred young people turned in more than a thousand comics; and Pendleton, Oregon, where 140 kids handed over more than 1,250 comics; as well as some suburban towns such as Little Neck, New York, where youngsters brought in 3,661 comics; and a few small cities, including Norwich, Connecticut, home of Mrs. Charles B. Gilbert, former national president of the Auxiliary, where hundreds of participants gathered some five thousand comics for burning. In Hyde Park, New York, the Auxiliary arranged for young readers to swap their own comics for other comics chosen by a committee; some 325 children took part, exchanging more than two thousand comics. As the leader of the event explained the unit's thinking, "We [did] not stress to the children the fact that some comics are objectionable, for our dealings with children have taught us that this would only increase their interest in something we are trying to stamp out."

In Wakeman, Ohio, for instance, several of the kids involved in the Book Swap had no special interest in comic books until they learned that adults in town were against them. Robert Jackson, a fourth-grader at the Townsend-Wakeman School, where the Swap was conducted, would remember going to one of the few area stores that carried comics, Larson's Hardware; it had two magazine racks, one on the near side of the cash-register counter, for the "good" books about costumed heroes and talking animals, and one on the far side, for the "other stuff." A sign above the second rack said, "No Children." Jackson had found the tools and guns in the store more alluring than either rack of magazines until the Swap concluded with a bonfire of the mysterious forbidden comics. "That's when I started to think, Hey, I wonder if I'm missing something."

For handing in ten comic books, Jackson received a nice hardcover edition of Baum's *The Wizard of Oz*, which had a letter from Mrs. Carl W. Zeller, the national chairman of the National Child Welfare Committee of the Auxiliary, pasted on the inside front cover of the book. It read:

I thank God that I am an American.
   I love my Country. I love my fellow man.
   I obey the Commandments of God.

I respect authority and the law.

I respect the rights of others.

I read good books that inspire me to be a good citizen, and refrain from reading books devoted to horror, hatred, violence, crime and other evils that destroy the spirit of America. This book is an award given me for living up to the above code.

The winner of the prize for delivering the most comics at Wakeman, Ted Yaworsky, never objected to the books he collected, but gathered them for the reward; he received a dollar, and six others divvied four dollars among them. "That was a lot of money in those days," Yaworsky said. Thinking of the Swap as a trade, he participated enthusiastically without knowing the Auxiliary's intentions. "They never told us they were going to destroy the books," he said. "That's not what they said. They said we should bring in all our books, and we'd get a prize, and then they put them all together in a big pile and they told us, 'Okay, we're going to burn them, because these are bad,' and I got really mad. What if I liked those comics? Did that make me bad? It got me mad.

"It was more or less like a dictatorship thing—'We're going to destroy all this! It's evil! You're evil!' It was like your witch hunts. It made me really mad. I wanted to tell them, but nobody asked us, and we were kids, and those were the days when you weren't supposed to talk unless you were talked to. That deal made me want to talk—it made me want to holler." The day after the bonfire, the local paper, the *Chronicle-Telegram*, published a photo of the comics in flames above the headline "1,427 Comics 'Taboo' As Book Swap Ends." Yaworsky, noted as first-prize winner, was not quoted; nor were any other students. At the end of that year, the *Chronicle-Telegram* reported, "'Book Swap' Top Story in Wakeman for 1955."

Former Legion Auxiliary president Gilbert, in the book she later wrote about the organization, quoted Zeller on the success of Operation Book Swap: "Not only was the original intent of the project realized, but also excellent public relations were established at home and abroad." However, the event in Gilbert's own city of Norwich generated more controversy than goodwill after it caught the attention of the nearby New York press. Two days before the Norwich unit was scheduled to burn the comics contributed by some four hundred Connecticut children, the *New York Post* sparked an editorial fire with an article headlined "Legion Auxiliary Sets Comic Book Burning." It quoted Gilbert as admitting, "There are overtones to book burning that aren't good," while she insisted that the burning would proceed as scheduled. When the American Book Publishers Council and the American Civil Liberties Union responded with complaints, the headlines shifted, first to "Comics 'Book Burning' Hit in Norwich Legion Drive," then to "Protests End Plan to Burn Comic Books." The swap went on, with the five thousand comics trucked to the city dump for disposal. The next day, an AP photo (published prominently in several papers in the Northeast) showed a pair of cute tikes, Lisa Drobnes and John Chiangi, tossing bundles into the back of a pickup truck loaded with comic books as Mrs. Gilbert and two other members of the Norwich Auxiliary watched, beaming. Chiangi, pondering the day as a middle-aged man, could remember little other than the fact that the adults were "very serious," and the children "did what we thought we were supposed to do." He "thought there was something very wrong about it, even then," Chiangi said, "but I didn't really understand what we were doing. It was the American Legion. We figured we were doing something patriotic."

■　■　■

Comic books were an adaptable demon. While American patriots rallied to stop them from spreading unconventional and probably Communist ideas, a leader of the rising Socialist movement in the UK led the English in a campaign to banish American comics. Peter Mauger, an activist and regular contributor to two Communist Party organs, the

Daily Worker and *Arena*, stirred up a furor over crime and horror comics imported from the United States (or reprinted, legally or illegally, by publishers in the UK). To Mauger and sympathizers in his country, whose postwar fears centered on America's expanding role in Europe, crime and horror comics served as tangible evidence of the monstrous vulgarity of American popular culture; they represented the sociopolitical plague of cultural imperialism.

A special issue of *Arena* "devoted to the American threat to British culture, to all that is good and vital in our national tradition" published a speech by Mauger on crime and horror comics. Mauger identified the books simply as "American comics," as if crime and horror were synonymous with America. "These magazines, which boast of spreading the American way of life throughout the globe, also deal in sadism, whippings, torture, and a rather vulgar form of visual pornography," said Mauger, as *Arena* quoted him. "Comics stress cruelty . . . Comics glorify power . . . Comics portray fantasies of the future, all fascist in character . . . The lessons that are constantly reiterated are that human nature is aggressive and ruthless—even if on the side of justice."

As early as May 1952, Mauger was arguing his case to the UK masses in popular magazines such as *Picture Post*. "Should US 'Comics' Be Banned?" he asked, purely rhetorically; and by the summer of 1954, English newspapers were blaring the answer. For nearly two weeks that August, the *Daily Dispatch* of London ran daily stories calling for a ban on lurid, American-made comics. The headlines were nearly identical to those in the United States, with the currency exchanged: "Drive Out the Horror Comics: Help us to fight 'sex and crime at a shilling a time.'" One *Dispatch* piece urged a solution as familiar as legislation in the United States: "Make Bonfires of Them." By November 1954, *The Times* of London, which was generally more temperate, had taken up the call for action against comic-book imports. "The problem which now faces society in the trade that has sprung up of presenting sadism, crime, lust, physical monstrosity, and horror to the young is an urgent and a grave one," pronounced *The Times* in an editorial. "There has been no more encouraging sign of the moral health of the country than the way in which public opinion has been roused in condemnation of the evil of 'horror comics' and in determination to combat them."

In January 1955, the British cabinet announced support for legislation to ban horror comics, ostensibly to reduce a potential impetus to crime, despite the fact that juvenile arrests were in decline throughout the UK. The resulting bill, called the Children and Young Persons (Harmful Publications) Act, would prohibit the sale or the publication of "horror comics" explicitly; in addition, it would bar all publications which "would tend to incite or encourage to the commission of crimes or acts of violence or cruelty, or otherwise to corrupt, a child or young person into whose hands it might fall." The penalty would be up to four months in prison or a fine up to one hundred pounds. It passed, after six hours of debate, on February 22, 1955.

On the same day, Americans returned to burning comic books. The teachers at St. James Catholic School in Decatur, Illinois, led the student body in a public burning of comics on the school grounds. Kids waved signs saying, "Burn the Bad, Read the Good" and "Read the Good Ones," as they tossed copies of *Action Comics* (Superman), *Marvel Tales* (Captain Marvel), *Startling Comics*, and others into the pyre. The same week, a Girl Scout troop in Indiana, Pennsylvania, launched a campaign to "rid the homes of Indiana" of "improper" comic books. The girls petitioned area residents and news dealers to hand over all comics in their possession that lacked the CMAA's seal of approval. Called Operation Clean-Up, the drive sought "the banishment of comic books not approved by the Comics Code Authority," according to the *Indiana Evening Gazette*. The books were burned at a ceremony the scout troop called a Bonfire of the Future.

Less than two years after the publication of Ray Bradbury's vision of future bonfires, *Fahrenheit 451*, the comic-book burnings of 1955, like the many that preceded them in the mid-to-late 1940s, were an inversion of Bradbury's prophesy. In the philistine dreamscape of *Fahrenheit 451*, a fascistic government institutionalized book burning, banishing all publications that expressed ideas or had artistic merit. The only volumes left unscathed were those deemed of practical value or those beneath contempt: trade journals, pornography, and comic books.

15. Murphy's Law

Charles F. Murphy had three children of his own, ages fourteen, fifteen, and twenty at the end of 1954. Like other young people, they read comic books, and on occasion they would bring home comics that their father considered unacceptable. Murphy, who was as good a Samaritan as any Girl Scout in Indiana, Pennsylvania, would burn the books. "But my kids always found replacements the minute my back was turned," Murphy said. In his public role as administrator of the Comics Code, Murphy applied no less fervor than he did at home, with more sophisticated methods of destruction. He saw his mission for the CMAA as a "sweeping . . . purification drive," and he pursued it more zealously than many in the comics business had expected. Murphy had been "hired to be a figurehead, like a rubber stamp," according to Carmine Infantino, an artist who was penciling Western and war comics for National/DC at the time. "He took the whole industry by surprise. Nobody expected him to come in and really change things. Even after the Code was written up, it was supposed to be more of a symbol. Nobody thought he was going to come in and really enforce it."

During the Code authority's first two months of operation, Murphy and his staff of five (all college graduates, the CMAA pointed out, and all women) screened 440 issues of 285 comic-book titles; they rejected 126 stories outright and called for changes in 5,656 panels of art. Member publishers discontinued thirty-eight titles that could not meet the Code's restrictions—not only horror and crime comics, but romances. Now required to "emphasize the value of the home and the sanctity of marriage," romance comics could no longer provide an outlet for young women (and men) to come to terms with conflicting impulses and points of view. Dana Dutch could no longer write scripts for stories such as "I Gave the Boys the Green Light" and "Tourist Cabin Escapade." Nor could any writers challenge any "respected institutions"—marriage, school, family, religion, government, or others—in stories that could "create disrespect for established authority." To writers such as Arnold Drake, the coauthor of *It Rhymes with Lust*, the Code "robbed the medium of the integrity it had and whatever purpose" it had as "an escape hatch" for young readers. "Comics were just a product to the people who ran the Code," said Drake. "They weren't an art form. If we had been working under the Code at the time, we never could have done *It Rhymes with Lust*. We could only have done *It Rhymes with Inanity*." A few minutes after saying that, Drake thought of a good rhyme: "Insanity."

On the stories they accepted, Murphy's censors enforced the minutiae of the Code fastidiously. About a fourth of the revisions called for in the Code's first two months were intended to desexualize the female characters by streamlining their proportions or adding more clothes. ("Ladies in the Comic Books to Be in Height of Style," announced a headline in the *Roanoke World News*; comic-book women would now "look like so many dress models on Christian Dior," reported the article. "Flat in front.") For an issue of *Love Problems and Advice Illustrated*, the opening "splash page" art for one story, "Love Flirt," was published with the head of an attractive young woman floating in a full-page square of solid black; the character's entire body had been brushed over with ink. Throughout the tale to follow, black patches covered sections of panels, and word balloons had cryptic blank spaces where dialogue had been whited out—censored like letters from prison, as if comic-book artists and writers really were convicted gangsters, mailing their stuff from Sing Sing. A young man, approaching a woman at a party in "Love Flirt," said, "Come on"—blank space—"Let's dance"—sizable blank space. The whited-out areas ended up suggesting unspeakable, mysteriously titillating thoughts. Yet, since the Code had no restrictions on the appearance of men, heroes bulged as ever, in costumes that amounted to skin paint; the male body now had exclusive domain over the comics' reduced erotic landscape.

Murphy's censors were faithful to the letter of the Code and indifferent to its effects. Sometimes publishers in the CMAA would reprint stories that had originally been issued prior to the enactment of the Code, and the "before" and "after" versions provide some evidence of the censors' thinking. For instance, one story, "Mack Martin Investigator," drawn by Rudy Palais and first published in the May 1948 issue of *Super Mystery Comics*, showed the hero bopping an opponent on the head with a piece of office equipment. "Ever hear of a Dictaphone, stupid?" Martin asked. An emphatic "Bang" appeared above the head of the victim, who groaned "Ugh" as he shot a pistol into the air. In the same story, revised for publication in the January 1956 issue of *Penalty Comics*, the machine was whited out, giving the attacker empty hands. There was no "Bang," no "Ugh," no gun blast. But the dialogue—"Ever hear of a Dictaphone, stupid?"—remained. Inane to begin with, the line was not improved by being made an inexplicable non sequitur.

Many of the revisions called for by the Code authority were matters of softening, even sweetening, the imagery, often in ways contrary to both the intentions of the story and the essence of the Comics Code. In the original version of the *Super Mystery Comics* story, one of the bad guys had angular features and a receding hairline. In the revision, he was ruggedly handsome and had a full head of hair; the character became more appealing and sympathetic. Much the same, countless heavies and wenches and ghouls were redrawn with nicer hairdos, better skin (or simply some skin, instead of skeletal bones), neater clothes, and happier faces. Images of Satan were invariably changed, with horns and fangs removed; the resulting character was no longer pure evil, just somewhat less pleasant than other fellows.

For a press conference demonstrating the Code authority's work, Murphy had a pair of comic-book panels enlarged on a sheet of posterboard. The left showed a demonic shrew with wild straw hair and a shriveled simian face. The right had that character redrawn as a plain-featured, ordinary woman with hair that could use a brushing; she appeared to be wearing lipstick. As evidence that she was the Code's idea of a hag, there was a mole on her face—a small mark near her mouth, like the ones Marilyn Monroe and Peggy Lee had. The Comics Code, as it was enforced in Murphy's office, denied evil its evilness. Blurring distinctions between good and bad, it purged the comics of not only the presence of Satan but the need for God.

Above all, the Code was a wholesale abrogation of the authorial prerogative, which was something precious to many comic-book creators, especially artists. "The wonderful thing about comics, to me, was that I never got any work back," recalled Jay Scott Pike, a romance specialist. "You were left totally on your own. It was so free—it was fantastic. Then the Comics Code came along, and, because I was doing mostly jungle girls and romance [comics], I had to make all the breasts smaller, and the jungle girls were always flying through the air on vines, and now they had to have skirts on, and the skirts could never go up. The laws of physics didn't apply. I know they were only jungle girls, and they were ridiculous to begin with, but that was kind of what made the whole thing worth doing for me. They didn't have to make sense. They could be whatever I wanted them to be, just because that's what I wanted, and now that was gone."

Everyone working in comics during the first years of the Code seemed to come away with a pet story about the Murphy office and its rigid, seemingly arbitrary demands. The artist Russ Heath submitted a drawing of a baseball player at bat, taking a hard, full swing, and he was ordered to remove the sweat from the batter's brow. John Severin had to white out the dagger in a villain's hand, while the slash in his victim's chest was permitted to stay, giving the impression that the bad guy had stabbed the other fellow with his fingers. Dick Ayers was a regular artist on *The Rawhide Kid*, a character named for the bullwhip he always carried; under the Code, the Rawhide Kid lost the whip and took up farming. Joe Edwards, an artist on *Archie*, was told to lower the skirts and loosen the blouses on Betty and Veronica.

"I'll never forget that Murphy and what he put us through," said Frank Thorne, who was drawing comic-book adaptations of the *Tom Corbett, Space Cadet* TV show in the early 1950s. "He was a great big bumbling idiot . . . the führer of the Comics Code."

Dick Giordano, who wound up engaged full-time in the task of shuttling pages between the CMAA office and the Charlton studios, extended his animosity to the Code staff, as well as to Murphy. "The Code was restrictive in the extreme!" said Giordano. "My contact was with the reviewers, who I've always believed were chosen for their capacity to uphold the Code by being as snotty as they felt for having the misfortune to have to read comics for a living and deal with the cretins who produced them."

Herb Rogoff, who was an editor at Ziff-Davis, found dealing with Murphy's office so frustrating that he protested to his superiors. "The biggest insult of all was the having to go through a censor," said Rogoff. "This was absolutely outrageous—the Comics Code. They had a bunch of old biddies, ex-schoolteachers, up there, sitting up there and telling us what we had to do. They blue-penciled everything. You could find anything that's objectionable if you're looking for it.

"We had a picture of a woman in a three-quarters view. So we had the outline of one breast, and then we had the half circle that showed the other breast. They wanted that out. Now, I said, 'This is madness. Are you going to change the anatomy of a woman?' They said, 'You don't have to be that explicit.' I said, 'Are you trying to teach kids that a woman does not have two breasts? What is your intent here?' They said, 'That is lascivious.' It was infuriating, it was demeaning, and it was insulting."

Rogoff complained to his bosses at Ziff-Davis. " 'Why don't we just tell them to go foof themselves?' I said. 'Oh,' the big boss said. 'The printers won't print.' I said, 'Are you kidding?' He said, 'No, they're scared. They won't print without the seal, and the distributors won't ship without the seal, and the newsstands won't sell without the seal. Without the seal, we're out of business,' and then I understood how big and bad this thing had gotten." The challenge was not one of salvaging artists' freedom of expression, but one of saving their jobs.

James A. FitzPatrick, the New York State assemblyman, found the Comics Code inadequate. After his testimony at the second session of Hendrickson committee hearings on comic books and juvenile delinquency, FitzPatrick decided to conduct his own legislative hearing on comics under the auspices of the state Joint Legislative Committee to Study the Publication of Comics, which he chaired. Conducted in the offices of the New York Bar Association in Midtown Manhattan on February 4, 1955, the hearing called as witnesses Charles F. Murphy, who defended the CMAA vigorously; Helen Meyer, vice president at Dell, who chastised the CMAA for laxity and said she would not join the association until it adopted a code calling for "elimination" rather than the "regulation" of objectionable comics; Fredric Wertham, who augmented his well-rehearsed material with props—a bullwhip and a knife, which he claimed to have purchased through advertisements in comics bearing the CMAA seal (although, under oath, he said he could not recall the titles of the comics); and Francis W. H. Adams, the New York City Commissioner of Police, who said he had found a direct link between comic books and juvenile crime and called for new comics legislation. After the testimony, FitzPatrick's staff dimmed the lights and screened a short film about horror comics produced for

CBS television. As Murphy summed up his view of the day's findings, "There is yet much to be done" to "eliminate this menace."

On March 21, FitzPatrick presented his committee report to the state legislature. It concluded that the CMAA had proved ineffectual and that the Comics Code was a mechanism unequipped to eradicate the "horror, sex, and brutality" in comics. Issues of comic books "currently upon the stands and bearing the authority's seal of approval contain an abundance of the same type of material termed objectionable by the authority and purportedly eliminated," the report asserted. "Our files are replete with comic books evidencing the fact that violence and brutality constitute the dominant theme of many publications currently stamped with the approval of the authority." As a result, FitzPatrick told the assembly, he was introducing a package of strong new measures, one provision of which would flatly outlaw the publication of controversial comics in their state of origin.

"Freedom without obligation is anarchy," FitzPatrick said. "We should not countenance any confusion of liberty with license and should move against those who persist in corrupting the minds and morals for profit."

He proposed sweeping legislation to

- prohibit the publication or the distribution of lurid comics, defined as those "devoted to or principally made up of pictures or accounts of methods of crime, or illicit sex, horror, terror, physical torture, brutality, or physical violence";
- bar the sale of any such books to those under the age of eighteen;
- ban the use of the words "crime," "terror," "horror," or "sex" in comic-book titles.

On March 22, the state assembly approved the bill unanimously; and on May 2, Governor Averell Harriman signed it into law. Violations would be punishable by a year in jail or a $500 fine, or both. The

UK law banning horror comics went into effect in four days after Harriman's action.

The New York State law was a paralyzing blow to the comic-book trade. Some eighty comic books were now illegal because of their titles: *Crime Does Not Pay*, *Police Against Crime*, *Terror Illustrated*, *Terrors of the Jungle*, *Tales of Horror*, *Weird Horrors*, and dozens more. (No comic sold over the counter had ever had the word "sex" in its title.) The FitzPatrick Act's restriction on title language in comics, applied to other books, would have banned Dostoyevsky's *Crime and Punishment* and Simone de Beauvoir's *The Second Sex*. Moreover, its prohibitions of accounts of "methods of crime" and "physical violence" could apply to virtually every detective, Western, war, or superhero comic, not to mention M. C. Gaines's Bible comics, had they still been in print. Even the talking-animal funnies (including the Disney titles but especially *Tom and Jerry* and those based on the Warner Bros. cartoons) were packed with slapstick roughhousing that could qualify as physical violence. (What Jerry did to Tom was outright torture.) The FitzPatrick Act essentially outlawed comic books, with the possible exception of *Archie*.

Laws in other states picked up comics after publication, regulating their distribution and sale. By fall 1955, bills on comic books had passed in the legislative bodies of California, Connecticut, Illinois, Maryland, Montana, Nevada, New Jersey, North Carolina, Ohio, Oklahoma, Oregon, Texas, and Washington, as well as in New York. In Connecticut, a comprehensive law prompted by *The Hartford Courant*'s fervent campaign against lurid comics would make it a crime not only to sell comic books dealing with "lust, violence, horror, passion, or obscenity" to minors, but also to advertise such books or display them in public. (After passing the legislation, the Connecticut assembly voted unanimously for resolutions commending the *Courant* and Irving Kravsow.) Nevada, New Jersey, and Ohio set out to outlaw both the public display and the sale of such comics to minors, but ignored advertising. Illinois and Maryland concentrated on the sale of comics depicting "sex, crime, violence or immorality" to minors. (Maryland added "the use of narcotics" to the list.) North Carolina passed a law much like those in Illinois and Maryland, though it had no age restrictions. In Montana, it became a crime, punishable by a mandatory jail sentence for a second offense, to sell or distribute "offensive" comic books. Oklahoma took a circuitous route, granting mayors and municipal governing bodies the power to bring suit against anyone selling or distributing "obscene" comics to minors. Washington State opted to require licenses of comic-book dealers, with the stipulation that a license could be suspended or revoked if a seller carried a comic-book depicting "sex or violence." In addition, at least six states (California, Idaho, Illinois, New Jersey, Oregon, and Texas) outlawed tie-in sales of objectionable comics. The legal engineering was wondrous in its variety, yet simple in its intent: to do something—anything—about those nasty comic books. No fewer than five more states—Arizona, Louisiana, Massachusetts, New Hampshire, and Pennsylvania—had comic-book legislation in the works; and at least three others—Vermont, Rhode Island, and Texas—had set up committees to study the issue and report by the next legislative session. (A few states which had already passed some comics legislation, such as California, had additional bills under development.)

In nine other states—Delaware, Indiana, Iowa, Kansas, Minnesota, New Mexico, South Dakota, Utah, and Wisconsin—legislation on comic books had been proposed but voted down or not acted upon. A key figure in the legislative debate in Wisconsin, Reuben C. Peterson, a public advocate, argued so vociferously against the legislation that he was booed out of the Madison statehouse. "I wasn't what you would call a rabble-rouser," Peterson recalled. "But they went too far over those comic books. They weren't using their heads. I tried to tell them that we have such a thing as the First Amendment. They forgot about that, and they shot me down—they shot me down but good. They were hootin' and hollerin' and booed me out of the place." Still, Peterson appeared to have helped influence enough votes to prevent the legislation from passing.

In another state that rejected comic-book legislation, Kansas, the editor of one newspaper, the *Great Bend Daily Tribune*, acclaimed the decision in an editorial titled "Modern Witch Burning":

> The witch-burning days are returning to the United States in this year 1955—if they were ever completely gone . . . There is a lot more to this business of censorship than the current situation, which was created by the appearance of comic books, many of which are weird, disgusting and revolting. Whether or not the books should be permitted on the newsstand is the immediate problem, but whether or not censorship is the way to keep them off is a matter that deserves a great deal of study, for censorship is a fearful thing . . . It is poppycock to think that it is necessary to resort to laws to make America greater by banning comic books . . . This is a matter for the home, the school, the church, and other family influences—not the legislatures.

Antipathy toward comics so permeated all those institutions that in many places it rendered moot the question of comic books' right to the newsstand. The comics business was collapsing under pressure not only from the schools, the churches, and the legislatures, but also from the distributors and the industry's own desperate, overzealous attempt to regulate itself. There were fewer and fewer comics to purchase, and those available were so bowdlerized that they were losing their idiosyncratic appeal to young people. They no longer had much besides color pictures that television could not provide in full motion. "All the dark craziness that made comics so interesting and so successful [was] stripped away," said Harry Harrison, the artist and writer. "They were so juvenile that *Howdy Doody* was more interesting." Television gained the audience that "comics was losing . . . by its own doing," Harrison said. "TV didn't kill the comics. [It] didn't have to. The job was already done."

In 1952, approximately five hundred comics titles were published in the United States; three years later, about three hundred were published. In 1953, Harry "A" Chesler closed his shop. In 1954, Fiction House (home of the jungle queens and female artists) went out of business; so did the four companies Stanley P. Morse operated under various company names (Aragon, Gillmore, Key, Stanmor); so did Comics Media (*Danger, Death Valley*) and Timor (*Blazing Western, Crime Detective*) and Stanhall (*G.I. Jane*). Harvey, one of the major publishers of horror comics, survived by replacing its line with a roster of kiddie titles (*Baby Huey, Little Dot, Casper,* and *Hot Stuff*). The fact that Hot Stuff was literally a little devil, complete with horns and a tail, and that Casper was a ghost, a junior citizen of the undead, was offset by their unremitting cuteness.

Joe Simon and Jack Kirby, faced with dwindling commissions by comics publishers, tried forming their own comic-book company, Mainline Publications, in 1954, only to find the business climate suffocating. Although the titles they created—a pair of Westerns, *Bullseye* and *Western Scout*; a romance, *In Love*; and a couple of others—were tame, the major comics distributors declined to take them on. "We couldn't get a decent distributor, because all the laws about selling comics had all the news dealers scared out of their wits—they were afraid to put comics on the newsstands," said Joe Simon. "So our own choice was to go with Leader News, which was the distributor of Bill Gaines's comic books, and with all the protests going on and the parents groups and the educational groups raising hell and the laws and the hearings and so forth, Leader News was in shambles. Our books weren't being sold. They never even got on the newsstands. Jack and I were pulling our hair out, and finally we just couldn't take it anymore, and we couldn't afford to keep producing comics that never got unwrapped, and we had to pull the plug on our company."

While the business of crime, horror, and romance comics collapsed, the public outcry against them and the calls for further comic-book legislation continued unabated. On October 9, 1955, the film that had been screened at James A. FitzPatrick's hearing on comics was broadcast nationally on the television series *Confidential File*. The program, a prototype of the broadcast newsmagazine, took up one topical subject—invariably, something a bit unsavory, such as prostitution or child molesting—each week. The host, Paul Coates, a columnist for the *Los Angeles Times* with the cocksure authority of the district attorney in a B movie, interviewed experts on the issue of the week; as they answered, Coates nodded knowingly, occasionally raised his right eyebrow, and scrawled notes on a pad. The centerpiece of each episode was a staged documentary-style sequence, directed by Irvin Kershner (a one-time documentarian for the federal government who would go on to make the noir classic *Stakeout on Dope Street* and, many years later, *The Empire Strikes Back*). For the *Confidential File* show on comic books, Kershner shot a sequence about a group of young adolescent boys who kept a stash of horror comics hidden in the woods. The footage had no ambient sound, like home movies of the day. It followed the kids as they gathered under the cover of trees to trade and read comics. "But they're not reading anything constructive," Coates intoned in a voice-over. "They're reading stories devoted to adultery, to sexual perversion, to horror, to the most despicable of crimes . . . One of the wonderfully appealing things about children is that they haven't yet come to the age where reality and unreality are divorced. The emotional impact of something they read in a comic may be much the same as a real-life situation they witness."

The boys grew more agitated as they turned the pages. "Maybe you can accept this fact, maybe not, but it is a fact . . . horror and crime comics upset kids," Coates said. "I'm not talking about any subtle distortion of their emotional makeup—I think that occurs, too—but there's a more noticeable, immediate effect. You can see the tension develop as the story gets more gruesome, and if it's a bad one, the kid is a mass of jangled nerves by the time he's through it." Rabid from their comics reading, the kids rushed off together and found an innocent young acquaintance, whom they lured into the woods. "This is the beginning of the game of violence," Coates announced gravely.

The staged footage accelerated in pace, showing the boys proceeding to tie the little guy to a tree, to gag him with a handkerchief, and to torture him with branches, lit matches, and a pen knife. "They didn't think it up all by themselves, of course," Coates continued in the voice-over. "They had an excellent manual, a regular do-it-yourself pamphlet: a crime and horror comic book. And they learned their lesson well." Ambient sounds from the scene on camera—the cackle of the boys taunting their prey while he screamed in terror—broke into the show's soundtrack and rose steadily in volume.

"And remember, these are not the faces of an isolated group of kids," Coates said. "These are not delinquents, not criminals. These are the faces of your sons. These boys are playing and yet they're not playing. Such games have ended in death many times . . . Men are getting rich off the comic books that teach kids this kind of activity. I don't know how you like it, but it makes me kind of sick."

In the program's interview segments, Coates talked with a few boys (no girls) who read comics, one comic-book artist (Ellis Eringer, a humor specialist who had taken a few horror assignments but disliked the genre), and Estes Kefauver. Coates and Kefauver sat at adjacent sides of a small table. Unlike the other guests, who interacted eye-to-eye with Coates during the interviews, Kefauver waited for Coates to finish each question, then turned to his left and spoke directly to the camera. For the segment with Kefauver, a pole hanging an American flag had been added to the *Confidential File* set, behind the senator. Kefauver said he believed the comic-book problem called for new legislation, and he gave a brief account of the New York hearings on comics and juvenile delinquency, adjusting the facts considerably. "This comic-book business is really big business," Kefauver said. "All of our testimony from psychiatrists and children themselves show that it's very upsetting, that it has a bad moral effect, and that it is directly responsible for a substantial amount of juvenile delinquency and child crime." In fact, both the expert testimony and the documentary evidence submitted at the hearings varied significantly in their judgments, and the committee spoke with no children; it had set a policy of precluding the testimony of minors.

The writer of the program, A. J. Fenady, had not seen a transcript of the hearings before preparing Coates's questions and "basically threw the guy some softballs," he said, because "[Kefauver] wanted to use this soapbox to run for president" in the 1956 election. "The comic-book scare was the big thing he had going for him," Fenady recalled, "and he knew how to use it."

Soon after the *Confidential File* broadcast, Kefauver began a world tour, meeting leaders of more than a dozen nations, looking presidential, picking up headlines, and building a defense against potential criticism for his inexperience in foreign affairs. He announced his candidacy formally that December, throwing his coonskin hat into a ring—four times, for the cameras. Adlai Stevenson would win the nomination again, leaving Kefauver in an unexpected brawl with an upstart contender, the thirty-eight-year-old senator from Massachusetts, John Kennedy, for the vice presidential slot. Kefauver won the dubious privilege of accompanying Stevenson in being duly routed by Eisenhower and Nixon, thereby setting up Kennedy as the frontrunner in 1960. After his election, Kennedy said wryly, "I guess I owe a lot to Estes."

16. Out of the Frying Pan and into the Soup

Bill Gaines and Al Feldstein promoted their "clean, clean line" of comics as EC's "New Direction," and that it was: straight down. Abandoning crime and terror for wholesomeness and virtue, they introduced seven titles in January 1955 (cover-dated April): three formulaic safe bets (*Valor*, about knights and gladiators and heroes of the like from mythic history; *Piracy*, about swashbucklers; and *Aces High*, about flyers); a few offbeat experiments geared to older readers (*MD*, about medicine; *Extra!*, about the newspaper business; and *Psychoanalysis*, about a field with which Gaines now had nearly as much experience as Fredric Wertham); and one restrained successor to EC's old "New Trend" comics, *Impact*, which Feldstein described, in a note in the premier issue, as carrying on "our most cherished tradition . . . THE SURPRISE ENDING!" In addition, they kept producing both humor books, *Mad* and *Panic*, and revamped *Weird Science-Fantasy* as the less weird and fantastical *Incredible Science Fiction*. Gaines and Feldstein explained the new line in a note of introductory hype published in each title's premier issue:

> What had we at E.C. done to merit the marvelous support you, our reader, gave us and continued to give us? The answer, to our way of

thinking, was that we respected you, our public! We respected your tastes, your judgment, your standards and, above all, your intelligence. We tried something new in comics. We used only the best art work available . . .

Even as time went on, and the subject matter of some of our old "New Trend" magazines became a topic of debate, criticism, and censure, the quality standards we had set in the beginning were diligently adhered to. Now, many of our old "New Trend" magazines are dead . . . But it was not the standards of entertainment we'd set in those magazines that were buried . . . merely the subject matter!

Yet EC's standards had changed. While much of the art in the New Direction comics—especially the angular, stylized panels by Bernard Krigstein and the obsessively filigreed pages by Al Williamson and his studio partners—matched or exceeded that of the best New Trend books, the stories—most of them by Feldstein and the freelance writers Carl Wessler, Sid Oleck, and the writer-artist Johnny Craig—had none of the old comics' antic bite. With few exceptions (among the most notable, Gaines and Feldstein's fatalistic narrative of a concentration-camp survivor encountering his former tormentor in a subway station, "Master Race," originally intended for *Crime SuspenStories* but published in the first issue of *Impact*), the writing was serious-minded, but conventional, simplistic, and overly earnest. "Listen," Feldstein explained, "we had cold feet, and we were just trying to stay in business. It was sanitized stuff, and it was just an attempt to put out a decent comic book that would sell, not realizing, of course, that we were tainted and didn't have a chance. As a matter of fact, the whole field was now tainted, and it was murder for everybody. But all we knew was that we were dying."

EC published the first issues of its eviscerated new line without participation in the CMAA. "I felt that I couldn't put out anything really decent—anything worth any entertainment so far as the intelligent quotient above an eight-year-old is concerned—and go through the association, unless it was just plain cold potatoes, you know, real mush," Gaines said in 1955. When most of those first issues were returned to EC in unopened bundles, Gaines panicked and decided to join the association he had publicly derided, submitting his new comics to Murphy's office for approval. "Everybody in the industry went through it, and if you didn't, you got clobbered at the wholesale level," Gaines recalled in a 1969 interview. "I tried not to join it, and my first few New Direction magazines in each title were put out without the new seal. We sold like 15 percent, which is *catastrophic*. So I joined the association, and the sales went up . . . [to] 20 or 25 percent, which is *still* catastrophic . . . I couldn't put out a title that wasn't losing money. Every single New Direction comic, *every single one of them*, lost money." By the end of the year, Gaines said, "I had run out of money."

The last comic book EC would ever publish was the February 1956 issue of *Incredible Science Fiction*, issued in November 1955. Feldstein, the editor, submitted the pages to Charles F. Murphy late in the summer of 1955. "Murphy always read our stuff himself," Feldstein said. "I'd go in there with the pages, and all the little old ladies were reading everything else, and I'd have to wait until Murphy personally read our pages." That issue of *Incredible Science Fiction* included a story, written by Jack Oleck and illustrated by Angelo Torres, about mutants. Murphy rejected it outright. "You can't have mutants," he said, as Feldstein remembered.

"So I went back to the office, and I said, 'Bill, what are we going to do? We got a deadline.' He said, 'Well, let's pull out an old one'—one that we already used before the Code but was clean enough to pass. So I dug out one of my favorite pieces." Written late in 1952 and originally published the following spring, the story, "Judgment Day!" was one of what Feldstein called his "preachies"; a science-fiction allegory about race, it followed an astronaut from Earth as he inspected a planet populated by self-replicated robots, some painted orange and some blue, but identical mechanically. When the Earthman saw that the orange ones had subjugated the blue ones to poverty and servitude, he declined to welcome the robots into the galactic union. The last panel of the story showed the astronaut back in his spaceship; with his helmet removed, we see that he is black-skinned. "In the 1950s, when I wrote it, that was a pretty strong message," Feldstein said. "You know, a message of hope for the future of what was then a terribly segregated society." Indeed, when "Judgment Day!" was first published the *Chicago Defender* devoted an editorial to recounting the story, which the newspaper praised for combining "the lure of color and fantasy with educational propaganda."

Murphy read the pages impassively. "He got to the last panel," Feldstein said, "and he looked up at me, and he said, 'No. You can't have a Negro.'

"I said, 'Why not?'

"He said, 'You can't have a Negro.'

"I said, 'Where in the Code does it say that I can't depict a Negro?'

"He said, 'I say you can't have a Negro.'

"I said, 'That's the point of the whole story.'

"'No.'

"So I said, 'Bye.'"

Feldstein returned to the EC office and protested to Gaines. "I said, 'Bill, this is impossible. It just can't work. They are after our ass, and they're going to find any excuse to give us a hard time.' And Bill called up Murphy and said, 'What the hell is going on?'

"And Murphy said, 'You can't have a Negro.'

"And Bill said, 'Okay. I'm going to have a press conference, and I'm going to tell the public that the comic-book authority is a racist authority that will not permit black people to have equal depiction' or something like that." After a pause to reflect, Murphy granted Gaines permission to publish the story, on the condition that the beads of perspiration on the black astronaut's face be removed. (Feldstein's text ended with a purple flourish: "And the instrument lights made the beads of perspiration on his dark skin twinkle like distant stars . . .")

Gaines said, "Fuck you," hung up on Murphy, and published the story intact.

"That was Bill's last act as a comic-book publisher," said Feldstein. "He was upset and he had had it and he was broke and he was mad as hell. I don't think Bill Gaines would have published a comic book if Fredric Wertham and Estes Kefauver came into his office holding hands and they said, 'Bill, we want to apologize. We were wrong, and you were right. Please come back and give us more horror comics.' I think he would have kicked them out on their asses. He had had it."

Although Gaines gave up comic books, he held on to *Mad* by publishing it as a magazine, rather than a comic, thus averting the Comics Code, comic-book distributors, and the legislative restrictions on comics. "*Mad* could never have gone through the association," Gaines later explained. "I don't think there's any way we could have worked with those people over there, and it would have wrecked the book." He stayed in business by making a business out of kicking the asses of Wertham, Kefauver, and all of institutional authority through the pages of his most original and successful publication. In July 1955, Gaines repackaged *Mad* in magazine format; he repriced it at twenty-five cents, a price thought too dear for young children; he abandoned color on the inside pages in favor of more serious-looking and economical black and white; and he encouraged Harvey Kurtzman, who stayed on as *Mad*'s editor (for a while), to broaden the contents to satirize not only comics, TV shows, and movies, but the whole of a society that had no place for Bill Gaines's beloved EC. *Mad* became, in Lyle Stuart's words, "a big fuck-you at the powers that almost did him in.

"You know how adversity sometimes does the trick? Bill said, 'What do we know about magazines?' I said, 'We'll learn.' I didn't know any more than he did. I was more interested, really, in keeping him from collapsing, because he was in despair. He felt he hadn't done anything wrong, and what was he being condemned for? What had he done? What was so terrible? He needed some hope again, and he got very hopeful once the first issue of the magazine edition of *Mad* was put together." (After canceling the New Direction line, Gaines experimented briefly with a series of illustrated magazines for adults, called Picto-Fiction, but abandoned them after a few issues, the last of which Gaines could not afford to bind and had shredded instead.)

To Gaines, publishing *Mad* magazine was, at least in part, an act of cultural retribution. "Bill Gaines was anti-establishment—he did not like coercion in any way, shape, or form," said Stan Hart, a graduate scholar in Elizabethan theater who soon became one of *Mad*'s regular writers. "*Mad* was the conduit for Bill's survival, and I think survival is the best revenge. Bill was forced into having only *Mad*, and I think that also played into his anti-establishment sympathies. I mean, the whole business that led to those hearings and the boycott—that offended him terribly, and I think that found its expression in *Mad*."

From its debut in the magazine section of the newsstands in 1955, *Mad* honored its charter to squirt soda in the face of mainstream America. The premier effort (billed on the cover as "First Issue: The New *Mad*," but numbered 24 so Gaines could piggyback the old *Mad*'s postal license) had pieces spoofing Ernest Hemingway (a text story, "Out of the Frying Pan and into the Soup," by parodist Ira Wallach) and Dale Carnegie–style self-improvement guides ("How to Get the Job You Want by Thinking Positively and Also Get Ahead by Learning My Five Rules That Will Give You a New and Unbelievably Positive Personality and Help You Achieve Success," by Roger Price, a humorist then well-known for his "Droodles"—silly abstract drawings whose meanings were intentionally obtuse, a near craze in the early 1950s), and fake advertisements that simultaneously mocked pillars of American commercial culture, such as Band-Aids and Jell-O, and Madison Avenue's cynical exploitation of the public's willing gullibility. As a mish-mash of topical parody made for young eyes, the magazine version of *Mad* was a mutation of the college humor magazine, a genre which, in 1955, was itself an institution more than 120 years old. (The *Harvard Lampoon*'s spoof of *Life* ran in 1896, nearly sixty years before *Mad*'s.) Still, *Mad* struck teenagers of the 1950s as something wholly new, because the targets of its satire were of the moment; because Kurtzman molded the contents like Play-Doh; because there was nothing like it on the newsstands—*College Humor*, the national anthology of said material, which had sold 800,000 copies per month at its peak in the 1920s, had ceased publication in 1943; because teenagers had not yet gone to college and discovered campus magazines; and because *Mad*, produced by comic-book people who knew how to think like kids, spoke directly to teenagers—proudly adolescent, *Mad* was *high-school* humor.

The first issue of the magazine also included, as an apparent space-filler, a portrait of a dim-looking kid above the phrase "What? Me Worry?" It would take another year for him to settle in as the magazine's mascot and be anointed as Alfred E. Neuman. The ardent stupidity and quiescence that Alfred embodied was always a front, a ruse to weaken the enemy's resistance: *Hey, let the kid read it—it's just a dumb joke book*. In fact, *Mad* took the world more seriously than popular adult magazines of the 1950s such as *Pageant*, and it provoked young people to worry a great deal about grown-up matters such as the Cold War, duplicity in politics and business, and social issues such as race relations.

For a TV parody in that issue, "Is This Your Life?," Will Elder produced a full-page illustration of the fictive program's studio audience. In vintage Elder chicken-fat style, the aisles were bursting with more than a hundred faces—Douglas MacArthur; the Lone Ranger; Irving Berlin and Liberace poring over a score of a piano concerto by Spike Jones; Abraham Lincoln; Martin and Lewis; Marlon Brando as Marc Antony, slashed and bloodied; Aunt Jemima; Edward R. Murrow, buried to his chest in cigarette butts; and, in the front row, next to Marilyn Monroe, Estes Kefauver, happily engrossed in a horror comic. (The back page of the book says "Comic Code 33 $X + = 6 = X0 - B + 5$.") Two rows behind Kefauver was Frank Costello, snarling and sweating; and behind him was his attorney, whispering in Costello's ear. Asked years later what Costello's lawyer was saying, Elder replied, "He was telling him, 'Don't worry about the murder and prostitution. Just don't tell 'em you like comic books.'"

■ ■ ■

While *Mad* survived by jumping to the magazine section of the newsstands, death swept the comic-book racks. Between 1954 and 1956, more than half the comic books on the newsstands disappeared; the number of titles published in the United States dropped from about 650 to some 250. By the end of 1955, when EC discontinued all its comics (retaining only *Mad*), five other publishers went out of business: Star (*Intimate Secrets of Romance*), Sterling (*Captain Flash, Tormented*), Toby Press (*Billy the Kid, Super Brat*), the comic-book division of the United Features syndicate (*Nancy & Sluggo*), and Eastern Color, M. C. Gaines's old company, where, in 1933, *Famous Funnies* had started the comic-book business. In 1956, Lev Gleason finally gave up *Crime Does Not Pay* and folded his operation. (Sales of Gleason's comics had dropped from 2.7 million per month in 1952 to 800,000 per month in 1956.) That year, Ace (*Crime Must Pay the Penalty, Atomic War!*), Avon (*Davy Crockett, Bachelor's Diary*), Premier (*Criminals on the Run, Nuts!*), and Superior (*Ghost Rider, My Secret Marriage*) all closed shop as well. In an interview conducted in 1955, Al Feldstein said, "Let's face it, the industry's dying, the comics industry. All they need is a spade to bury it."

When 1956 began, Feldstein was one of hundreds of writers, artists, and editors who found no more work or nominal work in the medium to which they had devoted their professional lives. "Everybody was punished," said Carmine Infantino. "It was like the plague. The work dried up, and you had nowhere to go, because comics were a dirty word. You couldn't say you were a comics artist, and you had nothing to put in your portfolio. If you said you drew comic books, it was like saying you were a child molester. It was a nightmare, especially for a lot of people who got into comics in the first place because, you know, that was where we could go."

Out of the Frying Pan and into the Soup

Stan Lee, the top editor at Timely/Atlas/Marvel, announced to his artists in April 1957 that he was "closing up." At the start of that year, the company published eighty-five comics titles; the publisher, Martin Goodman, discontinued all but sixteen—a mix of teen, romance, Western, and war comics—and had them distributed by its rival, National/DC. "Martin went to Florida, and he just said, 'Stan, we have to let the staff go, because of this, that, and the other—you tell 'em,'" Lee recalled. "For the record, it had everything to do with distribution, but that was the symptom, not the disease. The real reason, at the bottom of it all, was [that] everybody was running scared. The panic syndrome.

"I was the one who had to fire the staff. It was the toughest thing I ever did in my life. I had to tell them, and I was friends with these people. So many of them, I had dinner with them at their homes—I knew their wives, their kids, and I had to tell them this. It was, as I say, the most horrible thing I ever had to do." Lee summoned each of the major Timely artists—Joe Sinnott, Dick Ayers, Gene Colan, Martin Nodell, Morris Weiss, Frank Bolle, John Romita—to his office, and he told them, one by one, "I'm sorry, but there's no more work for you. It's over," as he recalled. "They were in shock, I was in shock." After each conversation, Lee went to the bathroom.

Those with special affection for the form, such as Pete Morisi, were devastated. "I loved comics—I loved everything about them, and I was proud of the work I was doing, but I felt ashamed to be doing it. You couldn't admit to anybody that you were a comic-book artist. You had to say you were 'an artist.' When people heard 'comic books,' that meant you couldn't be an artist," said Morisi, who gave up comics, took a civil-service test, and ended up as a police dispatcher in Brooklyn. "When the ax came down, it killed me. The fix was in. The comics were dead. I was heartbroken."

Mike Sekowsky worked for a while as a bagger at a grocery store. John Severin took work in a match factory. Dick Ayers found a job as a security guard. "I had to feed my family, but it was humiliating," Ayers said.

"I had devoted my whole life to mastering something that I thought was something of quality, and now I couldn't practice it anymore because it was considered something criminal. When I was a security guard, I thought, Well, this is ironic, because I'm supposed to be protecting something, and the whole country is trying to protect kids from me."

Harry Harrison, an artist who had collaborated with Wally Wood for EC and other publishers, had no work for a year. "There was nothing," Harrison said. "Actually, there was work, if you wanted to do juvenile crap. But if you took your work seriously at all and had any pride in what you did, there was nothing for you. Comics artists were walking the streets. People just vanished—disappeared. Top people, not just the marginal people—great talents. They were ruined." Eventually, Harrison decided to abandon art and pursue his second passion, writing.

Jack Cole, the creator of Plastic Man, one of the artists Wertham targeted in *Seduction of the Innocent* for his effectively frightful depiction of a morphine addict's nightmare—a drug pusher about to pierce the dope user's eyeball with a hypodermic needle—for *True Crime Comics*, found lucrative work drawing lusty cartoons for *Playboy*. In August 1958, Cole bought a .22-calibre rifle and shot himself dead, for reasons unknown. (The most credible theories about Cole's motives involve marital trouble, probably connected to Cole's drift into Hefner's circle of swingers, and debt; on the day of his suicide, he wrote a letter to Hugh Hefner saying "Sorry for owing you so much.")

Feldstein, Morisi, Ayers, Sekowsky, Severin, and some others passionate about comics hoped to return to the field—and did, in time. Kurtzman ended up leaving *Mad* to work for Hugh Hefner, and Gaines asked Feldstein to take over the magazine. Morisi kept his dispatcher's job but moonlighted in comics under a pseudonym. Hundreds more left comic books forever after the purge of the 1950s. Janice Valleau Winkleman finally took her father's advice and abandoned comics. "They thought we were awful people, and it wasn't right," Winkleman said. She devoted herself to her family and gave up drawing, even for pleasure, for several years. By the early sixties, she felt compelled to do something in art again and took a painting class at a community center near her home in New Jersey. On the first day of class, she sketched a figure, and the teacher brought it to the front of the class as an example of what not to do. "He said it was terrible—he said it looked like a comic book," Winkleman recalled.

Fred Guardineer, who had done crime stories (including "The Wild Spree of the Laughing Sadist" for *Crime Does Not Pay*) and Westerns for several companies, gave up comics for good and worked as a mailman on Long Island. Warren Broderick, who had collaborated with Harry Harrison for several publishers, became an ambulance driver. "Warren was a dear, gracious man and a very sensitive man—he left the business with enormous regret, and I never heard from him again," said Harrison.

Industrial art, commercial art, and advertising sustained some, such as Jack Kamen, Mort Leav, Marc Swayze, and Pierce Rice, for the duration of their working days. "I made a fine living and, if I say so myself, I was well respected among my peers in the advertising business," said Leav. "But the work was work. It wasn't comics. You couldn't be as creative. It wasn't fun. You don't have the freedom . . . I missed comic books for the rest of my life." By the end of the crackdown, in the late 1950s, more than eight hundred people who had been working in comics at the start of the decade had left the field, never to make another comic-book panel.

They did no spying for rival governments; they traded no atomic secrets. Unlike their rough counterparts in the Red Scare, the artists and writers caught up in the comic-book controversy were never charged with espionage, treason, contempt of Congress or court, or obstruction of justice. What they did was tell outrageous stories in cartoon pictures, a fact that makes their struggle and their downfall all the more strange and sad.

This is not to say that the victims of the comics purge were innocent; they were no more so than the young people Fredric Wertham accused them of seducing. Though they were not traitors, the makers of crime, romance, and horror comics were propagandists of a sort, cultural insurgents. They expressed in their lurid panels, thereby helping to instill in their readers, a disregard for the niceties of proper society, a passion for wild ideas and fast action, a cynicism toward authority of all sorts, and a tolerance, if not an appetite, for images of prurience and violence. In short, the generation of comic-book creators whose work died with the Comics Code helped give birth to the popular culture of the postwar era.

When comic-book publishing recovered, in the early 1960s, it did so by retrenching, shifting back to the heroic doings of superheroes, who have dominated mainstream comics ever since. With television now the preeminent form of mass entertainment, comic books became specialty items for adolescent boys and collectors. "I knew how to keep it simple," said Stan Lee, who revived Marvel Comics in the sixties by developing a new batch of hypertrophied costumed heroes. "We wanted to give kids a good time and give them something positive to enjoy. We didn't want to change the world."

Epilogue

Sauve, a walled amassment of gray stone along the Vidourle River, in the South of France, is, like many medieval villages, a fortress. Built to ward off intruders, it also shuts out time. The town has not changed appreciably in hundreds of years, apart from the arrival of cars. There are no signs of modern commerce—no chain stores, no billboards, few brand names anywhere. The buildings, narrow and clustered in jagged rows, are of unpainted masonry and have miniature shuttered windows dotted here and there. If you walked down the road that zig-zags around Sauve and knew which door to knock on, you could ask to see Robert Crumb, the American cartoonist. The housekeeper, following standing orders, would say he was out of town, and she would be right, figuratively speaking. Although Crumb has lived in Sauve since 1990 and, on most days, is on the second floor of his house drawing, reading, listening to music, squabbling with his wife, Aline, or otherwise enjoying himself, he has never really occupied the village. He does not speak much French, and he likes to stay indoors, in his studio, in which he has re-created the atmosphere of another place in another time: the popular culture of America in the 1920s. Shelves stacked with tens of thousands of 78-rpm records, virtually all from the first decades of sound recording, fill one side of the room. A glass-fronted bookcase holds a collection of toys and artifacts from the twenties: a Little Nemo figurine, a Felix the Cat doll . . . Framed picture sleeves from vintage records and portraits of old-time musicians paper the walls. The place is a temple of displacement—a fortress of cultural and temporal isolation, very much at home in Sauve, after all.

The only visible deviations from twenties fetishism are a second bookcase full of comic books, many of them by Robert Crumb, a few by his contemporaries, but most from the early 1950s: a collection of EC's and other comics of the pre-Code period. On the coffee table in the middle of the room on a Sunday in 2003 were some of Crumb's reading materials: a copy of the current issues of *The New Yorker* and *Leg Show* (the porn magazine), and two volumes of *Little Lulu* comics. "I was already an avid comics reader and an EC fan by the age of nine years old, when *Mad* first came out, but I wasn't allowed to bring comic books like that home—comic books with drawings of sexy girls and stuff like that were off-limits in my house. You could look at them on the newsstands, but you couldn't bring them home," said Crumb, sitting straight-backed in a chair of thin wood, painted black. He looked professorial in the long salt-and-pepper beard that he decided to grow after the release of the 1994 documentary *Crumb* made him too recognizable to too many strangers for his comfort. He was immobile when he spoke; his hands were folded in his lap, and his eyes were round and white behind thick, wire-framed glasses. "To me, EC was the culmination of everything that kind of came before it in comics. The art quality was the tops, and they had the best storytelling in comics. They were also the most serious comics in the fifties, and they were forbidden, and that made them all the more exciting."

As a teenager in suburban Delaware during the late 1950s, Crumb, with his older brother Charles, wrote and hand-printed his own fanzine, *Foo*, devoted to EC comics, Kurtzman's *Mad*, and the best of other pre-Code comics. They were members of a generation of comics readers slightly younger than EC's original fans, who came to revere the comics that had been published immediately prior to their own adolescence, in part because of the comics' quality, but also because the books' martyrdom enhanced their romantic aura. "By the time I was old enough to appreciate EC and *Mad* magazine, it was all over—the great stuff was over. I just caught the tail end of the comic-book [version of] *Mad*," said Crumb. "That made me a nostalgist at a young age and a seeker of the culture of the past at a young age. A lot of cultural things declined through the fifties, and for me, as a kid, that made me start searching for the past."

Frustrated with the juvenility and the vacuity of the Code-approved comics of the 1950s and early '60s, Crumb and his peers found solace and inspiration in the pages of pre-Code comics; and those who grew up to be comic-book artists and writers themselves carried the work's irreverence, idiosyncrasy, and ambition into underground comics and the graphic-novel movement. "Me and other guys who ended up drawing underground comics grew up loving those crazy comic books of the pre-Code period, when the comics had a lot of vitality," said Crumb. "*Mad* was probably the biggest influence of all, because it was really the coming together of everything that was great in EC and some of the other comics before the Code. The first issue that I saw on the stands when I was a little kid confused me. I had never seen respectable American institutions made fun of publicly that way. Here was a publication making fun of highly respected American institutions in the square, military, post–World War II environment and doing so in a crude, weird way. Here was this vision of America that countered all the stifling, goody-two-shoes fifties-propaganda totalitarian vision that was put forth in the media, the schools, and everything. A big part of the appeal to me was that it was so strange and esoteric and outside of this mainstream, and yet it reflected that attitude in this beautiful way. The artwork was beautiful.

"EC and some of the others were doing the same thing, to a degree, but *Mad* brought it to a kind of perfection. It was such a weird, quirky, freaky thing. Me and my brother and a lot of people in our generation never got over it."

APPENDIX

NOTES

BIBLIOGRAPHY

ACKNOWLEDGMENTS

INDEX

Appendix

Among the artists, writers, and others who never again worked in comics after the purge of the 1950s were

KIMBALL AAMODT

FREDERICK ABAIR

ARTHUR ADLER

HARRY ADLER

JOHN C. ADLER

NINA ALBRIGHT

ROY ALD

HOWARD ALEXANDER

ELAINE ALLEN

E. ALLGOR

BILL ALLISON

GERALD ALTMAN

J. ALTSMAN

LOUISE ALTSON

AL ALVISON

SALLY ANDERSON

JUNE ANDRUS

LARRY ANTONETTE

PERRY ANTOSHAK

GEORGE APPEL

JOAN APPLETON

MARIO AQUAVIVA

RUTH ARCARO

JOE ARCHIBALD

FRANK ARMER

BUSY ARNOLD

MARTY ARNOLD

RICHARD ARNOLD

MICHAEL ARTHUR

STANLEY ASCHMEIER

RAFAEL ASTARITA

JEAN ATKINS

RUTH ATKINSON

LEE BACHELOR

MART BAILEY

JOHN BAKER

E. BALTER

MANNIE BANKS

FRANK BARBER

VALERIE BARCLAY

NAT BARNETT

TOM BARON

CHARLES BARR

ADOLPHE BARREAUX

JOHN BARRON

ART BARTSCH

KEN BATTLEFIELD

BOB BEAN

CHARLES BEAUMONT

FRANK BEAVEN

EUGENIA BEDELL

ARTHUR BEEMAN

JOHN BELCASTRO

JOHN BELFI

HARRY BELIL

FRED BELL

ROBERT LESLIE BELLEM

AL BELLMAN

JOAN BEN-AVI

LORETTA BENDER

HELEN BENNETT

THOMPSON L. BENNETT

ANDREW BENSEN

JESS BENTON

BILL BENULIS

ANGELA BERG

JACK BERRILL

PHIL BERUBE

HARRY BETANCOURT

ADE BETHUNE

ELAINE BIERMAN

SAMUEL BIERMAN

JACK BINDER

PHILIP BIRCH

CHARLES BIRO

CHARLES BISHOP

MICHAEL BLEIER

AUDREY BLUM

JOHN BLUMMER

GLORIA BLYE

HERMAN BOLLIN

IVY BOLTON

LARZ BOURNE

LEIGH BRACKETT

MICHAEL BRAND

BERNARD BRANNER

R. BRAUN

ARMOND BRAUSSARD

ALAN BRENNAN

GEORGE BRENNER

BERNARD BRESLAUER

RICHARD BRICE

WARREN BRODERICK

STEVE BRODIE

BEN BROWN

JIM BROWNE

H. BROWNELL

CARL BUETTNER

Appendix

JOHN BULTHUIS

DICK BURDICK

MARY BURKE

BILL BURNETT

BOB BUTTS

GLORIA BYE

JOHN P. BYLY

JACK BYRNE

KURT CAESAR

DICK CALKINS

ROBERT CALLENDER

CORA CALNOUN

ORESTES CALPINI

DON CAMERON

THOMAS CAMPION

AL CAMY

ANTONIO CANALE

CATHERINE CAPOSELLA

RICHARD CARAIF

GEORGE CARLSON

VIC CARRABOTTA

R. CARREA

AL CARRENO

EDD CARTIER

JOHN CARTNER

BERNARD CASE

RICHARD CASE

JOHN CASSONE

TONY CATALDO

BOB CAVANAUGH

ART CAZENEUVE

LOUIS CAZENEUVE

VERA CERRUTI

ELLIS CHAMBERS

KEN CHAMPIN

RAY CHAN

LAFE CHARLES

PIERRE CHARPENTIER

LESLIE CHARTERIS

RAY CHATTON

SIDNEY CHENKIN

PAT CHERR

HARRY "A" CHESLER

LILLIAN CHESTNEY

HELEN CHOU

JIM CHRISTIANSEN

HING CHU

ELEANORE CLAIRE

ROLLAND COE

BOB COHEN

SOL COHEN

ELLEN COLE

JACK COLE

JOHN COMPTON

VESTA CONDON

WILLIAM CONGREVE

HAL COOPER

PAUL COOPER

SAM COOPER

BOB CORREA

BARNARD COSNECK

BOB COTTERILL

BRANT CRAIG

GERTRUDE CRAMPTON

EDA CRIST

RACHAEL CROFT

ED CRONIN

BETTY CUMMINGS

TONY D'ADAMO

JOSEPH DAFFRON

RALPH DAIGH

CAROLL DALY

JOHN DALY

HARRY DAUGHERTY

H. B. DAVEY

DICK DAVIS

OMAR DAVIS

RICHARD DAVIS

ROSS DAVIS

WOODY DAVIS

WALTER DAVOREN

BERT N. DEAN

TOM DeANGELO

A. DeBETHUNE

J. DECKTER

JIM DEE

A. DeKEROSET

HAROLD DELAY

MAURICE DEL BOURGO

MARTIN DeMUTH

GLORIA DENNIS

BOB DESCHAMPS

RAPHAEL DeSOTO

ANN DeSTEFFANO

DAVID DETIEGE

BURR DETT

CHARLES DEXTER

BERNARD DIBBLE

JIMMY DICKSON

ANAHID DINKJIAN

JOHN DIRKS

BILL DISCOUNT

ED DOBROTKA

TOM DOERER

VIC DONAHUE

HOBART DONAVAN

JOE DOOLIN

CLARENCE DOORE

STEPHEN DOUGLAS

ESTHER DOUTY

VIC DOWD

VIC DOWLING

LAWRENCE DRESSER

IRVING DRESSLER

PETER DRIBEN

MICK DUBIN

STEVE DUBIN

ED DUNN

JACK DUNNING

DANA DUTCH

LEONARD DWORKINS

AL EADEH

TOM EAGLIN

WILLIAM EATON

WILLIAM EKGREN

JILL ELGIN

RALPH ELLSWORTH

JAY EMMETT

FRED ENG

RENALDO EPWORTH

MICHAEL ESTROW

GIL EVANS

PHILIP EVANS

VIC EVANS

F. J. EVERS

AL FAGALY

BLANCHE FAGO

VINCE FAGO

BARBARA FAIRBANKS

RALPH FARLEY

TOM FARLEY

JACK FARR

JERRY FASANO

AL FASS

GORDON FAWCETT

ROSCOE FAWCETT

WILFRED FAWCETT

GENE FAWCETTE

HANK FELSEN

ERNIE FENNER

PABLO FERRO

W. Y. FERROL

LOUIS FERSTADT

OTTO FEUER

NEVIN FIDLER

EILEEN FIEL

JOHN FINNERTY

S. FINOCCHIARO

NICHOLAS FIRFIRES

JOHN FISCETTI

HARRY FISK

BILL FIX

RAYMOND FLANAGAN

CHARLES FLANDERS

HY FLEISHMAN

HOMER FLEMING

FRANK FLETCHER

E. E. FODERA

VINCE FODERA

FRANK FOGARTY

GEORGE FOLEY

CARL FORMES

VICTOR FOX

ARTHUR FRAMSON

LEE FRANK

LEONARD FRANK

NICK FRANK

GEORGE FRESE

BILL FRIEDMAN

SOPHIE FRIEDMAN

AUGUST FROELICH

MONROE FROELICH

BURT FROHMAN

FRANK FROLLO

HAL FROMM

NORMAN FRUMAN

JOE GAGLIARDI

JERRY GALE

BEN GALLOWAY

TOM GALLOWAY

JOE GALOTTI

RUDY GARCIA

ROGER GARIS

JIM GARY

ARTHUR GATES

PAUL GATTUSO

WALTER GEIER

WOODY GELMAN

JOHN GENTILELLA

DAVE GERARD

MICHAEL GERBOSI

EMIL GERSHWIN

SID GERSON

JOE GEVANTER

JOHN GIFFIN

SAM GLANKOFF

LEV GLEASON

AL GLEICHER

BOB GLOBERMAN

H. L. GOLD

ED GOLDFARB

LOUIS GOLDKLANG

EDMOND GOOD

DAVID GOODMAN

EVELYN GOODMAN

JEAN GOODMAN

AL GORDON

GEORGE GORDON

DAN GORMLEY

JAY GOUDE

JOHN GRAHAM

ALLEN GRAMMAR

BOB GRANT

DOUGLAS GRANT

EDWIN GREEN

ALFONSO GREENE

JOE GREENE

VERN GREENE

GEORGE GREGG

AL GRENET

WILLIAM GREW

HARLEY GRIFFITHS

SY GRUDKO

ELEANER GRUPSMITH

FRED GUARDINEER

DON GUNN

PAUL GUSTAVSON

MAURICE GUTWIRTH

SIDNEY GWIRTZMAN

CLARK HAAS

ED HAAS

GEORGE HAAS

LEO HAGLER

EMERSON HALL

THEDA HALL

MILT HAMMER

JOHN HAMPTON

BONNIE HANO

GWEN HANSEN

LAVERNE HARDING

ALLEN HARDY

W. G. HARGIS

CLINT HARMON

THURSTON HARPER

RUTH HARRIS

HARRY HARRISON

FRANK HARRY

C. L. HARTMAN

HANK HARTMAN

STUART HAWKINS

DAVID HEAMES

JACK HEARNE

MIRIAM HECHT

CHARLES HEDINGER

MEL HELITZER

VERN HENKEL

H. L. HERBERT

RAE HERMAN

VIC HERMAN

ERWIN HESS

BARBARA HEYMAN

BOBBIE HEYMAN

ANDREA HILL

BETTY HILL

LOUISE HILL

RUSS HILL

ROGER HOAR

PAUL HODGE

SYD HOFF

PHYLLIS HOFFMAN

JIM HOLDAWAY

ARNOLD HOLEYWELL

ALVIN C. HOLLINGSWORTH

MATT HOLLINGSWORTH

LEN HOLLREISER

RED HOLMDALE

LAWRENCE HOPE

ORA HOPE

FRANCES HOPPER

RAY HOULIHAN

CHARLES HOUTS

MARTIN HOWARD

MARVIN HOWARD

VIRGINIA HUBBELL

BILL HUDSON

EUGENE HUGHES

ETTA HULME

DOROTHY HUNTER

EDWIN HUNTER

S. M. IGER

JIM INFANTINO

GRAHAM INGELS

MEDIO IORIO

WILLIAM I. IRWIN

MARGARET ISBELLA

ARTHUR JAMESON

LEON JASON

AL JETTER

LINO JEVA

E. HARPER JOHNSON

RYERSON JOHNSON

WALTER JOHNSON

FRANK JUPO

ED JURIST

DAVID KAHN

RICHARD KAHN

JACK KAMEN

EUGENE KANE

HAL KANTER

HUBIE KARP

PAUL KAST

RUBY KAST

L. KATO

R. KAY

RUSSELL KEATON

PHIL KEENAN

DAN KEENE

DICK KEENE

DOROTHY KELLER

CHAD KELLY

Appendix

BOB KENT

GEORGE KERR

DAN KEYES

HENRY CARL KIEFER

H. W. KIEMLE

MALCOLM KILDALE

WOODY KIMBRELL

BERESFORD KING

DON KING

ROBIN KING

WARREN KING

A. L. KIRBY

MARION KIRBY

STEVE KIRKEL

ALICE KIRKPATRICK

IVAN KLAPPER

ISIDORE KLEIN

CLAYTON KNIGHT

MILT KNOPF

BILL KOFED

EVE KORIDOR

PETER KORTNER

ALEX KOSTUK

ALEX KOTZKY

ERNIE KOVACS

JOHN CHESTER KOZLAK

FRANK KRAMER

JERRY KRAMER

RAY KRANK

DICK KRAUSE

NATALIE KRIGSTEIN

NORMAN KURNICK

HENRY KUTTNER

BILL LA CAVA

WILLIAM LACKEY

BOB LAMME

HARRY LAMPERT

KEN LANDAU

BOB LANDER

A. M. LANGWORTHY

JOHN LANIER

STEVE LANSING

BOB LANZA

CLAUDE LAPHAM

HOWARD LARSEN

CHARLES LAUE

DENNIS LAUGEN

JIM LAVERY

MORT LAWRENCE

MARJORIE LAZARUS

MORT LEAV

HAROLD LEDOUX

FRANK LEE

KEN LEEDS

JOHN LEEWING

HENRY LEIFERANT

STAN LEIN

LEN LEONE

MARIO LEONE

GENE LESLIE

JEAN LEVANDER

LEO LEVESQUE

BEN LEVIN

MORT LEVIN

TSUNG LI

WILLIAM LIEBERSON

AL LIEDERMAN

FRANK LITTLE

IRENE LITTLE

WALLY LITTMAN

HAL LOCKWOOD

EARL LONSBURY

DICK LOOMIS

ADRIAN LOPEZ

DAN LOPRIENO

PAULINE LOTH

STAN LOUIS

GABE LUCHETTI

MIKE LUCHETTI

EDWIN LUKAS

AL LUSTER

BOB MACK

N. MACK

DON MacLAUGHLIN

BOB MacLEOD

VINCE MADAFFERI

BILL MADDEN

J. MAKOWSKI

JOE MANEELY

ISABEL MANGUM

MOE MARCUS

GEORGE MARKO

JESSE MARLAN

BILL MARLOWE

CHET MARTIN

HAZEL MARTIN

JOHN MARTIN

S. MARTIN

ROBERT MARTINOTT

LESLIE MASON

CAL MASSEY

JOAN MAURER

LEN MAURER

JOHN MAYO

RALPH MAYO

JAY McARDLE

BOB McCARTHY

RAY McCLELLAND

MARION McDERMOTT

JAMES McKELL

CHUCK McKIMSON

ROBERT McKIMSON

JIM McLAUGHLIN

AL McLEAN

TOM McNAMARA

FRANK McSAVAGE

FRED MEAGHER

RAYMOND MELLON

ABRAHAM MENIN

ANN MEREDITH

JESSE MERLAN

SAM MERWIN

OTTO MESMER

G. MEYERIECKS

JEFF MICHAELS

GEORGE MIGHT

MELVIN MILLAR

JOE MILLARD

CHUCK MILLER

HARRY MILLER

FRANK MINTON

JOHN MITCHELL

ED MOBILE

ED MOLINE

DAVID MONEYPENNY

BOB MOORE

CLAUDE MOORE

ED MOORE

HELEN MOORE

RUTH MOORE

SANFORD MOORE

DICK MOORES

TOM MORRISON

FRED A. MORTON

SY MOSKOWITZ

STEVE MUFFATTI

ED MURPHY

LORRAINE MURPHY

T. A. MURPHY

JOE MUSIAL

ROBERT NANOVIC

FRANK NAPOLEON

VINCE NAPOLI

PETER NELSON

RALPH NEWMAN

ZOE NEWMAN

BILL NEWTON

ROD NICHOLS

ARTHUR WILLIAM NUGENT

GEORGE OLESON

JACK OLESON

MARJORIE OLSEN

VICTOR OLSON

BILL O'MALLEY

PAUL OREN

JOHN O'ROURKE

P. O'SULLIVAN

RALPH OWEN

AL OWENS

JIM PABIAN

LEROY PAIGE

MAC PAKULA

WALTER PALAIS

ART PALETTE

HARRY PARKHURST

ROMANA PATENAUDE

VIC PAZMINO

MARJORIE PEARSON

LYNN PERKINS

JEROME PERLES

MARTIN N. PERRY

HARRY PETER

MAX PETERMAN

ERIC PETERS

FRED PETERS

THELMA PETERS

JACK PETRAZZO

KEATS PETREE

ART PINAJIAN

NED PINES

ROBERT PIOUS

MAX PLAISTED

W. POLSENO

WALTER POPP

JOHN PRENTICE

CHARLES PRESTON

JOAN PRINGLE

VIRGINIA PROVISIERO

DONALD QUEEN

CHARLES QUINLAN

SIDNEY QUINN

CHARLES RAAB

YVONNE RAE

HARRY RAMSEY

CONNIE RASINSKI

LOUIS RAVIELLI

AL REID

JIM REILLEY

KEN REILLY

BENTON RESNICK

GUS RICCA

BENTON RICE

BOB RICE

KENNETH RICE

PIERCE RICE

EDNA RICHTER

PETE RISS

TONY RIVERA

MARIO RIZZI

PAUL ROBINSON

RUTH ANN ROCHE

CHARLES RODGERS

BOB ROGERS

BOODY ROGERS

JESSE ROGERS

GORDON ROSE

HAL ROSEN

SAUL ROSEN

HOWARD ROSENBERGER

MAURICE ROSENFELD

TED ROSENFIELD

MARTIN ROSENHECK

MARTIN ROSS

ROSALIND ROSS

JIM ROTEN

ALDO RUBANO

MANN RUBIN

RUTH RUHMAN

RHETT RUTLEDGE

B. SAFRAN

HENRY SAHLE

ROBERT SALE

JOE SAMACHSON

HAROLD SANDBERG

LARRY SANGER

BEN SANGOR

FRANCIS SANGOR

RONALD SANTI

MARIE SARAFIANOS

LARRY SAUNDERS

BILL SAVAGE

CHRIS R. SCHAARE

ROY SCHATT

TOM SCHEUER

HENRY SCHLOSSER

HELEN DOIG SCHMID

B. SCHNEIDER

IRWIN SCHOFFMAN

RAY SCHOTT

WILLIAM SCHREIBER

HANNA SCHREIBERG

LOUIS SCHROEDER

TED SCHROEDER

GUS SCHROTTER

JAMES SCHUCKER

AL SCHUSTER

FRED SCHWAB

AL SCHWARTZ

LEW SCHWARTZ

H. W. SCOTT

THURMAN SCOTT

WALT SCOTT

SUZANNE SEABORNE

HAL SEEGER

BOB SEEVERS

JOY SELIGSOHN

ZEKE SELIGSOHN

ART SEYMOUR

IRWIN SHAPIRO

JACK SHAPIRO

HENRY SHARP

EARL SHERWAN

GORDON SHIRREFFS

MERCEDES SHULL

PEN SHUMAKER

MORRIS SIEGEL

NANCY SIEGEL

FRANK SIEMINSKY

BERNIE SILLS

ABE SIMON

S. SIMON

SAM SINGER

JOHN SINK

MARION SITTON

ELIZABETH SLOAN

RICHARD SMALL

ED SMALLE

AL SMITH

CARL SMITH

CHRISTINE SMITH

MARTIN SMITH

RICHARD SMITH

ROY SMITH

W. B. SMITH

MARCIA SNYDER

ROBERT SOLOMON

PAUL SOMMER

MILTON SORUL

BEVERLY SOUSER

JOE SPAINSKY

IRV SPECTOR

RICHARD SPEED

JOHN SPRANGER

EMILIO SQUEGLIO

ARCHER ST. JOHN

JOHN STARR

LEONARD STARR

DICK STEELE

RANDY STEFFEN

HARRY STEIN

MILT STEIN

SAUL STEIN

IRVING STEINBERG

NORMAN STEINBERG

HARRIS STEINBROOK

JULES STEINER

CHARLES STERN

LEONARD STERN

ROGER STERN

CHARLES STEWART

RAY STILL

ALBERT STOFFEL

LEE STOKES

E. C. STONER

HAL STRAUBING

MYRON STRAUSS

LIN STREETER

LOU STRICKOFF

CHARLES STRONG

BOB STUART

MYRON SUAREZ

MIKE SUCHORSKY

JOE SULMAN

CHARLES SULTAN

CECIL SURRY

MARC SWAYZE

SAM SWESKIN

ZOLTAN SZENICS

PAUL TALBOT

LEE TARRANT

HERB TAUSS

LEE TEAFORD

DAVID TENDLAR

HILDA TERRY

ALBERTA TEWKS

MARTIN THALL

E. THAYER

RAY THAYER

FRANK THOMAS

A. THOMPSON

BEN THOMPSON

BRETT THOMPSON

BUD THOMPSON

JIMMY THOMPSON

RAY THORLEY

JOHN THORNTON

BERTHOLD TIEDEMAN

RALPH TILLER

REUBEN TIMMINS

MURRAY TINKLEMAN

ANTONIO TOLDO

CHARLIE TOMSEY

FLOYD TORBERT

MEDIO TORRIO

MARRYLEN TOWNSEND

PAT TROY

BART TUMEY

PETE TUMLINSON

GIL TURNER

ROBERT TURNER

JIM TYER

AL TYLER

TED UDALL

ALLEN ULMER

CHARLES VERRAL

HERMAN VESTAL

GLENN VILLPU

CARLO VINCI

BARBARA CLARK VOGEL

ED VOLKE

PETER VOORHEES

LEO WALD

JOHN T. WALDEN	EDGAR WHEELAN
ED WALDMAN	DON WHITE
GEORGE WALDON	MALCOLM WHITE
ARTHUR WALLACE	WILLIAM WHITE
MARY WALLACE	EZRA WHITEMAN
LESLIE WALLER	BERT WHITMAN
ED WALOM	BOB WICKERSHAM
STAN WALSH	JIM WILCOX
JERRY WALTERS	LILY RENÉE WILHELMS
LINDA WALTERS	PRISCILLA WILLARD
BILL WALTON	WITMER WILLIAMS
BILL WARD	SAM WILLINSKY
GEORGE WARD	RAY WILLNER
KING WARD	EMERY WILSON
JACK WARREN	ED WINIARSKI
IVES WASHBURN	LEON WINIK
BOB WEBB	JANICE VALLEAU WINKLEMAN
FERRIS WEDDLE	CHARLES A. WINTER
WERNER WEIBEL	CHARLES W. WINTER
IRVING WEINSTEIN	BURT WOHL
CLEM WEISBECKER	RALPH WOLFE
MORRIS WEISS	JOSEPH WOLFERT
KERMIT WELLES	KAEM WONG
MANLEY WADE WELLMAN	BOB WOOD
DIXON WELLS	CATHERINE WOODS
PETER WELLS	SANDY WOOLF
WILLIAM WELTMAN	WILLIAM WOOLFOLK
JOAN WENZEL	MOE WORTHMAN
JANE WERNER	ROSE WYN
IRVING WERSTEIN	WILL YOLAN
G. H. WERTHEIMER	LES ZAKARIN
NORMAN WEXLER	PEGGY ZANGERLE

Appendix

LOUIS ZANSKY   DAN ZOLNEROWICH

WILLIAM ZELLER   RUBIN ZUBOVSKY

WILLIAM ZIMMERMAN   NICK ZURAW

Notes

This is a work of relatively recent history. Many of the participants in the events described here were available to provide firsthand accounts of those events when I was researching this book, in the first years of the twenty-first century. I was fortunate to interview more than 150 comic-book artists, writers, editors, publishers, readers, and others over a period of six years. Their recollections—weighed against documentary materials, contemporary accounts, and the vagaries of memory—were an invaluable resource. The testimony of the following informs this book: Kimball Aamodt, Lee Ames, Sergio Aragones, Dick Ayers, Milton Babinec, Valerie Baim, Kaye Bald, Ken Bald, Valerie Barclay, Frank Bolle, Frank Borth, Bill Bossert, Frank Bourgholtzer, Bob Boyajian, Joseph E. Buresch, John Calnan, Joseph Canny, Nick Cardy, Ann Cazeneuve, John Celardo, John Chiangi, Bob Clarke, Gene Colan, Robert Crumb, Jack Davis, Dick DeBartolo, Frances DiPreta, Tony DiPreta, Victor Dowd, Arnold Drake, Mort Drucker, Steve Duquette, Joe Edwards, Ann Eisner, Will Eisner, Will Elder, Mike Esposito, Jules Feiffer, Al Feldstein, A. J. Fenady, Martin Filchock, Creig Flessel, Gill Fox, Ramona Fradon, Bob Fujitani, Ruth Hamburger Fujitani, David Gantz, Walter Geier, Joe Giella, Joe Gill, Tom Gill, Dick Giordano, Dave Glanzman, Louis Glanzman, Sam Glanzman, Stan Goldberg, Al Grenet, Harry Harrison, Stan Hart, Irwin Hasen, Vincent Hawley, Russ Heath, Donald Heisserer, Carmine Infantino, JoAnne Jackson, Robert Jackson, Frank Jacobs, Al Jaffee,

Notes

Karen Jensen, Evelyn Kamen, Jack Kamen, Monsignor James D. Kane, Stanley Kauffmann, Fred Kida, Everett Raymond Kinstler, Denis Kitchen, Ivan Klapper, Lenore Klapper, Tom Koch, Arnie Kogen, Irving Kravsow, Joe Kubert, Adele Kurtzman, Sam Kweskin, Harry Lampert, Mort Leav, Stan Lee, Marvin Levy, Bob Lubbers, David Mace, George Mandel, Vanita Marlow, Fran Matera, Chuck Mazoujian, Nick Meglin, Jack Mendelsohn, Bonnie Miller, Helen Miller, Sheldon Moldoff, Jim Mooney, Louise Morisi, Pete Morisi, Stanley P. Morse, Dr. Rocco L. Motto, Frank Murphy, Martin Nodell, Paul Norris, Irv Novick, Sylvia Novick, Nicholas O'Dell, Bob Oksner, Rudy Palais, Walter Palais, Randolph Parker, Gordon Parks, Don Perlin, Fred Peters, Reuben C. Peterson, Jay Scott Pike, Al Plastino, Paul Plocinski, Pete Poplaski, Howard Post, Jerry Robinson, Herb Rogoff, John Romita, Merton Stanley Rothman, Ruth Schlicher, Al Schutzer, Alvin Schwartz, Julius Schwartz, John Severin, Marie Severin, Larry Siegel, Joe Simon, Betty Sinnott, Joe Sinnott, Shirley Norris Smith, Mickey Spillane, Emilio Squeglio, Bhob Stewart, Lyle Stuart, Ed Summer, Marc Swayze, Martin Thall, Frank Thorne, Angelo Torres, Alex Toth, Warren Tremaine, George Tuska, Leslie Waller, Blanche Weiss, Morris Weiss, Elmer Wexler, Ted White, Al Williamson, Ed Winkleman, Janice Valleau Winkleman, and Ted Yaworsky.

Prologue

3   *Sawgrass Village:* Interview Janice Valleau Winkleman and Edward Winkleman on location; interview Jane Sapere, May Management.

3   *Her daughter Ellen:* Interview Ellen Winkleman.

4   *"I like art":* Interview Janice Valleau Winkleman.

4   *"I wanted to be":* Ibid.

5   *"My God":* Ibid.

5   *between eighty million:* "Comics Debated As Good or Evil," *New York Times,* October 30, 1948; "Fighting Gunfire with Fire," *Newsweek,* December 20, 1948. Throughout this book, I used contemporary sources for statistics on comic-book sales, when they were available. In addition, I drew upon statistics published in *The Comic Book in America* by Mike Benton, *Encyclopedia of American Comics* by Ron Goulart, *Comix: A History of Comic Books in America* by Les Daniels, and *Comics Between the Panels* by Steve Duin and Mike Richardson. For additional data on comic-book sales, I am grateful to the comics historian Russ Maheras.

5   *more than twenty publishers:* For information on numbers of publishers, names of publishing companies, and titles of comics cited here and throughout this book, I am indebted to the research of John Jackson Miller, editorial director of the *Standard Catalog of Comic Books* and the *Comics Buyer's Guide*; Miller's main resource is contemporary data supplied by comics publishers to the Audit Bureau of Circulation.

6   *"Comic books are definitely":* Quoted in "Comic Books Are Called Obscene by N.Y. Psychiatrist at Hearing," *New York Herald Tribune*, October 28, 1947.

6   *"I think Hitler":* Quoted in *Report of the Subcommittee to Investigate Juvenile Delinquency of the Committee on the Judiciary*, U.S. Senate. This report will henceforth be referred to as *Report of the Subcommittee on JD*.

6   *"The time has come":* Quoted in "Horror in the Nursery," *Collier's*, March 27, 1948.

7   *"Depravity for Children":* *Hartford Courant*, February 14, 1954.

7   *"Horror in the Nursery":* *Collier's*, March 27, 1948.

7   *"The Curse of the Comic Books":* *Religious Education*, November–December 1956.

7   *More than a hundred:* "Modern Comics Hit by Mayors' Report," *New York Times*, November 25, 1948; "Regulation of Comic Books," *Harvard Law Review*, January 1955; Edward L. Feder, *Comic Book Regulation*.

7   *more than eight hundred people:* See note on sources for the Appendix.

7   *Page-one news:* "No Harm in Horror, Comics Issuer Says," *New York Times*, April 22, 1954; "Whether Crime 'Comic' Books Lead Child Astray Is Debated," *New York Herald Tribune*, April 22, 1954.

Chapter 1: Society Iss Nix

9   *Near the end:* For facts on the early history of comic strips, I am indebted to *The Comics: An Illustrated History of Comic Strip Art* by Jerry Robinson and *The World Encyclopedia of Comics*, edited by Maurice Horn, as well as to *The Smithsonian Collection of Newspaper Comics*, edited by Bill Blackbeard and Martin Williams, and *100 Years of Comic Strips*, edited by Blackbeard, Dale Crain, and James Vance.

9   *more than thirty daily newspapers:* "Daily Newspapers Published Within the Present Boundaries of New York City," *The Encyclopedia of New York City*.

10   *"De phonograph":* Reproduced in *100 Years of Comic Strips*.

10 *"Society iss nix":* Quoted in *Time*, December 1, 1947.

11 *"humor prepared"* . . . *"brutality":* "The Humor of the Colored Supplement," *Atlantic Monthly*, August 1906.

12 *"Are we parents":* "A Crime Against American Children," *Ladies' Home Journal*, January 1909.

13 *Other magazines:* Untitled article, *The Nation*, November 5, 1908 ("Material which in no other country in the world would be offered to anybody but infants or idiots, is here gravely thrust upon presumably intelligent readers . . ."); "The Comic Sunday Supplement," *Good Housekeeping*, May 1910 ("The comic supplement is a force which makes for lawlessness, debauched fancy, irreverence . . .").

13 *"eight pages of polychromatic":* New York Journal, October 17, 1896.

13 *millions of American:* Frank Luther Mott, *American Journalism: A History 1690–1960*.

14 *"colored Creole":* Patrick McDonnell, Karen O'Connell, and Georgia Riley de Havenon, *Krazy Kat: The Comic Art of George Herriman*.

15 *"With those who hold":* Gilbert Seldes, *The Seven Lively Arts*.

15 *After nightfall:* Interview Will Eisner, with corroboration and additional Eisner family history from Eliot Gordon, Eisner family historian (and husband of Will Eisner's late sister Rhoda).

16 *"The comic strips"* . . . *"ghetto":* Interview Eisner.

16 *also could emulate Segar:* Drawings by Reagan reproduced in "New York Day by Day," *New York Times*, August 19, 1982.

16 *"They were full of vivid":* Interview Creig Flessel.

17 *"I started out copying":* Interview Everett Raymond Kinstler.

18 *"He had drama":* Interview Eisner.

18 *his first publication:* Reproduced in Catherine Yronwode, *The Art of Will Eisner*.

18 *"My father had finally":* Interview Eisner.

18 Eve, *sponsored by Tetley Tea:* Yronwode, *The Art of Will Eisner*.

18 *"They wanted classy":* Interview Eisner.

19 *In February of that year:* Although the cover date of the first issue of *New Fun* was February 1935, it probably reached newsstands at least a month, perhaps several months, before then.

20 *"I see these magazines":* Letter from Wheeler-Nicholson to Siegel, quoted in Daniels, *Superman: The Complete History*.

20   *specialties of guile . . . bowed:* Veterans of early comics traded lore of Wheeler-Nicholson for decades; Creig Flessel, who did his first work for the major in 1936, could draw him from memory more than sixty years later.

20   *"The major was very quiet":* Interview Flessel.

21   *some antecedents:* For facts on the early years of comic books, I owe debts to several encyclopedic works of comics history: Benton's *The Comic Book in America*; Goulart's *Encyclopedia of American Comics* and *Great American Comic Books*; Daniels's *Comix: A History of Comic Books in America*; Duin and Richardson's *Comics: Between the Panels*; *Comics, Comix and Graphic Novels: A History of Comic Art* by Roger Sabin; and *A Smithsonian Book of Comic-Book Comics*, edited by Michael Barrier and Martin Williams.

22   *still contained old material:* A small Chicago publisher, Humor Publishing (also called Consolidated Publishing) issued at least three different black-and-white comic books, each centered on a different fictional detective, as early as 1933; distributed regionally and issued briefly, they were probably the first single-character comic books.

22   *"It was wide open":* Interview Joe Kubert. Kubert has told varying versions of the story of his introduction to the comics business at age ten, sometimes setting it at the comics shop run by Harry "A" Chesler, sometimes at MLJ; however, MLJ did not start operation until 1939, when Kubert was thirteen.

22   *"Bob was a very vapid":* Interview Eisner.

23   *"Of course":* Quoted in interview Eisner. Eisner told me this anecdote on three occasions, twice setting it in Manhattan, once in the Bronx. In one version, Kahn/Kane said, "They buy from everybody, even me."

23   *"Most comic books were publishing":* Ibid.

25   *"Will Eisner treated":* Interview Bill Bossert.

25   *"He was something":* Interview Eisner.

25   *"The camaraderie":* Interview Lee Ames.

26   *"I wanted to be":* Interview Nick Cardy.

26   *mural of athletes:* Reprinted in John Coates with Nick Cardy, *The Art of Nick Cardy.*

26   *"I found, first":* Interview Cardy.

26   *Audrey "Toni" Blum:* Interview Bossert, who married Blum while they were working in comics.

27   *"an Egyptian galley":* Interview Eisner.

27   *"Send an ambulance":* Reproduced in Yronwode, *The Art of Will Eisner.*

Notes

28   "*Muss 'Em Up was full*": Jules Feiffer, *The Great Comic Book Heroes.*

28   "*I believe they call*": Interview Flessel.

28   *a dummy issue:* Reproduced on the Grand Comic Database website. The GCD, a not-for-profit site operated by and for fans, was a useful source of information on the contents of long-out-of-print comics, here and throughout this book.

29   "*I thought it was good*": Quoted in Duin and Richardson, *Comics: Between the Panels.*

30   "*There's no question*": Interview Bob Oksner.

30   "*Champion of the Oppressed*": Action Comics, June 1938. On the first page of his first appearance in a comic book, Superman is introduced as "champion of the oppressed, the physical marvel who had sworn to devote his existence to helping those in need!"

30   *magazines, radio, and the movies:* Television, still experimental, would not make an impact in America until the World's Fair the following year, when RCA demonstrated prototype TV sets, housed in clear Lucite cabinets to prove that the equipment was really generating the pictures. Raymond Fielding, *Technological History of Motion Pictures and Television: An Anthology from the Pages of "The Journal of the Society of Motion Pictures and Television Engineers."*

31   *The special effects:* Advertisement, *American Artist,* April 1938.

31   *by its nineteenth issue . . . 300 cities:* Daniels, *Superman: The Complete History.*

31   *Amazing Man . . . Wonder Woman:* GCD.

Chapter 2: It Was Work

32   *Harry "A" Chesler, Jr.:* Information on Chesler and his studio came from veterans of the shop, including Creig Flessel, Gill Fox, Irwin Hasen, Jack Kamen, and Joe Kubert.

33   "*How much do you need*": Quoted in interview Fox.

33   "*Good work, kid!*": Quoted in interview Hasen.

33   "*That's when I learned*": Interview Hasen.

33   *By 1940, the population:* United States Bureau of the Census, *Historical Statistics of the United States, Colonial Times to 1970.*

34   *The number of comic books:* Research by John Jackson Miller, Russ Maheras.

34   "*It was a medium*": Interview Tom Gill.

34   "*Basically we*": Interview Jerrry Robinson.

35   *$15 to $25:* Interviews with Flessel, Fox, Hasen, Kamen, Kubert, Gill, Robinson, others.

35   *"Oh, it was like":* Interview Bob Lubbers.

35   *"A lot of guys":* Interview Mickey Spillane.

36   *"I decided":* Interview Al Jaffee.

36   *"When I went":* Ibid.

36   *"less grown-up" . . . "in those days":* Interview Jules Feiffer.

37   *"I really loved":* Interview Martin Thall.

37   *"Everything else" . . . "they fell apart":* Interview Ted White.

38   *"I made my bones":* Interview Eisner.

39   *"The comic strip, he explains":* Philadelphia Record, October 13, 1941.

39   *grandson of Midwestern homesteaders . . . literature:* Sterling North Society.

39   *literate independent paper:* Dick Griffin and Rob Warden, *Done in a Day: 100 Years of Great Writing from the* Chicago Daily News.

39   *there was an article:* "The North Family Reviews the Spring Flight of Juveniles," *Chicago Daily News,* May 8, 1940.

40   *The packing:* Ibid.

40   *"the adventures" . . . "ornithologist":* Ibid.

40   *"Virtually every child . . . negligence":* "A National Disgrace (And a challenge to American Parents)," *Chicago Daily News,* May 8, 1940.

43   *"My mother would":* Interview Sam Kweskin.

43   *"I remember that":* Ibid.

44   *Within a year . . . magazine:* "The Antidote to Comics," *National Parent-Teacher Magazine,* March 1941.

44   *"The 'comics' magazines":* Ibid.

44   *"the highly colored enemy" . . . "objectionable":* "The Comics Menace," *Wilson Library Bulletin,* June 1941.

44   *"The comic . . . folklore of the times":* Lauretta Bender and Reginald S. Lourie, "The Effect of Comic Books on the Ideology of Children," paper presented to annual meeting of the American Orthopsychiatric Association, New York, February 22, 1941. Papers of Lauretta Bender, Brooklyn College Library, Special Collections. While none of the New York papers covered this event, the *Los Angeles Times* published a short item on it, referring to Bender as a "woman physician," in the manner of the day, misquoting her, and snickering at her comments as "high-sounding." "Comics Held Beneficial for Children by Psychologist," *Los Angeles Times,* February 23, 1941.

Notes

45 *seven million . . . $2 million:* "They Call 'Em 'Comics,'" *Fitchburg Sentinel*, July 28, 1941.

45 *full-page house ad:* "Introducing the Editorial Advisory Board," *New Fun*, October 1941.

45 *Dr. Robert Thorndyke:* Mel Brooks would later use this name for the lead character, the director of the Psycho-Neurotic Institute for the Very, Very Nervous, in his 1977 Hitchcock spoof *High Anxiety*.

46 *Organized by M. C. Gaines:* "Funny Business," *Forbes*, September 1, 1943.

46 *"I reported to Shelly Mayer" . . . "so we did":* Interview Harry Lampert.

46 *"I worked at a couple":* Interview Martin Nodell.

47 *Less than four weeks: Weekly Comic Book, Chicago Sun*, June 2, 1940.

48 *Eisner interwove:* "Two Lives," *The Spirit*, December 12, 1948.

48 *a goofy nobody:* "Gerhard Shnobble," *The Spirit*, September 5, 1948.

48 *Adolf Hitler on a secret:* "The Tale of the Dictator's Reform," *The Spirit*, June 22, 1941.

49 *told from the point of view:* "The Killer," *The Spirit*, December 8, 1946.

49 *Another one took place:* "Ten Minutes," *The Spirit*, September 11, 1949.

49 *The text for another:* "Killer McNobby," *The Spirit*, June 1, 1941.

49 *Another had no dialogue:* "Hoagy the Yogi, Part Two," *The Spirit*, March 23, 1947.

49 *One meta-episode:* "Self Portrait," May 3, 1942.

49 *Jules Feiffer, who was:* Feiffer, *The Great Comic Book Heroes*.

49 *"I suppose he was Jewish":* Interview Eisner.

50 *"After the relatively innocent":* John Updike, quoted in *Comic Book Artist*, November 2005.

50 *Arnold, a former salesman:* Information on Busy Arnold and Quality Comics came from his artists, including Will Eisner, Gill Fox, Tony DiPreta, Bob Fujitani, George Tuska, and Janice Valleau Winkleman.

51 *"You could buy a lot":* Interview Tony DiPreta.

51 *There is a photo:* Courtesy of Winkleman.

51 *"Oh, Busy was all right":* Interview Winkleman.

51 *Phoenix Art Institute:* "Professional Schools" advertisements, *New York Times*, August 17, 1941.

52 *"The school was really":* Interview Winkleman.

52 *an exact duplicate:* "The Origin of Midnight," *Smash Comics*, January 1941.

Notes

Chapter 3: Crime Pays

53   *The small troupe:* Ephraim Katz, *The Film Encyclopedia*.

54   *"We should make a movie":* Quoted in Michael Freedland, *Cagney*.

54   *At the film's premiere:* Ibid.

55   *Timely's Sub-Mariner:* "The Sub-Mariner Goes to War," *Marvel Mystery Comics*, February 1940.

55   *the same company's . . . Captain America:* *Captain America Comics*, March 1941.

55   *"to pay for part":* Quoted in M. C. Gaines, "Youth and the War Effort," radio address broadcast on CBS series *Children Are Also People*, April 22, 1942, and published by All-American Comics as a pamphlet. Bender Papers.

55   *Hitler appeared:* Duin and Richardson, *Comics Between the Panels*.

55   *The youngest of several sons:* Information on Charles Biro's childhood came from the brothers Rudy Palais and Walter Palais.

56   *following Cagney:* James Cagney, *Cagney by Cagney*.

56   *"It was a rough-and-tumble":* Interview Rudy Palais.

56   *"I found out eventually":* Ibid.

57   *Grand Central School of Art:* "Professional Schools" advertisements, *New York Times*, August 17, 1941.

57   *"He was a very strong":* Interview Hasen.

58   *"Lev Gleason was a very clever":* Interview Jerry Robinson.

59   *Minot "Mickey" Jelke III:* "Oleo Heir Is Seized in Vice Raids Here," *New York Times*, August 16, 1952.

59   *"Bob Wood loved to hear":* Interview Pete Morisi. In August 1958, Bob Wood spent eleven days with a companion named Violette Phillips in a cheap hotel off Gramercy Park. During an argument, he beat her to death with a clothes iron. Wood never denied doing the killing. He was convicted of manslaughter and served three years in Sing Sing. "Cartoonist Held as Slayer," *New York Times*, August 28, 1958; "Gramercy Park Gets the Horrors: Editor of Mag Called 'Crime Does Not Pay' Murders Ad Woman in a Hotel Tryst," *New York Sunday News*, September 14, 1958; Duin and Richardson, *Comics: Between the Panels*.

59   *some of the stories:* "The Killer Who Hated Death," *Daredevil Comics*, September 1941; "Death Is the Referee," *Daredevil Comics*, October 1941.

60   *the $100 fee:* *Annual Report of the Postmaster General for the Fiscal Year Ended June 30, 1941*.

Notes

60   *"However unacceptable they may be"*: Josette Frank, *What Books for Children?*

62   *"consider[ed] them highly important"*: "The Director—1," *The New Yorker*, September 25, 1937.

62   *In May 1936*: Mike Benton, *The Illustrated History of Crime Comics*.

62   *A few months later*: Famous Funnies, October 1936.

62   *The jurisdiction of one*: "Calling All Cars," "The Purple Tiger, Part I," *More Fun*, July 1936.

62   *the other*: "Federal Men," "The Manning Baby Kidnapping," *New Comics*, January 1936.

63   *pulpy, noirish features*: "Muss 'Em Up," *Detective Picture Stories*, March 1937.

63   *homicide procedurals*: "The Murder of Miser Flint," *Detective Picture Stories*, April 1937.

63   *"Whatever you wanted"*: Interview Joseph E. Buresch.

63   *The logo . . . worth identifying*, Biro: *Crime Does Not Pay*, July 1942.

64   *"In consideration"*: Ibid.

65   *ghosted by*: Interview George Tuska.

65   *"It isn't often"*: *Crime Does Not Pay*, November 1947.

66   *a typical six-page story*: "The Wild Spree of the Laughing Sadist—Herman Duker," Ibid.

67   *"Not until [Biro] joined"*: Maurice Horn, *The World Encyclopedia of Comics*.

67   *"Biro was an egomaniac"*: Interview Morisi.

67   *bright, earthy . . . Hudson River barge*: Interviews Palais, Morisi. Also, "Virginia Bloch" (obituary), *Woodstock Times*, June 1, 2006.

68   *"She was a real smart cookie"*: Interview Palais.

68   *"He insisted"*: Interview Fred Kida.

69   *"Charlie didn't want to know"*: Interview DiPreta.

69   *"Do you think"*: "Who Dunnit," *Crime Does Not Pay*, November 1943.

69   *"Charlie used to yell"*: Interview Fujitani.

70   *In its debut year*: Benton, *The Illustrated History of Crime Comics*.

Chapter 4: Youth in Crisis

71   *"He wanted me to see"*: Interview Eisner.

72   *"The best I can do"*: Ibid.

72   *churches in some two thousand parishes*: "The Comics and Instructional Method," *Journal of Educational Sociology*, December 1944.

72 *heroic and episodic:* "The Boy Who Heard the Voice of God," *Picture Stories from the Bible,* Winter 1942; "Jonah and the Whale," ibid. (undated), 1942; "The Story of Jesus," ibid. (undated), 1942; "Paul's Four Journeys," ibid. (undated), 1946.

73 *Gaines said he had been . . . Eastern Color:* Frank Jacobs, *The Mad World of William M. Gaines.*

73 *a historical treatise: Narrative Illustration: The Story of the Comics,* 1942.

73 *"Originator of the comic book":* Ibid.

73 *he said he had been . . . the series:* "Funny Business," *Forbes,* September 1, 1943.

73 *Gaines followed through:* "Publisher Shares Profits," *New York Times,* December 30, 1943.

74 *In 1944, Gaines sold:* Interview Bill Gaines and Al Feldstein by early students of EC Larry Stark, Fred von Bernewitz, and Ted White, conducted December 28–30, 1955, August 6, 1956, and August 10, 1956. Published in Fred von Bernewitz and Grant Geissman, *Tales of Terror.*

74 *"Charlie always wanted":* Interview Ivan Klapper.

74 *"It was the strangest thing":* Ibid.

75 *Wonder Woman, appeared in 1942:* Letter from M. C. Gaines to Bishop John F. Noll, March 10, 1942. Bender Papers. Also, *The Acolyte,* issues 1942–1948.

75 *Founded in February 1939: The Drive for Decency in Print: Report of the Bishops' Committee Sponsoring the National Organization for Decent Literature,* 1939.

75 *John Francis Noll, the bishop . . . alarmed:* Ibid.; also, Richard Ginder, *With Ink and Crozier: The Story of Bishop Noll and His Work.*

75 *The next year . . . 900,000 votes:* Arthur M. Schlesinger, Jr., introduction to *The Writings and Speeches of Eugene V. Debs.*

75 *Noll launched . . . opinion against them:* Ginder, *With Ink and Crozier;* also, biography of Noll, website of *Our Sunday Visitor.*

76 *"I condemn":* Quoted in Ginder, *With Ink and Crozier.*

76 *"The traffic" . . . "social order":* Quoted in *The Drive for Decency in Print.*

76 *"black list":* Quoted in Ginder, *With Ink and Crozier.*

77 *"ultimate purpose":* Quoted in *The Drive for Decency in Print.*

77 *one-panel cartoon:* Reproduction, ibid.

77 *"While I am pleased":* Letter from Gaines to Noll, March 10, 1942. Bender Papers.

78 *Marston talked up:* "Are Comics Fascist?" *Time,* October 22, 1945.

78 *"Boys, young and old"*: "Our Women Are Our Future," *Family Circle*, August 14, 1942. In his 1928 book, *Emotions of Normal People*, Marston explained further: "Only when the control of self by others is more pleasant than the unbound assertion of self in human relationships can we hope for a stable, peaceful human society . . . Giving to others, being controlled by them, submitting to other people cannot possibly be enjoyable without a strong erotic element."

78 *"There is no reason"*: Letter from Noll to Gaines, March 13, 1942. Bender Papers.

79 *It opened . . . super pied Satan*: "Parents Must Control the Comics," *St. Anthony Messenger*, May 1944.

79 *"The comic book practice"*: Ibid.

79 *"There is anti-American"*: Ibid.

80 *eight-page pamphlet . . . satanic brew*: The Case Against the Comics, 1944.

80 *"A large number of comic books"*: Ibid.

81 *"weird names" . . . "characters of the Bible"*: "What's Wrong with the 'Comics'?" *Catholic World*, February 1943.

81 *a rumination*: "Are Comics Fascist?" *Time*, October 22, 1945.

81 *"paper incarnations"*: Quoted in "Priest Warns of Peril of Comic Books; Adopts Techniques for a Life of Christ," *New York Times*, August 24, 1946.

81 *"Every month 25,000,000"*: "Parents Must Control the Comics," *St. Anthony Messenger*, May 1944.

82 *"only a special FBI investigation" . . . "racketeering, and murder?"*: Ibid.

82 *"a coming generation"*: "A National Disgrace," *Chicago Daily News*, May 8, 1940.

83 *"This country is in deadly peril" . . . "gone before"*: "Youth . . . Running Wild," *Los Angeles Times*, June 27, 1943.

84 *17 percent . . . for vagrancy*: Ibid.

84 *"We cannot say"*: Katherine Lenroot, *Understanding Juvenile Delinquency*, U.S. Dept. of Labor, Children's Bureau, 1943.

85 *"Zoot Suit Riots"*: "Los Angeles Barred to Sailors by Navy to Stern: Zoot-Suit Riots," *New York Times*, June 9, 1943.

85 *vivid through film*: Youth in Crisis, videocassette, *March of Time: The American Lifestyles 1939–1950: Pt. 5*, Time/Life Video.

85 *"domestic upheaval" . . . marijuana cigarette*: Ibid.

Notes

86 *"This is a film"*: "Little Films with Big Ideas," *New York Times*, December 5, 1943.

86 *Senate hearings on the welfare*: "Wartime Health and Education, Part 1: Juvenile Delinquency," Congressional Information Services.

86 *issue of* Action Comics . . . *"Crazy Rhyme": Action Comics,* September 1945.

87 *cover of* Crime Does Not Pay . . . *on the strop: Crime Does Not Pay,* September 1945.

87 *The first several . . . "Readers Monthly"*: Benton, *The Illustrated History of Crime Comics.*

87 *fourteen-year-old boy . . . from a comic book:* "Boy Kills Self Showing Chum Gun Roulette," *Washington Post*, July 6, 1947.

88 *twelve-year-old named William Becker . . . comic books responsible:* "Jury Blames Hanging of Boy on Comic Books," *Washington Post*, September 16, 1947.

88 *A headline:* " 'Comics' Blamed in Death," *New York Times*, September 15, 1947.

88 *Allegheny County coroner . . . "weird adventures":* "Campaign Against Comic Books with Crime Base Ordered," *Charleroi (PA) Mail*, September 15, 1947.

88 *"the source of inspiration":* Quoted in "Chiefs Call Comic Books Crime Source," *Gettysburg (PA) Times*, July 24, 1947.

89 *"We should act":* Quoted in "Police Resolution Raps Comic Books," *Harrisburg (IL) Daily Register*, August 11, 1947.

89 *$100,000 in debt:* Lydia Ratcliff, research brief, dated May 8, 1958, for article "Maddiction," *Time*, July 7, 1958. Time Inc. library.

89 *"Charlie Gaines was trying":* Interview Mort Leav.

89 *Gaines had made sounder:* Ratcliff brief.

89 *In the third week:* Ibid.

90 *"He said, 'Listen, Ma' ":* Interview Lyle Stuart.

90 *On the afternoon of August 20:* Ratcliff brief; Jacobs, *The Mad World of William M. Gaines.*

90 *Jessie Gaines and her son . . . family business:* Ratcliff brief.

90 *Bill, reluctant . . . in his mind:* Interview Stuart.

90 *started going . . . at NYU:* Ratcliff brief.

90 *"smallest, crummiest":* Maria Reidelbach, *Completely Mad: A History of the Comic Book and Magazine.*

90 *"a mess of titles":* William M. Gaines, "Madman Gaines Pleads for Plots," *Writer's Digest*, February 1954.

91 *"If he was losing money"*: Quoted in Dwight Decker and Gary Groth, "An Interview with William M. Gaines," *Comics Journal*, May 1983.

Chapter 5: Puddles of Blood

92 *"the lowest, most despicable"*: Quoted in "The Case Against the Comics," *The Saturday Review of Literature*, March 20, 1948.

92 *"loaded with communistic"*: "Police Must Read Comics," *Charleroi* (PA) *Mail*, April 14, 1948.

93 *"Because no thought"*: "Junior Has a Craving," *The New Republic*, February 17, 1947.

93 *Detroit was the first*: "36 Comic Books Banned in Detroit as 'Corrupting,'" *Washington Post*, April 29, 1948.

94 *"outlawed"* . . . *"bloodshed, and indecency"*: "Comic Books Banned," *Traverse City* (MI) *Record-Eagle*, May 14, 1948.

94 *mayor of Mt. Prospect*: "Mt. Prospect May Ban Comic Books," *Roselle* (IL) *Register*, May 14, 1948; "Comic Books Banned," *Holland* (MI) *Evening Sentinel*, May 17, 1948.

94 *American Municipal Association reported*: "Three Cities Curb Comics," *New York Times*, May 25, 1948.

94 *Michigan state law . . . crime and bloodshed*: "Media Self-Regulation of Depictions of Violence," *Oklahoma Law Review*, Fall 1994.

94 *laws of this sort*: The twenty states were Connecticut, Illinois, Iowa, Kansas, Kentucky, Maine, Maryland, Massachusetts, Michigan, Minnesota, Missouri, Montana, Nebraska, New York, North Dakota, Ohio, Oregon, Pennsylvania, Washington, Wisconsin. Citations for the legislation are listed in the footnotes to the ruling, *Winters v. People of State of New York*, Supreme Court of the United States, 333 U.S. 507, March 29, 1948.

95 *"things intended for immoral use"*: "Act for the Suppression of Trade in, and Circulation of, Obscene Literature and Articles for Immoral Use," commonly known as the Comstock Act, passed by Congress on March 3, 1873.

95 *"Our youth are in danger"* . . . *"directed the thoughts"*: Anthony Comstock, *Traps for the Young*, 1883.

95 *"pictures and stories"*: Quoted in "Media Self-Regulation of Depictions of Violence," *Oklahoma Law Review*, Fall 1994.

95 *"pictures or descriptions"*: Quoted ibid.

Notes

95 *United States Supreme Court ruled: Winters v. New York.* Also, "State Law of 1884 on Lurid Books Killed by High Court as Too Vague," *New York Times*, May 30, 1948.

96 *"a collection of crime stories": Winters v. New York.*

96 *"We can see nothing":* Ibid.

96 *"We recognize the importance"* . . . *"publications give rise":* Ibid.

97 *"pictorial beatings"* . . . *"hand in hand":* Quoted in "Puddles of Blood," *Time*, March 29, 1948.

97 *"Comic books not only inspire":* Ibid.

98 *exquisitely credentialed:* "Fredric Wertham, 86, Dies; Foe of Violent TV and Comics," *New York Times*, December 1, 1981; Wertham testimony, *Report of the Subcommittee on JD.*

98 *1934 murder trial:* "Alienists' Testimony Is Usually 'Bunk,' Psychiatrist Swears at Murder Trial," *New York Times*, March 21, 1934.

99 *his first book:* Fredric Wertham, *The Brain As an Organ*, 1926.

99 *story of matricide:* Wertham, *Dark Legend*, 1941.

99 *adapted to the Off-Broadway stage:* "Bow Tonight Set for 'Dark Legend,'" *New York Times*, March 24, 1952.

99 *eight sensational murder cases:* Wertham, *The Show of Violence*, 1949.

99 *"describes at length":* "The Causes and Prevention of Murder—A Psychiatric Inquiry," *New York Times Book Review*, May 8, 1949.

99 *Through his friendship . . . psychiatric grounds:* "Ralph Ellison and the Law," *Oklahoma City University Law Review*, Fall 2001.

99 *again made news:* "Wertham Assails Ezra Pound Ruling," *New York Times*, November 27, 1949; also, "The Road to Rapallo," *American Journal of Psychotherapy*, October 1949.

100 *Devoted to correcting . . . any color in the United States:* "Harlem Pioneers with Mental Clinic," *Life*, February 23, 1948; "Minds & Spirits," undated clip in Time Inc. research file on Wertham.

100 *"This clinic":* Ralph Ellison, "Harlem Is Nowhere," *The Collected Essays of Ralph Ellison.*

100 *"We don't want to come here":* "Harlem Pioneers with Mental Clinic," *Life*, February 23, 1948.

100 *"His findings":* "Horror in the Nursery," *Collier's*, March 1948.

101 *"Lafargue researchers found"* . . . *"to see what it felt like":* Ibid.

101 *"We found that comic-book reading":* Quoted ibid.

101 *"in intent and effect"*: Ibid.

101 *"he called me a sissy"*: Quoted ibid.

102 *"In the basement of St. Philip's Episcopal Church"*: Ibid.

102 *"The publishers will raise"*: Quoted in "Horror in the Nursery," *Collier's*, March 1948.

102 *"who really wants an issue"*: Quoted in "Comics Poison Kids' Minds, Says Expert," New York *Daily News*, March 21, 1948.

102 *"some nonsense"* . . . *"kids happy"*: Interview Lampert.

103 *"Wow!"*: Quoted ibid.

103 *"I wouldn't brag"*: Quoted ibid.

103 *"One day, I came"*: Interview Kida.

103 *"We were too busy"*: Interview Eisner.

104 *"We just display them"*: Quoted in "Council Asks News Stands Eliminate Improper Books," *Hartford Courant*, June 15, 1948; interview Irving Kravsow.

104 *that June, comic books sold:* "Comics Debated as Good or Evil," *New York Times*, October 30, 1948; "Fighting Gunfire with Fire," *Newsweek*, December 20, 1948.

104 *"immorality and crime"* . . . *"minds of our children"*: Quoted in "Council Asks News Stands Eliminate Improper Books," *Hartford Courant*, June 15, 1948.

104 *"There are curvaceous Indian"*: Quoted ibid.

104 *"a scene of violence"*: Quoted ibid.

104 *"The police ought to be"*: Quoted ibid.

104 *"prohibit the display"* . . . *similar moves:* "Viscous [*sic*] Comic Books," *Bridgeport* (CT) *Post*, June 19, 1948.

104 *Milwaukee had set up:* "Milwaukee Police Find Comic Books Unfit for Children," *Sheboygan Press*, June 7, 1948.

105 *In Los Angeles:* "Drive Planned to Eliminate Crime Comics," *Los Angeles Times*, June 30, 1948.

105 *"These so-called"*: Quoted ibid.

105 *"How can we find"*: Quoted ibid.

105 *"like walking a legal tightrope"*: Quoted ibid.

105 *police and recreation departments* . . . *"those selling them"*: "Agree on City Plan to Censor Comic Books," *Chicago Daily Tribune*, July 22, 1948.

106 *"Even granting that comic books"*: "The Wrong Remedy," *Chicago Daily Tribune*, July 24, 1948.

Notes

106 *"It was the beginning of a time":* Interview Frank Bourgholtzer.

106 *Rochester, New York, district attorney:* "Fights Offensive Comic Books," *New York Times*, July 28, 1948.

106 *Bellingham, Washington:* "Fifty-four Comic Books Are Banned," *The News*, Mount Pleasant, Iowa, August 31, 1948.

106 *mayor of Sacramento:* "Sacramento Pushes Comic Book Curb," *Los Angeles Times*, August 15, 1948; "Sacramento's Lady Mayor Studies Comics in Move to Control 'Em," *Los Angeles Times*, August 25, 1948.

106 *"ban" the "pollution" . . . "trickery, and cruelty":* "Urges Comic Book Ban," *New York Times*, September 4, 1948.

107 *"Finger-pointing, paranoia":* Interview Bourgholtzer.

107 *HUAC had had a near brush:* "Barsky, 15 Others Are Found Guilty," *New York Times*, June 28, 1947; "Barsky, 10 Aides Sent to Prison, Fined for Contempt of Congress," *New York Times*, July 17, 1948.

107 *"Everybody knew" . . . "there was trouble":* Interview Morisi.

107 *the County of Los Angeles:* "Unfunny Comic Books Barred in Los Angeles," *New York Times*, September 23, 1948.

108 *"person, firm or corporation" . . . "mayhem":* Quoted in "Objectionable Books of Comics Disappear from Los Angeles Stands After New Law," *New York Times*, October 4, 1948.

108 *"pioneering" . . . "really comprehensive":* Quoted ibid.

108 *American Municipal Association:* "50 Cities Ban Off-Color Funnies," *New York Times*, October 5, 1948; "Ban on Comic Books Spreads as Cities Set Up Censorship," *Statesville* (NC) *Daily Record*, November 4, 1948.

108 *Separately, that day:* "Crime Comics Face State Ban," *Los Angeles Times*, October 5, 1948.

108 *According to the county coroner:* "Boy Shoots Brother to Death in Fight Over Comic Book," *Chicago Daily Tribune*, October 4, 1948.

109 *in Johnstown, Pennsylvania:* "Boy's Death by Hanging Laid to Comic Book," *Washington Post*, June 3, 1948.

109 *in New Albany, Indiana:* "Comic Books Inspire Torture of Playmate," *Washington Post*, August 19, 1948; "3 Boys Tell of Torturing Playmate, 7," *Chicago Daily Tribune*," August 19, 1948; "Comic Book Inspires Boys' Torture of Pal," *New York Times*, August 19, 1948.

110 *"You look like you come":* Quoted in "3 Held in Robbery Case," *New York Times*, August 9, 1948.

Notes

110 *dozens of costumed characters:* Research by Steven Tice, Jim Amash, and Thomas G. Lammers.

110 *crime had represented about 3 percent:* Ernst Gerber, *The Photo-Journal Guide to Comic Books, Vol. 2.*

110 *Thirty new crime titles:* "Seducers of the Innocent," *Comic Book Marketplace,* December 1998.

110 *Gleason mocked them:* House ad, *Crime Does Not Pay,* November 1947. The first issue of *Crime and Punishment,* cover-dated April 1948, was on newsstands in January.

111 *"Wertham and that":* Interview Palais.

Chapter 6: Then Let Us Commit Them

112 *80 million . . . $72 million:* "Fighting Gunfire with Fire," *Newsweek,* December 20, 1948.

113 *Hardcover book publishing:* "Publishers' Annual Statistical Report," *Publishers Weekly,* March 5, 1949.

113 *David Pace Wigransky:* Letters to the Editor: "Cain Before Comics," *The Saturday Review,* July 24, 1948.

113 *sharp boy:* "Police Force Door to Free Child, 4, Locked in Home," *Washington Post,* November 4, 1937.

113 *"Although sections":* Preface to "Cain Before Comics," *The Saturday Review,* July 24, 1948.

113 *"It is high time . . . about anything":* "Cain Before Comics," *The Saturday Review,* July 24, 1948.

114 *pages of responses:* Letters to the Editor, *The Saturday Review,* July 24, 1948; *The Saturday Review,* September 25, 1948.

114 *town of Spencer: West Virginia: A Guide to the Mountain State,* 1941; United States Census, 1950.

115 *"You could almost go":* Interview David Mace.

115 *"My mother and father":* Ibid.

115 *Nine years after RCA:* Norm Goldstein, *The History of Television.*

115 *"thrills and fun":* Interview Mace.

116 *"an evil effect":* Quoted in interview Mace.

116 *"She was":* Interview Mace.

Notes

116 *cool, dry, sunny:* Research by John Leslie, National Oceanic and Atmospheric Administration.

116 *a small mountain . . . facing the comics:* "Spencer School Pupils Wage War on Comic Books," *Charleston Daily Mail*, October 27, 1948; "Comic Books Are Committed to Fire After Impressive Ceremony at Elementary School on Monday," *Roane County Reporter*, October 28, 1948; "Grade School Students Burn Their Comic Books," *Times Record*, Spencer, October 28, 1948.

117 *"We are met here" . . . "commit them":* Quoted in *Roane County Reporter*, October 28, 1948.

117 *Associated Press:* "600 Students Hold Burial Rites for 2000 Comic Books," *Washington Post*, October 27, 1948; "Children Cremate 2,000 Old Friends—Their Comic Books," *Chicago Daily Tribune*, October 27, 1948.

117 *"She was really impressed":* Interview Mace.

117 *covered the national coverage:* "Spencer Graded School Is Famous," *Times Record*, November 4, 1948; "Grade School War on Comic Books Has Attracted National Interest," *Roane County Reporter*, November 4, 1948.

118 *"The burning of books . . . priority":* "Let's Burn a Book," *Charleston Daily Mail*, November 1, 1948.

118 *German Student Association:* Richard J. Evans, *The Coming of the Third Reich: A History*.

118 *during Catholic Book Week:* "Catholic School Pupils to Burn 'Undesirable' Comics," *Wisconsin Rapids Daily Tribune*, November 6, 1945; "The End of Superman," *Wisconsin Rapids Daily Tribune*, November 10, 1945.

119 *students of St. Gall's School:* "600 Pupils Prepare Petitions Asking Ban on 'Indecent Comics,'" *Chicago Daily Tribune*, December 7, 1947.

120 *In Binghamton:* For their memories of John Farrell, St. Patrick's Academy, and Binghamton in the 1940s, I am indebted to Joseph Canny, Monsignor James D. Kane, Paul Plocinski, and, especially, Vincent Hawley, who contributed important research on Binghamton history. Also, Obituary, John J. Farrell, Jr., *Binghamton Press*, October 31, 2001.

120 *"He was so damned funny":* Interview Paul Plocinski.

120 *"John was a well-read fellow":* Interview Joseph Canny.

121 *"It was very intimate":* Interview Monsignor James D. Kane.

122 *about 2,500 residents:* Marjory Barnum Hinman, *Court House Square: A Social History*.

122 *"Endicott house"* . . . *"wonderful and beautiful":* Interview Plocinski.

122 *Early in the twentieth century:* Hinman, *Court House Square.*

122 *"fairly judgmental"* . . . *"stuck together":* Interview Kane.

122 *"I will support the drive":* Quoted in "Students Burn Comic Books in Boycott Drive," *New York Herald Tribune,* December 11, 1948.

122 *"We had to go around":* Interview Plocinski.

123 *"I know a lot of dealers":* Quoted in "Burning Books Does Not Help, Pierson Says," *Binghamton Sun,* December 12, 1948.

123 *thirty-five Binghamton retailers:* Ibid.

123 *"We were very serious":* Interview Vincent Hawley.

124 *"We were crusaders":* Ibid.

124 *"I had been trading":* Interview Plocinski.

124 *cold and gray:* Research by Leslie, National Oceanic and Atmospheric Administration.

124 *Mother Anna Frances ended classes:* "Students Burn Comic Books in Boycott Drive," *New York Herald Tribune,* December 11, 1948.

124 *the picture:* Yearbook, St. Patrick's Academy, 1949.

125 *"An army of youth":* Quoted ibid.

125 *"I remember it very vividly":* Interview Canny.

125 *Associated Press:* "Comic Books Burned," *Washington Post,* December 10, 1948; "Catholic Students Burn Up Comic Books," *New York Times,* December 11, 1948.

125 *"I had no idea":* Interview Canny.

126 *"The action of the St. Patrick's pupils":* Reprinted from *Catholic Sun* in Yearbook, St. Patrick's Academy, 1949.

126 *"Banning books"* . . . *"acquainted with the problem":* Quoted in "Burning Books Does Not Help, Pierson Says," *Binghamton Sun,* December 12, 1948.

126 *"Another evil of our times":* Quoted in "Catholic Students Burn Up Comic Books," *New York Times,* December 11, 1948.

127 *"quick action"* . . . *"huge bonfire":* "Children of SS Peter-Paul School Burn Comic Books in Bonfire," *Citizen Advertiser,* December 22, 1948.

127 *"This action follows":* "The 'Comic' Book Bonfire," *Citizen Advertiser,* December 23, 1948.

127 *"The holidays came":* Interview Plocinski.

127 *as early as 1896 . . . for its members:* Kenneth A. Paulson, "Regulation Through Intimidation: Congressional Hearings and Political Pressure on America's

Notes

Entertainment Media," *Vanderbilt Journal of Entertainment Law and Practice,* Winter 2004.

128 *small group of comic-book publishers . . . 270 titles per month:* "Clean-Up Started by Comic Books As Editors Adopt Self-Policing Plan," *New York Times,* July 2, 1948; "Code for the Comics," *Time,* July 12, 1948.

129 *as its executive director:* "Fighting Gunfire with Fire," *Newsweek,* December 20, 1948.

130 *"a full-fledged fight" . . . "cavernous, swank":* Ibid.

130 *In a debate:* "Comics Debated As Good or Evil," *New York Times,* October 30, 1948.

130 *"beginning to develop":* Quoted ibid.

130 *By the end of 1948:* "Fighting Gunfire with Fire," *Newsweek,* December 20, 1948.

130 *"There are more morons":* Quoted ibid.

Chapter 7: Woofer and Tweeter

132 *Obsessed with measurements:* For this information on William M. Gaines and much of the material on Gaines and EC to follow, I am indebted to the EC veterans Jack Davis, Will Elder, Al Feldstein, Harry Harrison, Jack Kamen, Ivan Klapper, John Severin, Marie Severin, Shirley Norris Smith, Lyle Stuart, Angelo Torres, and Al Williamson.

133 *"In the beginning":* William M. Gaines, "Madman Gaines Pleads for Plots," *Writer's Digest,* February 1954.

133 *He concentrated on:* Ratcliff brief.

133 *Cohen thought:* This account of Cohen's role in EC's development is based mainly on interviews with Feldstein, with corroboration from Klapper and Stuart.

134 *a few pages:* "How Tunnels Are Constructed," *Science Comics,* May 1946.

135 *"I loved them":* Interview Al Feldstein.

136 *"I was a bit of a loner":* Ibid.

136 *"He checked out":* Ibid.

137 *"because everybody was":* Ibid.

137 *Although Gaines gave Feldstein:* Letter of agreement between William M. Gaines and Albert Feldstein, signed February 13, 1948. Feldstein's personal files.

138 *"'Come in,' he says":* Interview Feldstein.

138 *1947 Chrysler Town and Country:* Donald J. Narus, *Chrysler's Wonderful Woodie the Town and Country, 1941–1950.*

139 *RCA Berkshire television:* Robert Gerson, electronics writer and editor for *Television Digest* and *This Week in Consumer Electronics*; also, dealer brochures and photographs posted on television history website www.tvhistory.tv .com.

139 *"He was playing":* Interview Feldstein.

139 *"We took our work":* Ratcliff brief.

139 *Gaines had published: Blackstone the Magician Detective Fights Crime!,* Fall 1947; *Happy Houlihans,* Fall 1947; *Saddle Justice,* Spring 1948; *Fat and Slat,* Spring 1948; *Gunfighter,* Summer 1948; *International Comics,* November–December 1947; *International Crime Patrol,* Spring 1948; *Crime Patrol,* Summer 1948; *Animal Fables,* November–December 1947; *Moon Girl and the Prince,* Fall 1947; *Moon Girl,* Winter 1947–1948; *Moon Girl Fights Crime,* May–June 1949; *A Moon . . . A Girl . . . A Romance,* September–October 1949.

140 *"We were feeling our way":* Interview Klapper.

141 *Variations on gothic fright:* For insight into the early history of horror comics, I am indebted to the encyclopedic writing on the subject by comics historian Lawrence Watt-Evans.

141 *"I met with him":* Interview Sheldon Moldoff.

141 *"Bill said, 'Great' ":* Ibid.

141 *Later, Gaines published:* "The Werewolf's Curse," *Crime Patrol,* April–May 1949; "The Hanged Man's Revenge," *Crime Patrol,* July 1949.

141 *"I was thinking":* Interview Feldstein.

142 *"I used to go up":* Quoted in Decker and Groth, "An Interview with William M. Gaines," *Comics Journal,* May 1983.

142 *"We thought we'd be pretty safe":* Interview Feldstein.

143 *"highly pleased" . . . "menace of the comic books":* Quoted in "How the Comic Book Started," *Commonweal,* May 20, 1949.

143 *"The comics can be inspired" . . . "to do with them":* Letters, *Commonweal,* June 3, 1949.

143 *"national housecleaning":* "Parents Set Plan for Comics Curb," *New York Times,* November 30, 1948.

144 *"The criminal and sexual":* "Municipal Control of Comic Books," *American City,* December 1948. This article was adapted from a pamphlet by the same

Notes

author: Charles S. Rhyme, *Comic Books: Municipal Control of Sale and Distribution—A Preliminary Study*, 1948.

144 *ten-page handbook: Municipal Control of Objectionable Comic Books*, 1948.

144 *municipal government trade journal:* "Comic Book Control Can Be a Success," *American City*, January 1949.

144 *"rank with jazz music":* Quoted in "New Orleans to Supervise Comic Books," Associated Press, February 2, 1949. Text of New Orleans report courtesy of John Petty.

144 *"The wholesale condemnation" . . . "objectionable, and undesirable":* New Orleans report, courtesy of Petty.

144 *"throw Sherlock Holmes":* Quoted in "Delay Action on Crime Comics Ban," *Cleveland Plain Dealer*, May 3, 1949.

144 *"commission or attempted commission":* "Police Prepare Drive on Illegal 'Comics,'" *Cleveland Press*, May 10, 1949; "Votes Unanimous Ban on Crime Comic Sales," *Cleveland Plain Dealer*, May 10, 1949.

145 *William D. Dickey:* "Comic Book Sale Charge Will Take Druggist to Court," *Los Angeles Times*, April 23, 1949.

145 *Baltimore:* "Baltimore to Seek 'Objectionable' Comic Book Ban," *Washington Post*, January 14, 1949; "Baltimore Set for War on Crime Comics," *Washington Post*, March 2, 1949.

145 *Cleveland:* "Curb on Comics Good Start," *Cleveland Plain Dealer*, April 7, 1949.

145 *Milwaukee:* "Seek Ban on Comic Books," United Press, March 22, 1949.

145 *Sacramento:* "Council Will Consider Crime Comic Book Ban," *Sacramento Bee*, February 17, 1949; "City Adopts Law to Ban Crime Comic Books," *Sacramento Bee*, February 19, 1949.

145 *St. Louis:* "Would Outlaw Sale of Crime Comics," Associated Press, March 5, 1949.

145 *Falls Church:* "Falls Church Puts Curb on Comic Books," *Washington Post*, March 15, 1949.

145 *Nashua:* "Comic Book Suppression Talk Is Slated in City on Monday," *Nashua Telegraph*, March 11, 1949; "Name Comic Book Committee," *Nashua Telegraph*, April 4, 1949.

145 *Coral Gables:* "Comics—To Read or Not to Read?" *Wilson Library Journal*, May 1950.

Notes

145 *lead page-one:* "Crime Comic Book Ban Voted By City Council—$500 Fines, Term in Jail for Violators," *Sacramento Union,* February 19, 1949.

145 *"She was furious"* . . . *"collecting comic books":* Interview White.

146 *"badly printed"* . . . *"freedom of the press":* "700 Students See Hopes for Comic Books," *New York Times,* January 5, 1949.

146 *"precious chance":* Interview Merton Stanley Rothman.

146 *"The girls are scantily":* Quoted in "Juniors Sound Off on Comic Books: But Ban Them? Comes a Silence!" *New York World Telegram and Sun,* January 5, 1949.

146 *"It's important":* Interview Rothman.

147 *"Sale of some . . . Students":* Letters, *Herald-American,* February 23, 1949.

148 *grand public protest . . . torch to the books:* "Comic Criminals to Burn," *New York Times,* January 7, 1949.

148 *national office:* "Book Burning Scouts," Ironwood Daily Globe, January 14, 1949; "Burning of Comic Books Avoided," *New York Times,* January 16, 1949.

148 *a Girl Scout leader:* "Pupils Burn Comic Books to Open Girardeau Drive," *Southeast Missourian,* February 25, 1949; "Comic Books Burned," *Maryville Daily Forum,* February 25, 1949.

149 *"leading young people":* Quoted in "Pupils Burn Comic Books to Open Girardeau Drive," *Southeast Missourian,* February 25, 1949.

149 *"great big bonfire":* Interview Bonnie Wulfers Miller.

149 *"neither read nor purchase":* Quoted in "Pupils Burn Comic Books to Open Girardeau Drive," *Southeast Missourian,* February 25, 1949.

149 *student who played Superman:* Interview Donald Heisserer.

149 *"We were more or less":* Ibid.

On March 19, 1954, a similar comic-book burning took place at the St. Anthony parish school in Chicago. Students burned an estimated 1,238 comics of "the crime-school type," under the direction of the St. Anthony Junior Holy Name Society. "St. Anthony Pupils Burn Comic Books As Campaign Ends," *South End Reporter,* March 23, 1949.

150 *By March 1949:* untitled article, *Nation,* March 19, 1949.

150 *Benjamin F. Feinberg: The National Cyclopedia of American Biography,* Vol. 47, 1965.

150 *The comic-book legislation he proposed:* New York State Bill 551, Act to Amend the Education Law. Also, quoted in "State Bill to Curb Comic Books Filed," *New York Times,* January 14, 1949.

151 *the bill passed:* "State Senate Acts to Control Comics, *New York Times,* February 24, 1949.

Notes

151 *"Many people . . . to publish:* "Comic Book Censorship," *New York Times,* February 25, 1949.

151 *"We would be the first":* Untitled article, *Nation,* March 19, 1949.

152 *"The bill before me":* Quoted in "Comic Books Curb Vetoed by Dewey," *New York Times,* April 20, 1949.

152 *Canadian legislators:* "Canada's Comics Ban," *Time,* November 14, 1949.

152 *passed in both houses . . . "morals of such persons":* "Bill to Ban Comic Books Wins in Canadian Senate, *New York Times,* December 8, 1949; "The Press," *Time,* December 19, 1949.

152 *"There was no other explanation":* Quoted in *Report of the Subcommittee on JD.*

Chapter 8: Love . . . LOVE . . . LOVE!!

154 *"A force for good" . . . "Eradication of Crime":* Crime Does Not Pay, various issues, beginning in 1948.

154 *"former chief" . . . "good behavior":* Crime Does Not Pay, various issues, beginning in 1949.

155 *"Victor Fox was blowing":* Interview Morisi.

155 *adaptation of Longfellow:* "Skipper Hoy and That Wreck, the Hesperus," *Feature Presentations Magazine,* June 1950.

155 *"The crime trend":* Interview Morisi.

156 *"'Listen, Pete' . . . was in":* Quoted in interview Morisi.

156 *Although about thirty:* Research by Miller, Maheras.

156 *In a self-parody:* "The Love Story to End *All* Love Stories," *Modern Love,* August–September 1950.

157 *nearly a fifth:* Research by Miller, Maheras.

157 *heroines intended to appeal:* For insight into the underexplored history of women in comics, I am indebted to the essential work of Trina Robbins, Michelle Nolan, and Catherine Yronwode.

158 *"We always had":* Interview Winkleman.

158 *"Comic books were supposed":* Interview Joe Simon.

159 *"It was supposedly":* Ibid.

159 *biologist and zoologist:* "Dr. Kinsey Is Dead; Sex Researcher, 62," *New York Times,* August 26, 1956.

159 *former mayor of Winnipeg:* Jennifer McKnight-Trontz, *The Look of Love: The Art of the Romance Novel.*

Notes

160 *"The girls were always"*: Interview Kimball Aamodt.

160 *"Juvenile delinquency was"*: Ibid.

161 *a prolific writer*: Dana Dutch and his work were virtually unknown until comics historian John Benson's fine study, *Romance without Tears*.

161 *in which stories*: "I Joined a Teen-Age Sex Club," *First Love Illustrated*, July 1951; "My Mother Was My Rival," *My Love Secret*, August 1949.

161 *typical story by Dana Dutch*: "Thrill Seekers' Weekend," *Teen-Age Romances*, May 1954.

161 *Another Dutch script*: "I Set a Trap for a Wolf," *Blue Ribbon Comics*, June 1949.

162 *"We tried to avoid"*: Interview Walter Geier.

162 *"Ellie kissed me"*: "Just Good Friends," original typescript courtesy of Geier.

162 *"I wrote just about"*: Interview Geier.

163 *"When we think of romance"*: Interview Kinstler.

164 *"We heard there was money"*: Interview Arnold Drake.

164 *"We had been doing comic books"*: Interview Leslie Waller.

164 *"The attitude about comics"*: Interview Drake.

165 *a potboiler*: Drake, Waller, Matt Baker, Ray Osrin, *It Rhymes with Lust*.

165 *For the illustrations*: Interview Drake and Waller, as well as Baker's colleagues Lee Ames, Nick Cardy, John Celardo, Jack Kamen, and Bob Lubbers.

165 *"He could have been a movie star"*: Interview Lubbers.

166 *"All the women"*: Interview Celardo.

166 *"He wasn't that fast"*: Interview Ames.

166 *"You know that, oh that lazy"*: Ibid.

167 *"Matt was working"*: Interview Kamen.

167 *"Matt Baker was one of the first"*: Interview Drake.

167 *"We told St. John"*: Ibid.

167 *"Frankly, we were"*: Ibid.

168 *"She was greedy"*: Drake, Waller, Baker, Osrin, *It Rhymes with Lust*.

168 *"Could he live"*: Quoted in Geoffrey O'Brien, *Hardboiled America*.

168 *"Our publisher loved it"*: Interview Drake.

169 *"tendency toward normal"* . . . *"young devotees"*: "Comfort for Comics," *Newsweek*, January 9, 1950.

169 *"Last year's hysteria"*: "Anti-Comics Drive Reported Waning," *New York Times*, January 21, 1950.

169 *"Sanity is creeping"*: Quoted ibid.

169 *Canadian Parliament . . . equal zeal*: Ibid.

Notes

169 *Fredric Wertham's lieutenant:* "Psychiatrist Charges Stalling Tactics on Legislation to Control Comic Books," *New York Times,* January 24, 1950.

170 *"distorted picture"* . . . *"hatred and sadism":* Quoted ibid.

170 *she dismissed articles:* Josette Frank, "Some Questions and Answers for Teachers and Parents," and Henry E. Schultz, "Censorship or Self Regulation?" *Journal of Educational Sociology,* December 1949.

170 *a new study:* "Blame Parents on Delinquency, Not Movies, TV," *Chicago Daily Tribune,* May 19, 1949.

170 *"We should be less speedy":* Quoted ibid.

170 *TV broadcasting . . . sold TV sets:* Goldstein, *The History of Television.*

171 *Estes Kefauver:* Charles L. Fontenay, *Estes Kefauver: A Biography*; Joseph Bruce Gorman, *Kefauver: A Political Biography*; Harvey Swados, *Standing Up for the People*; "Tennessee, TV, and Kefauver Too," *Life,* March 24, 1952; "Professional Common Man," *Time,* September 17, 1956; "Estes Kefauver Is Dead at 60 After Heart Attack," *New York Times,* August 11, 1963.

171 *"a sort of by-himself boy":* Quoted in Fontenay, *Estes Kefauver: A Biography.*

171 *"I may be a coon":* Quoted in "Tennessee, TV, and Kefauver Too," *Life,* March 24, 1952.

172 *"Estes, don't you want":* Quoted in Fontenay, *Estes Kefauver: A Biography.*

172 *Approved on May 3:* Memoranda, records of the Special Committee to Investigate Crime in Interstate Commerce, U.S. Senate, National Archives.

172 *excluding Wertham:* Fredric Wertham, *Seduction of the Innocent.* Wertham wrote, "I was on vacation when I got a wire saying that the committee contemplated publication of a report on juvenile delinquency and wanted a written contribution from me for inclusion in the report. Of course I refused, replying that such a hasty publication without investigation was certainly not in the interests of the public."

172 *"Any overall study of crime":* Quoted in *Interim Report of the Special Committee to Investigate Crime in Interstate Commerce,* U.S. Senate.

172 *"No one can state":* Quoted ibid.

173 *"the incidence of crime"* . . . *"available to children":* Quoted ibid.

173 *"My own experience":* Quoted ibid.

173 *"Practitioners of the inexact science":* Quoted ibid.

174 *the news made the front pages:* "Many Doubt Comics Spur Crime," *New York Times,* November 12, 1950; "U.S. Survey Clears Comic Books of Breeding Teen-Age Criminals," New York *Sunday News,* November 12, 1950.

Notes

174 *"suggested some officials"*: Quoted in *Interim Report of the Special Committee to Investigate Crime in Interstate Commerce*, U.S. Senate. Also, "Comics Held No Factor in Delinquency," *Washington Post*, November 12, 1950; "Comics Not Held Delinquency Cause," *Los Angeles Times*, November 12, 1950.

174 *"Well, that puts"*: Quoted in interview Stan Lee.

Chapter 9: New Trend

175 *Shirley Norris:* Interview Shirley Norris Smith.

176 *imminent shift:* "Three Clues to TERROR," *Crime Patrol*, October–November 1949.

176 *cover of the next: Crime Patrol*, December 1949–January 1950.

176 *all four stories:* "The Corpse in the Crematorium," "Trapped in the Tomb," "The Graveyard Feet," and "The Spectre in the Castle," *Crime Patrol*, February–March 1950.

176 *duplicated this process: War Against Crime*, February–March 1950; *The Vault of Horror*, April–May 1950.

176 *"We were test-marketing"*: Interview Feldstein.

176 *"I was the first publisher"*: Quoted in *Report of the Subcommittee on JD*.

176 *During the war:* "Frankenstein Smashes the Nazis," *Prize Comics*, July 1944.

177 *devoted entirely: Spook Comics*, not dated, 1946.

177 *similar book: Eerie Comics*, not dated, 1947.

177 *process of replacing: Sub-Mariner Comics*, last issue, June 1949; *Amazing Mysteries*, first issue, May 1949.

177 *Timely virtually abandoned:* Lammers research.

177 *U.S. government intelligence: Bulletin of Atomic Sciences*, May/June 1998.

178 *"I was about to stop"*: Interview Bhob Stewart.

179 *first story:* "The Wall," *The Haunt of Fear*, May–June 1950.

179 *"We got a lot of mileage"*: Quoted in Jacobs, *The Mad World of William M. Gaines*.

179 *"I don't know"*: Interview Kamen.

180 *"Buster stories"*: Ibid.

180 *"I would dress"*: Ibid.

180 *giant alien cockroach:* "Revulsion!" *Weird Fantasy*, September–October 1950.

180 *baseball game:* "Foul Play!" *The Haunt of Fear*, June 1953.

180 *unrecognized artist:* "Portrait in Wax!" *The Vault of Horror*, April–May 1950.

Notes

180 *little boy:* "Horror of the School Room," *The Haunt of Fear*, May–June 1951.

180 *man with the basket:* "The Basket!" *The Haunt of Fear*, May–June 1951.

181 *mutant victims:* "Child of Tomorrow," *Weird Fantasy*, January–February 1951.

181 *"The EC approach":* Gaines, "Madman Gaines Pleads for Plots," *Writer's Digest*, February 1954.

181 *"Those were the happiest days":* Quoted in Rich Hauser interview with William M. Gaines, *Spa Fon*, 1969.

181 *"I read like a maniac":* Quoted in Decker and Groth, "An Interview with William M. Gaines," *Comics Journal*, May 1983.

181 *"I'd get this idea":* Quoted in Hauser, *Spa Fon*, 1969.

182 *"Al and I would sit":* Quoted in Jacobs, *The Mad World of William M. Gaines.*

182 *"I amazed myself":* Interview Feldstein.

183 *"This was the fun part":* Quoted in Reidelbach, *Completely Mad.*

183 *"You should know . . . over evil":* Gaines, "Madman Gaines Pleads for Plots," *Writer's Digest*, February 1954.

183 *"We tried to have an artist":* Interview Feldstein.

184 *big-game hunter:* "The Trophy!" *Tales from the Crypt*, August–September 1951.

184 *man who loves:* "Half Baked," *Tales from the Crypt*, February–March 1954.

184 *"Although the EC stories":* Mike Benton, *The Comic Book in America.*

185 *"Of course, Bill Gaines's books":* Quoted in "Newcon Panel 1978: Wood, Krigstein, Kurtzman," transcribed by Greg Sadowski, ed. by John Benson, *Squa Tront*, 2002.

185 *"I belong to low":* Quoted ibid.

185 *art form led him:* Sadowski, *B. Krigstein.*

185 *"I took the position":* Letter to Benson, June 1, 1975, quoted in Sadowski, *B. Krigstein.*

185 *stories barely worth:* "Conning the Confidence Man," *Justice Traps the Guilty*, June 1949; "The Huckster's Castle," *Crime Detective*, May 1951.

186 *He deepened:* "More Blessed to Give . . . ," *Crime SuspenStories*, September 1954; "The Catacombs," *The Vault of Horror*, September 1954.

186 *opening art:* "Monotony," *Crime SuspenStories*, May 1954.

187 *"I knew Bill":* Interview Feldstein.

187 *"EC was more like" . . . "screwed up":* Interview Al Williamson.

187 *"They had a tremendous":* Quoted in Decker and Groth, "An Interview with William M. Gaines," *Comics Journal*, May 1983.

188 *"Bill was incredibly kind":* Interview Davis.

188 *"No other publisher"*: Ibid.

188 *"Bill wanted to be Big Daddy"*: Interview Adele Kurtzman.

189 *"Everybody there was brilliant"*: Interview Marie Severin.

189 *"You have to be"*: Ibid.

189 *nearly one-third*: Benton, *The Comic Book in America*.

189 *More than a dozen*: Research by Miller, Maheras.

189 *twenty-five horror books*: Ibid.

189 *"There was a hell"*: Interview Lee.

190 *"The horror craze"*: Ibid.

190 *most successful publisher*: Goulart, *Encyclopedia of American Comics*.

190 *"Books came and went"*: Interview Lee.

190 *"You did what you had"*: Interview Stanley P. Morse.

190 *human brain*: Weird Mysteries, June 1953.

190 *pithily evocative*: "Hate," *Weird Chills*, September 1954; "Violence," ibid.

190 *"I don't know"*: Interview Morse.

191 *small river town*: "Walden, N.Y., Dealers Ban Comics on Crime," *New York Times*, February 15, 1952.

191 *"The entire industry . . . control such practices"*: 1951 findings cited in *Report of the New York State Joint Legislative Committee to Study the Publication of Comics*, March 1954.

191 *As with the legislation . . . 141 to 4*: "6 State Bills Seek Comic Book Curbs," *New York Times*, February 20, 1952; "Major Bills Lag in Albany; Jam Seen in Wind-Up Drive," *New York Times*, February 25, 1952; "Comic Book Curbs Voted in Assembly," *New York Times*, March 13, 1952.

192 *vetoed a month later*: "Governor's Veto Message," *New York State Legislative Annual*, 1952. Also, "'Comic' Book Curb Vetoed by Dewey," *New York Times*, April 15, 1952.

192 *"the effect on minors" . . . "so-called 'pocket books'"*: Quoted in *Report of the New York State Joint Legislative Committee to Study the Publication of Comics*, March 1954.

192 *In Maryland . . . year in jail*: "Prince Georges Opens War on Crime Comics," *Washington Post*, July 4, 1952; "3 Arrested in Drive on Crime Comics," *Washington Post*, July 8, 1952.

192 *"They didn't like"*: Interview Warren Tremaine.

Notes

Chapter 10: Humor in a Jugular Vein

193 *Al Vigoda . . . terms to Victor Fox:* Interview Thall.

193 *"I did the [comics] work":* Interview Stanley Kauffmann.

194 *"My work [in comics]":* Quoted in Andrew Wilson, *Beautiful Shadow: A Life of Patricia Highsmith.*

194 *Kurtzman had grown up:* Interview Adele Kurtzman, Will Elder, Al Jaffee; also, Harvey Kurtzman, *My Life as a Cartoonist.*

195 *"Even though I was young":* Kurtzman, *My Life as a Cartoonist.*

195 *"a comic on how to cure":* Quoted in "Newcon Panel 1978," *Squa Tront,* 2002.

195 *"The war books":* Ibid.

196 *"Watch me get that" . . . twin brother:* "War Story!" *Two-Fisted Tales,* January–February 1951.

196 *"In my war comics":* Quoted in "The 'Mad' Generation," *New York Times Magazine,* July 31, 1977.

197 *"I felt that people":* Quoted in Reidelbach, *Completely Mad.*

197 *Kurtzman often spent . . . Long Island:* Kurtzman, *My Life as a Cartoonist.*

197 *"He drove us":* Interview Davis.

197 *art for one story:* "Combat Medic," *Frontline Combat,* January–February 1952.

197 *"Harvey felt that he":* 1973 interview with John Benson, quoted in Grant Geissman, *Foul Play! The Art and Artists of the Notorious 1950s E.C. Comics!*

198 *"That's the real":* Quoted in Decker and Groth, "An Interview with William M. Gaines," *Comics Journal,* May 1983.

198 *Kurtzman would embellish:* Kurtzman, *My Life as a Cartoonist;* "The 'Mad' Generation," *New York Times Magazine,* July 31, 1977.

198 *"It was a face":* Kurtzman, *My Life as a Cartoonist.*

198 *"The average person":* Interview Eisner.

199 *"In the beginning":* Kurtzman, *My Life as a Cartoonist.*

199 *The first issue . . . idiocy around him: Mad,* October–November 1952.

201 *"Nobody complained":* Interview Morse.

201 *"When the decision":* Fredric Wertham, *Seduction of the Innocent.*

201 *writing about:* "The Body Maker," *Black Cat Mystery,* September 1952.

201 *"Now no holds":* Wertham, *Seduction of the Innocent.*

201 *"immoral, obscene" . . . "too gory":* "House Inquiry Set on Obscene Books," *New York Times,* November 30, 1952.

Notes

202 *United States Children's Bureau:* "Youth Delinquency Growing Rapidly Over the Country," *New York Times*, April 20, 1952.

202 *New York State Youth Commission:* "'51 Delinquency Cases Up," *New York Times*, May 2, 1952.

202 *"The public gets alarmed":* "Youth Delinquency Growing Rapidly Over the Country," *New York Times*, April 20, 1952.

202 *"We definitely feel":* Quoted in "Crime of Boy Linked to Lurid Magazines," *New York Times*, December 9, 1952.

203 *Bill Gaines read:* Interview Williamson.

203 *host of a popular:* Barry Gray, *10,001 Nights in Broadcasting; Contemporary Authors.*

204 *"Where's Marv Levy?":* Recording, *The Barry Gray Show*, November 8, 1952. Courtesy Marvin Levy.

204 *"No":* Ibid.

204 *"If you want to buy":* Recording, *The Barry Gray Show*, December 12, 1952. Courtesy Levy.

204 *"In the last decade":* Ibid.

205 *"In other words":* Ibid.

205 *"Well":* Ibid.

205 *"I'm sure you'll agree":* Ibid.

206 *"I think he had a point":* Interview Marvin Levy.

206 *"You don't know":* Interview Howard Post.

206 *"He was desperate":* Ibid.

207 *"lewd, lascivious":* Quoted in "Obscene and Other Objectionable Comics Are Targets for a Series of Albany Bills," *New York Times*, February 18, 1953.

207 *"lust, bloodshed":* Quoted in "Obscene Books Ban Pushed at Albany," *New York Times*, March 4, 1953.

207 *Governor Dewey declined:* "Governor Clears Desk of All Bills," *New York Times*, April 21, 1953.

207 *AP story:* "Here's Listing of '53 Bills Dewey Signed," *Syracuse Herald-Journal*, March 21, 1953.

207 *He would eventually approve:* New York State Assembly Bills no. 2839, no. 2174, no. 2753. Also, "Dewey Signs Bills on Obscene Books," *New York Times*, April 16, 1954.

207 *In Harrisburg . . . "obscene comic books" specifically:* Edward L. Feder, *Comic*

384

Notes

Book Regulation; "Investigation Group of Legislature May Check Laws, Comics," *Clearfield (PA) Progress*, May 20, 1953.

207 *"This is really serious"*: Quoted in "State Comic Book Sales Need Check," *Indiana (PA) Evening Gazette*, April 21, 1953.

208 *"The gentleman has a right"*: Ibid.

Chapter 11: Panic

209 *"The witch-hunt psychology"*: Interview Post.

210 *"It was a bad time"*: Interview Williamson.

211 *memorable EC story*: "A New Beginning," *Weird Science*, November–December 1953.

211 *trailer for a new film . . . jazzed-up hoodlums*: Trailer, *The Wild One*, 1953. http://movies2.nytimes.com/gst/movies/trailer.html

213 *juvenile crime*: "Youth Delinquency Down," *New York Times*, April 16, 1953.

213 *Eleven days later*: S. Res. 89, 83d Cong.

213 *"fifth horseman" . . . "Federal action"*: Robert C. Hendrickson Archive, Bird Library, Syracuse University. Also, quoted in part in "Fifth Horseman," *Washington Post*, April 12, 1953.

213 *subcommittee of the Committee . . . North Dakota*: Memoranda, Robert C. Hendrickson Archive, Bird Library, Syracuse University.

213 *when American prisoners . . . Americans' brains*: Rebecca Lemov, *World as Laboratory: Experiments with Mice, Mazes, and Men.*

214 *"It was getting" . . . "take the job"*: Interview Winkleman.

214 *a magazine her mother*: "What Parents Don't Know About Comic Books," *Ladies' Home Journal*, November 1953.

214 *Rabbits*: John Sheail, *Rabbits and Their History.*

215 *by the standard model*: Lydia Ratcliff, research brief, dated May 8, 1958, for article "Maddiction," *Time*, July 7, 1958. Time Inc. library.

215 *"The first three issues"*: Quoted ibid.

215 *The print run*: Ibid.

215 *"Mad #1"*: Gaines, "Madman Gaines Pleads for Plots," *Writer's Digest*, February 1954.

215 *"We began"*: Kurtzman, *My Life as a Cartoonist.*

216 *"[Gaines] began selling"*: "The EC 'Publisher of the Issue' William M. Gaines Alias Melvin," *Mad*, June–July 1953.

216 *the time . . . his wallet:* Interview Elder, Jaffee, John Severin, Marie Severin, David Gantz.

217 *"chicken fat":* Interview Elder.

217 *"pure mayhem":* Quoted in Will Elder, *Will Elder: The Mad Playboy of Art.*

217 *"Will was the one":* Kurtzman, *My Life as a Cartoonist.*

218 *"Harvey let me go":* Interview Elder.

218 *"I took Bill":* Interview Feldstein.

218 *"I used to say":* Ibid.

218 *"Mad is an imitation":* *Panic,* March 1954.

219 *"plundered all my techniques":* "An Interview with Harvey Kurtzman," *Comics Journal,* October 1981. Courtesy of Steve Stiles.

220 *"I had a good time":* Interview Elder.

220 *On December 18 . . . criminal prosecution:* "Santa Claus Comic Draws Holyoke Ban," *Springfield* (MA) *Daily News,* December 20, 1953; "Lampooning of Poem Brings State Protest," *Washington Post,* December 22, 1953.

221 *Gaines retaliated:* "State Bans 'Night Before'; Publisher Yanks Bible Tales," *Boston Daily Globe,* December 22, 1953.

221 *"The idea was":* Interview Feldstein.

221 *On Monday:* "Comic Book Ban Sought: Attorney Says Massachusetts Action Is 'Gross Insult,'" *New York Times,* December 28, 1953.

221 *"After it hit":* Interview Stuart. Several published accounts of this police visit to the EC offices refer to an article about the *Panic* controversy in the *New York World Telegram and Sun.* No such article was published in that paper in the years 1953 or 1954.

221 *While Norris handed:* Interview Stuart, Norris Smith.

221 *"They wanted":* Interview Stuart.

222 *"The cop came back":* Interview Norris Smith.

222 *"Do you know":* Interview Stuart.

222 *"Well, yes":* Interview Norris Smith.

222 *"You're under arrest":* Quoted ibid.

222 *arrest for violation:* New York statute 1141 renders punishable "a person who sells, lends, gives away, distributes or shows, or offers to sell, lend, give away, distribute, or show, or has in his possession with intent to sell, lend, distribute or give away, or to show, or advertises in any manner, or who otherwise offers for loan, gift, sale or distribution, any obscene, lewd, lascivious, filthy, indecent or disgusting book, magazine, pamphlet, newspaper, story paper,

writing, paper, picture, drawing, photograph, figure or image, or any written or printed matter of an indecent character."

222 *When the case:* Records of the proceeding in this case have survived; the account in this book is based on the recollections of participants Stuart and Norris Smith.

223 *"I couldn't believe":* Interview Norris Smith.

223 *"That was the thing":* Interview Feldstein.

223 *"Winchell didn't":* Interview Stuart.

223 *"their kids":* Ibid.

223 *still in the news:* "Depravity for Children—10 Cents a Copy!" *Hartford Courant,* February 14, 1954.

224 *"This morning":* "Design for Murder," *Hartford Courant,* December 14, 1954.

224 *an effete country boy:* "I Killed Mary," *Weird Mysteries,* January 1954.

224 *"series of articles":* "Depravity for Children—10 Cents a Copy!" *Hartford Courant,* February 14, 1954.

224 *"where juvenile delinquents"* . . . *"defy description":* Ibid.

225 *"No decent person":* Quoted in "Public Taste, Profit Used to Justify 'Horror' Comics," *Hartford Courant,* February 15, 1954.

225 *"I don't see anything wrong":* Quoted in "Public Taste, Profit Used to Justify 'Horror' Comics," *Hartford Courant,* February 15, 1954.

225 *"Is that the moral":* Quoted ibid.

225 *"Well":* Quoted ibid.

225 *"The guy":* Interview Morse.

226 *"You see, the profits":* Quoted in "Public Taste, Profit Used to Justify 'Horror' Comics," *Hartford Courant,* February 15, 1954.

226 *"This issue has been banned":* Quoted ibid.

226 *"We try to entertain":* Quoted ibid.

226 *one of the two major wholesalers . . . "sex" comics:* "State and City Officials Warn Comics Publishers to 'Clean Up,'" *Hartford Courant,* February 17, 1954; "Board of Education, Others Join Fight on Comic Books," *Hartford Courant,* February 19, 1954.

227 *"It is our sincere belief . . . hateful influence":* Quoted in "Board of Education, Others Join Fight on Comic Books," *Hartford Courant,* February 19, 1954.

227 *"I thought that their work":* Interview Kravsow.

227 *"I wanted to move":* Ibid.

Notes

Chapter 12: The Triumph of Dr. Payn

228 *"I write comic books":* Quoted in interview Eisner.

228 *"How dreadful":* Quoted ibid.

228 *"I had had it"* . . . *"them seriously":* Interview Eisner.

229 *Eisner had handed off:* Will Eisner, Jules Feiffer, and Wallace Wood, *The Outer Space Spirit.*

229 *"I was torn":* Interview Eisner.

229 *"When Dr. Wertham":* Ibid. Eisner, describing this broadcast more than forty years later, could recall the day of the week, Saturday, but not the date. Wertham is known to have appeared on several New York–based programs during this period, when his book *Seduction of the Innocent* was published. One of them was "Comic Books and Their Effect," the second of two programs on juvenile delinquency on the news-feature series *Eye on New York,* Channel 2, CBS affiliate, 3:00 to 3:30 p.m., May 22, 1954.

230 *teaser ads* . . . *"doing to your children?":* Advertisements, *Union Bulletin,* Walla Walla, WA, October 21, 22, 27, 1953.

230 *"How many [parents]":* "Sex and Sadism Rampant: It's Time Parents Awakened to Danger in Comic Books," *Los Angeles Times,* November 1, 1953.

231 *"Garishly presented":* Gershon Legman, *Love and Death.*

231 *"Unlike the other":* Gilbert Seldes, *The Great Audience.*

231 *"The influence of comic books":* Albert E. Kahn, *The Game of Death: Effects of the Cold War on Our Children.*

232 *"He was very serious":* Interview Gordon Parks.

232 *"cultural slaughter":* "A National Disgrace (and a Challenge to American Parents)," *Chicago Daily News,* May 8, 1940.

232 *hard-boiled fiction:* David Goodis, *Street of the Lost*; Kenneth Fearing, *Dagger of the Mind.*

233 *Wertham chose to release:* "What Parents Don't Know About Comic Books," *Ladies' Home Journal,* November 1953.

233 *"Revolution in Mothballs"* and *"Can This Marriage Be Saved?":* Ladies' Home *Journal,* November 1953.

233 *"the result of seven years"* . . . *"contact with them":* Publisher's Note in Fredric Wertham, *Seduction of the Innocent.*

233 *"If I find":* Wertham, *Seduction of the Innocent.*

234 *"Our researches have proved":* Ibid.

234 *"The role of comic books"*: Ibid.

235 *antecedent in the work*: Louis Proal, *Passion and Criminality: A Legal and Literary Study.*

235 *"tinge" . . . "their own business"*: Interview Robinson.

235 *"We established the basic ingredients"*: Wertham, *Seduction of the Innocent.*

236 *"With the big S"*: Ibid.

236 *"The contempt for law"*: Ibid.

237 *Wertham analyzed Richard Wright . . . "whole creative process"*: "An Author's Mind Plumbed for the Unconscious Factor in the Creation of a Novel," *New York Times*, September 24, 1944.

237 *"The writers of comic books . . . concoction"*: Wertham, *Seduction of the Innocent.*

239 *"To me, the most offensive"*: Interview Al Feldstein.

239 *"I am convinced"*: Wertham, *Seduction of the Innocent.*

240 *One page showed the cover*: *Crime SuspenStories*, December 1953–January 1954.

240 *tight close-up*: "Tabu," *Jungle Comics*, February 1948. The art was by Maurice Whitman.

240 *cover of Matt Baker's*: *Phantom Lady*, April 1948.

240 *psychiatrist resembling Wertham*: *Crime Detective Comics*, July–August 1949.

240 *two panels from the EC story*: "Foul Play!" *The Haunt of Fear*, June 1953.

240 *"That business"*: Interview Davis.

241 *"I read [Wertham's] book"*: Quoted in Rich Hauser interview with William M. Gaines, *Spa Fon*, 1969.

241 *"a horrible picture"*: Wertham, *Seduction of the Innocent.*

242 *"The whole idea"*: Interview Fujitani.

242 *"go find Wertham"*: Quoted ibid.

242 *"I said, 'Father' "*: Interview DiPreta.

242 *"[Wertham's] theory"*: "The Dark Fantastic," *New Republic*, May 3, 1954.

243 *"may well be the most important"*: Advertisement for *Seduction of the Innocent*, *New York Times*, April 26, 1954.

243 *"graphic inanity"*: "Sterling North Reviews the Books," *New York World Telegram and Sun*, April 13, 1954.

243 *"Dr. Wertham has read"*: "Nothing to Laugh At," *New York Times Book Review*, April 25, 1954.

243 *"Altogether, [the book]" . . . "foolish lives"*: "Keep Those Paws to Yourself, Space-Rat," *The New Yorker*, May 8, 1954.

Notes

Chapter 13: What Are We Afraid Of?

245 The account of the hearings of the Senate Special Committee to Investigate Crime in Interstate Commerce (chaired by Estes Kefauver) in this book is drawn from a variety of sources, including the following.

Books: *Report of the Special Committee to Investigate Crime in Interstate Commerce*, U.S. Senate; Estes Kefauver, *Crime in America*; Charles L. Fontenay, *Estes Kefauver: A Biography*; Joseph Bruce Gorman, *Kefauver: A Political Biography*; William Howard Moore, *The Kefauver Committee and the Politics of Crime, 1950–1952*; John Robert Greene, *The Failure of Ambition: Estes Kefauver and the Senate Crime Committee 1950–1952*.

Articles: "Crackdowns or Headlines?" *Washington Post*, February 21, 1951; "Senator Kefauver Wows 'Em on TV," *Washington Post*, March 5, 1951; "It Pays to Organize," *Time*, March 12, 1951; "Costello's Power in Politics, Crime Shown at Hearing," *New York Times*, March 13, 1951; "Can They Force You to Appear on TV," *Washington Post*, March 14, 1951; "Costello Again Defies Crime Probe by Silence," *Washington Post*, March 17, 1951; "TV Crime Session Almost Disrupts Red Cross Work," *Washington Post*, March 17, 1951; "Study of TV's Role in Congress Urged: Wiley Says 'Baby' May Turn into 'Monster'—Kefauver Backs Longer Inquiry," *New York Times*, March 25, 1951; "Sad News for TV Fans—Crime 'Show' Ends Today," *New York Times*, March 25, 1951; "Crime Hunt in Foley Square," *Time*, March 26, 1951; "Crime Found Top U.S. Subject," *Washington Post*, March 27, 1951.

Film: *March of Time* newsreels, February 1951, Time Inc. library.

Citations for quotations and information from other sources follow.

246 *pivotal moment:* Albert Abramson, *History of Television, 1942 to 2000*.

247 *"I didn't do":* Quoted in Kefauver, *Crime in America*.

247 *"I gotta refreshen":* Quoted ibid.

247 *"Mr. Costello doesn't care":* Quoted in David Halberstam, *The Fifties*.

248 *"The effect was unbelievable":* Kefauver, *Crime in America*.

248 *"The week of March 12":* "Who's a Liar," *Life*, April 2, 1951.

249 *"Senator Estes Kefauver is the nation's":* "Tennessee, TV, and Kefauver Too," *Life*, March 24, 1952.

250 *"The boss-run":* "Why Not Let the People Elect Our President?" *Collier's*, January 31, 1953.

Notes

250 *"Oh, no":* Quoted in Gorman, *Kefauver: A Political Biography.*

250 *Robert C. Hendrickson's committee on juvenile delinquency:* The account of this committee's hearings on juvenile delinquency and comic books is drawn from many sources, including the holdings of two archives: The Robert C. Hendrickson Archive, Bird Library, Syracuse University; and the records of the Subcommittee to Investigate Juvenile Delinquency of the Committee on the Judiciary, U.S. Senate, National Archives. Useful articles: "Comic Book Hearing Is Set," *New York Times,* February 21, 1954; "Hill to Probe Effect of Comic Books," *Washington Post,* February 22, 1954; "Senators to Press Delinquency Study," *New York Times,* March 15, 1954; "Hendrickson Backs Comic Book Probe," *Washington Post,* April 9, 1954; "Comic Book Hearing to Start Tomorrow," *New York Times,* April 20, 1954; "Comic Books and Delinquency," *America,* April 24, 1954.

Film: *March of Time* newsreels, April 1954, Time Inc. library.

For their firsthand accounts of the hearings, I am indebted to Irving Kravsow and Lyle Stuart; and for their memories of the events surrounding the hearings, I am grateful to Al Feldstein, Jack Davis, Will Elder, Harry Harrison, Jack Kamen, Stan Lee, John Severin, Marie Severin, Joe Simon, Shirley Norris Smith, and Al Williamson, among others.

Visual and oral descriptions are based on newsreel footage and photographs. All quotations from this set of hearings come from the *Report of the Subcommittee to Investigate Juvenile Delinquency of the Committee on the Judiciary,* U.S. Senate. Citations for other quotes and additional information follow.

250 *Hendrickson told reporters . . . "public entertainment":* "Why Youths Go Bad," *Evening News,* Newark, NJ, November 17, 1953.

251 *"Don't join": Remarks of the President of the United States at the Dartmouth College Commencement,* June 14, 1953, Dartmouth College Library.

251 *"a problem filled":* Quoted in "Ike Promises Full Aid to Hendrickson for Youth Crime Probe," *Courier Post,* Camden, NJ, November 27, 1953.

251 *Hendrickson's mail pile:* "Teen Probe to Study Effect of TV, Comics," *Washington Post,* March 24, 1954.

251 *"significant public concern":* "Comic Book Hearing Is Set," *New York Times,* February 21, 1954.

251 *last entry:* "State and City Officials Warn Comics Publishers to 'Clean Up,'" *Hartford Courant,* February 17, 1954.

251 *"He was not about"*: Interview Stuart.

252 *"ARE YOU A RED DUPE?"*: *The Haunt of Fear*, August 1954.

253 *"The American people"*: Hendrickson Archive, Bird Library, Syracuse University.

253 *"If some groups"*: Ibid.

254 *"Somebody came"*: Interview Morse.

254 *"Look at me"*: Interview Stuart.

255 *"He was eager"*: Ibid.

255 *cool spring morning*: Research by Leslie, National Oceanic and Atmospheric Administration.

255 *designed, in the early 1930s*: The Foley Square courthouse was designed by architect Cass Gilbert and built from 1933 to 1936. "Nine Seek to Build Court House Here," *New York Times*, January 7, 1933; also, www.nyc-architecture.com/SCC/SCC021.htm; www.cityrealty.com.

256 *"Crowded, busy, tense"*: Interview Stuart.

259 *"We may criticize . . . behavior"*: "The Comics and Delinquency: Cause or Scapegoat?" *Journal of Educational Sociology*, December 1949.

261 *more than thirty*: Estimate by John Jackson Miller.

262 *"Bill felt like"*: Interview Stuart.

262 *"This is all your fault"*: Interview Kravsow.

262 *"He was really"*: Ibid.

262 *"See that?"*: Interview Stuart.

262 *"Bill"*: Ibid.

263 *C. Wright Mills's review*: "Nothing to Laugh At," *New York Times Book Review*, April 25, 1954.

264 *"That's it"*: Interview Stuart.

269 *"He was losing it"*: Ibid.

270 *"Dexedrine keeps you hyper"*: Gaines interview with Mark Voger, *Comics Scene Spectacular* #7, 1992.

271 *"Stupid, stupid, stupid!"*: Interview Joe Simon.

271 *page-one story*: "No Harm in Horror, Comics Issuer Says," *New York Times*, April 22, 1954.

271 *"The high point"*: Max Lerner column (untitled), *New York Post*, April 22, 1954.

272 *Newspapers . . . in detail*: "Whether Crime 'Comic' Books Lead Child Astray Is Debated," *New York Herald Tribune*, April 22, 1954; "Good Taste in Comic

Books," *Lima* (OH) *News*, April 28, 1954; "The Uncomic Comic Books," *Walla Walla Union-Bulletin*, April 28, 1954; "Are Comics Horrible?" *Newsweek*, May 3, 1954; "Horror Comics," *Time*, May 3, 1954.

272 *idea of* taste: It would be another ten years until Susan Sontag would establish personal taste in matters high and low as a paramount aesthetic principle: "Taste governs every free—as opposed to rote—human response. Nothing is more decisive. There is taste in people, visual taste, taste in emotion—and there is taste in acts, taste in morality." "Notes on Camp," *Partisan Review*, Fall 1964.

272 *"It isn't that"*: "Are You a Red Dupe?" *The Haunt of Fear*, August 1954.

273 *"the defendant"*: Quoted in Gorman, *Kefauver: A Political Biography*.

Chapter 14: We've Had It!

274 *front-page news*: "No Harm in Horror, Comics Issuer Says," *New York Times*, April 22, 1954; "McCarthy Hearing Will Start Today; Hensel Included," *New York Times*, April 22, 1954.

274 *public-service features*: "Get a Box Seat to Nature's Wonders," *World's Finest*, July–August 1953; "How Safe Is Your Driving?" *World's Finest*, September–October 1953.

275 *"How can you do that?"* Interview Oksner.

275 *Dick Ayers . . . avoid embarrassment*: Interview Dick Ayers.

275 *upstate New York*: "Horror for Young Readers—All for the Price of a Dime," *Buffalo Evening News*, May 10, 1954; "Crime Stories Have Little Impact, Says Child Expert," *News*, May 11, 1954; "Opponent Calls Crime Tales a Blight on Nation's Morals," *News*, May 12, 1954; "Defender States His Case: 'Horror Never Hurt Anyone,'" *News*, May 13, 1954; "'Short Glance' at Crime Tales Is Turning Into a Long Look," *News*, May 14, 1954.

275 *had it entered*: *Congressional Record*, June 16, 1954.

275 *four-part series*: "Crime Pays as Theme of Comic Books," *Cleveland Press*, May 29, 1954; "Lessons in Bank Robbery and Jail Break Are Pictured in 'Comics' for Children," *Press*, May 31, 1954; "Police Told to Seize Lurid Comic Books," *Press*, June 1, 1954; "Juvenile Crimes Traced to Bad Comic Books," *Press*, June 2, 1954.

276 *Prodded by the series*: "Crime, Horror and Sex Comics," *Cleveland Press*, June 4, 1954.

276 *Conway made . . . second violations:* "Stores Near Schools Face Comics Hunt," *Cleveland Press*, June 2, 1954; "Arrests Are Ordered in Sex Comic Sales— Objectionable Books Will Be Listed for 'Get-Tough' Campaign," *Press*, June 5, 1954; "23 Comic Books Put on Police Purge List," *Press*, June 7, 1954.

276 *"I think . . . or office":* "Comic Books Blameless," Letters, *Cleveland Press*, June 5, 1954.

276 *received its own share:* Robert C. Hendrickson Archive, Bird Library, Syracuse University.

277 *"I need not tell you":* Records of the Senate Subcommittee on Juvenile Delinquency, National Archives.

277 *"A Special Editorial":* Published in five EC comics: *The Haunt of Fear*, September–October 1954; *Crime SuspenStories*, January 1955; *Shock SuspenStories*, January 1955; *Tales from the Crypt*, January 1955; *The Vault of Horror*, January 1955.

278 *"Recently, I received" . . . "delinquency scourge":* Typescript, Robert C. Hendrickson Archive, Bird Library, Syracuse University. This speech does not appear in the *Congressional Record*, suggesting that Hendrickson may not have given it while the Senate was in session.

279 *The second hearings:* Report of the Subcommittee on JD.

280 *"lascivious and lustful":* Quoted ibid.

281 *" 'I make myself sick' " . . . "federal level":* Quoted ibid.

281 *"halt circulation":* Quoted in "Ban Objectionable Matter," *Newport Daily News*, June 24, 1954.

282 *"condemning":* "Sheriffs' Meeting Here to Discuss Comic Books," *Washington Post*, June 28, 1954.

282 *"outlawing" . . . "children today":* Quoted in "Juvenile Court Judges Rap Some Comic Books," *Chicago Daily Tribune*, July 4, 1954.

282 *"war" . . . "offending comics":* Quoted in "GFWC to War on Lurid Comic Books," *Los Angeles Times*, July 8, 1954. Also, "Federation Juniors Urged to Battle Comic Book Threat," *Los Angeles Times*, August 6, 1954.

282 *"legislative action" . . . "horror themes":* Quoted in "Board of CCPT to Convene," *Los Angeles Times*, July 11, 1954; "CPT Grim Over Comic Book Peril," *Los Angeles Times*, July 15, 1954.

282 *more organizations:* "Comic Book Fight Mapped—Purple Heart Association Also Opposed to Red China in the U.N.," *Los Angeles Times*, August 17, 1954; "Auxiliary to Attack Poor Comic Books," *Los Angeles Times*, August 26, 1954;

"Thrill Comics Blamed on TV, Radio, Books," *Los Angeles Times*, August 20, 1954.

282 *"There was a sense"*: Interview Rocco Motto.

283 *"When I decided"*: Ibid.

283 *"The guy blew"*: Interview Jim Mooney.

283 *"The guy was helping"*: Ibid.

284 *"Get out of that"*: Interview Mike Esposito.

284 *"We were getting bundles"*: Interview Feldstein.

284 *"I said, 'Bill' "*: Interview Stuart.

285 *"Dear Fellow Comic Book Publisher"*: Photocopy of letter, Cartoon Research Library, Ohio State University, date obscured.

285 *"To everybody's surprise"*: "A Statement by William M. Gaines, Publisher of the Entertaining Comics Group: EC Will Drop Horror and Crime Comics," Cartoon Research Library, Ohio State University, September 14, 1954.

285 *Thirty-eight publishers . . . independent overseer*: Records of the Comics Magazine Association of America, Cartoon Research Library, Ohio State University.

285 *agreed to offer*: Interview Stuart.

286 *Among the early recommendations*: Records of the CMAA, Cartoon Research Library, Ohio State University.

286 *"This is not"*: Quoted in Diehl, *Tales from the Crypt*.

286 *"It was always"*: Quoted in Amy Kiste Nyberg, *Seal of Approval: The History of the Comics Code*.

286 *CMAA incorporated . . . and EC*: Records of the CMAA, Cartoon Research Library, Ohio State University.

286 *"code of ethics" . . . support the code*: "Comic Book Industry Names New York Judge As Code Administrator," *Wall Street Journal*, September 17, 1954.

286 *Charles F. Murphy . . . find work*: "Biography of Judge Charles F. Murphy," press release, prepared by Ruder & Finn Associates for the CMAA, Records of the CMAA, Cartoon Research Library, Ohio State University.

287 *"He was as clean"*: Interview Dick Giordano, via e-mail.

287 *press conference of his own*: Interview Stuart, Feldstein, Norris Smith. Also, *March of Time* newsreel, September 1954, Time Inc. library.

287 *"In January of 1950"*: "A Statement by William M. Gaines," Cartoon Research Library, Ohio State University, September 14, 1954; also, *March of Time* newsreel, September 1954, Time Inc. library.

287 *"I have decided"*: Ibid.

288 *"In recent months cleaned up"*: Ibid.

288 *"new line"* . . . *"clean line"*: Ibid.

288 *The decision*: "Publisher Halting His 'Horror' Comics," *New York Herald-Tribune*, September 15, 1954; "Publisher to Drop Crime and Horror 'Comic' Book," *Wall Street Journal*, September 16, 1954.

289 *"It came as a shock"*: Interview Feldstein.

289 *"He couldn't carry on"*: Ibid.

289 *"made the ultimate sacrifice"* . . . *"wine shop"*: Interview Stuart.

290 *"As a result . . . fewer rapes!"*: "In Memoriam," *The Haunt of Fear*, December 1954; *Crime SuspenStories*, March 1955; *Tales from the Crypt*, March 1955.

290 *"It will take"*: Quoted in "Statement by John Goldwater," press release, prepared by Ruder & Finn Associates for the CMAA, Records of the CMAA, Cartoon Research Library, Ohio State University. Dated October 27, 1954, the statement by Goldwater quotes Murphy and cites September 16, 1954, as the date for those quotes.

291 *"It is not only ready"*: "Statement by Charles F. Murphy," press release, prepared by Ruder & Finn Associates for the CMAA, Records of the CMAA, Cartoon Research Library, Ohio State University, October 27, 1954.

291 *"compares favorably"*: Ibid.

291 *"a landmark in the history"*: "Code of the Comics Magazine Association of America," adopted October 26, 1954, Records of the CMAA, Cartoon Research Library, Ohio State University.

291 *Policemen, judges . . . sanctity of marriage*: Ibid.

292 *"All elements"*: Ibid.

292 *"One of the reasons"*: Interview Geier.

293 *"disrespect for established authority"*: "Code of the CMAA."

293 *"the kind of thing"*: Interview Geier.

293 *"nationwide campaign"*: "Horror on the Newsstands," *Time*, October 27, 1954.

293 *Oklahoma City*: Ibid.

293 *Houston*: Ibid; also, "Comic Book Ban Assured," *Houston Chronicle*, August 25, 1954; "Major Publishing Firms Back New Crime Comic Law," *Chronicle*, August 27, 1954.

293 *"banning [of]"*: "Ridicule of Comic Book Law Is Smokescreen to Flout Decency," *Chronicle*, August 27, 1954.

Notes

293 *"hope to police":* "Horror on the Newsstands."

293 *bills outlawing . . . dozen states:* "Major Publishing Firms Back New Crime Comic Law," *Houston Chronicle,* August 27, 1954; "Columbus Weighs a Comic Book Law," *New York Times,* October 10, 1954; "Crime, Sex Comic Books Outlawed in E. Chicago," *Chicago Daily Tribune,* March 1, 1955; "House Gets Legislation to Curb Sale of Comic Books to Youths," *The Era,* Bradford, PA, March 4, 1955; "Monessen Legislator Caught in Middle Over Comic Book Bill," *Monessen (PA) Daily Independent,* March 17, 1955; "May Outlaw 'Horror' Books," *Indiana Evening Gazette,* May 25, 1955; "Comic Book Controls Passed by Assembly," *Reno Evening Gazette,* March 14, 1955; "State Sales Tax Signed into Law," *Reno Evening Gazette,* March 30, 1955; "House Passes Bill Creating Special Group to Study Comic Book Problem," *Newport Daily News,* April 2, 1955; "Meyner Gets Tie-in Bill: Forced Sale of Comic Books Forbidden by Measure," *New York Times,* August 5, 1955; "Senators Ban Comic Book Sale," Kennewick and Richland (WA) *Tri-City Herald,* April 14, 1955; "Comic Book Ban to Be Up for Ohio Senate Vote Today," *Cleveland Plain Dealer,* June 23, 1955; "Ohio Acts on Comic Books," *Cleveland Plain Dealer,* May 25, 1955; "Ban on Horror Comics Approved by Legislature," *Ohio State Journal,* June 24, 1955; "Assembly Votes Curbs on Comics," *Bridgeport Telegram,* June 7, 1955; "Comic Books Barred: Connecticut Halts the Sale of Editions Dealing in Violence," *New York Times,* July 19, 1955; "12 States Enact Laws to Curb Horror, Sex, Crime Comic Books," *Bridgeport Telegram,* July 11, 1955. Also, Feder, *Comic Book Regulation.* For legal citations on state acts passed, see note "Laws in other states," pertaining to page 312.

293 *calls to replace . . . Parents and Teachers:* "Board of CCPT to Convene," *Los Angeles Times,* July 11, 1955.

293 *soon joined:* "Board Supports Horror Comic Ban," *Los Angeles Times,* November 16, 1954.

293 *Los Angeles County . . . law in February 1955:* "Supervisors Call for Comic Book Ordinance," *Los Angeles Times,* November 17, 1954; "Law Banning Crime Comic Books Prepared," *Los Angeles Times,* February 15, 1955; "County Acts for Crime Comics Ban," *Los Angeles Times,* February 16, 1955.

294 *state senate approved . . . bill on April 21:* Cal. Stat. 1955, c. 214. Also, "Major Actions on Bills in Sacramento," *Los Angeles Times,* April 22, 1955.

294 *while the state legislature:* Feder, *Comic Book Regulation.*

294 *"By Knowing Worthy Publications"*: "Graham PTA Topic to Be Comic Books," *Chicago Daily Tribune*, January 20, 1955.

294 *"Do You Know What Your Children Are Reading?"*: "Comic Book Lecture at PTA Feb. 21," *Oconomowoc (WI) Enterprise*, February 17, 1955.

294 *newspaper columns*: "Impoverishing the Youthful Mind," *Newport Daily News*, November 30, 1954; "Are Comic Books Menace or Nuisance?" *Washington Post*, November 8, 1954.

294 *Gallup Poll . . . "young people"*: "TV and Comics Crime Blamed in Delinquency," November 22, 1954.

295 *"When one is not able"*: "Teenager Defends Comic Book Fans," *Los Angeles Times*, March 14, 1955.

295 *"well on their way"*: Ibid.

295 *Ilg and Ames devoted*: "Comic Book Stirs Further Discussion," *Los Angeles Times*, March 16, 1955.

295 The portrait of Ruth Lutwitzi and her activities is drawn primarily from recollections of her daughters Helen Miller and Ruth Schlicher, as well as from memories of her friend Vanita Marlow and her acquaintances Milton Babinec and Karen Jensen.

295 *"She was always running"*: Interview Schlicher.

296 *"She picked that up"*: Interview Marlow.

296 *Canton, Ohio . . . any comic was accepted*: "Committee Offers Swap of Good Books for Bad," *Canton Repository*, August 3, 1954; "Book Swap Scheduled for First Two Days of Fair," *Repository*, August 31, 1954; "1,000 Books on Order for Comic Swap October 29," *Repository*, October 5, 1954; "Children Get Free Bus Rides for Book Swap," *Repository*, October 19, 1954; "30,000 Comics Given Up in Operation Book Swap," *Repository*, October 30, 1954.

296 *American Legion's adaptation*: "Legion Auxiliary Cites Canton in Book Swap Plan," *Canton Repository*, October 13, 1954.

297 *"a stab in the right direction"*: Quoted in Mrs. Charles B. Gilbert, *The American Legion Auxiliary Vol. IV.*

297 *"literary diet of crime"*: Quoted ibid.

297 *"She had 'em marked up"*: Interview Miller.

297 *A rural school*: Interview Babinec, Jensen.

297 *That day . . . 127 comics*: "'Operation Book Swap' Is Launched at Stone Bank Against Comic Books," *Waukesha Daily Freeman*, March 14, 1955; "Operation Book Swap," *Oconomowoc Enterprise*, March 17, 1955.

Notes

297 *"I don't know where"*: Interview Babinec.

298 *"Dear Young Reader . . . That's America"*: " 'Operation Book Swap' Is Launched at Stone Bank Against Comic Books," *Waukesha Daily Freeman*, March 14, 1955.

298 *"I thought it was terribly"*: Interview Babinec.

298 *"hundreds of thousands"*: Gilbert, *The American Legion Auxiliary Vol. IV.*

298 *Fulton, New York:* "Horror Books Will Be Swapped," *Syracuse Herald-Journal*, April 15, 1955.

298 *Palatine, Illinois:* "Operation Book Swap," Chicago *Daily Herald*, December 9, 1954.

298 *Wakeman, Ohio:* "Comics 'Swap' Set Up," *Chronicle-Telegram*, February 24, 1955.

298 *Pendleton, Oregon:* Gilbert, *The American Legion Auxiliary Vol. IV.*

298 *Little Neck, New York:* Ibid.

299 *Norwich, Connecticut:* "Legion Auxiliary Sets Comic Book Burning," *New York Post*, February 25, 1955.

299 *Hyde Park, New York:* Gilbert, *The American Legion Auxiliary Vol. IV.*

299 *"We [did] not stress"*: Quoted ibid.

299 *In Wakeman:* "Wakeman Book Swap to Start," *Chronicle-Telegram*, March 2, 1955; "531 'Comics' Burned in Swap at Wakeman," *Chronicle-Telegram*, March 5, 1955. For information on the Wakeman events, I am indebted to JoAnne Jackson and Robert Jackson, who researched the records of the local American Legion Auxiliary, Post 689, and supplied me with copies of the organization's minutes, as well as copies of pages of the book he received in exchange for ten comic books.

299 *Robert Jackson . . . "missing something"*: Interview Robert Jackson.

299 *"I thank God . . . above code"*: Letter from Mrs. Carl W. Zeller, the national chairman of the National Child Welfare Committee of the Auxiliary, to "Bobby Jackson," not dated, courtesy of Jackson.

300 *"That was a lot of money"*: Interview Ted Yaworsky.

300 *"They never told us"*: Ibid.

300 *"It was more or less"*: Ibid.

300 *a photo:* "1,427 Comics 'Taboo' As Book Swap Ends," *Chronicle-Telegram*, March 11, 1955.

300 *end of that year:* " 'Book Swap' Top Story in Wakeman," *Chronicle-Telegram*, December 31, 1955.

Notes

300 *"Not only was"*: Quoted in Gilbert, *The American Legion Auxiliary Vol. IV.*

301 *"there are overtones"*: Quoted in "Legion Auxiliary Sets Comic Book Burning," *New York Post*, February 25, 1955.

301 *headlines shifted:* "Comics 'Book Burning' Hit in Norwich Legion Drive," *Bridgeport Post*, February 26, 1955; "Protests End Plan to Burn Comic Books," *Post-Standard*, Syracuse, February 27, 1955.

301 *five thousand comics:* "Norwich Drive on Comics a Success As Children Rush to Trade 10 for a Classic," *New York Times*, February 27, 1955.

301 *an AP photo:* "Protests End Plan to Burn Comic Books," *Post-Standard*, February 27, 1955.

301 *"very serious"* . . . *"something patriotic"*: Interview John Chiangi.

301 *Peter Mauger* . . . *Arena:* Martin Barker, *A Haunt of Fears: The Strange History of the British Horror Comics Campaign.*

302 *"devoted to the American threat"*: "The USA Threat to British Culture," *Arena*, June–July 1951.

302 *"These magazines"*: Quoted ibid. Also, "Should US 'Comics' Be Banned?" *Picture Post*, May 17, 1952; "Horror Comics: Is This the End?" *Picture Post*, November 20, 1954. "Drive Out the Horror Comics: Help us to fight 'sex and crime at a shilling a time,'" *Daily Dispatch*, August 11, 1954; "Make Bonfires of Them," *Daily Dispatch*, August 20, 1954.

302 *"The problem which"*: Editorial, *The Times* (London), November 12, 1954.

303 *"would tend to incite"*: Halsbury's *Statutes of England*, 3rd ed. 45 (1955 supp.).

303 *The penalty* . . . *February 22, 1955:* Barker, *A Haunt of Fears.*

303 *The teachers* . . . *the pyre:* "Pupils Burn Comic Books: Month-Long Drive Ends in Bonfire," *Decatur Daily Review*, February 24, 1955.

303 *Girl Scout troop* . . . *Bonfire of the Future:* "Girl Scouts Here Launch Anti-Comic Book Drive," *Indiana* (PA) *Evening Gazette*, February 21, 1955.

A few months before this wave of comic-book burnings, on September 19, 1954, an additional burning was conducted in the Southtown area of Chicago. Under the direction of the Citizens Committee for Better Juvenile Literature, members of the Campfire Girls, the Girl Scouts, and the Boy Scouts destroyed comics in a bonfire on the grounds of the Drexel Park Presbyterian Church. "Launch All-Out War on Comics," *Southtown Economist*, September 19, 1954.

304 *philistine dreamscape:* Ray Bradbury, *Fahrenheit 451.*

Notes

Chapter 15: Murphy's Law

305 *Charles F. Murphy had three . . . burn the books:* "Comic 'Czar's' Formula," *Los Angeles Times*, December 4, 1954. Murphy told the paper, "I've burned comic books in my time."

305 *"But my kids":* Quoted ibid.

305 *"sweeping . . . purification drive":* Quoted ibid.

305 *"hired to be":* Interview Carmine Infantino.

306 *During the Code . . . romances:* "'New' Comic Books to Be Out in Week," *New York Times*, December 29, 1954.

306 *"emphasize the value":* "Code of the CMAA."

306 *scripts for stories:* "I Gave Boys the Green Light," *Teen-Age Diary Secrets*, September 1949; "Tourist Cabin Escapade," *Teen-Age Temptations*, October 1952.

306 *"create disrespect for established authority":* "Code of the CMAA."

306 *"robbed the medium" . . . "Insanity":* Interview Drake.

306 *About a fourth:* "'New' Comic Books to Be Out in Week," *New York Times*, December 29, 1954.

306 *"look like so many" . . . "Flat in front":* "Ladies in the Comic Books to Be in Height of Style," *Roanoke World News*, October 28, 1954.

306 *opening "splash page":* "Love Flirt," *Love Problems and Advice Illustrated*, November 1955. An excerpt from the censored version of this story was published in Duin and Richardson, *Comics: Between the Panels*.

307 *some evidence:* "Mack Martin Investigator," *Super Mystery Comics*, May 1948, reprinted in a different form in *Penalty Comics*, January 1956. Panels of both versions of this story were reprinted in Benton, *The Illustrated History of Crime Comics*.

308 *For a press conference:* "'New' Comic Books to Be Out in Week," *New York Times*, December 29, 1954.

308 *"The wonderful thing":* Interview Jay Scott Pike.

309 *The artist . . . took up farming:* Interview Ayers, Joe Edwards, Russ Heath, John Severin.

309 *"I'll never forget":* Interview Thorne.

309 *"The Code was restrictive":* Interview Giordano, via e-mail.

309 *"The biggest insult":* Interview Herb Rogoff.

309 *"We had a picture":* Ibid.

Notes

310 *" 'Why don't we just' ":* Ibid.

311 *"There is yet":* Quoted in "Whip, Knife Shown as 'Comics' Lures," *New York Times*, February 5, 1955; "Legislators attack comics code violations; industry czar sharpens clean-up," *Printers' Ink*, February 11, 1955.

311 *"horror, sex, and brutality" . . . "approval of the authority":* Report of the Joint Legislative Committee to Study the Publication of Comics, March 1955.

311 *"Freedom without obligation":* Quoted in "Comic Book Code Called Failure," *New York Times*, March 22, 1955.

311 *sweeping legislation:* New York State Assembly Bill no. 2789.

311 *Governor Averell Harriman signed:* " 'Comic' Book Ban Signed," *Washington Post*, May 3, 1955; "Lewd Book Curbs in Effect," *New York Times*, July 1, 1955.

311 *The UK law:* Barker, *A Haunt of Fears.*

312 *Some eighty comic books:* Estimate by John Jackson Miller.

312 *Laws in other states:* The following bills had passed in state legislative bodies by fall 1955. California: Cal. Stat. 1955, ch. 214; Connecticut: Conn. G.S. 3293d (1955 supp.); Idaho: Idaho Bill no. 60; Illinois: Ill. Rev. Stat. Ch. 38 Sect. 472. 69th Gen. Assembly; Maryland: Md. Ann. Code Art. 27, 421; Montana: Act to Amend Sect. 94-3601, 94-2601, Revised Codes of Montana, 34th Leg. Assembly; Nevada: Nevada State Law AB243; New Jersey: Act 2A:15-3.1; North Carolina: Act of May 23, 1955, ch. 1204, G.S. 14189; Ohio: Ohio Rev. Code 2903.10; Oklahoma: Title 11, ch. 1, Sect. 1, 25th State Leg.; Oregon: Act of May 23, 1955, ch. 494; Texas: Ch. 120, H.B. no. 23; ch. 423 S.B. 423; ch. 107 H.B. no. 302; Washington: Washington Acts 1231, ch. 282. Also, "12 States Enact Laws to Curb Horror, Sex, Crime Comic Books," *Bridgeport Telegram*, July 11, 1955. Also, Feder, *Comic Book Regulation*; "Regulation of Comic Books," *Harvard Law Review*, January 1955; "Crime Comics and the Constitution," *Stanford Law Review*, March 1955; "Delinquency, Comic Books and the Law," *Ohio State Law Journal*, 1957.

313 *"I wasn't what":* Interview Reuben C. Peterson.

314 *"The witch-burning":* "Modern Witch Burning," *Great Bend Daily Tribune*, July 22, 1955.

314 *"All the dark craziness":* Interview Harrison.

314 *In 1952:* Research by Miller, Maheras.

315 *"We couldn't get":* Interview Simon.

Notes

315 *series* Confidential File: Multiple episodes screened at the Library of Congress. For this study of the *Confidential File* episode on comic books, the LOC provided the author with a videocassette of the program. All quotes from that episode and descriptions of the images come from that videocassette.

318 *"basically threw the guy" . . . "how to use it":* Interview A. J. Fenady.

318 *Kefauver began a world tour . . . for the cameras:* Fontenay, *Estes Kefauver: A Biography.*

318 *"I guess I owe":* Quoted in Swados, *Standing Up for the People.*

Chapter 16: Out of the Frying Pan and into the Soup

319 *"New Direction":* Valor, Piracy, MD, Extra!, Psychoanalysis, Impact, Incredible Science Fiction, all April 1955.

319 *"What had we at E.C. . . . merely the subject matter!":* Publisher's note, ibid.

320 *among the most notable:* "Master Race," *Impact,* April 1955.

320 *"Listen":* Interview Feldstein.

320 *"I felt that I couldn't":* Interview with Gaines and Feldstein by Stark, von Bernewitz, and White, conducted December 28–30, 1955, August 6, 1956, and August 10, 1956. Published in von Bernewitz and Geissman, *Tales of Terror.*

321 *"Everybody in the industry":* Quoted in Hauser interview with Gaines, *Spa Fon,* 1969.

321 *"Murphy always read":* Interview Feldstein.

321 *a story:* "Judgment Day!," *Incredible Science Fiction,* February 1956.

321 *"You can't have" . . . "segregated society":* Interview Feldstein.

322 *"the lure of color and fantasy with educational propaganda":* "Comics and Propaganda," *Chicago Defender,* February 7, 1953.

322 *"He got to the last" . . . "something like that":* Interview Feldstein.

322 *"And the instrument lights":* "Judgment Day!," *Incredible Science Fiction,* February 1956.

323 *"Fuck you" . . . "had had it":* Interview Feldstein.

323 *"Mad could never have gone":* Quoted in Decker and Groth, "An Interview with William M. Gaines," *Comics Journal,* May 1983. In this interview, Gaines described the ability of the new *Mad* to avoid the Comics Code authority as a "lucky result" of the switch to the magazine format. He said here that the

decision to change formats began as an attempt to appease Kurtzman, who
was threatening to leave *Mad* to work for *Pageant* magazine.

323 *"a big fuck-you"*: Interview Stuart.

323 *"You know how adversity"*: Ibid.

324 *"Bill Gaines was anti-establishment"*: Interview Stan Hart.

324 *"First Issue: The New Mad"*: Mad, July 1955.

324 *college humor magazine*: Dan Carlinsky, *A Century of College Humor*.

324 *The* Harvard Lampoon's *spoof*: Ibid.

325 College Humor, *the national anthology*: Ibid.

325 *"He was telling him"*: Interview Elder.

326 *Between 1954 and 1956 . . . all closed shop*: Research by Miller, Maheras.

326 *"Let's face it"*: Interview with Gaines and Feldstein by Stark, von Bernewitz,
and White, conducted December 28–30, 1955, August 6, 1956, and August
10, 1956. Published in von Bernewitz and Geissman, *Tales of Terror*.

326 *"Everybody was punished"*: Interview Infantino.

327 *"closing up"*: Interview Lee.

327 *that year . . . rival, National/DC*: Thomas G. Lammers, *Tales of the Implosion*.

327 *"Martin went to Florida"*: Interview Lee.

327 *"I was the one"*: Ibid.

327 *" 'I'm sorry, but' "*: Ibid.

327 *"I loved comics"*: Interview Morisi.

327 *"I had to feed"*: Interview Ayers.

328 *"There was nothing"*: Interview Harrison.

328 *frightful depiction*: "Murder, Morphine and Me," *True Crime Comics*, May
1947.

328 *In August 1958*: "Jack Cole, Comic Strip Creator, Shot to Death," *Chicago Sun-
Times*, August 14, 1958. Also, Spiegelman, *Jack Cole and Plastic Man*.

328 *"Sorry for owing"*: Letter of August 13, 1958, reprinted in Spiegelman, *Jack
Cole and Plastic Man*.

328 *"They thought we were awful"*: Interview Winkleman.

329 *"He said it was terrible"*: Ibid.

329 *"Warren was a dear"*: Interview Harrison.

329 *"I made a fine living"*: Interview Leav.

330 *"I knew how"*: Interview Lee.

Notes

Epilogue

331 *walled amassment:* This description of Sauve, Robert Crumb, and his home there is based on the author's observations on location.

332 *"I was already"* . . . *"more exciting":* Interview Robert Crumb.

333 *"By the time":* Ibid.

333 *"Me and other guys . . . never got over it":* Ibid.

Appendix

337 The list of artists, writers, editors, letterers, and others involved in comic-book making who never again worked in the field was put together over several years' time by a team of researchers. Steven Tice did the bulk of the painstaking work, with invaluable help from Jerry Bails, who devised a new software program specifically for the task. Jon Lovstad of the Grand Comic Database assisted considerably. Important contributors also include Jim Amash, Jon B. Cooke, and Roy Thomas.

Bibliography

Abramson, Albert. *History of Television, 1942 to 2000*. McFarland, 2003.

Annual Report of the Postmaster General for the Fiscal Year Ended June 30, 1941. U.S. Government Printing Office, 1941.

Barker, Martin. *A Haunt of Fears: The Strange History of the British Horror Comics Campaign*. University Press of Mississippi, 1992.

Barrier, Michael, and Martin Williams, eds. *A Smithsonian Book of Comic-Book Comics*. Smithsonian Institution Press and Harry N. Abrams, 1981.

Barson, Michael, and Steven Heller. *Teenage Confidential: An Illustrated History of the American Teen*. Chronicle Books, 1998.

Beaty, Bart. *Fredric Wertham and the Critique of Mass Culture*. University Press of Mississippi, 2005.

Benson, John, ed. *Romance Without Tears*. Fantagraphics Books, 2003.

Benton, Mike. *The Comic Book in America: An Illustrated History*. Taylor, 1989.

———. *The Illustrated History of Crime Comics*. Taylor, 1993.

Blackbeard, Bill, Dale Crain, and James Vance, eds. *100 Years of Comic Strips*. Barnes & Noble Books, 2004.

Blackbeard, Bill, and Martin Williams, eds. *The Smithsonian Collection of Newspaper Comics*. Smithsonian Institution Press and Harry N. Abrams, 1977.

Bradbury, Ray. *Fahrenheit 451*. 50th Anniversary Edition. Del Rey, 1987.

Cagney, James. *Cagney by Cagney*. Doubleday, 1976.

Bibliography

Callahan, Bob, ed. *The New Smithsonian Book of Comic-Book Stories: From Crumb to Clowes*. Smithsonian Institution, 2004.

Canemaker, John. *Winsor McCay: His Life and Art*. Harry Abrams, 2005.

Cardy, Nick, with John Coates. *The Art of Nick Cardy*. Vanguard Productions, 2001.

Carlinsky, Dan, ed. *A Century of College Humor*. Random House, 1971.

Carrier, David. *The Aesthetics of Comics*. Pennsylvania State University, 2000.

Cassell, Dewey, Aaron Sultan, and Mike Gartland, eds. *The Art of George Tuska*. TwoMorrows Publishing, 2005.

Children's Bureau, U.S. Department of Health, Education and Welfare. *Some Facts About Juvenile Delinquency*. U.S. Government Printing Office, 1953.

———. *Understanding Juvenile Delinquency*. U.S. Government Printing Office, 1949.

Comstock, Anthony, and J. M. Buckley. *Traps for the Young*. Funk & Wagnalls, 1883. Reprint by Kessinger Publishing, not dated.

Couch, N. C. Christopher, and Stephen Weiner. *The Will Eisner Companion*. DC Comics, 2004.

Daniels, Les. *Comix: A History of Comic Books in America*. Outerbridge & Dienstfrey, 1971.

———. *Superman: The Complete History*. Chronicle Books, 1998.

DeBarto, Dick. *Good Days and MAD: A Hysterical Tour Behind the Scenes at MAD Magazine*. Thunder's Mouth Press, 1994.

Debs, Eugene V. *The Writings and Speeches of Eugene V. Debs*. Hermitage Press, 1948.

Diehl, Digby. *Tales from the Crypt*. St. Martin's Press, 1996.

Disbrow, Jay Edward. *The Iger Comics Kingdom*. Blackthorne, 1985.

Drake, Arnold, Leslie Waller, and Matt Baker. *It Rhymes with Lust*. St. John, 1950.

The Drive for Decency in Print. Our Sunday Visitor Press, 1939.

Duin, Steve, and Mike Richardson. *Comics Between the Panels*. Dark Horse Comics, 1998.

Eisner, Will. *Hawks of the Seas*. Dark Horse Comics, 2003.

———. *The Outer Space Spirit*. Kitchen Sink Press, 1983.

———. *Shop Talk*. Dark Horse Comics, 2001.

Elliott, Mabel A. *Crime in Modern Society*. Harper & Brothers, 1952.

Ellis, Doug, John Locke, and John Gunnison. *The Adventure House Guide to the Pulps*. Adventure House, 2000.

Bibliography

Ellison, Ralph. *The Collected Essays of Ralph Ellison*. Modern Library, 1995.

Evanier, Mark. *Mad Art: A Visual Celebration of the Art of Mad Magazine and the Idiots Who Created It*. Watson-Guptill, 2002.

Evans, Richard J. *The Coming of the Third Reich: A History*. Penguin Press, 2003.

Feder, Edward L. *Comic Book Regulation*. Bureau of Public Administration, University of California, Berkeley, 1955.

Feiffer, Jules. *The Great Comic Book Heroes*. Bonanza Books, 1965.

Fielding, Raymond. *Technological History of Motion Pictures and Television: An Anthology from the Pages of "The Journal of the Society of Motion Pictures and Television Engineers."* University of California Press, 1984.

Fontenay, Charles L. *Estes Kefauver: A Biography*. University of Tennessee Press, 1980.

Frank, Josette. *Comics, Radio, Movies—and Children*. Public Affairs Committee, 1949.

————. *What Books for Children?* Doubleday, Doran & Company, 1937.

Freedland, Michael. *Cagney*. Stein and Day, 1975.

Gabler, Neal. *Winchell: Gossip, Power and the Culture of Celebrity*. Vintage, 1995.

Garriock, P. R. *Masters of Comic Book Art*. Images Graphiques, 1978.

Garrison, Karl C. *Psychology of Adolescence*. Prentice-Hall, 1951.

Geissman, Grant. *Foul Play! The Art and Artists of the Notorious 1950s E.C. Comics!* Collins Design, 2005.

Gilbert, Mrs. Charles B. *The American Legion Auxiliary Vol. IV*. American Legion Auxiliary, 1970.

Gilbert, James. *A Cycle of Outrage*. Oxford University Press, 1986.

Ginder, Richard. *With Ink and Crozier: The Story of Bishop Noll and His Work*. Our Sunday Visitor Press, not dated.

Goldstein, Norm. *The History of Television*. Random House, 1991.

Gorman, Joseph Bruce. *Kefauver: A Political Biography*. Oxford University Press, 1971.

Goulart, Ron. *Comic Book Culture: An Illustrated History*. Collectors Press, 2000.

————. *Comic Book Encyclopedia: The Ultimate Guide to Characters, Graphics, Novels, Writers, and Artists in the Comic Book Universe*. HarperCollins, 2004.

————, ed. *Encyclopedia of American Comics*. Promised Land Productions, 1990.

————. *Great American Comic Books*. Publications International, 2001.

————. *The Great Comic Book Artists*. Volume 2. St. Martin's Press, 1989.

Gray, Barry. *10,001 Nights in Broadcasting*. Simon & Schuster, 1975.

Bibliography

Griffin, Dick, and Rob Warden, eds. *Done in a Day: 100 Years of Great Writing from the* Chicago Daily News. Swallow Press, 1977.

Groth, Gary, and Greg Sadowski, eds. *Will Elder: The Mad Playboy of Art*. Fantagraphics Books, 2003.

Halberstam, David. *The Fifties*. Fawcett Columbine, 1993.

Harrison, Hank. *The Art of Jack Davis!* Stabur Press, 1987.

Harvey, Robert C. *The Art of the Comic Book: An Aesthetic History*. University Press of Mississippi, 1996.

Heer, Jeet, and Kent Worcester, eds. *Arguing Comics: Literary Masters on a Popular Medium*. University Press of Mississippi, 2004.

Heins, Marjorie. *Not in Front of the Children: "Indecency," Censorship and the Innocence of Youth*. Hill and Wang, 2001.

Hendrickson, Robert C. *Youth in Danger*. Harcourt, Brace, 1956.

Hinman, Marjory Barnum. *Court House Square: A Social History*. Self-published, 1984.

Horn, Maurice, ed. *The World Encyclopedia of Comics*. Avon Books, 1977.

Jackson, Kenneth T., ed. *The Encyclopedia of New York City*. Yale University Press, 1995.

Jacobs, Frank. *The Mad World of William M. Gaines*. Lyle Stuart, 1972.

Kahn, Albert E. *The Game of Death: Effects of the Cold War on Our Children*. Cameron & Kahn, 1953.

Katz, Ephraim. *The Film Encyclopedia*. Harper Perennial, 1998.

Kauffmann, Stanley. *Albums of Early Life*. Ticknor & Fields, 1980.

Kefauver, Estes. *Crime in America*. Greenwood, 1968.

Kinsey, Alfred, et al. *Sexual Behavior in the Human Male*. W. B. Saunders, 1948.

Kinstler, Everett Raymond, and Jim Vadeboncoeur, Jr. *Everett Raymond Kinstler: The Artist's Journey Through Popular Culture—1942–1962*. JVJ Publishing, 2005.

Kurtzman, Harvey. *My Life as a Cartoonist*. Minstrel Books, 1988.

Lammers, Thomas G. *Tales of the Implosion*. Self-published, 2005.

Legman, Gershon. *Love & Death*. Hacker Art, 1963.

Lemov, Rebecca. *World as Laboratory: Experiments with Mice, Mazes, and Men*. Hill and Wang, 2006.

Lenroot, Katherine. *Understanding Juvenile Delinquency*. U.S. Government Printing Office, 1943.

Lent, John A., ed. *Pulp Demons: International Dimensions of the Postwar Anti-Comics Campaign*. Associated University Press, 1999.

Bibliography

Lupoff, Dick, and Don Thompson, eds. *All in Color for a Dime*. Krause, 1997.

The MAD Archives. Volume 1. DC Comics, 2002.

Marston, William Moulton. *Emotions of Normal People*. Persona Press, 1928.

McCay, Winsor. *Little Nemo in Slumberland*. Sunday Press Books, 2005.

McDonnell, Patrick, Karen O'Connell, and Georgia Riley de Havenon. *Krazy Kat: The Comic Art of George Herriman*. Abradale Press, 1986.

McKnight-Trontz, Jennifer. *The Look of Love: The Art of the Romance Novel*. Princeton Architectural Press, 2002.

Moore, William Howard. *The Kefauver Committee and the Politics of Crime, 1950–1952*. University of Missouri Press, 1974.

Mott, Frank Luther. *American Journalism: A History, 1690–1960*. Macmillan, 1942.

Narus, Donald J. *Chrysler's Wonderful Woodie the Town and Country, 1941–1950*. Marjac Enterprises, 1973.

The National Cyclopedia of American Biography. Volume 47. James T. White & Co., 1965.

1949 National Catholic Almanac. St Anthony's Guild, 1949.

Noble, William. *Bookbanning in America*. Paul S. Eriksson, 1990.

Nyberg, Amy Kiste. *Seal of Approval: The History of the Comics Code*. University Press of Mississippi, 1998.

O'Brien, Geoffrey. *Hardboiled America: Lurid Paperbacks and the Masters of Noir*. Da Capo, 1997.

Preston, Charles. *Juvenile Delinquency*. Dell, 1956.

Proal, Louis. *Passion and Criminality: A Legal and Literary Study*. Emperial Press, 1905.

Reidelbach, Maria. *Completely Mad: A History of the Comic Book and Magazine*. Little, Brown, 1991.

Robbins, Trina. *The Great Women Cartoonists*. Watson-Guptill, 2001.

Robbins, Trina, and Catherine Yronwode. *Women and the Comics*. Eclipse Books, 1985.

Robinson, Jerry. *The Comics: An Illustrated History of Comic Strip Art*. G. P. Putnam's Sons, 1974.

Sabin, Roger. *Comics, Comix & Graphic Novels*. Phaidon, 2002.

Sadowski, Greg. *B. Krigstein*. Fantagraphics Books, 2002.

Savage, William W., Jr. *Commies, Cowboys, and Jungle Queens*. Wesleyan University Press, 1998.

Bibliography

Schelly, Bill. *The Golden Age of Comic Fandom*. Hamster Press, 1995.

Schwartz, Julius, with Brian M. Thomsen. *Man of Two Worlds*. HarperCollins, 2000.

Seldes, Gilbert. *The Great Audience*. Greenwood, 1970.

———. *The Seven Lively Arts*. Sagamore Press, 1957.

Sennitt, Stephen. *Ghastly Terror! The Horrible Story of the Horror Comics*. Headpress, 1999.

Simon, Joe, with Jim Simon. *The Comic Book Makers*. Vanguard, 2003.

Skal, David J. *The Monster Show: A Cultural History of Horror*. Penguin, 1994.

Spiegelman, Art, and Chip Kidd. *Jack Cole and Plastic Man*. DC Comics, 2001.

Steranko, James. *History of Comics*. Volume 1. Supergraphics, 1970.

———. *The Steranko History of Comics*. Volume 2. Supergraphics, 1972.

Stewart, Bhob, ed. *Wally Wood: Against the Grain*. TwoMorrows Publishing, 2003.

Swados, Harvey. *Estes Kefauver: Standing Up for the People*. Dutton, 1972.

Theakston, Greg. *The Lou Fine Reader*. Pure Imagination, 2003.

Thompson, Ilse, ed. *Your Vigor for Life Appalls Me: Robert Crumb Letters, 1958–1977*. Fantagraphics Books, 1998.

United States Bureau of the Census. *Historical Statistics of the United States, Colonial Times to 1970*. Basic Books, 1976.

Von Bernewitz, Fred, and Grant Geissman. *Tales of Terror*. Fantagraphics Books, 2001.

Wertham, Fredric. *Dark Legend*. Duell, Sloane & Pearce, 1941.

———. *Seduction of the Innocent*. Rinehart, 1954.

———. *The Show of Violence*. Doubleday, 1949.

West Virginia: A Guide to the Mountain State. Oxford University Press, 1941.

Wilson, Andrew. *Beautiful Shadow: A Life of Patricia Highsmith*. Bloomsbury, 2003.

Wood, Wally. *The Marvel Comics Art of Wally Wood*. Thumbtack Books, 1982.

Wright, Bradford W. *Comic Book Nation*. Johns Hopkins University Press, 2001.

Wright, Nicky. *The Classic Era of American Comics*. Contemporary Books, 2000.

Yeates, Thomas, Mark Schultz, and S. C. Ringgenberg, eds. *Al Williamson: Hidden Lands*. Dark Horse Books, 2004.

Yronwode, Catherine. *The Art of Will Eisner*. Kitchen Sink Press, 1982.

Zipes, Jack, et al., eds. *The Norton Anthology of Children's Literature: The Traditions in English*. Norton, 2005.

Acknowledgments

First and always, I thank my wife, Karen, for her immeasurable help and support.

To Jake, hearty thanks for laying the groundwork. To Torie, special gratitude for all the diligent work.

Then, my literary family: my editors Jonathan Galassi and Paul Elie, the latter of whom worked closely with me on this, our third book together, month after month, year after year. And my agent, Chris Calhoun, a combat buddy who saved me more times than I deserved.

I began the research for this project at the University of Chicago, while I was serving as the Robert Vare Nonfiction Writer in Residence. For that gift, I thank Robert Vare, and I am also grateful to Larry Norman, the chair of the English Department during my time at the school. Five years later, I finished writing the book while teaching at the S. I. Newhouse School of Public Communications at Syracuse University. For their invaluable support, I thank Dean David Rubin and Bob Lloyd, my department chair and guardian angel at SU.

For his aid and good counsel, I thank Leon Wieseltier, my editor at *The New Republic*, who held my post while I was writing this.

For encouraging the book early on and assigning essays that helped get me started, I am indebted to the late Barbara Epstein of *The New York Review of Books*. For commissioning a story on Will Eisner that informed this text, I thank David Remnick of *The New Yorker*; and for overseeing pieces on *Mad* and Robert

Acknowledgments

Crumb, parts of which led to passages here, I am grateful to David Friend of *Vanity Fair*.

My researcher at the University of Chicago, Anna Brenner, stuck with the project after graduation and ended up doing much of the tough research. I am also indebted, as ever, to Dierdre Cossman, the St. Jude of historical research. For additional help with research, I thank Ryan Fitzpatrick, Claire Duffett, Lauren Kay, Nathan Carlile, Julie Hoffman at the Stark County District Library in Ohio, Sean O'Heir, Dorian Tenore-Bartilucci and Vinnie Bartilucci, Vincent Hawley, Sarah Pye, Vern Morrison, and Elizabeth Edmonds.

I am greatly indebted to the many artists, writers, and others involved in the events in this book whom I interviewed over six years' time. Among them, I owe special thanks to Ann Eisner and her late husband Will, and to Michelle and Al Feldstein.

I thank the hardest-working man in the comics business, Steve Tice, for transcribing many of my interview tapes and for doing much of the painstaking labor involved in compiling the list of names, the Comics Code memorial, in the Appendix.

A great many comics experts and collectors were kind to share information and offer advice over the years. Chief among them were Jim Amash, Jerry Bails, Mike Benton, John B. Cooke, Digby Diehl, Steve Duin, Mike Feldman, Danny Fingeroth, Grant Geissman, Mark G. Heike, Thomas G. Lammers, Bill Leach, Russ Maheras, John Jackson Miller, Frank Motler, Lou Mougin, John Petty, Trina Robbins, David Siegel, Bhob Stewart, Steve Stiles, Ed Summer, Roy Thomas, Ted White, and Sam Viviano.

I am grateful to people at a number of institutions where I conducted research: Rodney A. Ross at the Center for Legislative Archives, National Archives; Bruce Kirby at the Manuscript Division of the Library of Congress; Dr. Lucy Caswell and Dennis Toth at the Cartoon Research Library, The Ohio State University; Edward L. Galvin, Nicolette A. Schneider, and the staff at the Special Collections Research Center, Bird Library, Syracuse University Library; Holly Koenig at the Comics Magazine Association of America; Eric W. Robinson at the newspaper microfilm department at the New York Public Library; Susan Tyler Stinson and Robert J. Hodge at the Belfer Audio Laboratory and Archive at Syracuse University; Randall W. Scott at the Special Collections Division, Michigan State University Library; Marianne Labatto at the Brooklyn College Library Archives and Special Collections Division; and Michael Martin at the Onondaga Historical Association.

Acknowledgments

Librarians and archivists at other institutions conducted some research on my behalf. Chief among them were Rina Wright and Joseph J. Hovish at the American Legion; Joann Regets of Saints Peter and Paul Church School in Auburn, New York; Belinda Harris at *The Roanoke Times*; Jeanine Thubauville at the Thomas Crane Public Library in Quincy, Massachusetts; and Margaret G. Wollitz at the Decatur Public Library.

For reading an early draft of the manuscript and providing invaluable insight on legal matters, I thank Roy Gutterman at SU. For important legal research, I am also grateful to Dee Gager and Jennifer Holtz.

For reading an early draft of the manuscript and offering editorial advice, I thank Robert G. Dunn; for fine copyediting, I thank Suzanne Fass and Susan Goldfarb; and for writerly counsel almost every day, I thank John Carey.

For essential help with the art and photo insert, I am indebted to Mitch Blank, Larry Elin, Daniel Herrick, and Todd Sodano.

For contributions of all sorts, I thank my parents and also my in-laws, Dr. Carol and John Oberbrunner; Joanne Hajdu, who laid the groundwork for the groundwork and still pitches in; and also Boyd Addlesperger, Marc Andreottola, Paul Buhle, Susanne Carbin, Aaron Cohen, Zarina Feinman, Dan Friedell, Paula Gabbard, Eliot Gordon, Patti Graziano, Chuck Hajdu, Jihae Hong, Lori Hostuttler, JoAnne and Robert Jackson, Abby Kagan, Michael Kubin, Ann Marie Lonsdale, Jon Lovstad, Ron Mann, Keelin McDonell, Sean McNaughton, Tom McNulty, Cathy Gaines Mifsud, Steven Mintz, Chloe Schama, Marcelyn Skerpca, Cara Spitalewitz, Jeanine Thubauville, Alfredo Trejo, David Unger, Dave Wagner, Lawrence Watt-Evans, Justine Whitaker, Ellen Winkleman, Margaret G. Wollitz, and Jerry Zelada.

Index

Index

Index

Index

Index

Index

Index

Tarzan, 17, 29, 30; movies, 128
Teen-Age Romance, 161, 276
teen comics, 210, 327; see also *Archie*
Teen Plan, Inc., 287
television, 115, 139, 162, 170–71, 214, 314, 358*n*; anti-comics program on, 310–11, 315–18; comic-book adaptations of shows on, 309; crime shows on, 251; FCC regulation of, 291; parodies of, 200, 215, 325; Senate hearings broadcast on, 174, 245–73; Wertham on, 229, 241
Terror Illustrated, 312
Terrors of the Jungle, 312
Terror Tales, 140–41
Terry and the Pirates, 17, 174
Thall, Martin, 37
Thimble Theater, 14, 16
This Magazine Is Haunted, 141
Thorndyke, Robert, 45
Thorne, Frank, 309
Thrasher, Frederic M., 259–60
Thrilling Adventures, 20
Thrilling Comics, 55
Tiger Girl, 157
Timely/Atlas/Marvel, 130, 133, 194, 261, 275, 283, 286; closing of, 327; horror-oriented comics published by, 177, 189–90; and Senate hearings, 172, 174, 254
Timely Comics, 43, 55; see also Timely/Atlas/Marvel
Time magazine, 81, 97, 246, 272, 293
Times (London), 302–303
Timor Comics, 315
Tiny Tot Comics, 89, 133, 219, 225, 241, 281
Tobey, Charles W., 172
Toby Press, 285, 326
Tolson, Clyde, 62
Tom and Jerry, 312
Tomb of Terror, 189
Tom Corbett, Space Cadet, 309
Topsy Turvy, 57
Tormented, 326
Torpey, John W., 226
Torres, Angelo, 321
Toth, Alex, 160, 163
Toulouse-Lautrec, Henri de, 11
Toy, Harry S., 92, 93

Traps for the Young (Comstock), 95, 232
Treasury Department, U.S., 250
Tremaine, Warren, 192
True Crime Comics, 110, 328
true-crime genre, 59–60, 64, 96
Truman, Harry S, 171, 249
Tufts University, 78
Tunney, Gene, 45, 77
Tuska, George, 65
Two-Fisted Tales, 178, 188, 195–96, 198

UFO sightings, 112
Ulysses (Joyce), 266
Understanding Juvenile Delinquency (Lenroot), 84
United Features, 326
United Press International (UPI), 174
United States Conference of Mayors, 144
Unsane, 218
Updike, John, 50

Valleau, Janice, *see* Winkleman, Janice Valleau
Vallee, Rudy, 50
Valor, 319
vaudeville, 15
Vault of Horror, The, 176–78, 180, 186, 224, 286
Victorianism, 12
Vigoda, Al, 193
violence, 42–43; response of well-balanced children to, 45; young readers' fascination with, 143; *see also* crime comics; horror comics
Viscardi, Nicholas, *see* Cardy, Nick
von Schmidt, Harold, 26

Wallach, Ira, 324
Walla Walla Union Bulletin, 230
Waller, Leslie, 163–65, 167–68
Walloch, Donna Jean, 119
Wall Street Journal, 106
Walter, Ralph, 148
Wanted, 110
War Against Crime, 142, 176
war comics, 178, 188, 195–98, 327
Warner, Jack, 54

Index

Illustration Credits

Grateful acknowledgment is made for permission to reprint the images in the illustration insert following page 214.

page 1, top left: Courtesy Will Eisner Studios and Denis Kitchen Art Agency; *top right*: Arnold Drake collection; *bottom*: Courtesy Will Elder.

page 2, top left: Courtesy Will Elder; *top right*: Courtesy Will Eisner Studios and Denis Kitchen Art Agency; *bottom*: Courtesy Wendy Gaines Bucci and the Gaines Estate.

page 3, top: Photograph by Clarence E. Olson, courtesy Arielle North Olson; *middle left*: Photograph by Gordon Parks.

page 4, top: Ron Mann collection, courtesy Sphinx Productions, Inc.; *bottom*: St. Patrick's Academy yearbook, Vincent Hawley collection.

page 5, top left and top right: The Repository (Canton).

page 6, top left: Photograph by Alfred Eisenstaedt, Getty Images; *top right*: Courtesy Wendy Gaines Bucci and the Gaines Estate.

page 7, top: Cartoon Research Library, The Ohio State University.

page 8: Courtesy Will Elder.

All uncredited images are in the public domain.